Irene Levin
Martin B. Sussman
Editors

Stepfamilies:
History, Research, and Policy

Stepfamilies: History, Research, and Policy has been co-published simultaneously as *Marriage & Family Review,* Volume 26, Numbers 1/2 and 3/4 1997.

Pre-publication
REVIEWS,
COMMENTARIES,
EVALUATIONS . . .

"**T**he editors begin by asking whether the stepfamily should continue to be a distinct unit of analysis. The answer supplied by the rich information in this volume is a resounding 'YES.'

This book challenges researchers to think about the next generation of research into stepfamilies. One prominent theme is that more attention should be paid to children's lives. Several contributors stress that better information is needed about the relationships between children and adults, and relationships among children themselves, within stepfamilies. It is also recommended that more information should be collected about stepfamilies from the child's point of view. The contributors illustrate these issues through careful demonstrations from their own research."

David Cheal, PhD
Professor of Sociology
University of Winnipeg
Winnipeg, Manitoba, Canada

More pre-publication
REVIEWS, COMMENTARIES, EVALUATIONS . . .

"**A** couple of decades ago the question was raised whether we are witnessing the death of the family. On our way to the third millennium it seems that the family is still living, prospering, constantly changing, appearing in a variety of forms but not losing its vital energy. This enhanced dynamism perplexes the students of the family who try to define the 'typical' form and essence of the modern family. The family appears in so many shapes and contexts that it escapes the definitions and the models of the past. In order to understand it we have to change our thought and research modes and try to adapt to the ideas of complexities and chaotic order. Divorce, cohabitation, remarriage, single parenthood and unisex couples are not signs of family pathology or the breakdown of familism.

Taking into account the proportion of divorces and remarriages in Western societies a large percentage of children and adults will have the experience of living some period of their life in a stepfamily. The book 'Stepfamilies': History, Research, and Policy' is a timely endeavor to focus on this type of relationship. The book contains 18 papers written by American and European scholars.

The book has an internal coherence that provides a taste of new ways of approach to the study of the complexities of family life. Each paper presents the stepfamily from a different approach, proof that there are as many stepfamilies as its members–there is the children's stepfamily and there is the family of the step- and the biological father, and the step- and biological mother. There are references to the seldom-mentioned figures of stepsiblings and stepgrandparents. Several papers deal with the large variety of stepfamilies and their dynamics and the assumption that during their life span members of a family–adults and children–may live in a variety of household compositions and step relationships.

The importance of the book transcends the specific issue of stepfamilies by contributing ideas, methods and approaches that can be fruitful for the study of the entire field of family theory and research. The book can well serve as text for courses on family within the framework of sociology, social work, law and public policy."

Rivka W. Bar-Yosef
Professor of Sociology, Emerita
The Hebrew University, Jerusalem, Israel

"This book contains, unusually, precisely what the title suggests–a wide range of individually valuable and stimulating chapters that form a wonderfully rich menu from which readers will find exciting and satisfying selections.

Chapters include: historical reviews from both the distant past and comparisons of 1984 and the present; explorations of stepfamily variations; detailed accounts of how society views stepfamilies, detailed accounts of how stepfamilies view themselves; accounts of how children view stepfamilies; how step-siblings view each other; explorations of gender and therapy; important discussions of abuse within stepfamilies and the legal response to stepfamilies; the policy perspective; a valuable account of the United Kingdom National Stepfamily Association; family life education for stepfamilies; and comparisons of step- and foster-families.

Central themes emerging from this rich collection are the question of whether and how stepfamilies should be compared to other forms of families, especially the popularly supposed 'nuclear family,' and whether stepfamilies might best be understood as developmental projects in themselves.

This volume not only charts progress in studying stepfamilies to the present but also points to a range of rich topics for further study and development. Whist built upon firm foundations of carefully gathered evidence, this book does not fail to integrate a wide variety of disciplines and push the frontiers of knowledge to the limits. A valuable collection that will appeal to all those concerned with stepfamilies whether from the human services perspective, education, or policy oriented research."

Jon Bernardes, PhD
Principal Lecturer in Sociology
University of Wolverhampton
Castle View Dudley
United Kingdom

Stepfamilies:
History, Research, and Policy

Stepfamilies: History, Research, and Policy

Irene Levin
Marvin B. Sussman
Editors

The Haworth Press, Inc.
New York • London

Stepfamilies: History, Research, and Policy has also been published as *Marriage & Family Review,* Volume 26, Numbers 1/2 and 3/4 1997.

The Haworth Press, Inc., 10 Alice Street, Binghamton, NY 13904-1580 USA

Cover design by Thomas J. Mayshock Jr.

Library of Congress Cataloging-in-Publication Data

Stepfamilies : history, research, and policy / Irene Levin, Marvin B. Sussman, editors.
     p. cm.–(The Marriage & family review series)
     "Has also been published as Marriage & family review, volume 26, numbers 1/2 and 3/4 1997"–T.p. verso.
     Includes bibliographical references and index.
     ISBN 0-7890-0337-6 (alk. paper).–ISBN 0-7890-0338-4 (alk. paper)
     1. Stepfamilies. I. Levin, Irene. II. Sussman, Marvin B. III. Marriage & family review. IV. Series.
HQ759.92.S7 1997
306.85–dc21   97-39585
                                                                       CIP

INDEXING & ABSTRACTING

Contributions to this publication are selectively indexed or abstracted in print, electronic, online, or CD-ROM version(s) of the reference tools and information services listed below. This list is current as of the copyright date of this publication. See the end of this section for additional notes.

- *Abstracts in Social Gerontology: Current Literature on Aging,* National Council on the Aging, Library, 409 Third Street SW, 2nd Floor, Washington, DC 20024

- *Abstracts of Research in Pastoral Care & Counseling,* Loyola College, 7135 Minstrel Way, Suite 101, Columbia, MD 21045

- *Academic Abstracts/CD-ROM,* EBSCO Publishing Editorial Department, P.O. Box 590, Ipswich, MA 01938-0590

- *Academic Search: database of 2,000 selected academic serials, updated monthly,* EBSCO Publishing, 83 Pine Street, Peabody, MA 01960

- *AGRICOLA Database,* National Agricultural Library, 10301 Baltimore Boulevard, Room 002, Beltsville, MD 20705

- *Applied Social Sciences Index & Abstracts (ASSIA) (Online: ASSI via Data-Star) (CDRom: ASSIA Plus),* Bowker-Saur Limited, Maypole House, Maypole Road, East Grinstead, West Sussex RH19 1HH, England

- *CNPIEC Reference Guide: Chinese National Directory of Foreign Periodicals,* P.O. Box 88, Beijing, People's Republic of China

- *Current Contents: Clinical Medicine/Life Sciences (CC:CM/LS) (weekly Table of Contents Service), and <u>Social Science Citation Index.</u> Articles also searchable through <u>Social SciSearch,</u> ISI's online database and in ISI's <u>Research Alert</u> current awareness service,* Institute for Scientific Information, 3501 Market Street, Philadelphia, PA 19104-3302 (USA)

- *Expanded Academic Index,* Information Access Company, 362 Lakeside Drive, Forest City, CA 94404

(continued)

99469

- *Family Studies Database (online and CD/ROM)*, National Information Services Corporation, 306 East Baltimore Pike, 2nd Floor, Media, PA 19063

- *Family Violence & Sexual Assault Bulletin,* Family Violence & Sexual Assault Institute, 1211 East South East Loop, Suite 130, Tyler, TX 75701

- *Gay & Lesbian Abstracts,* National Information Services, Inc., 306 East Baltimore Pike, 2nd Floor, Media, PA 19063

- *Guide to Social Science & Religion in Periodical Literature,* National Periodical Library, P.O. Box 3278, Clearwater, FL 34630

- *IBZ International Bibliography of Periodical Literature*, Zeller Verlag GmbH & Co., P.O.B. 1949, d-49009 Osnabruck, Germany

- *Index to Periodical Articles Related to Law,* University of Texas, 727 East 26th Street, Austin, TX 78705

- *INTERNET ACCESS (& additional networks) Bulletin Board for Libraries ("BUBL") coverage of information resources on INTERNET, JANET, and other networks.*
  - <URL:http://bubl.ac.uk/>
  - The new locations will be found under <URL:http://bubl.ac.uk/link/>.
  - Any existing BUBL users who have problems finding information on the new service should contact the BUBL help line by sending e-mail to <bubl@bubl.ac.uk>.
  The Andersonian Library, Curran Building, 101 St. James Road, Glasgow G4 0NS, Scotland

- *MasterFILE: updated database from EBSCO Publishing,* 83 Pine Street, Peabody, MA 01960

- *PASCAL, c/o Institute de L'Information Scientifique et Technique. Cross-disciplinary electronic database covering the fields of science, technology & medicine. Also available on CD-ROM, and can generate customized retrospective searches.* For more information: INIST, Customer Desk, 2, allee du Parc de Brabois, F-54514 Vandoeuvre Cedex, France; http://www.inist.fr

- *Periodical Abstracts, Research I (general & basic reference indexing & abstracting data-base from University Microfilms International (UMI), 300 North Zeeb Road, P.O. Box 1346, Ann Arbor, MI 48106-1346),* UMI Data Courier, P.O. Box 32770, Louisville, KY 40232-2770

(continued)

- *Periodical Abstracts, Research II (broad coverage indexing & abstracting data-base from University Microfilms International (UMI), 300 North Zeeb Road, P.O. Box 1346, Ann Arbor, MI 48106-1346),* UMI Data Courier, P.O. Box 32770, Louisville, KY 40232-2770

- *Population Index,* Princeton University Office Population, 21 Prospect Avenue, Princeton, NJ 08544-2091

- *Psychological Abstracts (PsycINFO),* American Psychological Association, P.O. Box 91600, Washington, DC 20090-1600

- *Sage Family Studies Abstracts (SFSA),* Sage Publications, Inc., 2455 Teller Road, Newbury Park, CA 91320

- *Social Planning/Policy & Development Abstracts (SOPODA),* Sociological Abstracts, Inc., P.O. Box 22206, San Diego, CA 92192-0206

- *Social Science Source: coverage of 400 journals in the social sciences area, updated monthly,* EBSCO Publishing, 83 Pine Street, Peabody, MA 01960

- *Social Sciences Index (from Volume 1 & continuing),* The H.W. Wilson Company, 950 University Avenue, Bronx, NY 10452

- *Social Work Abstracts,* National Association of Social Workers, 750 First Street NW, 8th Floor, Washington, DC 20002

- *Sociological Abstracts (SA),* Sociological Abstracts, Inc., P.O. Box 22206, San Diego, CA 92192-0206

- *Special Educational Needs Abstracts,* Carfax Information Systems, P.O. Box 25, Abingdon, Oxfordshire OX14 3UE, United Kingdom

- *Studies on Women Abstracts,* Carfax Publishing Company, P.O. Box 25, Abingdon, Oxfordshire OX14 3UE, United Kingdom

- *Violence and Abuse Abstracts: A Review of Current Literature on Interpersonal Violence (VAA),* Sage Publications, Inc., 2455 Teller Road, Newbury Park, CA 91320

(continued)

SPECIAL BIBLIOGRAPHIC NOTES

related to special journal issues (separates)
and indexing/abstracting

☐ indexing/abstracting services in this list will also cover material in any "separate" that is co-published simultaneously with Haworth's special thematic journal issue or DocuSerial. Indexing/abstracting usually covers material at the article/chapter level.

☐ monographic co-editions are intended for either non-subscribers or libraries which intend to purchase a second copy for their circulating collections.

☐ monographic co-editions are reported to all jobbers/wholesalers/approval plans. The source journal is listed as the "series" to assist the prevention of duplicate purchasing in the same manner utilized for books-in-series.

☐ to facilitate user/access services all indexing/abstracting services are encouraged to utilize the co-indexing entry note indicated at the bottom of the first page of each article/chapter/contribution.

☐ this is intended to assist a library user of any reference tool (whether print, electronic, online, or CD-ROM) to locate the monographic version if the library has purchased this version but not a subscription to the source journal.

☐ individual articles/chapters in any Haworth publication are also available through the Haworth Document Delivery Services (HDDS).

ABOUT THE EDITORS

Irene Levin, PhD, is Associate Professor in the Graduate School of Social Work and Social Research at Oslo College in Oslo, Norway. She is the author of three books, *Stepfamilies: Variations and Manifold, To Understand Everyday Life with a Symbolic Interactionistic Perspective,* and *Relations,* all of which were published in Norwegian. She has also written a number of book chapters and articles for national and international publications. Before beginning family research in the early 1980s, she worked as a family therapist for several years. In 1988, she became the first alumna of Bryn Mawr College invited to give the prestigious annual memorial Anita Lichtenstein Lecture. In 1991, she organized the XXVI international seminar of the Committee on Family Research in Norway on the theme of "What Is Family?" A book review editor for many years, Dr. Levin is a member of several professional national and international organizations and a board member of several professional journals.

Marvin B. Sussman, PhD, is UNIDEL Professor of Human Behavior Emeritus at the College of Human Resources at the University of Delaware. He is also a member of the CORE Faculty of the Union Graduate School of Union Institute in Cincinnati, Ohio. A member of many professional organizations, he received the 1980 Ernest W. Burgess Award of the National Council on Family Relations. In 1983, Dr. Sussman was elected to the prestigious Academy of Groves for scholarly contributions to the field, and, in 1984, he was awarded a lifelong membership for services to the Groves Conference on Marriage and the Family. A recipient of the Distinguished Family Award of the Society for the Study of Social Problems (SSSP), he was honored with the Lee Founders Award, the SSSP's highest professional award, in 1992. The author or editor of 30 books and more than 220 articles on family, community, rehabilitation, health and aging, and organizational transformation, Dr. Sussman's contributions to research and education in the family and aging fields were recognized in 1992 with the State of Delaware Gerontological Society Award.

Stepfamilies:
History, Research, and Policy

CONTENTS

ALL HAWORTH BOOKS AND JOURNALS
ARE PRINTED ON CERTIFIED
ACID-FREE PAPER

Introduction

Marvin B. Sussman
Irene Levin

What can editors say about a volume on stepfamilies which has not already been said by the contributors in the pages that follow? Not too much. Editors have the prerogative to be redundant, praiseworthy, scandalous and obstinate in words and deeds. After all, editors are in control of the process. Yet negativism which is the forte of the majority of editors (such a grandiose statement will get me in trouble) escapes a few. Here authors are honored for their contributions to the body of knowledge; taking advantage of the constructive criticism of reviewers and consequently improving their papers immensely; their tolerance of the complexities and vagaries of publishing. "Yes, it is to be published in 1997–definitely."

There are a few features in this collection which are notable and require a brief discussion. Eight of the 18 papers are authored by international scholars. This means that perceptions of reality may vary widely since respective writers conceptualize their research within the context of their cultural identities, particularistic training and experiences in their societies. Collaborative work in recent decades has reduced the impact of this cultural specificity. A paradigm of intercultural and interdisciplinary thought and process is beginning to emerge. Marker variables such as agreed definitions of varied forms of families and social class are becom-

Marvin B. Sussman is UNIDEL Professor of Human Behavior, Emeritus, University of Delaware, Newark, DE, and a member of the Core Faculty, Union Institute. Irene Levin is Associate Professor in the Graduate School of Social Work and Social Research at Oslo College, Oslo, Norway.

[Haworth co-indexing entry note]: "Introduction." Sussman, Marvin B., and Irene Levin. Co-published simultaneously in *Marriage & Family Review* (The Haworth Press, Inc.) Vol. 26, No. 1/2, 1997, pp. 1-4; and: *Stepfamilies: History, Research, and Policy* (ed: Irene Levin and Marvin B. Sussman) The Haworth Press, Inc., 1997, pp. 1-4. Single or multiple copies of this article are available for a fee from The Haworth Document Delivery Service [1-800-342-9678, 9:00 a.m. - 5:00 p.m. (EST). E-mail address: getinfo@haworth.com].

1

ing standardized and used increasingly in national and cross-national studies. Yet one cannot erase the cultural imprinting that is a consequence of professional socialization in the early years of the author's career.

The incidence and prevalence of stepfamilies is increasing in all societies paralleling the increases in the divorce and separation rates. Normalization of stepfamilies is likely to occur as it has in relation to divorce. The phenomenon of stepfamilies is increasing sufficiently to be internalized as less than an extraordinary family form. Before divorce became so prevalent, it was treated as a rare and startling event where the participants were often stigmatized and given the message that they were failures as human beings.

As the divorce rates increased it became an almost everyday activity, a terrible experience for many involved in separation and divorce, but with lessened stigmata, viewed as a situation undesirable and in some instances unhealthy but not an unusual event.

The creation of a stepfamily usually as a consequence of divorce is becoming less of a pathological event as its incidence increases. Learning that a family has stepchildren does not create any strong reaction or rejection. Discovering that the Jones family is one that has stepchildren and stepparents, does not unleash rhetoric which claims that this state of being is less fulfilling when compared to non-stepfamilies.

It is appropriate to discard the model of research which compares step- with non-stepfamilies. Attention should be given to research which deals with the internal dynamics of families where there are stepchildren. By doing this, one recognizes, honors and empowers this family form and avoids comparisons with a so-called ideal type of family–the traditional family of procreation.

Another concern is that individuals as they move over the life cycle may experience being in a stepfamily either as a step- or non-stepchild. The length of time in the stepfamily may extend over many of the formative years. In one possible scenario, you could start out life in a nuclear family of procreation; a divorce occurs and in three or four years, you may be in a single parent family. Economics and other conditions may require that your mother, you and your siblings return to the family of orientation and you move into a three, four or even five-generational household. Subsequently, your mother remarries and you and your two siblings move into another household with her new husband and his two children. The stepfamily is not a timeless, continuous condition for individuals as they move over the life cycle.

Given this high incidence of stepfamily formation, it is likely that the legal bases that will provide the policies and functions of stepfamilies are likely to change. Common law decisions by judges and various jurisdictions are likely to expand their perceptions to include (with the best interest of the child) doctrine with the best interest of the family and kin group members. For example, grandparents are increasingly involved in caregiving with their natural and step-grandchildren and until very recently, the courts did not give any legal rights to grandparents but instead blessed them with moral rights. This meant that grandparents could not be involved with their grandchildren or great-grandchildren unless permission was given by the parents. This is being changed in the various jurisdictions where grandparents have taken on the major caregiving responsibilities where their own children, because of AIDS or addictions are unable to provide such care. The assumption that parents are the best and natural caretakers of their children is being eroded. The "best interest" doctrine is increasingly encompassing other members of the kin family who have taken on childbearing responsibilities.

A convoluted, non-traditional family system is emerging in the 21st century. Stepfamilies will be nuclear units within a larger kin network along with other nuclear units living in the same household or propinquitous to other units which will function as unified or semi-autonomous structures. Individuals will find such extensive relationships to be supportive of their physical, social, economic and spiritual needs. The units within the system of relationships will maintain their own work and financial activities and can opt for limited or extensive involvement in the larger grouping of nuclear units. Such creative communities of families will be slow in coming but will be formidable in empowering non-traditional family forms which include the stepparent family.

The absorptive capacities of societies worldwide to integrate "deviant" family forms, to normalize these structures into the mainstream of "family" is increasing over time. Societies proceed with this process of integration for a variety of reasons including economic, political, humanistic and social. Ultimately the legal system authenticates this normative process. It accords to the stepfamily rights, privileges and responsibilities which are given to the nuclear family.

Beyond this is a fundamental question as to whether the stepfamily will continue to be a unit of analysis as witnessed by the great variety of articles in this volume. Will the issues treated by authors of various perspectives, intellectual persuasions and their specializations resonate with the problems and concerns of individuals in other family forms? Families indistinguishable in major characteristics and sharing a common genesis will create conceptual and theoretical problems for many creative social scientists.

One activity of investigators is to label individuals, groups, conditions and processes for identification purposes. Usually associated with a label given to a group are implied behaviors, images and myths, for example, the stepfamily, single parent family, extended generational household; each has presumed behaviors and identities which may not be in consonance with reality. When people believe that such "deviant" families are a product of the malfunctions of its members, labeling in this instance may create the behaviors people associate with this family form. One is invoking the self-fulfilling prophecy.

The stepparent as well as others who differ and stray from the traditional nuclear family of procreation may be cast into a larger kin network either by choice or circumstances. This phenomenon described previously in this paper will become an increasing event in the 21st century. Family units, mostly nuclear, may be linked together in a sharing network. It will behoove the social scientist to look at the impact of this development for its members and the consequences of the legalization of such forms. Will the techniques and strategies developed by this larger unit enable it to deal effectively with groups and bureaucracies outside of the family? The research unit of analysis moves into this larger playing field with complexity and rapid change occurring within this enlarged "new" family system. Will it have the capabilities to deal with the outside world is a major question.

Stepfamilies
from a Historical Perspective

Roderick Phillips

INTRODUCTION

As the articles in this volume attest, stepfamilies have come to constitute a prominent feature of the modern Western family system. Depending
on the use to be made of the data, the incidence of stepfamilies is
expressed in various ways, but it is generally given as the proportion that
households containing stepfamilies represent among all households or as
the proportion of children living in stepfamilies. It is variously estimated
that in the United States about one in six (17 percent) of married-couple
family households is a stepfamily (Orleans, Palisi, Caddell, 1989: 371),
and that about one child in six is a stepchild (Burchardt, 1989: 293). These
are, of course, broad-based statistics that hide significant variations by
region, class and by ethnic group, but they indicate the dimensions of the
phenomenon in what might well be the country with the highest incidence
of stepfamilies in the Western world.

Statistics on a nationwide basis, such as those cited above, are not
available for much earlier generations, and historians generally have to
make do with what they can discover for individual communities. The findings vary immensely, as we would expect. Peter Laslett's survey of censuses
in nineteen English communities between 1599 and 1811 revealed that of

Roderick Phillips is Professor of History, Carlton University, Ottawa, Ontario,
Canada.

The author wishes to thank Janine Lanza (Cornell University) who generously
provided material from her research on widowhood.

[Haworth co-indexing entry note]: "Stepfamilies from a Historical Perspective." Phillips, Roderick.
Co-published simultaneously in *Marriage & Family Review* (The Haworth Press, Inc.) Vol. 26, No. 1/2,
1997, pp. 5-18; and: *Stepfamilies: History, Research, and Policy* (ed: Irene Levin and Marvin B.
Sussman) The Haworth Press, Inc., 1997, pp. 5-18. Single or multiple copies of this article are available
for a fee from The Haworth Document Delivery Service [1-800-342-9678, 9:00 a.m. - 5:00 p.m. (EST).
E-mail address: getinfo@haworth.com].

6,668 children resident in households, some 284 (four percent), were living in households that contained a stepparent. But, as Laslett points out, the range was far greater than this combined figure might suggest. His analysis of ecclesiastical censuses in the English village of Clayworth (Nottinghamshire) showed that in 1676 there were 154 resident children, of whom 50 (33 percent) were orphaned. Only seven of these orphans were living in stepfamilies, which meant that some five percent of all resident children were stepchildren. Twelve years later a census of the same community showed 162 resident children, and that roughly the same percentage were orphaned (56 children, representing 35 percent). On the other hand, the number of children resident in stepfamilies had by 1688 quadrupled to 32, raising the proportion of stepchildren in the resident child population to 20 percent.

Just how many households in Clayworth these stepfamilies represented at each census is not stated, but the average number of children in households with children was about 2.1, and this suggests that there might have been 3 households containing stepfamilies in 1676 and 15 in 1688. On this basis, stepfamilies would have accounted for 3 percent of the community's 98 households in 1676, and 16 percent of the 91 households in 1688 (Laslett, 1977: 87 [Table 2.8], 88 [Table 2.11], 164 [Table 4.1], 166 [Table 4.2]). In other words, one in six households in that latter year probably contained a stepfamily. These figures, for a small Nottinghamshire community at the end of the seventeenth century are the same as estimates for the United States three hundred years later. Indeed, just as stepfamilies are recognized as common in modern Western society, so they were in the past. In his survey of the English family in the early modern period, Ralph Houlbrooke notes that "the experience of living in a reconstructed family must have been a common one" (Houlbrooke, 1984: 215).

Yet this apparent continuity from the past to the present masks differences that are so far-reaching in their implications that it is questionable whether we are able to make any meaningful comparisons between stepfamilies in the present and their historic forerunners. This is a caution that applies as much to stepfamilies in the fairly recent past (as recent as the early twentieth century) as to the more distant periods. The most evident difference–which is both a manifestation of underlying demographic change and the source of important shifts in the social and cultural implications of stepfamilies–is that the great majority of stepfamilies in modern Western society result from the marriage or cohabitation of mothers and fathers of children whose other parent is still living. Of these the largest group by far is composed of families formed by the remarriage of divorced men and women. To this extent the incidence of divorce and rates of remarriage by the divorced are key variables in the frequency of modern stepfamilyhood.

In the past, on the other hand, stepfamilies resulted from quite different conditions and had different implications. Far more frequently than today, stepfamilies were the product of remarriages made possible by the death of a spouse, and to this extent it was not divorce and remarriage but the rate of mortality and frequency of remarriage by the widowed that were the variables that largely explained the incidence of stepfamilies. Moreover, unlike their modern counterparts, children who lived in stepfamilies in the past rarely had more than one living biological parent.

This short article will consider the broad circumstances that gave rise to stepfamilies in the past and examine their implications. It will also survey attitudes toward stepfamilies, stepparents and stepchildren, and suggest some of the contours of stepfamily experience. The article will be broadly based on secondary material from early modern and modern Europe, and will also draw on evidence from pre-twentieth century France.

THE DETERMINANTS OF STEPFAMILIES

The frequency of stepfamilies in the past depended upon variables whose number and relative significance not only varied by region and class but also shifted over time. It is likely that before the nineteenth century the main variables were marital fertility (the likelihood that couples would have children), mortality (the point at which a marriage was dissolved by death), and nuptiality (the likelihood that a widow or widower would remarry). In the great majority of cases, a household containing a stepfamily was formed when a number of preconditions were satisfied: when a couple had at least one child, when one of the parents died (leaving a surviving spouse and dependent child), and when the surviving spouse remarried and took the child into the newly-formed household. It was precisely these conditions that led to the formation of the stepfamily households in seventeenth-century Clayworth.

Circumstances that favored the possibility of satisfying these conditions thus increased the incidence of stepfamilies. Of course circumstances, such as famines, that increased mortality might simultaneously depress fertility and nuptiality as men and women delayed forming couples and adding to existing families. But it is important to note that conditions that optimized the formation of stepfamilies were sequential, just as the preconditions were sequential. As an example we can look to the "demographic crises" that regularly struck many parts of early modern Europe. These crises, generally provoked by harvest failures, produced a high level of mortality as people not only starved to death but died of diseases to which malnutrition made them more vulnerable. At the same time, the number of marriages declined as women and men delayed forming new households in times of hardship, and the number of conceptions fell, in part as a result of the reduction in marriages, in part because couples delayed adding to their families when resources were scarce. Once the subsistence crisis had passed and mortality returned to pre-scarcity rates, however, there were generally short-term increases in the number of marriages and conceptions above the pre-crisis level that went some way toward compensating for the lower numbers during the crisis. Demographic crises, then, might well have led to a sharp increase in the proportion of stepfamilies in a specific population by producing an unusually high number of widows and widowers who remarried as soon as conditions improved (Goubert, 1960: II, 56ff.).

There were, of course, other variables, and fertility and nuptiality must be understood in their social, economic, and cultural contexts. Both were influenced by their environment (as the experience of demographic crises demonstrates) but there were also underlying social imperatives that must be considered. One was the sheer necessity for many women and men to remarry after widow(er)hood in pre-industrial populations. The key here was the household economy that bound all members of a family household in a set of interrelated economic relationships such that each member of a household depended upon the contribution of the others for his or her survival. The married couple were at the center of the household economy, and wife and husband carried out tasks that were often defined by gender and which were complementary. The relationships thus created bound husband and wife into a relationship of reciprocity and interdependence that went far beyond the economic sphere, but that was nonetheless fundamentally economic (Medick, 1981: 38-73; Wall, 1986: 261-94).

An important implication of this marital economy was that the death of either spouse had a devastating economic effect, apart from any social and emotional impact (it is impossible to separate one from the others very clearly). As many historians have noted, the death of a spouse had a dramatic effect on the domestic economy. Olwen Hufton, for example, writes that "the loss of either party in a marriage would also certainly wreck the entire fabric of the family economy" (Hufton, 1975: 17). The need to reconstitute the family economy lay behind the imperative for widows and widowers to remarry and to remarry quickly. One result was that a high proportion of marriages in pre-twentieth-century Europe included at least one partner who had been married and widowed. A study of one community in eastern France over the period 1670-1840 found that more than a third of marriages (37 percent) included a previously-married spouse. Seventeen percent were spinster-widower marriages, 8 percent involved bachelors and widows, and 12 percent saw widows and widowers marry (Bideau, 1980: 30, Table 2).

The rapidity of remarriage in many preindustrial societies has often drawn the attention of historians (Cabourdin, 1978: 305-32; Dupaquier, 1981, *passim*). In the English community of Earls Colne from the sixteenth to eighteenth centuries, for example, 60 percent of widowers who remarried had done so within a year of their wives' deaths, and on average these men waited only five months before contracting a new marriage. Widows in the community married less rapidly (Macfarlane, 1986: 235). In the French village of Thezels-Saint-Sernin in the eighteenth century (1700-1792), almost half the widowers who remarried did so within seven months of their wives' deaths. Again, widows married less rapidly but more than a third had remarried within 18 months of being widowed (Valmary, 1965: 102-3).

Not all widows and widowers were equally likely to remarry. Some must have been under greater pressure than others to reconstitute a family economy, and some must have been more attractive than others as marriage partners. The evidence strongly suggests that age at widowhood was a critical variable in the likelihood of remarriage. Bideau's study of Thoissey showed that the proportion of widows who remarried declined with age: some 60 percent of those under 30 at the time of widowhood remarried, but this was true of only 43 per cent in their thirties, 14 percent of those in their forties, and ten per cent of those in their fifties (Bideau, 1980: 35, Table 5).

The presence of dependent children was no doubt a critical variable. We can speculate that a widower with dependent children might be under immense pressure to remarry so as to provide a woman to look after them, while a widowed mother might well have quickly sought a new husband to replace the income lost by the death of her husband. On the other hand, a widow with children was very likely not an attractive marriage proposition; in Earls Colne, widows with children married less rapidly than those without (Macfarlane, 1986: 235). It is no accident that the bulk of the poor population of preindustrial Europe consisted of women (never married, widowed, or deserted) and their dependent children. Although we should not want to push this idea too far, it might be suggested that, from the perspective of widows, poverty must frequently have been the result of the inability or unwillingness of women to reenter marriage–that is, their inability or unwillingness to create stepfamilies. Quite possibly, the frequency of stepfamilies and the incidence of poverty were linked, in early modern society, in an inverse relationship.

A widowed mother who was able to contribute tangibly to a new marriage was, however, a different proposition. Possession of property, for example, might more than compensate for the burden of children, and in nineteenth-century Norway Eilert Sundt noted that widows with property married more often and more rapidly than those without (Drake, 1969: 136). Similarly, widows who had rights to guild membership were likely to be attractive as marriage partners for skilled workers.

Stepfamilies in preindustrial Europe were, then, generally a result of the socio-economic and demographic regime within which the family household was the basic economic unit, to which marriage was fundamental, and where high rates of mortality prevailed. From this perspective the stepfamily was integral to Western society, and it should not be surprising that they were frequently to be found. It ought, in fact, to be more surprising to encounter low rates of stepfamilyhood, such as that found in Clayworth in 1676, than the high rates that prevailed in the same community twelve years later.

We should bear in mind that even though the great majority of stepfamilies in the period under discussion were made possible by death, some were (like modern stepfamilies) the result of remarriage following divorce. Divorce, legalized in most of Protestant Europe in the sixteenth century, and in other parts between the eighteenth and twentieth centuries, remained rare until the last seventy years, but it did reach significant levels in some places. In 1792, for example, divorce was legalized in France and made easily and cheaply available to husbands and wives on a more or less equal basis. The result was some 20,000 divorces (an astonishing number for the time) throughout the country during the following decade, most in the first two or three years as men and women whose marriages had broken down years earlier took advantage of the new law (Phillips, 1988: 256-60). The legalization of divorce enabled many men and women to contract new marriages and thus to form stepfamilies; in the Norman city of Rouen, which had one of the highest divorce rates, 28 percent of men and 25 percent women who divorced eventually remarried (Phillips, 1981: 83). There was, however, a tendency for divorced couples to be without children: two thirds of divorcing couples in Rouen had no children under the age of majority (21 years), and to this extent even the relatively high incidence of divorce in France in the last decade of the eighteenth century can have had little impact on the frequency of stepfamilies (Phillips, 1981: 78, Table 2.14). If the figures for Rouen are generalized, the 20,000 divorces might have resulted in the formation of no more than 2,000 stepfamilies throughout the whole of France.

The example of Clayworth, however, alerts us to the fact that the incidence of stepfamilies must have varied markedly over time, generally in tandem with (though lagging behind) trends in mortality and nuptiality. Because of the variability of the conditions that gave rise to stepfamilies, there is no useful generalization about the incidence of stepfamilies in the past. To suggest that a certain percentage of households were composed of stepfamilies would be a meaningless generalization that concealed far more than it revealed.

Not only did stepfamilies in the past originate in demographic and social conditions that were markedly different from those of the second half of the twentieth century, but their meaning for their members also varied. In the past a stepparent *replaced* rather than *added to* an existing parent. Even granted that in modern times a non-custodial parent might be physically or socially absent from his or her child, the sheer difference between having and not having a living parent or former spouse or partner cannot but have altered the meaning of the stepfamily for both parents and children.

In addition, stepfamilyhood was only one phase that a family might experience. The family formed by the remarriage of a widow with a child would cease to be a stepfamily if her husband predeceased her (disparities in ages at remarriage meant that women often had a good chance of outliving two or three husbands) or if the child died. If the couple had another child in addition to the wife's by her previous marriage there the stepfamily would exist in tandem with the other.

ATTITUDES TOWARD STEPFAMILIES

In view of the centrality, even necessity, of stepfamilies to the pre-industrial European demographic regime, the reputation of stepfamilies is astonishingly negative; they were regarded neither positively nor neutrally, but in general as something to be avoided or, if they took place, as likely to be disastrous. In the sixteenth century one Norwich (England) widow, Katherine Andrews, informed her widower suitor that she could not marry him because doing so would form a stepfamily: "I will never be a stepmother, for I understand ye have children, and that should cause us never to agree" (Houlbrooke, 1984: 211). In the early nineteenth century a French legislator had this to say about stepfamilies: "Experience proves only too clearly that second marriages are generally disastrous for the children of the first marriage. The law does not suppose that a father has the same tenderness, the same care, for his children by his first marriage" (Vezin, 1803: 8).

These comments, which are examples of commonly-expressed attitudes toward stepfamilies in the early modern period, suggest two principal effects of stepfamilies. The first is that stepchildren suffer, and the point is often made that they suffer at the hands of stepmothers. It is possible that widowed men with children were more likely than widowed women with children, and that there were more stepmothers than stepfathers in European populations. It is possible, too, that stepmothers received more attention because they were more involved than fathers with the day-to-day business of child-raising. Whatever the reason, stepmothers had a thoroughly negative association in the period, and there is no evidence that biological mothers and fathers were differentiated in anything like the same manner. The stepmother has come down to us as a figure of cruelty and evil, constantly plotting to harm her stepchildren in a myriad ways. It is notable that the French word *maratre* means both "stepmother" and a "cruel or harsh mother," and that in English "stepmother" is often preceded by "wicked."

The second implication of stepfamilyhood is that the tension or outright conflict between stepparent and stepchild(ren) would result in tension or conflict between the spouses. The implications of this belief are far-reaching. It suggests, for one thing, that parents cared more for their children than their spouses insofar as they were prepared to risk the spousal conflict that taking a child's side might entail. The popular conception of stepfamilies, in short, was of an institution characterized by tension and conflict as stepparents and stepchildren battled for resources of all kinds, from emotional to material.

As for stepchildren, they are portrayed in tradition as children who do not belong, or whose quality of belonging is not much greater than that of orphans. This is surely significant because while the essence of being an orphan is that a child is deprived of at least one, and generally two, parent(s)–that is to say, orphans are defined by deprivation–stepchildren are defined by reference to a parent figure, the person who had married their biological parent. That a relationship defined by reference to an extant figure should popularly be thought of as "belonging" no more than one defined by reference to deprivation is a powerful statement about the meaning of the stepfamily in Western culture.

THE EXPERIENCE OF STEPFAMILIES

The experience of stepfamilies in the past is difficult to recapture. That of the early twentieth century can be recovered to some extent by oral historians, but earlier than that the sources upon which historians can draw are spotty and not necessarily representative of general experience. One of the most useful sources, court records dealing with stepfamilies, is almost invariably biased toward tension and conflict; harmonious families are rarely involved in the litigation involving marriage, family discipline, or inheritance, that constitutes the core of family-based cases.

The tension and conflict that commentators described or predicted in stepfamilies certainly emerge as the dominant themes from accounts of life in such households that were recorded in legal records. Stepchildren, for example, were often cited as causes or catalysts of conflict in divorce cases that were heard in France during the 1790s. Although it was often argued that children were a force for marital harmony in so far as they represented a common interest on the part of husbands and wives, almost all the children (10 out of 14 cases) involved in marital disputes leading to divorce in Rouen were children of an earlier marriage by the husband or wife. In one case a man beat his wife bloody because (as he himself said), she "refused to dress his child"–that is, his child by one of his two previous marriages. In this case the apparent neglect of the child by the stepmother appears rather as a catalyst for conflict, for the couple involved had a history of tension: the wife was reported as having alleged "that he [her husband] had caused the death of his first two wives and that he would kill her too" (AD Seine Maritime, LP7098, 4 June 1793). In another divorce case, however, ill-treatment of stepchild appears to have been more essentially involved in matrimonial conflict. When a step-mother beat her stepdaughter, the latter cried out and a neighbor witnessed the father "come down to the cries of his daughter, armed with a saber, and say to his wife, 'slut, you are trying to kill my daughter.' He raised the sabre but the witness placed his hand on the man's arm and the sabre fell" (AD Seine Maritime, LP6737, 13 August 1798).

Such examples suggest that when remarriages were in conflict, alliances might occur between children and their biological parents and fissures between stepchildren and stepparents. This principle was well illustrated in the Rouen divorce cases by the case of the Michels, husband and wife, each of whom had been married before and each of whom brought a son by the previous marriage to their new household. When an argument broke out between the two boys–now half-brothers–"the husband and wife Michel came and each took the side of their child. Citizen Michel called his wife a slut and a whore, and she replied 'Damn you, I have to defend my son'" (AD SEine Maritime, LP6735, 15 November 1796).

These cases would probably not have surprised anyone, for there seems to have been an expectation that stepfamilies meant trouble. But there was even a suggestion that men who had children in successive marriages were less solicitous about the children of the first.

What lay at the base of these tensions within families? The divorce cases that provide the above examples do not reveal the source of conflict; it was enough to show conflict and violence in order to obtain a divorce. We can only speculate on the reasons for antipathy between stepparents and stepchildren.

A likely source was property, for in most French legal codes (there were many different codes before a uniform law was introduced during the French Revolution) the remarriage of woman or man with children complicated inheritance. Part of the children's patrimony was diverted to their stepmother or stepfather, while the inheritance a husband or wife could expect was reduced by the entitlements of his or her stepchildren. Overall, it is likely that if there was to be resentment over the effects of remarriage and the creation of a stepfamily from the perspective of inheritance, we should expect the stepparent to feel it more keenly than a young stepchild. Provisions in some marriage contracts attempted to deal with these issues. An example is one arranged in 1709 between Louis Buisson and Anne Dory, a widow with two daughters (aged twelve and seven) from her first marriage. The contract allowed that the girls could live in the new household until they reached the age of 20 (even though the age of majority was 25), but that the costs of their upbringing would be a charge on the money they had inherited from their father. They would have no claim on the assets of their mother's second marriage (Archives Nationales, Minutier Centrale, etude XVII/517, February 4, 1709). This, and other similar cases, not only excluded stepchildren from succession, but also prevented them from inheriting from their biological parent after he or she had remarried. On the other hand, any children born to the couple after the remarriage were specifically entitled to inherit. This highlights an important dimension of stepfamilyhood that is often neglected: that children in such families are simultaneously children and stepchildren. In the case just cited, the legal status of Anne Dory's children as her new husband's stepchildren overwhelmed what would have been their legal status as her children had she not remarried.

We get a sense of official unease about the potentially harmful effects of stepfamilyhood on children's property rights from the fact that in sixteenth-century France a series of laws set out to protect the property interests of children by limiting the extent to which remarrying widows could transfer property to their new husbands. (The laws referred specifically to widows, because women were thought to be more foolish or gullible than men.) A 1560 edict on second marriages forbade any widow who remarried to give more of her goods or money to her new husband (or to her new husband's children or other relatives) than given to any one of her children or grandchildren. (The edict was provoked by a scandalous case in which one of wealthiest widows in Paris married a younger man and not only transferred her fortune to him but did all she could to prevent her seven children from inheriting from her.) The law was reinforced in 1576 by another, the Edict of Blois, which expressed particular concern about socially unequal marriages, notably those between a well-off widow and a man of lower social status (Gager, 1996: 63-6).

Clearly these laws bore on a range of issues, but they did express concern about the effects of stepfamilies. One anxiety was the harmful effects that remarriage had on the children when a parent remarried. Another was that a widow should not be able to transfer the family property, built up or conserved by her dead husband, to another man, her subsequent husband. There is a sense here that remarriage/stepfamilyhood (at times they become inseparable for analytical purposes) were harmful to family property when it was viewed from the perspective of acquisition and consolidation by males and transmitted between generations defined biologically. Remarriage and the formation of stepfamilies interfered with these conceptions of the family.

STEPFAMILIES AND OTHER FAMILIES

The anxiety that seems to have surrounded stepfamilies does not appear to have applied to other forms of family formation that included children. One recent book has drawn attention to the incidence of adoption in early modern France, a practice thought to have been absent between the sixteenth and twentieth centuries (Gager, 1996). Adoption in Paris during the sixteenth and seventeenth centuries took two principal forms. The first was a private transfer of authority over a child from one set of parents to another. These transactions were formalized by a notarial contract in which the adoptive parents agreed to assume all responsibility for the child's welfare, upbringing, and education, and which often guaranteed the child's right to inheritance. The second form was institutional, the adoption by a man, woman, or a couple of a child that was housed in a charitable institution. The children concerned here were generally orphans or had been abandoned, and it is thought that most of the latter were nonmarital births.

The frequency of adoptions at this time is uncertain (records relating to them are not centralized), but it is evident that they represented a significant means of family formation that responded to imperatives similar to those that underlay the formation of stepfamilies. This is especially clear in the case of orphaned or abandoned children, who were made available for adoption by the death or disappearance of a parent, which was also a precondition of stepfamily formation. Even private adoptions could arise from mortality, actual and imminent. In 1605, for example, a woman adopted her three-month-old goddaughter whose father had died and whose mother was on the verge of dying. The woman, who had no children of her own, signed a contract in which she promised to raise, educate, apprentice and dower her adopted daughter, and to pass on to her all her property (Gager, 1996: 71).

Similarly, economic motivations often underlay adoption. In its private form, adoption generally witnessed the movement of a child from financially distressed parents to an individual or couple in better circumstances. Seen from this perspective adoption was an alternative to child-abandonment (often resorted to by indigent parents and was a form of social mobility for a child).

Adoptive parents were almost all childless, and to that extent adoption provided a direct heir, an important resource in a society that attached importance to the transmission of property and culture from generation to generation. Adoption, then, provided an alternative form of parenthood and, in the broader sense, of family formation, in a society in which the family was they key economic and cultural institution. We should not overlook the importance of children in the family economy as part of the desire to add a child to a family, although Gager concludes that adoption was probably not exploited as a means of obtaining free labor.

Adoptive children were quite different from stepchildren, it is true. In many of the Paris cases studied by Kristin Gager the children were adopted by relatives–aunts, uncles, grandparents, and by godparents–and even by neighbors. But adoption could provoke tensions similar to those that surrounded stepfamilies. The arrival of an adopted child interfered with pre-existing expectations of succession, for example, and in a number of cases litigation was undertaken by relatives whose successoral rights as collateral heirs the adopted child had replaced. So it was in stepfamilies. An example was the 1751 process of dividing the estate of Thomas Besnard, who was succeeded by his second wife, their six children, and his son from his first marriage. It transpired that when Besnard had remarried, he had held on to the property of his deceased wife, and when he in turn died, his son from that marriage had to litigate in order to retrieve his share of his mother's estate before it was divided among his half-siblings (the children born in his father's second marriage) (Archives Nationales, Minutier Centrale, etude LXXVII/235). The son in this case was fortunate because there remained goods and money from the first marriage. In other cases it was quite conceivable that wealth carried over to a second marriage could be lost in bankruptcy or dissipation by any number of means. Litigation by collateral heirs against adoptive children raised different questions, of course, but both stepfamilies and adoptive families focused attention on the effects of family re-formation on family relationships defined by consanguinity and affinity.

In addition to formalized adoption, other methods of adding children to households were known to early modern French society. Children could be fostered or taken in as apprentices, but in these cases authority over them was limited and they were not integrated into the family in the formal sense that adoption represented. There appears to have been some encouragement for people to add to their families. The administrators of some of Paris's charitable institutions were known to display children in the hope that passers-by would see one they wanted to take home and look after.

Such practices raise at least two important points. First, the spectrum of family formation on which stepfamilyhood lay was, in the early modern period, wider than historians have often recognized. Second, there appears to have been broad social acceptance of the addition of children to families by means other than procreation, and this throws the often negative attitudes toward stepfamilyhood into even sharper relief.

CONCLUSION

The historical incidence of stepfamilies and their implications clearly deserve more attention than they have received so far. Stepfamilies appear to have occupied a position at the intersection of a number of social, economic, and cultural characteristics of the European family system, such that even though they can be seen as the necessary outcome of the pre-industrial socio-demographic regime, their existence gave rise to many forms of anxiety. They appear to have represented tensions between spouses and to have created roles for children (as children and stepchildren) that proved difficult to reconcile. The replacement of "stepfamily" by other terms (like "blended family") and the apparent decline of "stepfather" and "stepmother" in common usage might well speak to a reaction against their historically negative connotations, even though it could be that families formed by remarriages or the cohabitation of previously-cohabiting parents continue to pose problems analogous to those posed by families called "stepfamilies." Not the least of the questions facing historians are the timing and reasons for the fading of "stepfamilies" from popular language, and the cultural reconfiguration of families that result from the remarriage or successive cohabitation of women and men who are parents at the time of transition.

BIBLIOGRAPHY

AD Seine Maritime. Archives Départementales de la Seine Maritime (Rouen).
Archives Nationales. Archives Nationales (Paris).

Bideau, Alain. 1980. "A Demographic and Social Analysis of Widowhood and Remarriage: the Example of the castellany of Thoissey-en-Dombes." *Journal of Family History 5.*

Burchardt, Nastasha. 1989. "Structure and relationships in stepfamilies in early twentieth-century Britain." *Continuity and Change 4.*

Cabourdin, Guy. 1978. "Le Remariage." *Annales de Dmographie Historique* 1978: 305-32.

Drake, Michael. 1969. *Population and Society in Norway, 1735-1865.* Cambridge: Cambridge University Press.

Dupaquier, Jacques. 1981. *Marriage and Remarriage in Populations of the Past.* London.

Gager, Kristin Elizabeth. 1996. *Blood Ties and Fictive Ties: Adoption and Family Life in Early Modern France.* Princeton: Princeton University Press.

Goubert, Pierre. 1960. *Beauvais et le Beauvaisis de 160 à 1730.* Paris: Presses Universitaires de France.

Houlbrooke, Ralph. 1984. *The English Family, 1450-1700.* London.

Hufton, Olwen. 1975. "Women and the Family Economy in Eighteenth-Century France." *French Historical Studies 9*: 1-22.

Laslett, Peter. 1977. *Family Life and Illicit Love in Earlier Generations.* Cambridge: Cambridge University Press.

Macfarlane, Alan. 1986. *Marriage and Love in England, 1300-1840.* Oxford: Blackwell.

Medick, Hans. 1981. "The Proto-Industrial Family Economy," in Peter Kriedke, Hans Medick, and Jurgen Schlumbohm (eds.), *Industrialization Before Industrialization.* Cambridge: Cambridge University Press.

Orleans, Myron, Palisi, Bartolomeo J., and Caddell, David. 1989. "Marriage Adjustment and Satisfaction of Stepfathers: Their Feelings and Perceptions of Decision-Making and Stepchildren Relations." *Family Relations 38.*

Phillips, Roderick. 1981. *Family Breakdown in Late Eighteenth-Century France: Divorces in Rouen, 1792-1803.* Oxford: The Clarendon Press.

Phillips, Roderick. 1988. *Putting Asunder: A History of Divorce in Western Society.* New York: Cambridge University Press.

Valmary, Pierre. 1965. *Familles paysannes au XVIIIe siècle en Bas-Quercy.* Paris: Presses Universitaires de France.

Vezin. 1803. *Rapport fait par Vezin, au nom de la section de législation . . . relatif à la puissance paternelle.* Paris: Imprimerie nationale.

Wall, Richard. 1986. "Work, Welfare and the Family: An Illustration of the Adaptive Family Economy," in Lloyd M. Bonfield, Richard M. Smith, and Keith Wrightson (eds.), *The World We Have Gained: Histories of Population and Social Structure.* Oxford.

Stepfamilies in 1984 and Today–
A Scholarly Perspective

Marilyn Ihinger-Tallman
Kay Pasley

Almost two decades have passed since family scholars began to systematically investigate the phenomenon of remarriage and stepfamily formation. Divorce and its consequences attracted the attention of family scholars in the early 1970s; however, little attention was paid to the fact that most divorced people also remarried. Researchers were slow to show interest in marital transitions beyond that of divorce. Some early exceptions were Bernard (1956), Bohannan (1970), and Duberman (1975). Further, most researchers were slow to acknowledge the differences between stepfamilies and first-marriage families. This acknowledgment came first from clinicians and others in the helping professions who brought these differences to the attention of researchers (see as examples, Berkowitz, 1970; Bitterman, 1968; Fast & Cain, 1966; Visher & Visher, 1978a & 1978b). We credit Cherlin's 1978 article that suggested remarriage was an "incomplete institution" as the catalyst that called attention to the difficulties inherent in remarriage and the stepfamilies that form after remarriage to researchers.

During the 1980s and early 1990s, research interest in remarriage and stepfamilies grew dramatically. Reviews of this literature document the increased interest in these families (see Cherlin & Furstenberg, 1994;

Marilyn Ihinger-Tallman is Professor and Chair of Sociology at Washington State University, Pullman, WA. Kay Pasley is Associate Professor of Human Development and Family Studies at the University of North Carolina-Greensboro, Greensboro, NC.

[Haworth co-indexing entry note]: "Stepfamilies in 1984 and Today–A Scholarly Perspective." Ihinger-Tallman, Marilyn, and Kay Pasley. Co-published simultaneously in *Marriage & Family Review* (The Haworth Press, Inc.) Vol. 26, No. 1/2, 1997, pp. 19-40; and: *Stepfamilies: History, Research, and Policy* (ed: Irene Levin and Marvin B. Sussman) The Haworth Press, Inc., 1997, pp. 19-40. Single or multiple copies of this article are available for a fee from The Haworth Document Delivery Service [1-800-342-9678, 9:00 a.m. - 5:00 p.m. (EST). E-mail address: getinfo@haworth.com].

19

Coleman & Ganong, 1990; Ihinger-Tallman, 1988; Pasley & Ihinger-Tallman, 1992, 1995). Here we review some of the major findings from this body of research and comment on the state of our knowledge. First, we discuss the methodological improvements that resulted in a more sophisticated understanding of the complexity surrounding stepfamily life. Then we address several consistent findings in the research literature that provide a foundation of "known facts" about remarriage and stepfamilies. Next, we summarize the findings from the empirical literature that emphasizes both the characteristics of the population and the key relationships formed in stepfamilies. We also discuss the most frequently studied topic, the effects of remarriage on children. Lastly, we offer some recommendations for future research efforts. One caveat must be recognized in this overview. The specific studies discussed are not inclusive of all studies on the topic but are used in an illustrative manner.

METHODOLOGICAL OBSERVATIONS

In the past 10 years more sophisticated designs have been used in research studies of remarriage and stepfamilies than was true previously. Now most research addresses the complexities of stepfamily structure. Earlier, scholars had recommended that research designs move beyond simple between-group comparisons to include more refined groupings and explore within-group comparisons (Coleman & Ganong, 1990; Esses & Campbell, 1984; Pasley & Ihinger-Tallman 1992; Price-Bonham & Balswick, 1980). For example, the earliest studies only differentiated first-married families from remarried families, as if all families in these two structures were the same. If greater differentiation occurred within groups it was typical to compare simple and complex stepfamilies or stepfather and stepmother families (Ganong & Coleman, 1987). Recent studies have included more specific differentiations in structural complexity and other key factors, e.g., that reflect the diversity of stepfamilies (see as examples, Hetherington & Clingempeel, 1992; Fine, Voydanoff, & Donnelly, 1993; Pruit, Calsyn, & Jenson, 1993).

Further, recent studies commonly include additional information that specifies the conditions under which stepfamily behavior is enacted. For example, studies of the effects of living in a stepfamily on child outcomes often include information on how old the child was when the remarriage occurred, whether remarriage followed parental divorce or the death of a parent, and custodial arrangements. Other improvements include (a) tests for interaction effects or a wide variety of control variables, (b) selection of samples that distinguish stepfather from stepmother families, (c) comparisons that differentiate families where stepchildren are "living-in" or "living-out," and (d) use of first families and/or single-parent families as comparison groups (Crosbie-Burnett, 1991; Gold, Bubenzer, & West, 1993; Haurin, 1992; Hetherington, 1993; Marks & McLanahan, 1993).

There appears to be a trend toward addressing more complicated research questions about family processes within different family structures. Many scholars have examined the effects of various parenting behavior as one indicator of family process on child outcomes (e.g., Amato, 1994; Anderson, Hetherington, Reiss, & Howe, 1994; Kurdek, Fine, & Sinclair, 1995). Other recent studies emphasize the role of social cognitions as part of a cognitive process affecting children's behaviors (Fine & Kurdek, 1994).

We note that many of these change came about primarily because data from several national studies (e.g., National Survey of Families and Households) were made available to researchers. For example, these data offer information based on representative samples with oversampling of divorced and remarried families. Other national or state surveys also provide data using large, random samples that permit comparisons between and within groups. Included in several longitudinal studies are data useful to researchers interested in remarriage and stepfamilies. Examples include the 1990 Family and Friends Survey (Canadian), the Michigan Study of Adolescent Life Transitions, National Longitudinal Surveys of Labor Market Experience of Youth, Panel Study of Income Dynamics, National Survey of Children, and National Education Longitudinal Survey. Some of these datasets provide more detailed information on family structure than do others. However, for the research community, even with their limitations these data permit the exploration of important empirical questions that have remained unanswered due to small samples that did not permit group comparison. The use of these newly available datasets also allows scholars to raise empirical questions that were not able to be addressed in the past, such as those related to change that takes place over time. Thus, many of the methodological recommendations called for earlier have been heeded. We would argue that the knowledge about stepfamilies that has been collected to date will be very useful to students, teachers, lawyers, judges, policy-makers, clinicians, and those in the other helping professions.

CONSISTENT FINDINGS FROM THE RESEARCH

When the wealth of information on remarriage and stepfamilies is examined, some consistencies emerge. We discerned at least five trends that speak to the development of what could be called empirical generalizations. These trends and generalizations are discussed below.

One trend suggests that norms have begun to develop regarding expectations about the stepparent role. Much of the literature on stepparents is derived from studying stepfathers and stepfather families, mostly due to their common occurrence. Findings from several studies show that there is consensus about the degree of stepfather involvement in parenting stepchildren, such that early in the remarriage stepfathers are expected, by both mothers and stepfathers, to be less involved with children (e.g., Amato, 1987; Bray & Berger, 1993; Furstenberg & Cherlin, 1994; Santrock & Sitterle, 1987; Schwebel, Fine, Renner, 1991). This lower involvement has been described as a disengaged style of stepparenting and viewed as healthy and desirable (Bray, Berger, Silverblatt, & Hollier, 1987; Hetherington & Clingempeel, 1992). We also know that there is (a) wide variation in the nature of behaviors deemed acceptable for stepfathers compared to biological fathers (Furstenberg & Cherlin, 1994; Marsiglio, 1992) and (b) stepparenting behaviors are more similar to those of biological parents when children are younger (Marsiglio, 1992). Furthermore, it appears that attitudes and beliefs about roles are formed early in the remarriage and remain stable over time (e.g., Bray, Berger, & Boethel, 1995; Furstenberg, 1987).

A second trend evident in many studies is that time is needed for a stepfamily to develop a sense of family cohesion (emotional closeness) that results in stepfamily integration (e.g., Bray, 1988a; Hetherington, 1991). That there is less closeness in stepfamilies compared to first-families has been well documented (e.g., Anderson & White, 1986; Bray, 1988; Pill, 1990; Pink & Wampler, 1985; Smith, 1991). On the average it seems to take between three and five years for family cohesion to develop and family integration to occur. Related research (Keshet, 1990) shows that remarried couples evaluate their marriage more highly if they do not adhere to expectations about loyalty (one indicator of high cohesion) and family boundaries that are typical of first-married families. It has been argued that stepparents realize that *less* cohesion is healthy for a well-functioning stepfamily and do not set family unity as a goal early in the remarriage (Bray et al., 1987; Hetherington & Clingempeel, 1992; Pink & Wampler, 1985; Smith, 1991; Waldren, Bell, Peek, & Sorell, 1990).

Third, almost all of the research substantiates that the stepmother-stepchild relationship is the most difficult of all stepmember relations, more problematic than the stepfather-stepchild relationship (Ahrons & Wallisch, 1987; Ambert, 1986; Fine et al., 1993; Hobart, 1987; Ihinger-Tallman, 1988). Scholars have suggested several reasons for this difficulty. Furstenberg (1987), for example, argued that because nonresident mothers are more involved with their children postdivorce competition between the mother and stepmother "looms larger." Fathers in the households in his study reported that dealing with their former spouses placed additional strain on their current marital relationship and interfered with the step-mother's relationship with the child. Guisinger, Cowan, and Schuldberg (1989) suggested that the greater involvement of stepmothers in the care of stepchildren results in more opportunities for limit-setting and conflict, a finding supported by Fine and his associates (1993).

Fourth, most studies that examine differences based upon the gender of children find that stepfather-stepdaughter relations are conflictual and neg-ative compared to stepfather-stepson relations, and when combined with a resident stepmother are even more so (Bray, 1988a; Clingempeel, Brand & Ievoli, 1984; Hetherington, 1987, 1991; Hetherington, Cox, & Cox, 1982; Santrock, Warshak, Lindbergh, & Medows, 1982). This may be particu-larly true for early adolescent girls (Hetherington, 1993; Hetherington & Clingempeel, 1992). A recent study by Lee, Burkan, Zimiles, and Ladeswki (1994) found that girls in stepfather families and single-father families were more likely to have behavioral problems than were boys in these families, although no differences were found when emotional prob-lems were examined. When behavioral and emotional problems were combined, girls in father-stepmother families were at greatest risk for problems.

Lastly, it is a well-established finding that children leave the family home sooner when they reside in stepfamily households rather than single-parent or first-family households (Aquilino, 1991; Goldscheider & Gold-scheider, 1989; Kiernan, 1992; Wiser & Burch, 1989). Hetherington (1987) suggested that girls especially had more positive relationships with parents who don't remarry. Other scholars (Aquilino, 1991; Wiser & Burch, 1989) argued that early home-leaving by stepchildren may reflect one means of dealing with problematic or conflictual relationships in the stepfamily.

In summary, 18 years ago Cherlin (1978) wrote that remarriage was an incomplete institution. He called attention to the differences between par-enting one's biological children and parenting someone else's children and the lack of norms associated with this behavior. We argue here that we are witnessing the development of expectations and standards associated with raising children who are not one's own. We agree with Cherlin and Furs-tenberg (1994) that remarriage is not yet institutionalized, but we believe the consistencies reported over and over in the literature are signs that norms have begun to emerge.

In the paragraphs below we summarize findings that are less strongly substantiated but that provide additional information about life as it is experienced in stepfamilies. We conclude with some insights derived from this body of research.

THE CURRENT PICTURE: WHO REMARRIES?

The remarriage rate in the United States currently is about 40%, suggesting that 4 out of 10 people who marry today are entering a marriage in which at least one of the adults has been married before (Norton & Miller, 1992). Further, if a bride or groom has been previously married, in 61% of the cases he or she is marrying someone who also has been married before (Wilson & Clarke, 1992). As has been the case throughout history, men remarry more frequently and more quickly than do women, and this disparity increases with increasing age (Pasley & Lofquist, 1995).

Our post-modern era is characterized by sequential marriage. About one-third of all currently-married people have been married at least once before. It may be that eventually the majority of people will be married more than once during their lifetime if the rate of divorce for first marriages continues at the present pace (estimates vary between 56% and 62%) (Bumpass, 1990; Norton & Miller, 1992). Further, about 60% of remarried couples now dissolve their unions, and couples are divorcing sooner than they did in the 1980s. The median duration of a first marriage was 6.3 years for women aged 20-54 in 1990 compared to 7.9 in 1980 (Glick & Lin, 1987; Norton & Miller, 1992). Looking at specific age categories illustrates this decline very clearly. For young women ages 25-29, the median duration of marriage before divorce was 4.0 years in 1980; in 1990 it was 3.4 years. For older women ages 40-44, the same figures are 9.7 and 7.6 respectively (Norton & Miller, 1992).

Pasley (1995) summarized some of the key factors associated with the probability of remarriage. Being employed increases the odds of remarriage for women, whereas higher levels of education reduce the odds for women, but not for men. The presence of children does not appear to deter remarriage for men or women. Looking at racial differences, white women are more likely to remarry than women of color. Recent evidence (Kitson & Holmes, in press) suggests that divorced women with fewer economic resources are likely to remarry sooner while the opposite is true for men.

In spite of high divorce rates, the percent of divorced persons who remarry suggests that the institution of marriage in the United States continues to be valued. Thus, although the overall marriage and remarriage rates have slowed, among younger people who divorce most remarry within about two years. As has been noted by others, this suggests that it is a particular partner who is rejected rather than the institution of marriage itself. Further, the practice of marrying holds in spite of increasing numbers of people who choose to cohabit. Cohabitation delays the onset of marriage, but most people ultimately do marry, and remarry.

KEY RELATIONSHIPS IN STEPFAMILIES

If spouses were parents in a former marriage, remarriage brings with it unique experiences and a new conceptualization of family. This family has a label–stepfamily–and many studies document the extent to which a stepfamily is negatively stereotyped in many American minds (Bryan, Ganong, Coleman, & Bryan, 1986; Coleman & Ganong, 1987; Ganong, Coleman, & Jones, 1990; Ganong, Coleman, & Mapes, 1990). In the following paragraphs we review the findings on the key relationships within the stepfamily.

Husband-Wife Relations

Many studies have focused on the degree of marital quality, happiness, or satisfaction reported by remarried couples, typically using first-married couples as a comparison (Anderson & White, 1986; Glenn, 1981; White & Booth, 1985). The findings suggest few differences. Using meta-analytic techniques, Vemer, Coleman, Ganong, and Cooper (1989) systematically compared 34 studies assessing marital quality/satisfaction in order to determine the effects of five factors on marital satisfaction, including marriage order, gender, gender of stepparent, stepfamily structure, and presence/residence of stepchildren. No differences were found between stepfather and stepmother families, those who had residential and nonresidential children, and those in simple and complex stepfamily structures.

It has been argued that it is neither the structural complexity nor the presence/absence of children in the home per se that impacts the marital relationship. Rather, the ways in which couples interact around these issues are the key to understanding marital relationships in general and marital relationships in remarriages specifically (Visher & Visher, 1988; Pasley, Dollahite, & Ihinger-Tallman, 1993). Scholars have begun to explore these complex issues. There is some research to support the multiple ways in which children, for example, affect marital outcomes. Research shows that several variables affect marital quality, including beliefs about the stepparent role (Kurdek & Fine, 1991), spousal consensus over how to enact the stepparent role (Bray et al., 1995; Roberts & Price, 1989), and agreement on decisions pertaining to child rearing (Bray et al., 1995;

Kurdek, 1991; Orleans, Palisi, & Calddel, 1989). Working out a mutually satisfying stepparent-stepchild relationship affects marital quality (Brand & Clingempeel, 1987; Bray et al., 1995; Crosbie-Burnett, 1984; Hobart, 1988), as does deriving an equitable arrangement around child care and family work (Guisinger et al., 1989). The birth of a common child affects marital quality in complex ways depending on where stepchildren reside (Ambert, 1986; Ganong & Coleman, 1988). In one study, a common child positively influenced marital stability for up to ten years (Wineberg, 1992).

Stepparent-Stepchild Relations

There has been a good deal of research on the stepparent-stepchild relationship. Most findings suggest that if a stepparent and stepchild can work out a relationship that is *mutually* satisfying whether it be warm or detached, then not only is marital satisfaction enhanced as noted earlier, but stepfamily adjustment also is fostered. This literature backs the conclusion that the nature of the stepparent-stepchild relationship provides a vital key to understanding stepfamily life, as well as child outcomes (such as early "nest-leaving" and involvement in sexual behavior).

The literature overwhelmingly suggests that relationships with stepchildren are more difficult for stepmothers than stepfathers (Brand et al., 1988; Furstenberg & Nord, 1985; Lee et al., 1994; MacDonald & DeMaris, 1996; Quick et al., 1995; White, 1993). However, a mediating factor of this relationship is the residence of children. When stepchildren reside with stepmothers, the stepmothers are more likely to report feelings of security and close partnership with their husbands compared to stepmothers with non-resident stepchildren (Furstenberg & Spanier, 1984; Quick, McKenry, & Newman, 1995; Visher & Visher, 1979).

Both stepmothers and stepfathers report engaging in fewer activities with stepchildren. They report that they communicate less well with stepchildren compared to their own biological children, and they feel they provide less warmth and express fewer positive feelings toward stepchildren than biological parents do toward their children (Ganong & Coleman, 1994; Thomson et al., 1992). Further, MacDonald and DeMaris (1996) found stepmothers had a more difficult time rearing stepchildren than did stepfathers regardless of time spent in parenting activities or household tasks. Whether or not they had given birth to a child fathered by the current husband did not alter these results.

Ganong and Coleman (1994) reviewed a number of studies and found inconsistent findings concerning the effects of the birth of a new child on steprelationships. For example, the presence of a new baby was found to negatively affect the stepmother-stepchild relationship (Ambert, 1986; Santrock & Sitterle, 1987), have no effect on the stepmother-stepchild relationship (Ahrons & Wallisch, 1987; Ganong & Coleman, 1988), positively effect the stepfather-stepchild relationship (Ambert, 1986; Hobart, 1988), and have little effect on any stepfamily relation (Ahrons & Wallisch, 1987; Ganong & Coleman, 1988). Clearly this is a topic that calls for more research before conclusions can be drawn.

Rearing stepdaughters seems to be particularly challenging for stepparents (e.g., Ganong & Coleman, 1995; Hetherington, 1989, 1991; Peterson & Zill, 1986; Vuchinich, Hetherington, Vuchinich, & Clingempeel, 1991). For example, Vuchinich and his associates (1991) found that daughters in stepfamilies avoid conflict with stepfathers, but when conflict is initiated against them, they are oppositional, and this behavior persists through time. Girls also were less responsive to their mothers. Some evidence suggests that daughters are at greater risk for behavioral problems than sons, and girls in stepmother families are at greatest risk for experiencing both behavior and emotional problems (Lee et al., 1994).

Many of the parenting behaviors commonly advocated in first-marriage families (e.g., authoritative parenting style) are less effective in stepfamilies, in the short run. Findings reported by Hetherington and Clingempeel (1992) suggest that stepchildren's externalizing and socially competent behaviors "were driving changes in the parenting of their new stepparents and that children's socially competent behavior also affects changes in warmth expressed by mothers in remarried families" (p. 197). Early on, parental strategies were more reactive. That is, mothers and stepfathers were more negative in their interactions with children that resulted, in part, in more negative behavior elicited by children.

Sibling Relations

According to Ganong and Coleman (1994), approximately 75% of all children who live in a stepfamily have at least one sibling, and 20% have a half-sibling. It is impossible to report an accurate number of stepsiblings because, while we know that about 15% of stepfamilies include the children of both parents (i.e., both parents are stepparents), there is no way of determining how many stepsiblings reside in other homes.

Research on stepsibling relationships is limited relative to other topics of family study. However, several studies provide information about these important family relationships. Looking at adult siblings and using data from the National Survey of Families and Households, White and Riedmann (1992) reported overall contact with adult siblings was lower when there were stepsiblings or half-siblings in the family while growing up.

Adults kept in contact with their step- and half-siblings, but to a lesser degree than they did with their full sibs. They lived closer to full siblings. Those with step- or half-siblings came from larger families, tended to have fewer years of schooling, were more likely to be African-American, were younger, and left the home at an earlier age than those with full siblings. Among adults who lived in a stepfamily, contact with half- or stepsiblings was considerably reduced if they had lived with a stepmother rather than a stepfather.

Lynn White (1994) used these same data to report on sibling solidarity among adults who grew up in either a first-family, a single-parent family, or a remarried family that followed divorce. She found that sibling solidarity was not diminished by divorce and remarriage: respondents who grew up in stepfamilies were likely to regard a sibling as a best friend, but there was no overall effect of parents' remarriage on solidarity among siblings. In addition, divorce and remarriage did not differentiate sibling contact or support given or received by one's parents.

Anderson and Rice (1992) did find sibling relationships less close in remarried families compared to other family types. Adolescents in remarried families appeared to disengage rather than bond with one another, irrespective of any normal developmental process of teenage withdrawal. They also reported that children who were experiencing stress with their mothers' recent remarriage directed more of their negative behavior towards siblings. However, their relationships with siblings and stepsiblings improved over the 26 months of the study. Zill (1988) reported that half-siblings had a negative influence on stepsiblings, and Ganong and Coleman (1993) found children's relationships with half-siblings somewhat more positive than relationships with stepsiblings.

Relations with Grandparents

Grandparents can be a source of needed stability for children during and after a parental divorce. Often, however, the extent of support is dependent upon which parent the grandparent is related to. When a child resides with his or her mother after divorce, relations with paternal grandparents tend to lessen (Cherlin & Furstenberg, 1986; Marks & McLanahan, 1993) unless the nonresident father maintains contact with the children. Current estimates from data from the National Longitudinal Survey of Youth, 1988 survey, indicate only 27.2% of children whose parents were divorced visited with their fathers at least once a week (King, 1994). Another national data set, the National Survey of Families and Households (Sweet, Bumpas, & Call, 1988) showed this figure to be 26.5% as reported by resident mothers; 32.5% of nonresident fathers reported they visited their children at least once a week. Looking at the opposite end of the continuum, 29.1% of mothers and 19.7% of fathers reported that the father visited "not at all." The percent of "never" visits in the National Longitudinal survey was 30.7%.

Lawton, Silverstein and Bengston (1994) reported data from a nationally representative sample of 1500 adult children who were questioned about the relationship with their parents. When parents were remarried they tended to live further away, there were fewer visits and telephone calls, and less closeness was felt towards them. This distanced behavior infers lessened grandparent-stepgrandchild contact and closeness.

Spitze, Logan, Glenn, and Zerger (1994) found telephone contact, visiting, babysitting, and offers of help from one's parents were lowest for remarried daughters compared to married or divorced daughters. Other studies confirm that parent-grandparent involvement is diminished after remarriage (Booth & Edwards, 1992; Clingempeel, Colyar, Brand & Hetherington, 1992). Eggebeen (1992) also found having at least one stepgrandchild inhibited giving assistance (measured in the form of advice, money, childcare or household assistance) to one's adult children.

Only a few studies have examined stepgrandparent relationships and thus no trends are available. However, there is little indication that stepgrandparents are a dependable source of support for children. For example, data from the National Survey of Children (Furstenberg & Spanier, 1984), indicate only 7.5% of remarried respondents reported the older generation had no difficulty accepting new stepgrandchildren. Cherlin and Furstenberg (1986) found that "the younger that children were when their parents remarried, the more the grandparents reported feeling that the children were like biological grandchildren" (quoted in Cherlin & Furstenberg, 1994, p. 368). Henry, Ceglian and Mathews (1992) found different expectations for stepgrandmothers than for grandmothers. The former were perceived by their adult daughters to be less instrumental, less expressive, and more remote in their relationships with stepgrandchildren than were biological grandmothers. Cherlin and Furstenberg (1992) found the stepgrandparent-stepgrandchild relation was contingent on the child's residence. When the child lived in the adult child's household, relations were closer than when the child lived in the home of the other parent. These constraints aside, these authors concluded that the amount of effort put into building a relationship is the determining factor of closeness between steprelatives.

A longitudinal study examining grandparent-grandchild relations over time found children in single-parent families were more involved with grandparents than were children in either first-married or remarried families (Clingempeel et al., 1992). Few gender differences were found, and then only under conditions of pubertal growth for boys which was associated with closer relationships with grandfathers over time.

CHILDREN'S ADJUSTMENT IN STEPFAMILIES

Much of the literature addressing children's adjustment in stepfamilies has come from cross-sectional studies, with a few notable exceptions. The Hetherington and Clingempeel (1992) study followed a group of target children (9-11 years old) in nondivorced, divorced single-mother, and stepfather families over 26 months. They found that children in divorced and remarried families were reported to have more externalizing behavior problems than those in first-marriage families. Both stepfathers and mothers saw children as less competent and more problematic in their scholastic performance and prosocial behaviors; however, teachers did not consistently share the level of concern of parents and stepparents. Thus, these authors argued that behavior problems may be more common at home than at school. As in other studies (Baumrind, 1989; Bray, 1990; Hetherington, 1989), Hetherington and Clingempeel noted that initial reported adjustment difficulties remained as children moved toward adolescence, and some behavior problems emerged during adolescence. Younger children appeared to adjust better to their parents' remarriage as well (Hetherington, 1989; Bray, 1990).

Bray and Berger (1993) reported findings from a cross-sectional, longitudinal study of first-marriage and stepfather families with a target child between the ages of 6 and 8 years. They found that children in stepfamilies of 6 months duration and those in stepfamilies of 5-7 years duration had more behavior problems, stress, and lower social competency than children in first-marriage families. Importantly, however, they noted that a large majority of children in stepfamilies were functioning within a normal range on all adjustment indicators.

Findings from the National Survey of Children (Zill, Morrison, & Coiro, 1993) show that after controlling for the effects of socioeconomic and demographic characteristics "youth in disrupted families were twice as likely to exhibit problems as youth from nondisrupted families" (p. 91). They concluded that remarriage did not have a protective effect, but that it ameliorated some effects for those children who experienced marital disruption early and for whom the remarriage remained intact. They suggested that a remarriage following parental divorce that occurs later in the child's life is more problematic for children's adjustment, a conclusion that is supported by the studies of Hetherington (1988) and Bray (1990) noted earlier.

Other studies have reported useful information about child adjustment and various factors that affect child outcomes. For example, a Michigan study of adolescent adjustment in stepfamilies (Barber & Lyons, 1994) examined some family processes known to affect children. They found adolescents in stepfamilies reported similar levels of permissiveness and family democratic decision-making compared to adolescents in first-families, but they reported more family conflict and less family cohesion. This latter finding is supported by earlier studies with both children and adult respondents (e.g., Bray & Berger, 1993; Smith & Morgan, 1994). Furthermore, Hoffman (1994) found older teens (14-17 years of age) living in stepfamilies were reported to be less attached to their families than were teens from nondivorced families–a finding that also helps explain the greater frequency of home leaving in these adolescents.

Regarding child outcomes specifically and using data from the National Survey of Families and Households, Gorman and Korste (1994) reported that young adults who had lived with a stepparent rather than two biological parents were more likely to form an intimate union before age 20. The unions entered were more likely to be cohabitational rather than legal marriage. Upchurch (1993) found that living in a stepfamily was associated with the likelihood of dropping out of school, giving birth while a teen, and being less likely to attain post secondary schooling. Coffman and Roark (1992) reported adolescents in stepfamilies were less apt to participate in extracurricular activities, read books, spend time with friends, spend time with family, and keep a summer job. A study comparing adolescents in non-divorced, remarried, or single-parent families (DuTroit, Nel, & Steel, 1992), found family structure did not influence either positively or negatively children's personality development. Other research shows that children in stepfamilies are not at greater risk for certain health issues, such as obesity (Lissau & Sorenen, 1994). However, as discussed earlier, child outcomes differ for children living with stepfathers versus stepmothers. Fine and Kurdek (1992) reported higher levels of self-esteem and fewer social problems among stepchildren living with stepfathers compared to those living with stepmothers.

Many of the outcomes reported here also are associated with single-parent households. It is difficult to know the relative contribution of parental remarriage to poor child adjustment. It may well be that most of the negative effects can be attributed to predivorce conditions as suggested by Furstenberg and Teitler (1994) or postdivorce effects (e.g., reduced income, multiple transitions that accompany divorce), of which parental remarriage is only one.

One caution must be added to this discussion. The picture is bleak if findings from studies of clinical samples are examined (Amato & Keith, 1991; Ganong & Coleman, 1987). Recent research compared clinical and nonclinical stepfamilies to identify the ways in which those seeking or involved in clinical services differ from nonclinical families. Brown, Green, and Druckman (1990) found more conflict, less expressiveness, less satisfaction with the stepparent role, and less role reciprocity by the stepchild in response to the stepparent's initiatives in clinical stepfamilies. Bray (1992) compared the family relationship processes and children's adjustment in a small sample of clinical and nonclinical stepfather families. He found that parents in clinical stepfamilies reported children as having more problem behaviors, less prosocial behaviors, and being more shy and withdrawn than children in nonclinical stepfamilies. Clinical stepfamilies were observed to have more negative and less positive parent-to-child interactions. Ganong and Coleman (1987) and Amato and Keith (1991) suggest that the results from clinical studies not be generalized to the larger stepfamily population.

CONCLUSIONS

The research reviewed here offered no surprises, and no new controversies have arisen. In general, the research conducted over the past decade has begun to specify the components of family relationships with more precision. The antecedent conditions under which stepfamily relationships develop or are maintained are being examined with more sophisticated methods of data gathering and analysis. For the most part, theoretical frameworks as guides to research are still lacking, with notable exceptions from Giles-Sims (1995) and Fine and Kurdek (1995). A few scholars have advocated that research be designed to include all family members (Fine & Kurdek, 1995; Ganong & Coleman, 1995), and an interesting new approach includes an examination of the psychological dimensions inherent in family processes (Fine & Kurdek, 1995). The entire range of family processes that may be important to our understanding the effects of remarriage and stepfamily life is only beginning to be explored (Bray, 1992; Hetherington & Clingempeel, 1992).

Several excellent longitudinal studies have moved the study of remarriage and stepfamilies beyond cross-sectional analysis. These include the Virginia Longitudinal Study of Divorce and Remarriage (Hetherington & Clingempeel, 1992), the Developmental Issues in Stepfamilies Research Project (Bray, 1988b), and the National Survey of Families and Households (Sweet et al., 1988). Results from these studies have provided additional insight into change over time in stepfamily relationships.

One important outcome that is evident from this overview of recent research is the consistency in certain behaviors on the part of stepfamily members. While enacted behavior is not the same as behavioral expectations (i.e., normative standards), nevertheless it may be time to recognize the issue of norms-in-formation.

Finally, we suggest that at least some researchers have begun to frame the study of marriage and the family in terms of structural formation, transitions, and reformation of structure (i.e., remarriage and stepfamilies). These studies focus on such variables as transition events, time, community factors (e.g., education, legal institutions), and economic resources. This overarching structural focus does not exclude behavioral processes, for inherent in formation and transition is the study of communication, conflict formation and resolution, power and control, social support, boundary formation and maintenance, and psychological dimensions such as perceptions and attributions. We believe that continued work in this direction will begin to fill the remaining gaps in our knowledge and understanding of remarriage and stepfamily life.

REFERENCES

Ahrons, C. R., & Wallisch, K. (1987). Parenting in the binuclear family: Relationships between biological and stepparents. In K. Pasley & M. Ihinger-Tallman (Eds.), *Remarriage and stepparenting: Current research and theory* (pp. 225-256). New York: Guilford Press.

Amato, P. R. (1987). Family processes in one-parent, stepparent, and intact families: The child's point of view. *Journal of Marriage and the Family, 49,* 327-337.

Amato, P. R. (1993). Children's adjustment to divorce: Theories, hypotheses, and empirical support. *Journal of Marriage and the Family, 55,* 23-38.

Ambert, A. (1986). Being a stepparent: Live-in and visiting stepchildren. *Journal of Marriage and the Family, 48,* 795-804.

Anderson, E. R., Hetherington, E. M., Reiss, D., & Howe, G. (1994). Parents' nonshared treatment of siblings and the development of social competence during adolescence. *Journal of Family Psychology, 8,* 303-320.

Anderson, E. R., & Rice, A. M. (1992). Sibling relationships during remarriage. In E. M. Hetherington & G. W. Clingempeel (Eds.), *Coping with marital transitions* (pp. 149-177). Monographs of the Society for Research in Child Development, 57 (Serial No. 227).

Anderson, J. Z., & White, G.D. (1986). Dysfunctional intact families and stepfamilies. *Family Process,* 25, 407-422.

Aquilino, W. S. (1991). Family structure and home leaving: A further specification of the relationship. *Journal of Marriage and Family, 53,* 999-1010.

Amato, P. R. & Keith, B. (1991). Parental divorce and adult well-being: A meta-analysis. *Journal of Marriage and the Family, 53,* 43-58.

Barber, B. L., & Lyons, J. M. (1994). Family processes and adolescent adjustment in intact and remarriage families. *Journal of Youth and Adolescence, 23,* 421-436.

Baumrind, D. (1989, April). *Sex-differentiated socialization effects in childhood and adolescence in divorced and intact families.* Paper presented at the meeting of the Society for Research in Child Development, Kansas City, MO.

Berkowitz, B. J. (1970). Legal incidence of today's "step" relationship: Cinderella revisited. *Family Law Quarterly, 4,* 209-229.

Bernard, J. (1956). *Remarriage: a study of marriage.* New York: Russel & Russel.

Bitterman, C. M. (1968). The multimarriage family. *Social Casework, 49,* 218-221.

Bohannan, P. (1970). Divorce chains, households of remarriages, and multiple divorces. In P. Bohannan (Ed.), *Divorce and After,* pp. 128-139. Garden City, NY: Doubleday.

Booth, A., Brinkerhoff, D., & White, L. (1984). The impact of parental divorce on courtship. *Journal of Marriage and the Family, 46,* 85-94.

Booth, A., & Edwards, J. N. (1992). Starting over: Why remarriages are more unstable. *Journal of Family Issues, 13,* 179-194.

Brand, E., & Clingempeel, W. G. (1987). Interdependencies of marital and stepparent-stepchild relationships and children's psychological adjustment: Research findings and clinical implications. *Family Relations, 36,* 140-145.

Brand, E., Clingempeel, W. G., Bowen-Woodward, K. (1988). Family relationships and children's psychological adjustment in stepmother and stepfather families. In E. M. Hetherington, J. Arasteh (Eds.) *Divorce, Remarriage and Child Outcomes.* Hillsdale, NJ: Erlbaum.

Bray, J. H. (1988a). Children's development in early remarriage. In E. M. Hetherington & J. D. Arasteh (Eds.), *The impact of divorce, single parenting, and stepparenting on children* (pp. 279-298). Hillsdale, NJ: Erlbaum.

Bray, J. H. (1988b). *Developmental Issues in StepFamilies Research Project: Final report* (Grant No. RO1HD18025). Bethesda, MD: National Institute of Child Health and Human Development.

Bray, J. H. (1992). Family relationships and children's adjustment in clinical and nonclinical stepfather families. *Journal of Family Psychology, 6,* 60-68.

Bray, J. H. & Berger, S. H. (1993). Developmental issues in stepfamilies research project: Family relationships and parent-child interactions. *Journal of Divorce & Remarriage, 19,* (3/4), 197-220.

Bray, J. H., Berger, S. H., & Boethel, C. L. (1995). Role integration and marital adjustment in stepfather families. In K. Pasley & M. Ihinger-Tallman (Eds.), *Stepparenting: Issues in theory, research and practice* (pp. 69-86). Westport, CT: Praeger.

Bray, J. H., Berger, S. H., Silverblatt, A. H., & Hollier, A. (1987). Family process and organization during early remarriage: A preliminary analysis. In J. P. Vincent (Ed.), *Advances in family intervention, assessment, and theory* (pp. 253-279). Greenwich, CT: JAI Press.

Brown, A. C., Green, R. J., & Druckman, J. (1990). A comparison of stepfamilies with and without child-focused problems. *American Journal of Orthopsychiatry, 60,* 556-566.

Bryan, H., Ganong, L. H., Coleman, M., & Bryan, L. (1986). Person perception: Family structure as a cue for stereotyping. *Journal of Marriage and the Family, 48,* 167-174.

Bumpass, L. L. (1990). What's happening to the family? Interactions between demographic and institutional change. *Demography, 27,* 483-498.

Cherlin, A. (1978). Remarriage as an incomplete institution. *American Journal of Sociology, 84,* 634-650.

Cherlin, A. J., & Furstenberg, F. F., Jr. (1986). *The new American grandparent: A place in the family, a life apart.* Cambridge, MA: Harvard University Press.

Cherlin, A. J., & Furstenberg, F. F., Jr. (1994). Stepfamilies in the United States: A reconsideration. *Annual Review of Sociology, 20,* 359-381.

Clingempeel, W. S., Brand, E., & Ievoli, R. (1984). Stepparent-stepchild relationships in stepmother and stepfather families: a multimethod study. *Family Relations, 33,* 465-473.

Clingempeel, W. G., Colyar, J. J., Brand, E., & Hetherington, E. M. (1992). Children's relationships with maternal grandparents: A longitudinal study of family structure and pubertal status effects. *Child Development, 63,* 1404-1422.

Coffman, S. G., & Roark, A. E. (1992). A profile of adolescent anger in diverse family configurations and recommendations for intervention. *The School Counselor, 39,* 211-216.

Coleman, M., & Ganong, L. H. (1987). The cultural stereotyping of stepfamilies. In K. Pasley & M. Ihinger-Tallman (Eds.), *Remarriage and stepparenting: Current research and theory* (pp. 19-41). New York: Guilford Press.

Coleman, M., & Ganong, L. (1990). Remarriage and stepfamily research in the 80s: New interest in an old family form. *Journal of Marriage and the Family, 52,* 925-940.

Crosbie-Burnett, M. (1984). The centrality of the step relationship: A challenge to family theory and practice. *Family Relations, 33,* 459-464.

Crosbie-Burnett, M. (1991). Impact of joint versus sole custody and quality of co-parental relationship on adjustment of adolescents in remarried families. *Behavioral Sciences and the Law, 9,* 439-449.

Duberman, L. (1975). *The reconstituted family: A study of remarried couples and their children.* Chicago: Nelson Hall.

DuToit, J., Nel, E., & Steel, H. (1992). Personality traits of a group of young adults from different family structures. *Journal of Psychology, 126,* 407-410.

Eggebeen, D. J. (1992). Family structure and intergenerational exchanges. *Research on Aging, 14,* 427-447.

Esses, L. & Campbell, R. (1984). Challenges of researching the remarried. *Family Relations, 33,* 415-424.

Fast, I., & Cain, A. C. (1966). The stepparent role: Potential for disturbances in family functioning. *American Journal of Orthopsychiatry, 36,* 485-491.

Fine, M. A., & Kurkek, L. A. (1992). The adjustment of adolescents in stepfather & stepmother families. *Journal of Marriage and the Family*, 54, 725-736.

Fine, M. A., & Kurdek, L. A. (1995). A multidimensional cognitive-developmental model of stepfamily adjustment. In K. Pasley & M. Ihinger-Tallman (Eds.), *Stepparenting: Issues in theory, research and practice* (pp. 15-32). Westport, CT: Praeger.

Fine, M. A., Voydayoff, P., & Donnelly, B. W. (1993). Relations between parental control and warmth and child well-being in stepfamilies. *Journal of Family Psychology*, 7, 222-232.

Furstenberg, F. F., Jr. (1987). The new extended family: The experience of parents and children after remarriage. In K. Pasley & M. Ihinger-Tallman (Eds.), *Remarriage and stepparenting: Current research and theory* (pp. 42-61). New York: Guilford.

Furstenberg, F. F., Jr., & Nord, C. W. (1985). Parenting apart: Patterns of child rearing after marital disruption. *Journal of Marriage and the Family*, 47, 893-904.

Furstenberg, F. F., Jr., & Spanier, G. B. (1984). *Recycling the family: Remarriage after divorce*. Beverly Hills, CA: Sage.

Furstenberg, F. F., Jr., & Tietler, J. O. (1994). Reconsidering the effects of marital disruption: What happens to children of divorce in early adulthood? *Journal of Family Issues*, 14, 173-190.

Ganong, L. H., & Coleman, M. (1987). Effects of parental remarriage on children: An updated comparison of theories, methods and findings from clinical and empirical research. In K. Pasley & M. Ihinger-Tallman (Eds.), *Remarriage and stepparenting: Current research and theory* (pp. 94-104). New York: Guilford.

Ganong, L. H., & Coleman, M. (1988). Do mutual children cement bonds in stepfamilies? *Journal of Marriage and the Family*, 50, 687-698.

Ganong, L. H., & Coleman, M. (1993). An exploratory study of stepsibling subsystems. *Journal of Divorce & Remarriage*, 19(3/4), 125-142.

Ganong, L. H., & Coleman, M. (1994). *Remarried family relationships*. Newbury Park, CA: Sage.

Ganong, L. H., & Coleman, M. (1995). Adolescent stepchild-stepparent relationships: Changes over time. In K. Pasley & M. Ihinger-Tallman (Eds.), *Stepparenting: Issues in theory, research and practice* (pp. 87-104). Westport, CT: Praeger.

Ganong, L. H., Coleman, M., & Jones, G. (1990). Effects of behavior and family structure on perceptions. *Journal of Educational Psychology*, 82, 820-825.

Ganong, L. H., Coleman, M., & Mapes, D. (1990). A meta-analytic review of family structure stereotypes. *Journal of Marriage and the Family*, 52, 287-297.

Giles-Sims, J. (1995). Comparison of implications of the justice and care perspectives for theories of remarriage and stepparenting. In K. Pasley & M. Ihinger-Tallman (Eds.), *Stepparenting: Issues in theory, Research and Practice* (pp. 33-50). Westport, CT: Praeger.

Glenn, N. D. (1981). The well-being of persons remarried after divorce. *Journal of Family Issues*, 2, 61-75.

Glick, P. C., & Lin, S. L. (1987). Remarriage after divorce: Recent changes and demographic variations. *Sociological Perspectives*, *30*, 162-179.

Gold, J. M., Bubenzer, D. L., & West, J. D. (1993). Differentiation from ex-spouses and stepfamily marital intimacy. *Journal of Divorce & Remarriage*, *19*(3/4), 83-96.

Goldscheider, F. K., & Goldscheider, C. (1989). Family structure and conflict: Nest-leaving expectations of young adults and their parents. *Journal of Marriage and the Family*, *51*, 87-97.

Gorman, B. K., & Forste, R. (1994). The influence of childhood family structure on entry into cohabitation or marriage during adolescence. *Family Perspective*, *28*, 113-124.

Guisinger, S., Cowan, P. A., & Schuldberg, D. (1989). Changing parent and spouse relations in the first years of remarriage of divorced fathers. *Journal of Marriage and Family*, *51*, 445-456.

Haurin, R. J. (1992). Patterns of childhood residence and the relationship to young adult outcomes. *Journal of Marriage and the Family*, *54*, 846-860.

Henry, C. S., Ceglian, C. P., & Matthews, D. W. (1992). The role behaviors, role meanings, and grandparenting styles of grandmothers and stepgrandmothers: Perception of the middle generation. *Journal of Divorce & Remarriage*, *17*(3/4), 1-22.

Hetherington, E. M. (1987). Family relations six years after divorce. In K. Pasley & M. Ihinger-Tallman (Eds.), *Remarriage and stepparenting: Current research and theory* (pp. 185-205). New York: Guilford Press.

Hetherington, E. M. (1989). Coping with family transitions: Winners, losers, and survivors. *Child Development*, *60*, 1-14.

Hetherington, E. M. (1991). The role of individual differences and family relationships in children's coping with divorce and remarriage. In P. Cowan & E. M. Hetherington (Eds.), *Family transitions* (pp. 165-194). Hillsdale, NJ: Erlbaum.

Hetherington, E. M. (1993). An overview of the Virginia Longitudinal Study of Divorce and Remarriage with a focus on early adolescence. *Journal of Family Psychology*, *7*, 39-56.

Hetherington, E. M., & Clingempeel, W. G. (1992). Coping with marital transitions: A family systems perspective. *Monographs of the Society for Research on Child Development*, *57*(2/3, Serial no. 227).

Hetherington, E. M., Cox, M., & Cox, R. (1982). The effects of divorce on parents and children. In M. Lamb (Ed.), *Nontraditional families* (pp. 233-288). Hillsdale, NJ: Lawrence Earlbaum Associates.

Hobart, C. W. (1987). Relationships in remarried families. *Canadian Journal of Sociology*, *13*, 261-282.

Hobart, C. (1988). Perception of parent-child relationships in first married and remarried families. *Family Relations*, *37*, 175-182.

Hoffman, J. P. (1994). Investigating the age effects of family structure on adolescent marijuana use. *Journal of Youth and Adolescence*, *23*, 215-235.

Ihinger-Tallman. M. (1988). Research on Stepfamilies. In W. R. Scott & J. Blake (Eds.), *Annual Review of Sociology*, 14, (pp. 25-48).

Keshet, J. K. (1990). Cognitive remodeling of the family: How remarried people view stepfamilies. *American Journal of Orthopsychiatry, 60*, 196-203.

Kiernan, K. E. (1992). The impact of family disruption in childhood on transitions made in young adult life. *Population Studies, 46*, 213-234.

King, V. (1994). Nonresident father involvement and child well-being: Can dads make a difference? *Journal of Family Issues, 15*, 78-96.

Kitson, G. & Holmes, E., in press.

Kurdek, L. A. (1991). The relations between reported well-being and divorce history, availability of a proximate adult, and gender. *Journal of Marriage and the Family, 53*, 71-78.

Kurdek, L. A., & Fine, M. A. (1991). Cognitive correlates of satisfaction for mothers and stepfathers in stepfather families. *Journal of Marriage and the Family, 53*, 565-572.

Kurdek, L. A., Fine, M. A., & Sinclair, R. J. (1995). School adjustment in sixth graders: Parenting transitions, family climate, and peer norm effects. *Child Development, 66*, 430-445.

Lawton, L., Silverstein, M., & Bengston, V. (1994). Affection, social contact, and geographic distance between adult children and their parents. *Journal of Marriage and the Family, 56*, 57-68.

Lee, V. E., Burkan, D. T., Zimiles, H., & Ladeswki, B. (1994). Family structure and its effects on behavioral and emotional problems in young adolescents. *Journal of Research on Adolescence, 4*, 405-437.

Lissau, I., & Sorensen, T. I. A. (1994). Parental neglect during childhood and increased risk of obesity in young adulthood. *Lancet, 343*(8893), 324-327.

MacDonald, W. L. & DeMaris, A. (1996). The effects of stepparent's gender and new biological children. *Journal of Family Issues, 17*, 5-25.

Marks, N. F., & McLanahan, S. S. (1993). Gender, family structure, and social support among parents. *Journal of Marriage and the Family, 55*, 481-493.

Marsiglio, W. (1992). Stepfathers with minor children living at home: Parenting perceptions and relationship quality. *Journal of Family Issues, 13*, 195-214.

Norton, A. J., & Miller, L. F. (1992). Remarriage among women in the United States: 1985. *Studies in Household and Family Formation* (Series P-23, No. 169). Washington, DC: Government Printing Office.

Orleans, M., Palisi, B. J., & Caddell, D. (1989). Marriage adjustment and satisfaction of stepfathers: Their feelings and perceptions of decision making and stepchildren relations. *Family Relations, 38*, 371-377.

Pasley, K., & Lofquist, A. (1995). Remarriage. In D. Levinson (ed.), *Encyclopedia of marriage and the family* (pp. 581-584). New York: Macmillan.

Pasley, K., Dollahite, D., & Ihinger-Tallman, M. (1993). Bridging the gap: Clinical applications of research findings on the spouse and stepparent roles in remarriage. *Family Relations, 42*, 315-322.

Pasley, K., & Ihinger-Tallman, M. (1992). Remarriage and stepparenting: What the 1980s have added to our understanding of these families. *Family Science Review, 5,* 153-174.

Pasley, K., & Ihinger-Tallman, M. (1995). Building bridges: Reflections on theory, research, and practice. In K. Pasley & M. Ihinger-Tallman (Eds.), *Stepparenting: Issues in theory, research and practice* (pp. 239-250). Westport, CT: Praeger.

Pasley, K., & Ihinger-Tallman, M. (1987). An evolution of a field of investigation: Issues and concerns. In K. Pasley & M. Ihinger-Tallman (Eds.), *Remarriage and stepparenting: Current research and theory* (pp. 303-313). New York: Guilford.

Peterson, J., & Zill, N. (1986). Marital disruption, parent-child relationships, and behavior problems in children. *Journal of Marriage and the Family, 48,* 295-307.

Pill, C. (1990). Stepfamilies: Redefining the family. *Family Relations, 39,* 186-193.

Pink, J., & Wampler, K. (1985). Problem areas in stepfamilies: Cohesion, adaptability and the stepparent-adolescent relationships. *Family Relations, 34,* 327-335.

Price-Bonham, S., & Balswick, J. O. (1980). The noninstitutions: divorce, desertion, and remarriage. *Journal of Marriage and the Family, 42,* 959-972.

Pruett, C. L., Calsyn, R. J., & Jensen, F. M. (1993). Social support received by child in stepmother, stepfather, and intact families. *Journal of Divorce & Remarriage, 19* (3/4), 165-180.

Quick, D. S., McKenry, P. C., & Newman, B. M. (1995). Stepmothers and their adolescent children: Adjustment to new family roles. In K. Pasley & M. Ihinger-Tallman (Eds.), *Stepparenting: Issues in theory, research and practice* (pp. 105-125). Westport, CT: Praeger.

Roberts, T. W., & Price, S. J. (1989). Adjustment in remarriage: Communication, cohesion, marital and parental roles. *Journal of Divorce, 13*(1), 17-43.

Santrock, J. W., & Sitterle, K. A. (1987). Parent-child relationships in stepmother families. In K. Pasley & M. Ihinger-Tallman (Eds.), *Remarriage and stepparenting: Current research and theory* (pp. 273-299). New York: Guilford.

Santrock, J. W., Warshak, R., Lindbergh, C., & Meadows, L. (1982). Children and parents' observed social behavior in stepfather families. *Child Development, 53,* 472-480.

Schwebel, A. I., Fine, M. A., & Renner, M. A. (1991). A study of perceptions of the stepparent role. *Journal of Family Issues, 12,* 43-57.

Smith, T. A. (1991). Family cohesion in remarried families. *Journal of Divorce & Remarriage, 17,* (1/2), 49-66.

Smith, H. L., & Morgan, S. P. (1994). Children's closeness to father as reported by mothers, sons and daughters. *Journal of Family Issues, 15,* 3-29.

Spitze, G., Logan, J. R., Glenn, D., & Zerger, S. (1994). Adult children's divorce and intergenerational relationships. *Journal of Marriage and the Family, 56,* 279-293.

Sweet, J., Bumpass, L., & Call, V. (1988) *The design and content of the National Survey of Families and Households* (Working paper NSFH-1). Madison, WI: University of Wisconsin-Madison, Center for Demography and Ecology.

Thompson, E., McLanahan, S. S., & Curtin, R. B. (1992). Family structure, gender, and parental socialization. *Journal of Marriage and the Family, 54,* 368-378.

Upchurch, D. M. (1993). Early schooling and childbearing experiences: Implications for postsecondary school attendance. *Journal of Research on Adolescence, 3,* 423-443.

Verner, E., Coleman, M., Ganong, L. H., & Cooper, H. (1989). Marital satisfaction in remarriage: A meta-analysis. *Journal of Marriage and the Family, 51,* 713-725.

Visher, E. B., & Visher, J. S. (1978a). Major areas of difficulty for stepparent couples. *International Journal of Family Counseling, 6,* 70-80.

Visher, E. B., & Visher, J. S. (1978b). Common problems of stepparents and their spouses. *American Journal of Orthopsychiatry, 48,* 252-262.

Visher, E. B., & Visher, J. S. (1979). *Stepfamilies: A guide to working with stepparents and stepchildren.* New York: Brunner/Mazel.

Visher, E. B., & Visher, J. S. (1988). *Old loyalties, new ties: Therapeutic strategies with stepfamilies.* New York: Brunner/Mazel.

Vuchinich, S., Hetherington, E. M., Vuchinich, R., & Clingempeel, W. G. (1991). Parent-child interaction and gender differences in early adolescents' adaptation to stepfamilies. *Developmental Psychology, 27,* 618-626.

Waldren, T., Bell, N. J., Peek, C. W., & Sorell, G. (1990). Cohesion and adaptability in postdivorce remarried and first-married families: Relationships with family stress and coping styles. *Journal of Divorce & Remarriage, 14,* (1), 13-28.

White, L. (1994). Growing up with single parents and stepparents: Long-term effects on family solidarity. *Journal of Marriage and the Family, 56,* 935-948.

White, L. K., & Booth, A. (1985). The quality and stability of remarriages: The role of stepchildren. *American Sociological Review, 50,* 689-698.

White, L. K., & Reidmann, A. (1992). When the Brady Bunch grows up: Step/half- and fullsibling relationships in adulthood. *Journal of Marriage and the Family, 54,* 197-208.

Wilson, B. F., & Clarke, S. C. (1992). Remarriages: A demographic profile. *Journal of Family Issues, 13,* 123-141.

Wineberg, H. (1992). Childbearing and dissolution of the second marriage. *Journal of Marriage and the Family, 54,* 879-887.

Wiser, A. W., & Burch, T. K. (1989). The family environment and leaving the parental home. *Journal of Marriage and the Family, 51,* 605-613.

Zill, N. (1988). Behavior, achievement, and health problems among children in stepfamilies. In E. M. Hetherington & J. Arasteh (Eds.), *Impact of divorce, single parenting, and stepparenting on children* (pp. 325-368). Hillsdale, NJ: Erlbaum.

Zill, N., Morrison, D. R., & Coiro, M. J. (1993). Long-term effects of parental divorce on parent-child relationships, adjustment, and achievement in young adulthood. *Journal of Family Psychology, 7,* 91-103.

Confronting Nuclear Family Bias in Stepfamily Research

Susan J. Gamache

Assumptions from the nuclear family model permeate our view of the stepfamily (Coontz, 1992; Ganong & Coleman, 1994; Levin, 1993). As researchers, we are situated within a culture that holds the nuclear family as the golden standard against which all other family configurations are compared (Crosbie-Burnett, 1984; Ganong & Coleman, 1984). Post modern philosophers suggest that cultures contain dominant perspectives that exert a powerful influence on how knowledge is constructed (Gergen, 1990; Giddens, 1991; Shotter, 1990; Kvale, 1990; Peavy, 1993). Dominant cultural norms 'colonize' those of lesser power, encouraging some perspectives and discouraging others (White & Epston, 1990). Values and beliefs from the dominant perspective distort our vision and cloud our thinking when we attempt to examine experiences of the non-dominant culture. In this way, nuclear family thinking dominates our construction of the stepfamily (Clingempeel, Flescher, and Brand, 1987; Gross, 1986; Levin, 1993). As the stepfamily remains 'unistitutionalized' (Cherlin, 1978; Cherlin & Furstenburg, 1994) appropriate social structures are not in place to validate and support it and the nuclear family model remains the cultural standard by default. Continued use of the 'nuclear family map' (Ganong & Coleman, 1994; Levin, 1993) masks unique characteristics of

Susan J. Gamache is affiliated with the Department of Counselling Psychology, Faculty of Education, University of British Columbia, Vancouver, BC, Canada.

The support of the Social Sciences and Humanities Research Council of Canada in the development of this paper is gratefully acknowledged.

[Haworth co-indexing entry note]: "Confronting Nuclear Family Bias in Stepfamily Research." Gamache, Susan J. Co-published simultaneously in *Marriage & Family Review* (The Haworth Press, Inc.) Vol. 26, No. 1/2, 1997, pp. 41-69; and: *Stepfamilies: History, Research, and Policy* (ed: Irene Levin and Marvin B. Sussman) The Haworth Press, Inc., 1997, pp. 41-69. Single or multiple copies of this article are available for a fee from The Haworth Document Delivery Service [1-800-342-9678, 9:00 a.m. - 5:00 p.m. (EST). E-mail address: getinfo@haworth.com].

the stepfamily and encourages misrepresentations of the stepfamily in the stepfamily literature. Nowhere is this more evident than in the ambiguous and often confusing relationship between the stepchild and stepparent. What are stepparents? What types of relationships exist between stepparents and stepchildren? Stepfamily research has often sought to answer these questions by the deficit-comparison approach (Ganong & Coleman, 1984) which compares stepfamily relationships to their nuclear family counterparts and finds them lacking. Stepparents have been found to be less authoritative and more disengaged than biological parents (Hetherington & Clingempeel, 1992) and to have less positive relations with their stepchildren than biological parents (Fine, Voydanoff & Donnelly, 1993). Stepchildren have been found to be more disengaged, less well adjusted and to have more behavior problems than children in biological families (Bray, Berger, & Boethel, 1993; Bronstein, Clauson, Stoll & Abrams, 1993; Hetherington & Jodl, 1993; Zill, 1988; Zill, Morrison, & Coiro, 1993). Relationships between stepchildren and stepparents have been found to be more disruptive and conflictual (Barber & Lyons, 1993; Hetherington & Clingempeel, 1992; Kurdek & Fine, 1993b), more negative (Bray et al., 1993; Pruett, Calsyn & Jensen, 1993; Fine et al., 1993), less warm (Kurdek & Fine, 1993b) and less supportive (Fine et al., 1993; Pruett et al., 1993) than child-parent relationships in biological families.

Movement from a deficit-comparison model (Ganong & Coleman, 1984) to a normative-adaptive approach (Ganong & Coleman, 1994; Hetherington, Stanley-Hagen & Anderson, 1989) does not seem to have influenced the fundamental assumption that stepparents must adhere to a 'parental' relationship as defined by the nuclear family. Nor has this assumption been shaken by reviews of stepfamily research recommending less attention to comparing steprelationships to biological relationships and more attention to the exploration of what types of steprelationships work better than others (Ganong & Coleman, 1993; Ihinger-Tallman & Pasley, 1994). The steprelationship appears destined to be constructed according to the dominant cultural norm of the nuclear family, examined through the 'parental' lens, and found to be 'less than.'

Stepchild-stepparent[1] relationships are constructed as parental relation-

---

1. The literature on stepfamilies has been criticized for over emphasizing adult perspectives and underrepresenting children's experiences in stepfamilies. Language is a subtle yet powerful force in encouraging some perspectives and discouraging others. For these reasons, the usual expression 'stepparent-stepchild relationship' has been replaced with the reverse, the 'stepchild-stepparent relationship.' Equally, the descriptor 'adult-child' has been replaced with 'child-adult,' to encourage greater attention to children's perspectives.

ships by the research designs, instruments, scoring procedures, and sampling procedures. Research designs that compare stepparent-stepchild relationships to biological relationships implicitly assume that steprelationships are, or should aspire to, parental roles and responsibilities. It has been suggested that stepparents are more like in-laws or extended family (Cherlin & Furstenburg, 1994) and, like other adult 'non-parents,' are providers of socialization for children (Kurdek & Fine, 1993a), yet research designs continue to focus on the parental relationship as the only comparison group.

The lack of sophistication in conceptualizing the steprelationship is further encouraged by the paucity of research that builds on children's experiences in stepfamilies. Unfortunately, even though children are the ties without which stepfamilies would not exist (Bernstein, 1988), their perspectives are generally underrepresented (Crosbie-Burnett & Skyles, 1989; Gross, 1986) and not taken seriously in the development of basic conceptualizations of the stepfamily. Researchers (Hetherington, 1987b) and clinicians (Keshet, 1980; Papernow, 1988) agree that the experiences of children and adults in stepfamilies are often very different. While adults in stepfamilies often view their stepfamily in terms of the nuclear family model (Dahl, Cowgill & Asmundsson, 1987), children often construct their relationship with their stepparent in ways that are beyond the nuclear family model (Gross, 1986). The all too prevalent practice of not including children as important respondents in stepfamily research (Fine et al., 1993) adds implicit support to the continued use of the nuclear family model to understand stepchild-stepparent relationships.

Reviewers have criticized stepfamily research for the lack of standardized measures (Ganong & Coleman, 1994; Pasley, Ihinger-Tallman & Lofquist, 1994). Unfortunately, measures designed specifically for studying the stepfamily (Crosbie-Burnett, 1989) have not received wide spread support and lack the standardization reviewers suggest. Therefore, in order to satisfy the requirement for standardized measures, researchers have been obligated to use measures which have been developed from nuclear family assumptions and tested on nuclear family samples. Since the nuclear family model assumes a parental relationship between adults and children, the steprelationships must replicate this in order to achieve similar scores on these measures. To adhere to a different model puts the stepfamily at risk of being scored as less than. Furthermore, parenting scores for stepparents are sometimes combined with those of the biological parent for the sake of the analysis (Fine, Donnelly, Voydanoff, 1991; Kurdek & Fine, 1993b). To combine the two assumes they are similar enough to be additive.

Finally, sampling criteria frequently include demographic variables, family structure, time in the stepfamily, and the age of children at the time of the study. However, excluding studies which explicitly articulate the range of steprelationship styles, the type of relationship between the stepparent and stepchild is not generally discussed. The relationship is assumed to be parental and the purpose of the study to measure the extent to which the steprelationship mimics the custodial, biological relationship on the stated criteria. Although a few studies have attempted to correct for this in the sampling procedures (Bray, 1992; Bray et al., 1993; Bray, Berger, & Boethel, 1994; Gamache, 1992), different types of stepparent relationships are generally not acknowledged. The samples are therefore not homogenous for the parental status of the stepparent relationship, but include all stepparent relationships under one general rubric of 'stepparent.' Stepparent relationships with full parental status are combined with those of partial parental status and those with no parental status, thereby threatening the validity of the results.

Child-parent relationships from the nuclear family model continue to set the standard by which the stepchild-stepparent relationships are assessed. Specifically, stepchild-stepparent relationships are explicitly and implicitly conceptualized as attempts to replicate child-parent relationships in the nuclear family. Since parent-child relationships in nuclear families are, by definition, 'parental,' this assumption has been implicitly carried over to the research on stepfamilies. Alternate views of the steprelationship are hidden by this assumption and unavailable to us. The implicit and unspoken convention is that the steprelationship must aspire to full parental status as defined by the nuclear family, and that our job as researchers is to keep tabs on how close it comes to this pre-ordained goal, knowing in our hearts that few, if any, will ever reach it. In order to truly move from the deficit-comparison model to the normative adaptive perspective, the certitude that all stepchild-relationships aspire to full parental status must be suspended and replaced with a willingness to explore steprelationships outside the confines of the nuclear family model.

Moving beyond the nuclear family model means attempting to articulate constructs that have not yet been identified or defined. As Burgoyne and Clark (1984) suggest,

> the pervasiveness of the nuclear family norm is based on its taken-for-granted quality. It is so much part of the 'natural order' of things that . . . it is rarely possible to locate distinct, clearly articulated ideologies of the family except in situations when either an individual's family life or the family as an institution appears threatened. (p. 195)

The purpose of this paper is to attempt to do just that, to articulate constructs of relevance to stepfamily literature, without resorting to a 'threatened' or problem focused approach.

THREE INTERRELATED CONCEPTS

Three interrelated concepts will be proposed. Two of these concepts depart from the confines of the nuclear family model and as such may appear awkward or 'unnatural.' The third is a demographic variable of critical importance to the other two. The three concepts are: (a) a conceptualization of the stepchild-stepparent relationship that includes a range of possible relationships based on the degree to which the stepparent is considered a 'psychological parent,' (b) the age of the child at the beginning of the steprelationship as influential in determining the degree to which the stepparent is considered a 'psychological parent,' and (c) an acknowledgment of the 'one parent' vs. 'two parent' stepfamily household as a consequence of the range of possible stepchild-stepparent relationships.

Each of these concepts can be best conceptualized as a continuum (see Figure 1). The first concept describes a range of stepparent relationships based on the parental status of the stepparent. (This concept will be defined and discussed in the following section.) This continuum ranges from full parental status, that of a psychological parent, to no parental status, that of a relative stranger.[2] The second continuum describes the age of the child at the beginning of the steprelationship. It ranges from birth to adulthood. (Although this concept could include anytime post conception to adult children, it will be limited for the purposes of this discussion.) The third continuum, that of the parental status of the stepfamily household, ranges from a 'two parent' stepfamily household to a household including one 'parent' and another adult with no parental status.

It is to be expected that these concepts will seem unusual and perhaps, uncomfortable as they are not present in 'traditional' views of the family. However, these three concepts allow us to explore the stepfamily in a way that acknowledges and respects the perspectives of stepfamily members and builds on their experiences of stepfamily living, particularly those of children in stepfamilies. That these concepts seem cumbersome is both encouraging and discouraging. It is discouraging because it increases the difficulty of incorporating them into the existing stepfamily literature,

---

2. The term 'relative stranger' was originally used by Beer (1988). This double entendre not only suggests that the stepparent may feel like a stranger, relative to other family members, but also hints that the stepparent is indeed a relative after all.

FIGURE 1. Three Interrelated Concepts for Stepfamily Research

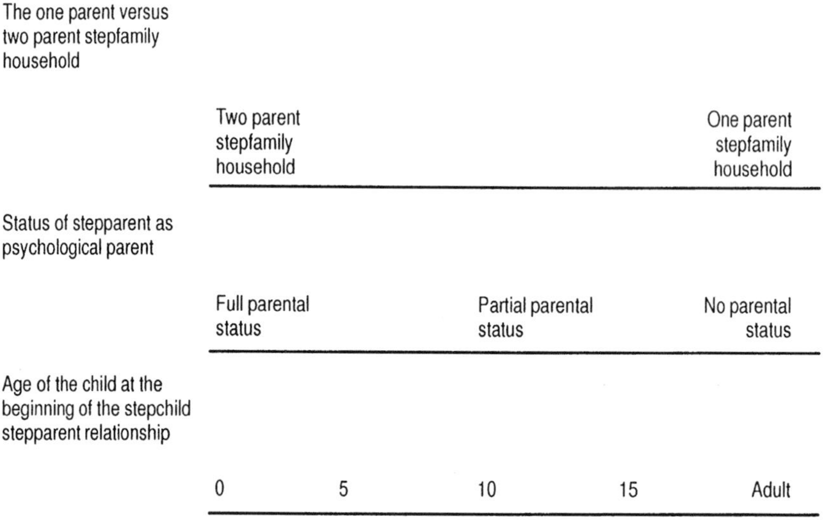

The one parent versus
two parent stepfamily
household

	Two parent stepfamily household		One parent stepfamily household

Status of stepparent as
psychological parent

	Full parental status	Partial parental status	No parental status

Age of the child at the
beginning of the stepchild
stepparent relationship

0	5	10	15	Adult

based as it is on the nuclear family model. On the other hand, it is encouraging because the awkwardness of working with these concepts may be indicative of having finally moved far enough away from the nuclear family model to begin to more accurately represent the experience of stepfamily members, particularly children.

A Range of Possible Stepchild-Stepparent Relationships

Reviews of the empirical literature suggest a broad range of relationships between stepchildren and their stepparents. While some stepparent relationships are experienced as extremely 'parent-like,' others are not (Cherlin & Furstenberg, 1994; Hetherington, Stanley-Hagan & Anderson, 1989). In addition, several researchers have provided a forum for stepfamily members to describe their families in their own terms and found stepparent relationships to be perceived in ways that are at times within the nuclear family model and at times dictated more by the perceived needs and desires of the family members than by social convention (Burgoyne & Clark, 1984; Erera-Wetherley, in press; Gross, 1986; Levin, 1990).

These initial findings suggest that stepfamily members can be described as organizing their family relationships around different themes. Levin

(1990) and Burgoyne and Clark (1984) report that the stepfamilies they studied chose to use the goals of the stepfamily as the organizing feature. The families in both studies saw themselves as attempting to recreate the nuclear family, to consciously avoid it, or to wait and see what happened without a conscious attempt to either replicate or avoid the nuclear family. Some families, the 'Not Really a Stepfamily' group (Burgoyne & Clark, 1984) saw themselves so much like a nuclear family that many stepfamily issues were not relevant to their family life. On the other hand, other families, the 'Innovation' group (Levin, 1990) were consciously working against recreating the nuclear family. These families blamed the structure of the nuclear family for the end of the first marriage.

However, even though the theme of attraction, aversion, or indifference to the nuclear family model is articulated, it appears that this theme is functionally expressed by the type of stepchild-stepparent relationship that exists or is desired, specifically, whether or not, or to what degree the stepparent acts as a 'parent' to the children. For example, Levin (1990) suggests that those that sought to recreate the nuclear family granted the stepparent full parental status while those that sought to create a family outside the nuclear family model did not. A member of the latter group reports, "The child has two parents and do [sic] not need another one" (p. 11). Equally, the 'Largely Successful Conscious Pursuit of an Ordinary Family Life Together' group described by Burgoyne & Clark (1984) sees the stepparent relationship as a functional expression of the attitudes behind the organization of the family. The authors report that "in their efforts to reconstitute an ordinary family life for their children, parents consciously attempt to adopt as full and normal a parental role as possible" (p. 193).

The extent to which the stepparent is seen to be or desired to be a 'parent' appears to be a recurring theme around which stepfamily members organize their conceptualization of their stepfamily (Burgoyne & Clark, 1984; Erera-Wetherley, in press; Gross, 1986; Levin, 1990). Erera-Weatherly (in press) focused on attitudes towards the stepchild-stepparent relationships and found a typology of five stepchild-stepparent relationship styles. The parental status of the stepparent seemed to be a central feature. For example, as in the study by Burgoyne and Clark, some stepchild-stepparent relationship were described by these adults as 'biological.' One adult reports, "I feel toward her daughters exactly the way I feel toward my [own] children" (Erera-Weatherly, in press).

The power of the parental status of the adults as a central feature in the stepfamily is further demonstrated in a study by Gross (1986). This study explored the extent to which 16-18 year olds constructed their relationships with the adults in their family according to the parental status of the stepparent, the custodial biological parent, and the noncustodial biological parent. She found two dichotomous elements operating simultaneously: the inclusion or exclusion of the stepparent and the inclusion or exclusion of the noncustodial biological parent as 'parents.' The inclusion of the custodial biological parent as a 'parent' was constant. The results suggested four mutually exclusive and exhaustive typologies: retention, reduction, substitution, and augmentation. In the 'retention' group, the biological parents were retained and the stepparent not included as a parent. In the 'reduction' group, neither the stepparent nor the noncustodial biological parent were included. For these teens, there was only one parent, the custodial, biological parent. The other biological parent had lost their parental status. In the two remaining groups (substitution and augmentation), the stepparent was considered very much a parent. In the 'substitution' group, the stepparent was perceived as a substitute for the non custodial biological parent. These children had two adults with full parental status, one biological and one step, synonymous with the adult members in the household. In the 'augmentation' group, the stepparent was included with the two biological parents. These adolescents granted parental status to three adults.

This study exemplifies the need to go outside the nuclear family model to accurately represent the experience of stepfamily members, particularly children. The parental status of the stepparent could not be assumed as 58% of the sample did not consider the stepparent a parent. The adults these stepchildren described as parents did not fall within the nuclear family model in 86% of the cases. Twenty-five percent of the sample had one psychological parent while 28% considered three adults as psychological parents. Of the 46% who included two psychological parents, 33% included a psychological parent in each of two households, while only 13% described the adults of their primary household as their parents.

In addition, although the typology presented two dichotomous choices, the anecdotal information suggests that stepparents can be considered 'parents' without having full parental status in all situations. One adolescent from the group in which the stepparent had been substituted for the noncustodial biological parent stated, "I really care about him, but I could never be as close to him as to my mother . . . ," ". . . sometimes he takes on the father role, at other times he doesn't" (Gross, 1986, p. 211).

Although far from definitive, these efforts at describing stepfamilies demonstrate the diversity in the stepparent relationship described by stepfamily members and raise fundamental questions concerning the basic conceptualization of stepchild-stepparent relationships. In contrast to the nuclear family model, there seems to be a range of child-adult relationships in stepfamilies based on the degree to which the stepparent relationship is granted full, partial, or no parental status. The degree to which the stepchild-stepparent relationship is perceived as parental appears to be a central, organizing feature of the stepchild-stepparent relationship and of the stepfamily itself.

Psychological parenthood. Given that stepfamily members appear to consider the degree to which stepparents are considered as psychological parents as a central feature in the experience of both children and adults in stepfamilies, it is perhaps a construct worthy of further refinement and systematic exploration by stepfamily researchers. Psychological parenthood appears to be independent of family structure or biological relatedness (Gross, 1986). It allows variability in the degree to which the steprelationship is experienced as parental without assuming that more is better and less is deficient. The concept of the 'degree of psychological parenthood' in the stepchild-stepparent relationships avoids the implicit assumption of a parental relationship yet does not exclude the possibility of this relationship being granted full parental status. The degree of psychological parenthood can change, increasing or even decreasing over time or in different circumstances.

The term 'social parent' has been used in the literature to describe the stepparent that functions as 'parent' (Burgoyne & Clark, 1984; Marsiglio, 1992). Marsiglio (1992) uses the term 'social parent' to differentiate stepparent relationships from 'blood' or biological parent relationships. However, the term 'social parent' carries an implicit limitation. While we are willing to call stepparents 'social parents' we are probably not willing to call biological parents 'social parents.' The term 'psychological parent' is a more neutral term. Relationships with both the biological parents and stepparents can include it as it suggests a psychological relationship rather than a paraphrase of the presence or absence of the biological relationship. The term psychological parent reflects a normative adaptive approach rather than implicitly hinting at a deficit-comparison perspective. Equally, reports from children in stepfamilies do not make this distinction. While the amount of 'parentness' in the stepchild-stepparent relationship may vary, the actual commodity, the 'parentness' of the relationship, seems to be the same according to the stepfamily members involved in the studies reported.

Exactly how to define psychological parenthood is open to investigation. In a study of families six years after divorce, Hetherington (1987b) describes dimensions of parenting which include warmth, control, monitoring, conflict and maturity demands. Parenting styles were clustered and found to parallel parenting styles earlier described by Baumrind in research on nuclear families (Baumrind cited in Hetherington, 1987b). One additional parenting style was added for some stepparents. Investigation of the degree to which the stepparent was considered a psychological parent was not the goal of the research. However, dimensions of relationship such as those described in this study could provide an opportunity to determine the relative power of these features in defining stepfamily members' experience of psychological parenthood in the stepparent relationship.

Stepfamily researchers may be able to further explore 'psychological parenthood' by examining the work of Furman and Buhrmester (1985, 1992). These authors have built on theories of social provisions (Weiss, 1974) to study dimensions of relationships between adults and children. Weiss (1974) proposed a theory of social provisions in which six dimensions of social relationships are defined: attachment, reliable alliance, enhancement of worth, social integration, guidance, and opportunity for nurturance. Furman and Buhrmester (1985) added four more dimensions to study relationships between children and adults: relative power, conflict, satisfaction, and importance of relationship. These ten dimensions of relationship proved to be valid and reliable in studying children's relationships with mothers, fathers, teachers, and other adults in their social networks (Furman and Buhrmester, 1985).

To date, little is known about which aspects of the stepparent relationship are central to the experience of psychological parenthood. Research by Lutz (1983) suggests that discipline is a critical aspect of the stepparent relationship for adolescents. Perhaps dimensions of power, conflict, and guidance suggested by Furman and Buhrmester (1985) are most salient for adolescents. In contrast, stepfathers are more likely to have 'fatherlike perceptions' when they are happy with their partner (Marsiglio, 1992). Perhaps dimensions of reliable alliance, enhancement of worth, and opportunities for guidance are more central for stepparents. Further research in this area has great potential to move stepfamily research beyond the nuclear family model and to generate an abundance of ideas with which to refine our thinking about stepparent relationships.

Although the critical dimensions of the stepparent relationship that contribute to the lived experience of psychological parenthood in stepfamilies cannot be articulated at this time, the concept itself appears to hold potential for stepfamily research. Given the theory and research described above, the extent to which the stepparent is considered a psychological parent may be best conceptualized as a continuum (see Figure 1). One end describes the steprelationship that functions as a psychological parent and the other end, those that function simply as an acquaintance or relative stranger. Between these two extremes lies a range of relationships that includes greater and lesser degrees of psychological parenthood, perhaps more like uncles and aunts, grandparents, in-laws, coaches, teachers, and friends of the family. As we do not criticize grandparents or coaches for not functioning exactly as parents, many stepparents can also be excused from this no-win comparison. Equally, extended family do carry responsibilities for children and, at times, take on roles that may be partially or fully parental. The use of the concept of psychological parenthood in stepchild-stepparent relationships grants this same flexibility for stepparents.

Factors That Influence Psychological Parenthood

Which factors influence the degree of psychological parenthood in the stepparent-stepchild relationship? Although the concept of psychological parenthood has not been explicitly and systematically dealt with, there is some evidence to suggest that a number of factors can contribute to the development of a parental relationship between stepparent and stepchild. In their review of stepfamily literature, Cherlin and Furstenburg (1994) list 4 factors: the age of the child at the beginning of the steprelationship, the frequency of contact with the same sex biological parent, the quality of the relationship between the stepparent and the biological parent in the household, and the child's temperament. Others have explored typologies of stepfamily relationships and have found additional factors. Gross (1986) found the age of the child at separation and remarriage, time since remarriage, visitation with and additional children to, the non-residential parent, and sex of the child as contributing factors. Erera-Weatherley (in press) focused on the expectations and behaviors of the stepparent, the stepchild, the spouse, and the non-residential parent. Levin (1990) examined attitudes towards the nuclear family, finding that those who sought to recreate the nuclear family created steprelationships as psychological parents. Those whose goal was to avoid creating another nuclear family did not see the stepparent as any type of parental figure. Burgoyne and Clark (1984) found that the principal contributor to the type of relationship that developed between the stepparent and stepchild was the stage in the family life cycle at the time of the divorce and remarriage. When the marital transitions took place early in the family life cycle, that is when children were younger, there was a greater likelihood that the stepchildren and stepparents developed a parental style of relationship.

These initial attempts to describe and discuss the degree of psychological parenthood in the stepparent-stepchild relationship have generated many factors worthy of further exploration. However, the single factor that has garnered greater support and virtually no contradictory evidence is the age of the child at the time the stepparent enters the family.

Age of the child at the beginning of the stepchild-stepparent relationship. The second of three interrelated concepts to be discussed in this paper is the influence of the age of the children at the time the stepparent enters the stepfamily on the degree of psychological parenthood that can reasonably be expected to be created between stepchild and stepparent. The combination of the age of the child at the time of remarriage and the degree of psychological parenthood in the steprelationship has received some attention in the clinical literature but scant systematic study from researchers.

Of the models described in the clinical literature, those proposed by Whiteside (1989) and Mills (1984) pay the most direct attention to the age of the children when the stepparent enters the stepfamily as significantly influencing the type of relationship that can be reasonably expected to develop between the stepparent and stepchild. In his proposed model for stepfamily development, Mills (1984) suggests that the initial age of the child acts as an indicator for the time frame necessary for the development of stepparent relationships that act as psychological parents. He suggests that steprelationships involving younger children can develop into parent-like relationships once the stepparent has shared a significant period of time with the child. Mills suggests a significant period of time as roughly defined by the age of the child at the time the stepfamily forms. That is, 3 years for a 3 year old, 6 for a 6 year old, etc. In other words, the stepparent must achieve half of the mutual history of the child and biological parent to fill a parental role. Using this model, the degree of psychological parenthood in the relationship between a stepchild and stepparent would vary along a continuum based on the age of the child at the beginning of the steprelationship (see Figure 1). Stepparent relationships that begin when the child is 2 or 3 would be expected to develop into relationships with a high degree of psychological parenthood. Mills further suggests that the parental choice is generally ruled out when the children are adolescents at the time the steprelationship begins.

Whiteside (1989) also addresses the impact of the age of the child when the steprelationship begins as critical in establishing reasonable expectations for the stepchild-stepparent relationship. Whiteside proposes an interaction between the age of the child at the time of the formation of the stepfamily and that of the stage of the remarried family. Four developmental stages are suggested for the child (Preschool, 0-5 yrs.; Middle, 6-12 yrs.; Adolescence, 13-17 yrs.; and Adult, 18 + yrs.), and three developmental stages for the remarried family (Early, 0-2 yrs.; Middle, 3-5 yrs.; and Later (6 + yrs.). The developmental stage of the child at the beginning of the process plays an important role in determining the type of relationship that can reasonably be expected to form. Whiteside (1989) suggests that preschool children can form strong bonds with a nurturing stepparent and that it is this situation that "a role approximating that of a biological parent role has the best chance of success" (p. 148). By the time these children are in the early years of elementary school, they will have known their stepparent for nearly half their lives and are likely to consider the stepparent as a permanent and important member of the family. However, if the child is an adolescent at the time of the formation of the stepfamily, the expectation of creating a parental steprelationship is counter-indicated. "In this combination of age and family stage, there should be no expectation that the stepparent will be able to assume an effective authoritative position directly in relation to the child"(p. 153).

One empirical study was found in which the influence of the age of the children at the beginning of the steprelationship was investigated for its influence on the 'parentness' of the relationship. In a unique research design, Marsiglio (1992) examined stepfathers' perceptions of the 'father-like' quality of their relationship with their stepchild. Using data from the National Survey of Families and Households, responses of 195 stepfathers were included in the study. The experience of 'stepfathering' seems to include varying degrees of psychological parenthood as perceived by the stepfather. The age of the stepchild at the beginning of the steprelationship was found to be a significant influence on the degree to which the stepfathers considered themselves psychological parents to their stepchildren. 'Fatherliness' among stepfathers was found in relationships with children who were younger at the time the stepfather entered the family.

Bray (1992) acknowledges the developmental status of the child at the beginning of the steprelationship as influential in a study comparing marital and family processes, children's behavioral adjustment, and the relationship between family process and children's psychosocial adjustment in clinical and non-clinical stepfather families. The age of the child at the time the steprelationship began was limited, in part, to create a more homogeneous sample. Twenty-four stepfather families that had been married at least one year participated. Each family contained a target child between 6 and 11 years at the time of the study. Children in the clinical stepfather families were found to have more behavior problems than the children in the non-clinical stepfamilies. Child-to-parent interactions were found to be more negative and less positive in stepfather families in which children demonstrated more behavior problems.

In examining the sample more closely, the children were 10 years of age or younger at the time of remarriage. Although this sample is more homogeneous in terms of the developmental stage of the child at the beginning of the steprelationship, according to Whiteside (1989) at least two developmental stages have been grouped together. According to Mills (1984) and Whiteside (1989), probable types of steprelationships for the older children in the sample would not include parent-like relationships. It is interesting to speculate what additional information may have been provided if the analysis had discriminated between the children by age at stepfamily formation. Mills (1984) suggests that problems arise when the stepparents move into parental roles too quickly with children who have outgrown their availability for more parents. What are the non-clinical families doing differently than the clinical families? Do their 'parenting' or 'non-parenting' styles vary with children of differing developmental status at the beginning of the stepparent relationship?

Hetherington (1987b) suggests that children who are younger when the stepfamily begins eventually accept a warm and involved stepparent while children 9-15 years of age are most resistant. However, if we consider the degree of psychological parenthood as variable influenced by the age of the children when the steprelationship begins, it may be that for the 9-15 year old group, the problem is not the 'step' but rather the 'parent.' If we agree that a 'parent-like' relationship is counter-indicated for this age group, then perhaps it is the 'parental' model that is at fault. Children who are younger when they begin the steprelationship are able to accept another 'parent' or 'parental figure,' thereby remaining within the nuclear family model and not appearing 'resistant.' Again, perhaps the 'step' is not the critical factor but the 'parent.' Perhaps children in this age group would establish a 'parental' type of relationship with any warm involved adult, such as a live-in aunt, uncle or older cousin.

Two areas of child development literature may inform this discussion: attachment theory and theories of social-personality development. As extensive discussion of these theories is beyond the scope of this paper, a brief overview will be provided.

Bowlby's (1982) theory of attachment integrates theories and research on mother-infant relationships from diverse disciplines to offer one of the best supported theories of socioemotional development available. Attachment theory suggests that within the first two years of life, infants establish strong bonds with a primary figure, usually the mother, through which they experience a pervasive sense of security. Attachment behaviors obtain and maintain proximity to the attachment figure. While attachments appear very strong in the first few years of life, it appears that attachments are somewhat reduced after the pre-school years (Parkes & Hinde, 1982).

Attachment theory would suggest that for the stepparent to develop a bond with the stepchild that includes a high degree of psychological parenthood, the steprelationship must begin early in the child's life, at a time when primary attachments are being formed. Attachments appear to be hierarchically organized in that infants can develop more than one attachment figure; however, the secondary attachment figures do not replace the primary attachment figure (Ainsworth, 1982). While the relationship with the stepfather does not replace the mother-infant bond in stepfather families, a second adult in the home who is committed to the children can positively influence children's development (Weiss, 1982).

Attachment theory would also suggest that children develop attachment styles in the mother-infant relationship that have enduring qualities (Weiss, 1982). Subsequent relationships, i.e., with the stepparent, may include the same relationship style, be it secure or insecure, as had developed in the first relationship. Children who have had secure early attachments may be better able to build strong bonds with stepparents.

Children's changing perspectives on social relationships are elaborated by the work of Furman and Buhrmester (Buhrmester & Furman, 1986; Furman & Buhrmester, 1985; 1992). As described earlier, these authors build on the theories of Sullivan and Weiss to investigate the changes in children's social relationships during childhood. From Sullivan's theory of Social-Personality Development these authors focused on the central theme of the interpersonal situation (Buhrmester & Furman, 1986) which suggests five developmental stages and critical relationships within normal social-personality development. While parents fulfill these roles in the early years, same sexed friends, and eventually opposite sexed partners eventually provide the social context for these emerging needs. Weiss's (1974) theory of social provisions further refines Sullivan's theory by specifying which types of social support children seek in their social networks. Age was found to play a significant role in determining which relationships children selected to provide different social provisions (Furman & Buhrmester, 1992). Children are found to look to parents for basic social needs in their early years and to then branch out to include friends and romantic partners. While parental figures are not rejected in the later years, it seems that children do not seek out additional adults with whom to establish close relationships as they get older, but increasingly look to peers as providers of basic social provisions.

Stepfamily researchers are in a unique position to explore adult-child familial relationships that begin at different points along the course of the child's development. The theory and research from this aspect of the child development literature would suggest that the social needs of the child when the stepparent relationship begins and the subsequent stages of the child's social development that occur while the stepparent and stepchild participate in familial life will have a significant impact on the type of relationship that is developed. The literature discussed to this point strongly supports the age of the child at the beginning of the steprelationship as an important factor influencing the relationship between a stepparent and stepchild. The younger the child at the beginning of the relationship, the more likely it is that the stepparent relationship will be considered a psychological parent. The older the child at the beginning of the stepparent relationship, the less likely the stepparent relationship will attain full parent status.

One Parent or Two Parent Stepfamily Households

The issue of psychological parenthood in the steprelationship begs yet another question of stepfamily researchers. This brings us to the third of three interrelated concepts to be addressed in this paper, that of 'one parent' versus 'two parent' stepfamily households. If we consider that some stepchild-stepparent relationships are experienced as full parental relationships and others are somewhat parental in nature or are not parental at all, it then follows that not all stepfamily households are 'two parent' households. Some stepfamily households will include two parents while others will include only one parent together with another adult of undetermined parental status. Many stepfamily households, it would seem, include two adults, but not two parents. While one adult is a biological and psychological parent (although the latter assumption could be questioned), the parental status of the second adult cannot be assumed.

The nuclear family model assumes that both adults in the household are 'parents' and as such execute parental responsibilities even though these responsibilities may differ by gender, lifestyles, age of children, etc. (Minuchin & Fishman, 1981). Both adults are simultaneously spouses and parents. To view the issues of parenting in the stepfamily we must let go of the nuclear family lens and open our sights to the realities of stepfamily living. If some stepfamilies include only one parent and another adult of partial parental status, very different models of parenting are required than those found in the nuclear family. Models of parenting in the stepfamily must allow for one biological/psychological parent plus another adult who may be at any point along our hypothetical continuum from psychological parent to relative stranger (see Figure 1). In addition, models of parenting must accommodate movement along the continuum (change in the degree of psychological parenthood) over the formative years of the children.

How do couples in stepfamily households 'parent' children if equal parental status is no longer assumed? Although little is known about exactly how these considerations play themselves out in daily stepfamily living, there appears to be a general consensus that parenting responsibilities must be separated out from the couple relationship. At the beginning of the stepfamily, both adults participate in the couple relationship but only the biological parent (to the exclusion of the stepparent) engages in the parenting of the children, especially regarding authority and discipline. Clinicians have addressed this issue and are generally in agreement that stepparents cannot assume a 'parental' role (Mills, 1984; Papernow, 1988; Whiteside, 1989). Mills (1984) suggests that the biological parent must retain the aspects of parenting that include authority, discipline and nurturing while the stepchild-stepparent relationship slowly develops enough strength to begin to assume these responsibilities.

This arrangement could be represented by the mechanism of two axes hinged together at a pivot point. The biological parent is the pivot point. The two axes are formed by the relationship with the marital partner to one side and the relationships with the children to the other side. The stepparent is connected to the biological parent by the spousal relationship and the children are connected to the biological parent by the child-parent relationship. The biological parent is the pivot point that connects the two axes. The stepparent is not connected to the stepchildren at the beginning of the stepfamily. This division of family life is tentatively supported by stepfamily research that suggests that marital relations do not have the central role in stepfamilies that they do in nuclear families (Crosbie-Burnett, 1984) and that marital satisfaction is not predictive of happiness in family life in stepfamilies as it is in nuclear families (Anderson & White, 1986). Similarly, the relationship between the children and their biological parent has been found to be stronger in stepfamilies than in nuclear families (Anderson & White, 1986).

The research literature has paid little attention to the fundamental shifts that the unequal parental status of couples in stepfamily households entails. Consequently, empirical exploration of different aspects of stepfamily living based on the unequal parental status of couples in stepfamily households is underdeveloped. The research that is available is generally found in studies that combine parental styles with stepfamily adjustment. In some cases, two or three of the concepts discussed in this paper are addressed.

Predicting Adjustment

It seems that the appropriate combination of the three concepts discussed, age of child at the beginning of the stepparent relationship, the degree of psychological parenthood in the stepparent relationship, and the consequent parenting style in the stepfamily household, is necessary to encourage positive stepfamily adjustment (Mills, 1984; Whiteside, 1989). Confusion and misunderstandings regarding these critical factors and how to effectively combine them may contribute to the ambiguity surrounding the stepparent role (Walker & Messinger, 1979; Crosbie-Burnett, 1984). The stepchild-stepparent relationship is a powerful influence on the well-being of the new couple and of the stepfamily itself (Crosbie-Burnett, 1984; Kelly, 1992; White & Booth, 1985). Mills (1984) suggests that one of the main contributors to conflictual stepchild-stepparent relationships in the stepfamily is the "precipitous assumption of the parental role by the stepparent" (p. 371). This cycle of conflict may prevent the stepchild-stepparent relationship from developing (Mills, 1984). Equally, a distant stepparent who does not accept a parental role may frustrate a young child's desire for attachment (Weiss, 1982).

Using standardized instruments and interviews with 20 stepfamilies, Kelly (1992) found several themes which differentiate well functioning stepfamilies from their clinical counterparts. The three concepts discussed appear to be central to the experience of successful stepfamilies. Well functioning stepfamilies approached authority and discipline in a way that separates parenting functions from the spousal relationship. The age of the child at the beginning of the steprelationship was also taken into consideration.

> Most families agreed that it is important for the biological parent to be in charge of the rules and discipline for her or his offspring, especially at first. Most families said that this general rule should be followed for teenagers as well. The stepparents who shared discipline successfully had been married a long time, the children were young, or special relationships had been established before the marriage. (p. 585)

Stepfamily members articulated the importance of protecting the biological child-parent relationship. Well functioning stepfamilies reported that it was important to set aside time for both the couple and the biological parent and child.

This study supports the three concepts and three continua proposed. The extent to which the stepparent functioned as a psychological parent evolved from not at all to 'shared parenting.' Relationship styles changed as the stepfamily developed such that the family moved along the continuum from a household in which there was only one 'parent' plus another adult with no parental status to a household with one 'parent' plus another adult with partial parental status. Age is confirmed as an important criterion for situating the family along the parenting continuum in two ways.

First, the successful stepfamilies suggest that the biological parent should be in charge of rules and discipline for the teenagers. Similarly, they observe that the couples who shared discipline successfully had children who were younger at the beginning of the steprelationship. A separation of the parenting and spousal functions of the adults is implicit in the reports of these stepfamilies. It would be interesting to know how the stepfamilies in the clinical group would situate themselves along these hypothetical continua and if a lack of coordination of these three aspects of stepfamily living are associated with excessively problematic experiences in stepfamily living.

In studying families six years after divorce Hetherington (1987b) found that stepfamilies in which stepfathers were more supportive of their partner's parenting style experienced more success in the stepfamily. "The new father [sic] should first work at establishing a relationship with the children and support the mother in her parenting" (p. 198). This arrangement would be situated at the far right of the third continuum, that of a single parent household with another adult with no parental status. "This period can then be effectively followed by more active, authoritative parenting . . . " This change represents a shift to the left on our hypothetical continuum, towards a stepfamily household with one psychological parent and another adult of partial parental status.

In a study of stepfather families, Bray (1992) provides further support for the separation of parental and spousal responsibilities. The clinical and non-clinical families could be differentiated by the existence of a working parental and marital arrangement. The non-clinical stepfather families had resolved issues such as discipline and authority with the children and had established a strong marital bond. In contrast, the clinical stepfather families appeared to be 'stuck' in their development and unable to resolve these issues.

It is noteworthy that an attempt was made to create a more homogeneous sample by limiting the families to those including a target child who was 6-11 at the time of the study. In examining the sample more closely, although the average length of time since the remarriage was 4 years, the children could have ranged from infants to 10 years of age at that time. Therefore differences in outcome based on the age of the children at the time of the remarriage are difficult to assess. Nevertheless, this study speaks to the importance of acknowledging unequal parental status in the stepfamily household and of resolving issues that derive from it for the marital couple.

Bray, Berger and Boethel (1994) conducted a unique study of stepparent role adjustment and marital adjustment in stepfather families in which the age of children at remarriage was held constant. All stepchildren were 6-9 at remarriage. Groups were defined by time since remarriage: 6 months, 2 years or 5-7 years. According to the developmental stages suggested by Whiteside (1989), these steprelationships would all fall within the same category, thereby encouraging a more homogeneous sample for the potential for the steprelationship to develop into a parental relationship.

Consistent with clinical perspectives, husbands and wives were happier in their relationship when stepfathers did not play a parental role during early remarriage and were not expected to quickly form a close relationship with the children. While this study provides information regarding one developmental stage, it precludes comparisons with others. How would results be different if the sample had included children who were 0-5 years or 10-15 years at remarriage? Also, the developmental stage of children 6-9 years would be positioned near the middle of our hypothetical continuam. Therefore, we would expect smaller effect sizes than if the extreme ends of the range had been included, i.e., children who had been very young or in late adolescence at the time of remarriage.

Three interrelated concepts have been presented which may assist stepfamily research in going beyond the nuclear family model. To date, the nuclear family model has dominated our thinking in stepfamily research. In spite of clinical models and exploratory studies which provide information to the contrary, the majority of stepfamily research implicitly or explicitly adheres to the nuclear family model in research designs. Each of the three concepts presented can be conceptualized as a continuum which includes a range of possibilities. Different positions along the three continua can be combined to describe stepchild-stepparent relationships in the stepfamily household. However, all combinations are not created equal. It would appear that some combinations of positions along the three continua have been demonstrated to encourage positive adjustment in stepfamilies more than others. The three concepts presented hold significant implications for stepfamily research.

STEPFAMILY RESEARCH

To shift from a deficit-comparison approach to a normative adaptive perspective in stepfamily research requires exploration of the uncharted territory beyond the boundaries of the nuclear family model. However, due to the pervasive nature of the conceptual limitations of the nuclear family model, this is a challenging, if not daunting task. The three concepts discussed have been an attempt to meet this challenge.

Implications for Future Research

1. From the extant literature, it would seem that the time has come to begin to 'unpack' the stepparent relationship. Rather than continue to compare stepparent relationships to their nuclear family counterparts, stepfamily research can benefit from going outside the bounds of the nuclear family model to investigate a range of stepchild-stepparent relationships based on varying degrees of psychological parenthood. Research designs could take into consideration that stepparent relationships may function as psychological parents, as relative strangers or as something in between these two extremes. Further empirical investigation is warranted for initial findings that suggest that the parental status of stepparent relationship is a fundamental organizing principle of the relationship with the stepchildren and of the stepfamily household. Exactly which dimensions of the child-adult relationship are experienced as fundamental to 'parenthood' from the perspectives of all family members? Answers to questions such as this would allow greater understanding of which types of relationships are associated with greater satisfaction and resolution, for whom, and in which circumstances. Instruments from other disciplines may assist researchers in this area.

2. Research on stepchild-stepparent relationships can benefit from including the age of the child at the beginning of the stepparent relationship as important aspect of the research design and criteria of the sample. It has been suggested that stepfamilies are a "complimentary weave of many strands of developmental time" (Whiteside, 1989, p. 135). To date, stepfamily research has largely ignored this aspect of 'developmental time.'

By exploring perspectives of stepparent relationships in accordance with the age of the child at the beginning of the stepparent relationship, we are acknowledging a fundamental feature of their experience, their developmental status. This opens the door to a multitude of questions. Following a child-driven model (Hetherington & Clingempeel, 1992), research designs could benefit from exploring the types of relationships children of different ages develop with their stepparent and vice versa. Which are more successful, for whom, and under what conditions? What do children at different ages have to offer their stepparents and vice versa? What do they need in order to establish strong bonds with each other? How do those needs change over time? How does the age of the child influence the length of time it takes to establish stepparent relationships of varying degrees of psychological parenthood? Does the presence or absence of non-custodial parents influence all age groups equally? For which ages are gender related issues most salient? At which developmental stage can children accept more than two parents? Understanding more about what children of different ages need to establish positive relationships with their stepparents and what stepparents need in order to feel satisfied with the stepparent role with children of different ages would contribute not only to the well-being of the stepchild-stepparent relationship but to that of the marital relationship and the entire family (Anderson & White, 1986; Bray, 1992; Bray et al., 1994; Crosbie-Burnett, 1984).

3. Stepfamily research could benefit from suspending the assumption that stepfamily households are necessarily 'two parent households.' Test scores for stepchild-stepparent relationships should be distinct from those for biological relationships and not cumulative. Equally, measures are needed for assessing stepfamily households that include a range of possible stepparent relationships that can be considered positive. How does unequal parenting status in a household translate into daily parenting practices? How are child-parent relationships affected by the introduction of a stepparent? How do successful stepfamily households handle differing degrees of psychological parenthood for different children in the same household? Implications regarding parenting practices and relationship skills of couples in stepfamily households warrant further investigations by stepfamily researchers.

Obstacles to Overcome

1. Challenges to the nuclear family model can be associated with the shift from the modern to the postmodern or postindustrial era. Reaching its peak in popularity in the 1950s, the nuclear family has dominated our conceptualization of 'the family' (Coontz, 1992; Ganong & Coleman, 1994; Ihinger-Tallman & Pasley, 1987; Levin, 1993). Family structures other than the nuclear family, such as the stepfamily, have been seen as deficient (Ganong & Coleman, 1984). Equally, the stepfamily remains 'uninstitutionalized' (Cherlin, 1978; Cherlin & Furstenburg, 1994) and as such without social guidelines to support stepfamily members. Stepfamily dynamics may be much better defined by relationships of the Postmodern, Post-industrial culture (Gergen, 1990; Hage & Powers, 1992; Shotter, 1990; Kvale, 1990). Post-industrial society demands adaptation to unpredicted relationship changes. Relationships are negotiated rather than fixed or scripted. In the postmodern world, relationships are to be created to suit the unique experience of a limitless variety of perspectives and histories.

Adjusting to a view of social structures in a postmodern or postindustrial era may challenge researchers. Comfortable ways of considering family may need to give way to perspectives that are more variable and less predictable. Nevertheless, information to help create high quality family relationships regardless of the structure of the family is more fitting with a postmodern perspective, and, it would seem, to enhancing stepfamily adjustment.

2. Considering the age of children at the time of the study as well as the age of the same children at the time of remarriage means more effort must be taken in selecting the sample. Fewer children will fit the profile than if just one of these variables is considered. Alternatively, a research design with more categories will require a larger sample to satisfy the requirements for statistical analysis. Adding yet another variable adds to the complexity already noted in the stepfamily literature (Ganong & Coleman, 1994).

3. If the concept of 'psychological parenthood' is to be useful to stepfamily research it must be defined and operationalized. Defining this construct and developing valid and reliable instruments to assess it are challenge prospects. Instruments for assessing the nuclear family do not need to consider child-adult relationships of varying parental status that begin when the child is 5, 10, or 15 years of age. The child development literature described above may provide a fresh look at child adult relationships that can offer stepfamily researchers a method of studying stepchild-stepparent relationships that is less restricted by the nuclear family model.

4. Language also remains to be invented to describe stepfamily relationships. True to postmodern sensitivities, language is not neutral but rather carries social judgment and can obscure critical issues for less powerful groups (Gergen, 1990). Terms such as 'stepparent-stepchild relationship' may make the task of moving to a child-driven model more difficult than the reverse, i.e., 'stepchild-stepparent relationship.' Attempting to create vocabulary that does not carry the preconceived notions of the nuclear family model to the stepfamily is an onerous task in itself. Terms such as 'psychological parenthood' and 'one versus two parent stepfamily households' seem awkward and uncomfortable. Yet the vocabulary drawn from the nuclear family brings with it restrictions and judgments. For example, the term 'stepparent' may be a misnomer. Stepparent relationships that have a high degree of psychological parenthood may be devalued by the use of 'step' while those with a low degree of psychological parenthood may be ill defined by the use of 'parent.' Stepfamily research needs more sophisticated and more sensitive terminology in order to refine our thinking and our discussions so that we can address the unique features of stepfamily experience more faithfully.

Benefits

1. The stepfamily literature has devoted considerable time to studying stepchildren. However, the majority of this work has been through the eyes of adults. The ways in which children construct their stepfamilies is

often based on their experience rather than any theoretical model (Gross, 1986). The few studies in which children's conceptualizations of stepfamilies were explored presented very different descriptions of roles and relationships within the family (Gross, 1986; Lutz, 1983). Children's perspectives may be very valuable in developing constructs with which stepfamilies can be viewed in normative terms. Research designs including the concepts described in this paper may be much more consistent with the perspectives children in stepfamilies have expressed.

2. Given the wide range of relationships that can be developed between stepchildren and their stepparent, the validity and reliability of the terms 'stepparent' and 'stepparenting' are at risk. Models of stepfamily adjustment that address the concept of a continuum of stepchild-stepparent relationships based on degrees of psychological parenthood may capture the experience of those in stepfamilies more accurately, thereby increasing the validity and reliability of the term 'stepparent.'

3. By creating samples that are more homogeneous for type of stepchild-stepparent relationship researchers should find a greater effects size for significant variables. The step literature includes findings that are at times contradictory (Erera-Weatherley, in press). Many other studies include small effect sizes which lead to speculation that the differences may be statistically significant but not meaningful (Ganong & Coleman, 1993).

For example, in a small exploratory study, Gamache (1992) found that by limiting the sample of young adult stepchildren to those who had become stepchildren in their adolescent years, approximately 70% of the variance in perceived well-being could be explained by 3 family process variables. The results of the study suggest that the well-being of these young adults was strongly associated with their experience of family relationships in which the biological child-parent relationship was not interfered with by the stepparent, the adolescent was not displaced in family roles and responsibilities, and a peer-like relationship between biological parent and child existed.

3. With the inclusion of a range of stepchild-stepparent relationships based on the age of the children at the beginning of the steprelationship, the dialogue between researchers and clinicians may be improved, thereby encouraging the on-going dialogue between these two professional communities. Historically, the communication between these two groups has been tentative at best (Ganong & Coleman, 1987; Ihinger-Tallman & Pasley, 1994). By becoming more sensitive to the type of stepchild-stepparent relationship under discussion, whether a psychological parent or relative stranger, research findings will be more easily incorporated to the

very real relationships facing the therapist (Pasley, Dollahite & Ihinger-Tallman, 1993). The theory and practice of family therapy are often biased in favour of the nuclear family to the detriment of the stepfamily (Browning, 1994; Gamache, 1995). Clinicians working with stepfamilies could greatly benefit from research that is more compatible with therapeutic practice.

As we look past the border of the nuclear family model to the uncharted territory beyond, it is difficult to envision where empirical investigation of the stepfamily must go in order to truly reflect a normative adaptive approach to stepfamily research. However, as we move from a modern, industrial society to a postmodern, postindustrial era, it is becoming increasingly important to be able to respond to social change in a way that does not pathologize an ever increasing number of families in our communities.

On the other hand, stepfamily members need accurate information about how to maximize their chances to create a positive family life. To date, stepfamily research has documented the risks of divorce and remarriage to children (Hetherington, 1987a) and adults (White & Booth, 1985). Nevertheless, stepfamily research has an equally important role to play in providing accurate and relevant information to help stepfamilies and other members of the community make these transitions successfully, thereby enhancing their potential to adapt to the dramatic changes of society today.

REFERENCES

Ainsworth, M. (1982). Attachment: Retrospect and prospect. In C. M. Parkes & J. S. Hinde (Eds.), *The place of attachment in human behavior* (pp. 3-30). New York: Basic.

Anderson, J. Z. & White, G. D. (1986). An empirical investigation of interactive and relationship patterns in functional and dysfunctional nuclear families and stepfamilies. *Family Process, 25,* 407-422.

Barber, B. & Lyons, J. (1994). Family processes and adolescent adjustment in intact and remarried families. *Journal of Youth and Adolescence, 23,* 421-436.

Beer, W. R. (Ed.) (1988). *Relative strangers: Studies of stepfamily processes.* Totowa, NJ: Littlefield, Adams & Co.

Bernstein, A. (1988). Unraveling the tangles: Children's understanding of stepfamily kinship. In W. Beer (Ed.), *Relative strangers: Studies of stepfamily processes* (pp. 83-111). Totowa, NJ: Littlefield, Adams & Co.

Bowlby, J. (1982). Attachment and loss: Retrospect and prospect. *American Journal of Orthopsychiatry, 52,* 664-678.

Bray, J. (1992). Family relationships and children's adjustment in clinical and nonclinical stepfather families. *Journal of Family Psychology, 6,* 60-68.

Bray, J., Berger, S., & Boethel, C. (1993, August). *Conflict following divorce and* remarriage: Impact on children. Paper presented at the 101st Annual Convention of the American Psychological Association, Toronto, Canada.

Bray, J., Berger, S., & Boethel, C. (1994). Role integration and marital adjustment in stepfather families. In K. Pasley & M. Ihinger-Tallman (Eds.), *Stepparenting: Issues in research, theory, and practice* (pp. 69-86). New York: Greenwood.

Bronstein, P., Causon, J., Stoll, M., & Abrams, C. (1993). Parenting behavior and children's social, psychological, and academic adjustment in diverse family structures. *Family Relations, 42*, 268-276.

Browning, S. (1994). Treating stepfamilies: Alternatives to traditional family therapy. In K. Palsey & M. Ihinger-Tallman (Eds.), *Stepparenting: Issues in Theory, Research, and Practice* (pp. 175-198). Westport, CT: Guildford.

Buhrmester, D. & Furman, W. (1986). Changing functions of friends in childhood: A neo-Sullivanian approach. In V. J. Derlega & B.A. Winstead (Eds.), *Friendship and social interaction* (pp. 41-62). New York: Springer-Verlag.

Burgoyne, J. & Clark, D. (1984). *Making a go of it.* Boston: Routledge & Kegan Paul.

Cherlin, A. (1978). Remarriage as an incomplete institution. *American Journal of Sociology, 84*, 634-650.

Cherlin, A. & Furstenburg, F. (1994). Stepfamilies in the United States: A reconsideration. *American Review of Sociology, 20*, 359-381.

Clingempeel, W. G., Flesher, M., & Brand, E. (1987). Research on stepfamilies: Paradigmatic constraints and alternative proposals. In J. P. Vincent (Ed.), *Advances in family intervention: Assessment and theory, Volume 4* (pp. 229-251). Greenwich, CT: JAI Press.

Coontz, S. (1992). *The way we never were: American families and the nostalgia trap.* New York: Basic.

Crosbie-Burnett, M. (1984). The centrality of the step relationship: A challenge to family theory and practice. *Family Relations, 33*, 459-464.

Crosbie-Burnett, M. (1989). *The stepfamily adjustment scale: The development of a new instrument designed to measure the unique aspects of stepfamilies.* Paper presented at the Theory Construction and Research Methodology Workshop, National Council on Family Relations, New Orleans, November, 1989.

Crosbie-Burnett, M. & Skyles, A. (1989). Stepchildren in schools and colleges: Recommendations for educational policy changes. *Family Relations, 38*, 59-64.

Dahl, A., Cowgill, K., & Asmundsson, R. (1987). Life in remarriage families. *Social Work, 32*, 40-44.

Erera-Weatherley, P. (in press). On becoming a stepparent: Factors associated with the adoption of alternative stepparenting styles. *Journal of Divorce and Remarriage.*

Fine, M., Donnelly, B., & Voydanoff, P. (1991). The relation between adolescents' perceptions of their family lives and their adjustment in stepfather families. *Journal of Adolescent Research, 6*, 423-436.

Fine, M., Voydanoff, P., & Donnelly, B. (1993). Relations between parental control and warmth and child well-being in stepfamilies. *Journal of Family Psychology, 7*, 222-232.

Furman, W. & Buhrmester, D. (1985). Children's perceptions of the personal relationships in their social networks. *Developmental Psychology, 21*, 1016-1024.

Furman, W. & Buhrmester, D. (1992). Age and sex differences in perceptions of networks of personal relationships. *Child Development, 63*, 103-115.

Gamache, S. (1992, November). *Young adult perceptions of stepfamily transition: The essential role of the single parent family within the stepfamily.* Paper presented at the National Council on Family Relations Conference, Orlando, Florida.

Gamache, S. (1995). Protesting the dominance of the nuclear family model: Creating space for the stepfamily. *Journal of Collaborative Therapies, 3*(2), 13-19.

Ganong, L. & Coleman, M. (1984). Effects of remarriage on children: A review of the empirical literature. *Family Relations, 33*, 389-406.

Ganong, L. & Coleman, M. (1987). Effects of parental remarriage on children: An updated comparison of theories, methods, and findings from clinical and empirical research. In K. Pasley & M. Ihinger-Tallman (Eds.), *Remarriage and stepparenting: Current research and theory* (pp. 94-140). New York: Guildford.

Ganong, L. & Coleman, M. (1993). A meta-analytic comparison of the self-esteem and behavior problems of stepchildren to children in other family structures. *Journal of Divorce and Remarriage, 19*, 143-163.

Ganong, L. & Coleman, M. (1994). *Remarried family relationships.* Thousand Oaks, CA: Sage.

Gergen, K. (1990). Toward a postmodern psychology. *The Humanistic Psychologist, 18*, 23-24.

Giddens, A. (1991). *Modernity and self-identity: Self and society in the late modern age.* Stanford, CA : Stanford University Press.

Gross, P. (1986). Defining post-divorce remarriage families: A typology based on the subjective perceptions of children. *Journal of Divorce, 10*, 205-217.

Hage, J. & Powers, C. (1992). *Post-industrial lives: Roles and relationships in the 21st century.* Newbury Park, CA: Sage.

Hetherington, E. M. (1987a, April). *Coping with family transitions: Winners, losers, and survivors.* Paper presented at the Meetings of the Society for Research in Child Development, Baltimore, MD.

Hetherington, E. M. (1987b). Family relations six years after divorce. In K. Pasley & M. Ihinger-Tallman (Eds.), *Remarriage and stepparenting: Current research and practice* (pp. 185-205). New York: Guildford.

Hetherington, E. M., Stanley-Hagan, M., & Anderson, E. (1989). Marital transitions: A child's perspective. *American Psychologist, 44*, 303-312.

Hetherington, E. M. & Clingempeel, G. (1992). Coping with marital transitions: A family systems perspective. *Monographs of the society for research in child development, 57*.

Hetherington, E. M. & Jodl, K. (1993, November). *Stepfamilies as settings for child development*. Paper presented at the National Symposium on Stepfamilies, University Park, PA.

Ihinger-Tallman, M. & Pasley, K. (1987). Divorce and remarriage in the American family: A historical review. In K. Pasley & M. Ihinger-Tallman (Eds.), *Remarriage and stepparenting: Current research and practice* (pp. 3-18). New York: Guildford.

Ihinger-Tallman, M. & Pasley, K. (1994). Building bridges: Reflections on theory, research, and practice. In K. Pasley & M. Ihinger-Tallman (Eds.), *Stepparenting: Issues in theory, research, and practice* (pp. 239-250). Westport, CT.: Greenwood Press.

Ihinger-Tallman, M., Pasley, K., & Lofquist, A. (1994). Remarriage and stepfamilies: Making progress in understanding. In K. Pasley & M. Ihinger-Tallman (Eds.), *Stepparenting: Issues in theory, research, and practice* (pp. 1-14). Westport, CT: Greenwood Press.

Kelly, P. (1992, Dec.). Healthy stepfamily functioning. *Families in Society: The Journal of Contemporary Human Services*, 579-587.

Keshet, J. (1980). From separation to stepfamily: A subsystem analysis. *Journal of Family Issues*, *1*(4), 146-153.

Kurdek, L. & Fine, M. (1993a). Parent and nonparent residential family members as providers of warmth and supervision to young adolescents. *Journal of Family Psychology*, *7*, 245-249.

Kurdek, L. & Fine, M. (1993b). The relation between family structure and young adolescents' appraisals of family climate and parenting behavior. *Journal of Family Issues*, *14*, 279-290.

Kvale, S. (1990). Postmodern psychology: A contraditio in adjecto? *The Humanistic Psychologist*, *18*, 35-54.

Levin, I (1990, July). *The stepfamily: Reconstruction, trial, or innovation*. Paper presented at XII World Congress of Sociology, Madrid, Spain.

Levin, I. (1993). Family as mapped realities. *Journal of Family Issues*, *14*, 82-91.

Lutz, E. P. (1983). The stepfamily: An adolescent perspective. *Family Relations*, *32*, 367-376.

Marsiglio, W. (1992). Stepfathers with minor children living at home: Parenting perceptions and relationship quality. *Journal of Family Issues*, *13*, 195-214.

Mills, D. M. (1984). A model for stepfamily development. *Family Relations*, *33*, 365-372.

Minuchin, S. & Fishman, H. (1981). *Family therapy techniques*. Cambridge, MA: Harvard University Press.

Papernow, P. (1988). Stepparent role development: From outsider to intimate. In W. Beer (Ed.), *Relative strangers: Studies of stepfamily processes* (pp. 54-82). Totowa, NJ: Littlefield, Adams & Co.

Parkes, C. M. & Hinde, J. S. (Eds.) (1982). *The place of attachment in human behavior*. New York: Basic.

Pasley, K., Dollahite, D., & Ihinger-Tallman, M. (1993). Bridging the gap. *Family Relations*, *42*, 315-322.

Pasley, K., Ihinger-Tallman, M., & Lofquist, A. (1994). Remarriage and stepfamilies: Making progress in understanding. In K. Palsey & M. Ihinger-Tallman (Eds.), *Stepparenting: Issues in Theory, Research, and Practice* (pp. 1-14). Westport, CT: Guildford.

Peavy, V. (1993). Envisioning the future: Worklife and counselling. *Canadian Journal of Counselling, 27,* 123-139.

Pruett, C., Calsyn, R., & Jensen (1993). Social support received by children in stepmother, stepfather, and intact families. *Journal of Divorce and Remarriage, 19,* 165-179.

Shotter, J. (1990). Getting in touch: The metamethodology of a postmodern science of mental life. *The Humanistic Psychologist, 18,* 7-22.

Walker, K. & Messinger, L. (1979). Remarriage after divorce: Dissolution and reconstruction of family boundaries. *Family Process, 18,* 185-192.

Weiss, R S. (1974). The provisions of social relationships. In Z. Rubin (Ed.), *Doing Unto Others* (pp. 17-26), Englewood Cliffs, NJ: Prentice-Hall.

Weiss, R. S. (1982). In C. M. Parkes & J. S. Hinde (Eds.), *Attachment in Human Behavior* (pp. 171-175). New York: Basic.

White, L. K., & Booth, A. (1985). The quality and stability of remarriages: The role of stepchildren. *American Sociological Review, 50,* 689-698.

White, M. & Epston, D. (1990). *Narrative means to therapeutic ends.* New York: Norton.

Whiteside, M. (1989). Remarried systems. In L. Combrinck-Graham (Ed.), *Children in family contexts* (pp. 135-160). New York: Guildford.

Zill, N. (1988). Behavior, achievement, and health problems among children in stepfamilies: Findings from a National Survey of Child Health. In E. M. Hetherington & J. Aresteh (Eds.), *Impact of divorce, single-parenting, and stepparenting on children* (pp. 325-369). Hillsdale, NJ: Lawrence Erlbaum Associates.

Zill, N, Morrison, D., & Coiro, M. J. (1993). Long-term effects of parental divorce on parent-child relationships, adjustment, and achievement in young adults. *Journal of Family Psychology, 7,* 91-103.

Step-Family Variations

Jan Trost

INTRODUCTION

The term step-family is not an old one at all. Fancher[1] tells us that she at age 30 married a widower aged 32 with three children. As the first notes of the wedding march sounded, her husband to be said: "Darling girl, I'm about to make an instant mother of you." One could say that she at the same time got an instant-family household or with today's terminology a step-family household. As De'Ath in this volume notes, the *term* step-family as such did not occur in the Concise Oxford Dictionary until the middle of 1995. The first time I have seen the term used was in a book by Anne W. Simon, published in 1964. Previously there was no term for the phenomenon, only for some parts of it, like step-mother, step-father, step-child, etc.

There are numerous ways of looking at what could be labelled as step-families. Since there are so many varieties and since valid data can never be found for all the varieties, I limit my presentation to numbers for just one kind of step-families: step-family households with minor children. I will further discuss the relevance of LAT (Living Apart Together) for the idea of step-families as well as the relevance of adult children and not only minors. Since most step-families are based upon remarriage, I also examine these data.

Step-families have as a main prerequisite that a not-married parent marries another adult, who at the time is not a parent together with the husband or wife (for simplicity I will use the terms married and marriages also for cohabiting couples since they are so common in Western societies

Jan Trost is Professor of Sociology, Uppsala University, Uppsala, Sweden.

[Haworth co-indexing entry note]: "Step-Family Variations." Trost, Jan. Co-published simultaneously in *Marriage & Family Review* (The Haworth Press, Inc.) Vol. 26, No. 1/2, 1997, pp. 71-84; and: *Stepfamilies: History, Research, and Policy* (ed: Irene Levin and Marvin B. Sussman) The Haworth Press, Inc., 1997, pp. 71-84. Single or multiple copies of this article are available for a fee from The Haworth Document Delivery Service [1-800-342-9678, 9:00 a.m. - 5:00 p.m. (EST). E-mail address: getinfo@haworth.com].

and the two phenomena now since some decades are social institutions alongside each other[2]). With this basic definition the social reality of step-families seems very simple, but as often is the case, social reality is much more complex than what at first seems simple. The not-married parent can be never married, widowed or divorced. The other adult can be either never married, divorced or widowed and he or she can also be a parent. The two adults might also have a child jointly.

The main aim of this article is to demonstrate the complexity and variability; thus to show that it is impossible to come to a conclusion of how many and what varieties there are. If one takes the perspective of social policy, the effect will be different from a perspective of a child's or of an adult's.

The basic definition combined with sharing a household, which also is the most common one, applies the perspective of traditional societies, looking at the phenomenon from outside and not from the social reality as such. The household is also used as the unit of analysis. It is a legalistic and simplistic way of defining a part of society. In this article to start with I will follow the traditional definition and thus look at frequencies of remarriages over the last two centuries in Sweden, followed by a section on household composition and finally I will take a look at other sorts of step-families than those limited to household structure.

REMARRIAGES

Technically speaking, there are three kinds of remarriages: both the bride and the groom are previously married, only the bride is previously married, and only the groom is. But since we do not accept bigamy, the background for the previously married has to be a dissolution of the previous marriage either by death of the other spouse or by a divorce. Thus one could say that there are six kinds of remarriages by background as illustrated in Figure 1.

FIGURE 1. Property space showing six varieties of step-family households.

Previously married	Death	Divorce
Both	1	2
Bride only	3	4
Groom only	5	6

Historically, however, a century ago almost no divorces existed for the simple reason that the law did not permit any divorces or at least all laws in Western countries either forbid divorce or they were very restrictive. In most of these countries the laws subsequently became more liberal and in many countries divorce became a social fact by numbers about 50 years ago. Still some few decades ago there were no divorces in, for example, Italy and Spain. In these sorts of countries legal separation has been a way of circumscribing the legal restrictions, but since the cohabiting relationships after such legal separations have never been true social institutions and since we never had them in Sweden, I will not deal with such sorts of semi-remarriages or pseudo-remarriages.

In Diagram 1 I show the relative number of marriages in Sweden that have been first marriages for both the bride and the groom. There one can see that two centuries ago as many as about 25 per cent of those who married, either the bride or the groom or both were previously married; thus these couples constituted remarried couples. Just one century ago the

DIAGRAM 1. Marriages where both are never married, Sweden, percent

Sources: Historisk Statistik 1967
Befolkningsrörelsen 1990

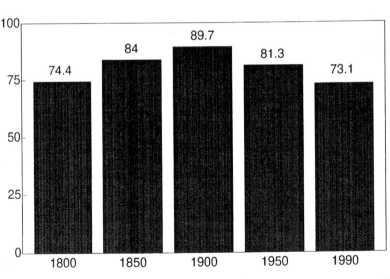

EREMARR

relative number of remarriages of all marriages formed had decreased to only ten percent after which the frequencies of remarriages have gone on increasing and reaches now more than one third of all marriages formed. This means that remarriages were common two centuries ago and that they are much more common now than a century ago and somewhat more common than two centuries ago.

The important difference is, however, that 200 years ago all remarriages were based upon the death of at least one spouse, 100 years ago the picture was the same but now at the end of the 20th century almost all remarriages are based upon a divorce by at least one of the spouses in the newly married couple. One could say that high mortality rates have been replaced by high divorce rates. For example, a couple of centuries ago the death of a mother or father of minor children was not at all unusual–today it is. On the other side, today divorces among fathers and mothers of minor children are not at all unusual–a couple of centuries ago they practically speaking didn't exist.

During the 19th century the death rates for men as well as for women decreased historically very rapidly and have gone on decreasing but with less pace. In Diagrams 2 and 3 are illustrated the changes in death rates for women and men. The mortality rates for men have decreased even more rapidly than for women. This means that what is often called the gender ratio switches from more men than women to the opposite in the later years of life. More baby boys are born than baby girls. Already at ages lower than 15 there were more females than males. However, now there are more males than females in Sweden up to an age of 57 and from 58 there are more females than males. This in its turn means that, relatively seen, there can be many more opposite gender couples in today's society than, say, a hundred years ago.

The decreases in death rates also mean that relatively seen much fewer young marriages are dissolved by the death of one of the spouses, customarily a parent to minor children. Now very few couples are dissolved by death where there are minor children. One could say that previously both the law, economic circumstances and social control prevented couples from divorcing. Now they don't. Added should be that previously couples did not have time to divorce until one of the spouses died–now the law, economic circumstances and social control does not prevent divorces, the partners of the couples now live long enough to divorce.

Cohabitation as a Social Institution Alongside Marriage

The data presented above are from official statistics and thus no data are included on informal relationships or cohabiting couple formations. Until

DIAGRAM 2. Death rates among females
(per 1,000 alive in the age class)

Sources: Historisk statistik, 1969
Befolkningsförändringar, 1990

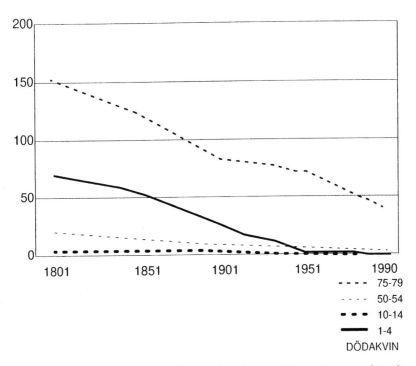

- - - - 75-79
- - - - 50-54
■ ■ ■ 10-14
■■■■ 1-4
DÖDAKVIN

the middle of the 1960s in Sweden (and until some five or ten years later in most of the other Western societies) non-marital cohabitation was no social issue nor was it an issue of figures. With this I mean that there were very few cohabiting couples (except for in Iceland[3]) and the very few that existed were never counted neither were they social issues at that time. Since around 1970 non-marital cohabitation has become common and a social institution in most Western societies.[4]

Cohabitation is somewhat special in these circumstances. On one side one can say that they are similar to or even equal to marriages in most respects and on the other side one can say that they constitute a very different social category. In, for example, Sweden, almost no couples marry without having cohabited for some months or years before marry-

DIAGRAM 3. Death rates among men
(per 1,000 alive in the age class)

Sources: Historisk statistik, 1969
Befolkningsförändringar, 1990

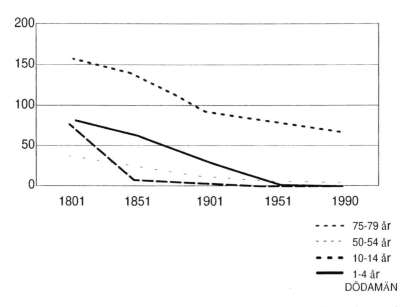

- - - - 75-79 år
- - - - 50-54 år
■ ■ ■ 10-14 år
━━━━ 1-4 år
DÖDAMÄN

ing. This means that during the last two decades or so, all newly married couples have lived together before marrying. Furthermore, the cohabiting couples constitute a very heterogeneous category in the meaning that, if we take a cross sectional view of them, some of them have cohabited for only some few days or weeks and some have cohabited for years and even for decades.

Compared to the traditional system of courtship, engagement and marriage, the system of cohabitation means that some of the newly formed cohabiting relationships are to be compared to the courtship period previous to the period of going steady, some are comparable to the going steady period, some are comparable to the engagement period, and some are comparable to the first part of the married period within the traditional system (cf. Diagram 4).

What implications does this have upon remarriages? As I stated in the introductory part of this article, I look upon marriage and cohabitation as two social institutions alongside each other. But to do so is in some

DIAGRAM 4. The "traditional" and the present system

"Traditional" system

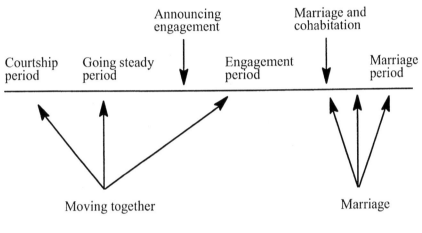

Present system

respects not fully realistic. Since some of the cohabiting relationships are more comparable to the courtship period and some to the going steady period it is very reasonable that we would find quite a few dissolutions of these cohabiting relationships as in all Western courtship systems. To look upon all re-cohabitations as equivalent to remarriages would not be reasonable. Only more marriage-like ones should be taken seriously in these respects. But since we are dealing with step-families here, only cohabiting relationships with a child are to be taken into consideration. In any case, we do not know how many are the cases of recohabitation and have to look upon the official figures as indicating changes in the social structure. We can take for granted that, with the low death rates and the historically very high divorce rates, the relative numbers of remarriages (including re-cohabitations) have been increasing and will probably go on increasing further in the near future.

This means that we can face an increasing number of step-families. Before coming into a discussion of what seriously could or should be looked upon as step-families, I will present some data on the household composition in Sweden related to step-family households.

HOUSEHOLD COMPOSITION

In Sweden[5] there were in 1992 about 1,850,000 children younger than 18 years of age. Of these 75 per cent live in nuclear families, i.e., they live with their fathers and mothers and if they have siblings of minor age, they all live there together. About 16 per cent live with their mother or father in what is usually classified as a one-parent family or household. About nine per cent remain; some two percent live with their mother or father who has remarried someone (or the parent cohabits with someone not a parent of the child), but no step-siblings or half-siblings. Some of the children live with half-siblings or step-siblings (about seven per cent) in the household. Finally, some very few children live in households with a step-parent and step- as well as half-siblings. Thus somewhat more than one child out of ten children live in step-family households. Noted should be that I have here only considered minor children, i.e., younger than 18 years old. If older children would have been included in the figures more children would be classified as living in step-families of various sorts.

Glick and Lin[6] take a different perspective when saying that in the USA, 1980, divorced and remarried women during their lifetime gave birth to one third of all their children after their (first) marriages and thus, two thirds of the children were born before their second marriage.

All data of this sort should be looked at with some skepticism since they are estimates of various kinds. For example, in some studies cohabiting couples are counted as cohabiting only if they officially are registered as residents at the same address. In other studies self-reports only are used as criteria, which can mean that some cohabiting couples don't report themselves as cohabiting; one reason for not doing so could be that the couple is sub-letting an apartment illegally; another reason, probably common in some parts of the world, could be that the official resident could risk losing housing support, child support or alimony.

In a Swedish study[7] (not the one mentioned above), where household is the unit of analysis, somewhat more than six per cent of all households with at least two inhabitants are step-family households. If one would include only households with at least one child younger than 18 years (thus excluding all couples without children) one would find that somewhat more than 13 per cent of these households are step-family households.

As a final remark in this section I want to stress that these figures are estimates based upon sources where the number of cohabiting couples are underestimated which means that the number of households classified as step-family households is underestimated. When looking at the child as the unit for analysis, the number of children estimated as living in step-families is also underestimated. Another momentum is that a child could be a step-child for almost 18 years, could be adopted by the step-parent and thus turn into a combination of a "biological" and an adopted child, could be a step-child only the last few months or so before turning 18 years of age. The situation for the step-parent is very similar. All households are in a process where one might know what has happened, but no one knows what will happen. We only know that if a child survives until major age, the child is no child anymore in these respects.

OTHER STEP-FAMILIES

Traditionally and as hinted at above, when looking at step-families almost everyone refers to the *household* unit as *the* unit of analysis. Furthermore, children are counted only if of *minor* age.

Not Limited to Household

Until now I have limited myself to the household, which is very common to do. But a step-family as any other variety of family can live distributed over several households and still be a family–depending upon perspective used.

In a Swedish study of about 1,000 adults (aged 20-59) one out of 935 said that there was a step-parent in the household; and this step-parent was also by the respondent defined as a member of the family. Another nine respondents had a step-parent in the self-defined family, who was not a member of the household. Step-children were more frequently occurring. Of the 935 respondents 26 (less than three per cent) had a step-child in the household, out of which 17 (65 per cent) also were members of both the family and the household; nine (35 per cent) were not members of the respondents' families even though they were members of the household. Looking from the perspective of the family, 34 (less than four per cent) had step-children in their families, of which 17 (50 per cent) were not members of the households and the rest, 17 or 50 per cent, were members of both the family and the household.

These data from adults clearly show that people's social reality is quite different from the outside perspective that technically classifies households as families and even as step-families. An example: A married couple has a child and they live together. After some time they divorce. The child stays with the mother in her household and visits the father more or less regularly, the parents might have joint custody or they might not. After some time the mother starts a cohabiting relationship and eventually marries. Thus the child now lives in a step-family household. The child might or might not define the step-father as a member of the child's family. The child might define the father as a member of the child's family. Even the father might start a cohabiting relationship and might eventually marry. The same child will still belong to the same step-family household. But she or he might also be seen by the father and by itself as belonging to the household of the father, too (although technically the child might have to be registered at the mother's home).[8] Now we could talk about the child as belonging to two step-family households. Social reality of this sort would hardly be included as reality in official statistics and other quantitative reports.

For me it is reasonable to include a new term and concept not dealt with previously here or elsewhere. Until now I have limited myself to marriages and cohabitations. For some readers to include cohabitation might seem odd, but as I have argued above, cohabitation is in so many countries a social institution alongside marriage so that the two have to be dealt with as parallel phenomena. The new term is LAT, which is an acronym for Living Apart Together.

LAT was first used in an article by the Dutch journalist Michiel Berkel in *Haagse Post*, October 14, 1978. He lived himself in a relationship where both he and his female friend wanted to be together for at least 24 hours a day, but for practical reasons they couldn't. He couldn't live with her and neither without her. He decided to write an article about the phenomenon. In a letter to me dated October 17, 1993, Michiel Berkel wrote, i. a.:

> At one of our editorial meetings, someone mentioned the term "Living Apart Together," referring to the Dutch motion picture. "Frank & Eva/Living Apart Together" directed by Wim Verstappen, made in 1973.
>
> For my article, I was trying to find an appropriate Dutch translation but I didn't manage to come up with something. Therefore I decided to use the abbreviation of the English words and voilà: that was the genesis of THE LAT RELATIONSHIP. (*De LAT relatie*), quickly a common term in the everyday language.

As Berkel wrote, the term LAT very rapidly became a term in everyday language in the Netherlands. For many of us within the international field of family studies the same term has come into use for our communication in English. Since the beginning of the 1990s most Swedes would agree with the meaning of the newly constructed Swedish term *särbo*, which means the same as LAT. (Similarly as with the Nordic origin of the English term neighbour, *nabo,* where *na* stands for close and *bo* for to live, in särbo *sär* means apart and *bo* to live.)

In a Swedish poll of about 1,000 adults about two percent said that they live in a LAT relationship of the sort here indicated. I would regularly define LAT as a not married couple with separate domicile, both defining themselves as a couple living under marriage-like conditions and also perceiving that at least their significant others define them as a couple of the same sort. Practically speaking, the couple would, for example, expect to be invited as a couple when married and cohabiting couples are and their social surrounding would also so expect and behave.

LAT relationships must have existed for long time but they have not until recently had a label and the phenomenon has not until recently been noticed socially, thus it has not been a concept in people's minds. I would say that there are a set of mechanisms behind the formation and continuation of LAT relationships.

One of them is the kind Berkel belonged to: Two divorced (or separated) persons with minor children, who both want to keep their households for the children's sake and not let a new partner move in. To start a living together would be to go too far, considering the children. When the children grow up and learn to know the new partner a moving together might be appropriate.

Another kind are those who both are widowed remaining in their households and with adult children not living together with the surviving parent. For these widowed persons to move might be too physically heavy and also too emotionally heavy thinking about the deceased and loved ex-spouse. Another rationale for remaining in two households would for some be a concern about adult children and grandchildren who come visiting their parent/grandparent–it should be possible for the children/grandchildren to come home to the parent/grandparent and not to someone else's home.

A third kind of arrangement is the long-distance LAT relationships. Typically the two had their jobs at different places when they met and, when they have become a couple, they want to keep their jobs, they might not be able to find reasonable jobs in the same area. For the time being a commuting LAT relationship might be most suitable.

Common for all these couples, of which some few examples have been presented here, is that they have their two households but otherwise we are talking about a very heterogeneous category; some would eat together daily and sleep together only sometimes, some would eat together only some days a week, some would be together all the time except for when children/grandchildren come visiting, just to mention some few varieties.

I will not here go further into the varieties of LAT relationships and the meanings of them. Important in the context of step-families is, however, to notice that quite a few of these relationships can be classified by some of those concerned as step-families. Even if not so classified, quite a few of the phenomena typical for step-families are present. For example, the parent has a new partner, this partner might have children of its own.

Important is also that the absolute as well as the relative numbers of LAT relationships most likely will increase. With high divorce and separation rates, more persons will be eligible for these relationships. With low mortality rates and high healthiness among elderly, these LAT relationships will increase. With a more differentiated labour market as well as more equity between the genders, the same will be our future reality.

As so often is the case a description and analysis of a social phenomenon might sound as if the phenomenon is stable and under no change. A married couple might divorce or one of the spouses might die. Similarly with a cohabiting couple, but added should be that the two can marry, which has at least some legal implications. With the LAT relationship even more can happen: their relationship might be ended by death of one of them or they might themselves end the relationship, they might move in together, and they might marry. In a short time perspective all these relationships can remain without interior structural changes but in the long run they will all change.

Children of Minor and Major Age

Traditionally, when talking about step-families not only common household is more or less taken for granted, but also that the children are minors and living in the household. However, minors can be defined in various ways. One can use the age until when the parents have to take responsibility for the children in at least some ways. Such a limit can be 18 years as in Sweden or 25 years as in Belgium. Even in these cases the limit is not absolutely clear. Thus, in Sweden the parents still have a financial responsibility later until age 20 if the child is studying at high-school level or similar. In Belgium the 25 year limit is not as high if the child is married and/or is financially capable on its own behalf.

My main interest here in this section is, however, children not living with the remarried parent and the children who are adults. Children can be viewed from various angles. One is to look upon them from a generational perspective, saying that a teenager 50 years ago is living under different conditions than a teenager does now. Another way is to look upon children as minors, which I have mentioned above. A third variety is to look at children from a relational perspective; children as relations.

In society we too often forget that a child usually is a child until both parents are deceased. If we take all children into account and not only those living in the parental household we will find an enormous variety of situations where a parent has started a new relationship of marriage, cohabitation or LAT.

The 70 year widow who has started a LAT relationship with a 75 year old widower might very well include her LAT in her family together with her children and her grandchildren. Her children might or might not include her new partner in their families. Her grandchildren might or might not include her partner in their families. If the two LATs move in together and become a cohabiting couple or if they marry, the children and the grandchildren might or might not change their definitions of their families.

This is one example only of possibilities where at least one of the new partners, be they married, cohabiting or LAT, has a child and where thus the term step, or to be more precise, the concept of step might be relevant. The concept might be relevant for one or for many of those concerned and thus a part of social reality. I fully agree with Cooley[9] when he said that " ... the imaginations which people have of one another are the *solid facts* of society, and to observe and interpret these must be a chief aim of sociology." Or as Dewey[10] argued, that social sciences and philosophy should deal with everyday situations and problems and not only play with abstract theories and abstract phenomena not existing in everyday life.

NOTES

1. Fancher (1962).
2. cf. Trost (1978, 1979, 1981).
3. cf. Bjørnson (1971) and Trost (1979). In Iceland cohabitation has been a common phenomenon for centuries, probably connected to a tradition to ignore the rules of Christianity. For example, when Iceland was Christianed a thousand years ago, they demanded to keep the right to abortion/infanticide and also to eat horse meat. Demands the pope accepted.
4. cf. Trost (1981).
5. Landgren Möller, Larsson & Sande (1996).
6. Glick & Lin (1987).
7. Statistiska centralbyrån (1990).
8. Levin (1994).
9. Cooley (1902 (1922, 62)).
10. Dewey (1920).

REFERENCES

Bjørnson, B. (1971) *The Lutheran Doctrine of Marriage in Modern Icelandic Society*, Oslo: Univeritetsforlaget.

Cooley, C. H. (1902 (1922)) *Human Nature and Social Order*, New York: Scribner's.

Dewey, J. (1920) *Reconstruction in Philosophy*, New York: Holt.

Fancher, B. H. (1962) I Was an "Instant" Mother, *Redbook Magazine*, March, 8-14.

Glick, P. C. & Sung-Ling, L. (1987) Remarriage after Divorce, *Sociological Perspectives*, vol. 30, 162-179.

Landgren Möller, E., Larsson, A. & Sande J. (1996) Barndomen, in *Fakta om den svenska familjen*, Stockholm: Statistiska centralbyrån, pp 24-43.

Levin, I. (1994) *Stefamilie–variasjon og mangfold*, Oslo: Aventura.

Simon, A. W. (1964) *Stepchild in the Family*, New York: Odyssey Press.

Statistiska centralbyrån (1990) *Barns familjeförhållanden*, Stockholm: Statistiska centralbyrån.

Trost, J. (1981) Cohabitation in the Nordic Countries: From Deviant Phenomenon to Social Institution, *Alternative Lifestyles*, 4, 401-427.

Trost, J. (1979) *Unmarried Cohabitation*, Västerås: International Library.

Trost, J. (1978) A Renewed Social Institution: Non-marital Cohabitation, *Acta Sociologica*, 21, 303-315.

How Society Views Stepfamilies

Lawrence H. Ganong
Marilyn Coleman

Researchers recently have shown an increased interest in the impact of societal views (i.e., norms, expectations, stereotypes, myths) on relationships in stepfamilies (Coleman & Ganong, 1987; Kurdek & Fine, 1991; 1993). This increased interest is due to a growing recognition that cultural beliefs about family life exert a strong influence on the ways in which people conduct themselves, evaluate their own situations, and expect to be regarded by others (Dallos, 1994). It is increasingly understood that societal views influence the level of social support stepfamilies receive, which in turn affects their abilities to function effectively (Cherlin, 1978). In this paper we will review research and theory regarding societal views of stepfamilies. Although most of the research we cite has been conducted in the United States, there is ample evidence that what is described in this paper is true for Canada (Messenger, 1984), Europe (Bernardes, 1993; Hughes, 1991; Levin, 1993; Nemenyi, 1992), Israel (Guttman & Broudo, 1989), and Australia (Webber, 1991).

There are two general perspectives regarding how societies view stepfamilies. One perspective views stepfamilies as generally ignored by societies. Stepfamilies tend to be excluded from legal and social policy considerations, and they are often disregarded by social institutions such as schools and religious systems. Cherlin (1978) referred to stepfamilies as incomplete institutions because they lack institutionalized guidelines and support to help them solve their problems. The second general way that

---

Lawrence H. Ganong and Marilyn Coleman are affiliated with the University of Missouri, Columbia, MO 65211.

[Haworth co-indexing entry note]: "How Society Views Stepfamilies." Ganong, Lawrence H., and Marilyn Coleman. Co-published simultaneously in *Marriage & Family Review* (The Haworth Press, Inc.) Vol. 26, No. 1/2, 1997, pp. 85-106; and: *Stepfamilies: History, Research, and Policy* (ed: Irene Levin and Marvin B. Sussman) The Haworth Press, Inc., 1997, pp. 85-106. Single or multiple copies of this article are available for a fee from The Haworth Document Delivery Service [1-800-342-9678, 9:00 a.m. - 5:00 p.m. (EST). E-mail address: getinfo@haworth.com].

85

societies view stepfamilies is to see them as less functional and more problematic than nuclear families. In this stigmatized view, stepfamilies and stepfamily members are stereotyped as possessing mostly negative traits and characteristics, and interactions within stepfamilies are thought to be generally harmful and unpleasant (Coleman & Ganong, 1987; Ganong, Coleman, & Mapes, 1990).

Both of these views, the *stepfamily as incomplete institution* and the *stepfamily as stigma*, are by-products of an idealization of nuclear families. The ideal family, at least in many Western societies, continues to be the middle-class, first-marriage nuclear family with a mother and father and two, sometimes three, children (Coontz, 1992). This ideal influences perceptions of how families should live and lowers motivations to develop other models of healthy family functioning, or even to accept that there are other models of healthy family functioning (Candib, 1989; Levin, 1993; Uzoka, 1979).

THE NUCLEAR FAMILY IDEOLOGY

As long-time researchers of stepfamilies, we are struck by the disparity between the restricted ways in which people think about families and the rich diversity and variety of the families in which they live. Although families exist in a wide variety of forms and family behaviors are extremely varied, the guidelines and norms for how to be a family are quite limited. This is the "model monopoly" of nuclear families (Levin, 1993) in that one family model, the first-marriage nuclear family, is seen as the standard to which others should be compared (Uzoka, 1979).

In the United States a great deal of nostalgia has been expressed for an imagined past in which families were better than they are now, and consequently, life was richer. The fact that this era never existed does not seem to matter to those who wax sentimentally about life when men were breadwinners, women were homemakers, children were cared for with love, and society worked well as a result (Coontz, 1992). In the idealized view of families, men and women play distinct and complementary roles, paid work for women is peripheral to their family work, and family members' activities and duties are clearly related to age and gender (Candib, 1989).

Farber (1973) has argued that the nuclear family is often seen not only as an ideal, but as a universal, necessary entity in nature. This equivalence of the nuclear family and the natural family can be traced back to Old Testament Hebrews (Farber, 1973), and this model has come to be associated with a moral, natural imperative. Other forms of family life are considered to be immoral, or at best, less moral, and carry with them heavy stigma.

Although in most Western societies the stigma of divorce and remarriage has likely been reduced due to the relatively high rates of divorce and remarriage, in the United States there is still an undercurrent of moral outrage directed towards those who divorce (Poponoe, 1993). This moral outrage is often extended to remarriages and stepfamilies, because most remarriages follow divorce. Although there is less tolerance for the open expression of views that disparage "alternative family lifestyles," deeply felt negative attitudes toward those in nonnuclear families are still held by many. In fact, in the United States support appears to be increasing for those who wish to express their moral repugnance for postdivorce families and stepfamilies. At the societal level, a thin veneer of civility hides the punitive nature of traditional mores that suggest those who don't conform to the family ideal should be disdained. Cultural adherence to the nuclear family ideology helps explain why policymakers and governments can intrude so thoroughly into family life at the time of legal divorce (e.g., deciding the frequency of parent-child contacts, deciding which parent will pay for what needs of children, and so forth), and yet be reluctant to provide support to divorced families and stepfamilies.

For many, there is compelling evidence that nuclear families are better than stepfamilies. For example, children in nuclear families tend to score better, on average, than stepchildren on measures of cognitive, psychological and social well-being (Poponoe, 1994). Social and behavioral scientists, as well as politicians, are particularly prone to cite group means as justifications for their beliefs, forgetting the huge range of diversity in family processes within and between different types of families, ignoring the complexity of stepfamilies, and excluding careful examinations and interpretations of the relatively small effect sizes between nuclear families and stepfamilies (Amato, 1994). Selectively recalling evidence to support their positions, some authors simultaneously maintain a belief in the nuclear family ideology while contending that they do not have an ideology; they simply base their beliefs on their interpretation of the available empirical evidence.

In recent years, a new rationale for the superiority of the nuclear family model has emerged. Sociobiologists or evolutionary theorists have argued that biological bases for family life furnishes all the rationale needed to support the superiority of nuclear families over stepfamilies and other families that are not based on genetically-related kin (Poponoe, 1994). The evolutionary perspective is that parents are shaped by evolutionary forces to discriminate in favor of their biological offspring. This puts stepchildren at risk and perhaps even jeopardizes their safety. Whatever the rationale for supporting the nuclear family model, this ideology has had a profound influence on societies' views about stepfamilies. We will now examine the two major ways that this mindset has impacted how societies view stepfamilies, by ignoring them and by stigmatizing them.

STEPFAMILIES AS INCOMPLETE INSTITUTIONS

Cultural adherence to the nuclear family ideology led Cherlin (1978) to argue that remarriage is an incomplete institution. He reasoned that the absence of guidelines and norms for role performance, the dearth of culturally established, socially acceptable methods of resolving problems, and the relative absence of institutionalized social support for stepfamilies contribute to greater stress, inappropriate solutions to problems, and higher divorce rates for remarried families. Several clinical writers have supported this view, noting that stepparents are often unsure of how to relate to their stepchildren, an uncertainty that is shared by other stepfamily members and by outsiders who interact with stepfamilies (Mills, 1984; Papernow, 1993; Visher & Visher, 1988). According to clinicians, cultural models about how families are supposed to be are based on nuclear families and, therefore, do not provide members of stepfamilies much assistance in anticipating problems and figuring out workable solutions to existing difficulties, since they are based on nuclear families (Coale Lewis, 1985; Visher & Visher, 1988).

Cherlin (1978) pointed to the lack of support from social systems, the absence of language to describe steprelationships, and the paucity of legal regulations as illustrations of how remarried families are incompletely institutionalized. In the next few pages we will examine evidence for each these areas.

Little Institutionalized Social Support

Social organizations, such as schools, youth groups, religious groups, and health care systems are based on policies and procedures designed primarily for nuclear families (Coleman, Ganong, & Henry, 1984a; Crosbie-Burnett, 1994; Ganong, 1993). Consequently, stepfamilies find minimal support from formal institutions of society, and they often encounter barriers. For example, stepparents who are involved in their stepchildren's schooling frequently find that schools make little allowance for the presence of stepparents. Enrollment forms may have places for parents' names only and teachers are ill-prepared for a child to have three or more adults (i.e., biological parents and stepparents) show up to discuss a child's progress in school (Coleman, Ganong, & Henry, 1984b). Although stepfamilies are ostensibly welcome to participate in these social organizations, few attempts, if any, are made to accommodate organizational practices in order to facilitate their participation (Ganong, 1993).

Health care institutions often have policies about access to patients. From our experiences in teaching nurses and nursing students, we have heard many stories about the inconsistent application of policies restricting hospital visits to family members only. Sometimes they are applied in such a manner that stepfamily members are not allowed to visit stepkin in the hospital because they are not biologically-related or legally-related kin and thus are not considered by health care providers to be family members.

These subtle social insensitivities serve as constant reminders to stepfamily members that their families are deficient. If they want to be accepted, stepfamilies find it easier to act like nuclear families. Unfortunately, this puts undue pressure on relationships within remarried families to imitate nuclear family relationships as closely as possible. Rather than providing buffers, the customs of social systems that interact with stepfamilies can increase their stress.

Absence of Appropriate Terms

In many postdivorce stepfamilies there are types of relationships for which there are no labels. Take the following scenario:

Bob and Susan are a divorced couple with two children, Bobby and Sue. Susan retained physical and legal custody of the children and Bob paid child support. Three years after their divorce, Bob remarried Linda, a divorced woman with a son, Leon. A year after that, Sue remarried Alan, a man who had never been married. They had a child together whom they named Tony.

There are no labels in English for the relationships between Linda and Susan, between Linda and Alan, and between Bob and Alan. Some have suggested that the relationship between a former spouse and current spouse be called the *husband-in-law* or *wife-in-law*, and some have even facetiously referred to these persons as *outlaws*, but these terms have not been widely used, and these relationships remain nameless (Ganong & Coleman, 1994). The relationship between Leon, the stepsibling of Bobby and Sue, and Tony, the half-brother of Bobby and Sue, also has no label.

When there are no terms for a relationship, it is because there is no societal expectation that such a relationship will exist. Nonetheless, even though fathers and stepfathers are not expected to communicate with each other or to develop any kind of relationship, relationships between residential stepparents and nonresidential parents are inevitable in situations in which: (a) divorcing parents share legal custody of children, and/or (b) children are physically members of two households, and/or (c) parents and stepparents in two households are contributing to the child's upbringing. Ironically, clinicians suggest that stepfamilies in which biological parents cooperate with each other and with stepparents are those that are creating positive family environments for their children (Visher & Visher, 1988), and yet potentially key relationships are left nameless by societies that do not expect them to exist.

Other language usage, such as describing biological parents as *real* or *natural* parents, implicitly conveys the message that stepparents (and adoptive parents, foster parents, and others) are *unreal* or *unnatural*. Identifying nuclear families as *normal, real,* or *traditional* similarly signifies that other families are *abnormal, unreal,* and *nontraditional*. The use of language can serve to powerfully legitimize certain family forms and place others on the fringe of acceptability. Moreover, language helps shape thinking, and language about relationships in stepfamilies may make it more difficult for family members to develop positive identities and satisfying relationships (Coleman & Ganong, 1987).

Nonexistent or Ambiguous Legal Relationships

Stepparents have been generally overlooked in federal and state laws in the United States; they have few legal responsibilities toward their stepchildren, and even fewer rights (Chambers, 1990; Fine & Fine, 1992; Mahoney, 1994).

> The preference for the nuclear family finds expression in the legal system through laws that create distinct protections, entitlements, and responsibilities for spouses, parents, and children . . . The traditional emphasis on the nuclear family has effectively prevented many individuals, who live in other family situations, from enjoying the same type of legal recognition and protection. (Mahoney, 1994, p. 1)

Although some recent changes in family law in the United States and other countries indirectly affect the legal relationship between stepparents and stepchildren (e.g., more states are allowing third party requests for postdivorce custody and visitation), there is little consensus regarding needed legal changes, and almost no political pressure on legislatures to alter existing policies and laws regarding steprelationships (Chambers, 1990; Mahoney, 1994). For the most part, stepparents' obligations to stepchildren are based on whatever family members want them to be. Although this flexibility can be seen as an advantage, it is likely that for many stepparents the absence of legal ties adds to their feelings of ambiguity and lack of control regarding their relationships with stepchildren. Clinicians and social scientists who examine legal issues contend that the absence of a legal relationship potentially serves as a barrier to the development of emotionally close stepparent-stepchild bonds (Fine, 1989; Visher & Visher, 1988).

Relative Absence of Guidelines and Norms for Role Performance and Problem-Solving

Perhaps the most important way the nuclear family ideal affects relationship process is through the absence of cultural norms that serve to guide relational behaviors in stepfamilies. Adults who believe there is only one natural, normal way to be a family may find it difficult to determine what their roles and responsibilities are when their family ceases to fit the cultural ideal. In particular, seeing the nuclear family model as the standard contributes to confusion about roles and responsibilities regarding stepchildren. What many stepfamilies do is imitate or attempt to reconstitute the nuclear family model (Visher & Visher, 1988), behavior Goldner (1982) has labeled "the retreat from complexity" (p. 205). Stepfamilies try to recreate the nuclear family because it is familiar and simpler to deal with than the reality of stepfamily complexity and ambiguity, and because they are supported in this by extended family, friends, and society as a whole.

According to the view of *stepfamilies as incomplete institutions*, perceptions of what a stepparent should do in a given situation are more variable than perceptions of what a biological parent should do in the same situation, and there is less societal consensus regarding expectations for stepparent role performance. Although few studies have been done to test these contentions, researchers have found that there is less consensus about the role of stepparents than there is about biological/adoptive parent roles (Rossi & Rossi, 1990; Schwebel et al., 1991). However, there is some indication that stepparents are seen as less obligated and less likely to engage in supportive parental behaviors than are parents, although evidence on this is mixed. Respondents in some studies indicated they thought that stepparents were as obligated to stepchildren as parents are to children, but only if the relationships between stepparents and stepchildren were emotionally close (Finch & Mason, 1990; Ganong & Coleman, 1996). It may be that role performance expectations for stepfamilies are similar to those for nuclear families in those cases where steprelationships emotionally resemble societal expectations for nuclear family relationships (e.g., close, loving). In order for stepfamilies to recreate themselves as nuclear families: (a) stepparents must assume parental roles, duties, and responsibilities, and (b) the family must be defined as only those living in the household. Stepparent adoption is one of the most widely used methods of achieving these tasks. Adoption laws in the United States require the noncustodial parent to yield or transfer parental rights and responsibilities to the adopting stepparent, the stepparent legally becomes a parent, and the stepfamily legally becomes a nuclear family. In our state, the biological parent's name is removed from the child's birth certificate and replaced with the name of the adopting stepparent, regardless of the age of the child being adopted. For these stepfamilies, the question of how family roles should be performed is answered by following cultural norms for first-marriage nuclear families. However, in most stepfamilies the nonresidential biological parent does not want to relinquish parental rights, and/or the stepparent does not wish to adopt. This means that for the majority of stepfamilies roles and relationships remain somewhat ambiguous and negotiable; trying to recreate the nuclear ideal may only add more problems.

THE SOCIAL STIGMA PERSPECTIVE

A second perspective is that stepfamilies and stepfamily roles (e.g., stepmother, stepchild) are social categories associated with generally negative attributes (Ganong, Coleman, & Mapes, 1990). Stepfamilies are stigmatized in a number of ways: through labels, cultural stereotypes, media images, and cultural myths. What all of these have in common is the view that stepfamilies are deviant and deficient compared to nuclear families.

Labels

Labels serve to identify persons as members of social categories. When stigma is associated with the social category, the avoidance of labels becomes part of the impression management strategy of group members who wish to avoid being associated with negative connotations. Forty years ago, family sociologist Jessie Bernard (1956) wrote, "Because of the emotional connotations of the terms stepchild, stepmother, stepfather, they are avoided . . . For they are, in effect, smear words" (p. 14). Unfortunately, there is both anecdotal and empirical evidence that her words are as true today as when she wrote them.

For example, a few years ago we wrote a book entitled *Remarried Family Relationships* (Ganong & Coleman, 1994). The book title was a matter of some discussion with the editor because there are myriad labels used to describe stepfamilies, and because many problems are associated with these labels. Among the labels for stepfamilies found in the professional literature: reconstituted, blended, reconstructed, reorganized, reformed, recycled, combined, rem, step, second-time around, merged, and remarried families. There are problems with all of them: some are awkward and conceptually unacceptable (e.g., reconstituted), some are used inconsistently to describe different types of families (e.g., blended sometimes is used as a generic term for all stepfamilies and sometimes it is used specifically to refer to families in which both adults are stepparents), some are inaccurate (e.g., not all stepfamilies are second-time around families), some are too vague (e.g., combined), some suggest odd labels for individual family positions (e.g., a reformed or reconstituted father, a merged or reorganized mother), and, of course, some carry negative connotations (e.g., stepfamily). The editor's choice prevailed in the title of our book, but we carefully defined who the book was about and used the terms *remarried family* and *stepfamily* interchangeably.

The proliferation of labels for stepfamilies is not a matter of social scientists being unable to agree on a suitable term. Rather, these terms represent attempts to relabel stepfamilies using more neutral, less negatively connotated labels in an effort to avoid stigmatizing them. However, most scholars use the term stepfamily, and pioneering stepfamily clinicians, John and Emily Visher, have long argued for the use of this label, partly in the hope that the continued use of the term will serve to normalize and de-stigmatize it (Visher & Visher, 1996). Although it is hard to determine if this has happened to any great degree outside of professional circles, the little research that has been done on stepfamily labels indicates that the term stepfamily still carries with it negative connotations (Ganong, Coleman, & Kennedy, 1990). For example, the term stepchild continues to be widely used in both professional and popular literature to refer to someone or something that is abused, neglected, or unwanted (Coleman & Ganong, 1987). In fact, this use of the term is not a metaphorical one, but is one of the definitions of the word found in standard English dictionaries.

Several labels have been applied to stepparents: other-parents, non-parents, half-parents, acquired parents, added parents, and second or third parents have been used in the professional literature (Ganong & Coleman, 1994). We have heard stepparents call themselves sociological or social parents, but many stepfamily members refer to stepparents simply as parents.

Some refuse to use the labels of stepmother and stepfather to identify themselves because the prefix *step* triggers such negative reactions (Fine, 1986; Ganong & Coleman, 1983; Ganong, Coleman, & Kennedy, 1990). Stepmothers and stepfathers often do not let outsiders know of their step-family status in an effort to avoid stigma (Dainton, 1993). Although this strategy may effectively avoid unpleasant reactions from others, it unfortunately excludes others from providing assistance, encouragement, and moral support. In hiding their step status to avoid stigma, members of stepfamilies may be unintentionally contributing to their social isolation (Pill, 1981). Daily encounters with language that seems to invalidate themselves and their families may add to the stress of stepfamily members.

Stereotypes

Stereotypes are defined as "products of normal everyday cognitive processes of social categorization, social inference, and social judgment" (Six & Eckes, 1991, p. 58). Stereotypes represent cognitive structures that consist of a set of beliefs about the personal attributes of a group of people (Leyens, Yzerbyt, & Schardon, 1994). These attributes may be predominantly positive, predominantly negative, generally neutral, or mixed.

Of course, individuals vary in the degree to which they subscribe to specific cultural stereotypes. The idiosyncratic cognitions of a person can result in unique attributes being added to or subtracted from widely-held cultural stereotypes, with the consequence that some attributes are more widely-agreed upon than others as characteristic of the stereotyped group (Devine, 1989). An individual's set of beliefs about a stereotyped group contains both commonly-held and idiosyncratic beliefs.

There is a small body of research on cultural stereotyping of stepfamilies and stepfamily members. Most of these studies compare people's perceptions of the commonly-held attributes of stepfamilies and stepfamily positions to what they see as attributions of nuclear families and nuclear family positions. There are more studies about stereotypes regarding individual family positions than there are of stereotypes about family units (Ganong et al., 1990).

Stereotypes of Stepmothers. Cultural stereotypes may be particularly relevant when applied to women, because women often define themselves and are defined by others based on their marital and parental statuses (Ganong & Coleman, 1995). Studies on attitudes toward motherhood (Hare-Mustin & Broderick, 1979) and on stereotypes about different "types" of mothers (Bryan et al., 1986; Etaugh & Study, 1989; Ganong, Coleman, & Riley, 1988; Riedle, 1991) indicate that marital and parental status are salient social categories by which women are stereotyped.

Several studies indicate that stepmothers are perceived more negatively than mothers in nuclear families (Bryan et al., 1985; 1986; Fine, 1986; Ganong et al., 1988; Ganong, Coleman, & Kennedy, 1990; Ganong & Coleman, 1983; 1995). In a recent study of the content of stereotypes about mothers of different marital statuses, it was found that several undesirable personal attributes (e.g., unkind, unreasonable) were perceived to be characteristic of stepmothers, and they were stereotyped as not being family-oriented, as disinterested and unskilled in raising children, and as unsuccessful marriage partners. Stepmothers were not only rated more negatively than mothers, they were thought to have fewer positive personality characteristics and to be less skilled at childrearing than women in general.

Stereotypes of Stepfathers. Although stepfathers have generally escaped the disparaging attention that stepmothers have received, at least in folklore and in fairy tales, most studies of the stereotypes of stepfathers have reported similar findings to those of studies on stepmothers. Stepfathers are judged less favorably than fathers (Bryan et al., 1985; 1986; Fine, 1986; Ganong & Coleman, 1983; Ganong, Coleman, & Kennedy, 1990), however they escape some of the scapegoating of stepmothers, perhaps, because the culturally gendered nature of family roles and responsibilities make women the central focus of cognitions and beliefs about families. Nonetheless, stepfathers do not escape the step stigma.

Stereotypes of Stepchildren. The negative image of stepchildren as neglected and unloved is widely held by helping professionals such as counselors, social workers, nurses, and teachers (Bryan et al., 1985; 1986; Glanz, Ganong, & Coleman, 1989; Guttman & Broudo, 1989; Sierbert, Ganong, Coleman, & Hagemann, 1986). This is not surprising, given the pejorative use of the term stepchild.

Stereotypes of Stepfamilies. There have been very few investigations of the perceptions of stepfamilies as groups, but the limited findings we have indicate that stepfamilies are viewed less positively than most other family forms. For example, Bryant, Coleman, and Ganong (1988) found that stepfamilies were evaluated more negatively than nuclear families. In a more recent study, we asked college students to write what they believed to be culturally stereotyped attributes of nuclear families, single-parent families, and stepfamilies (Ganong & Coleman, 1996). Listed below are typical responses. As a test of your ability to recognize cultural views of stepfamilies, put NF in front of the descriptors that you think were written about nuclear families, and SF in front of those that were given as descriptors of stepfamilies.

- Secure, stable, happy, moral, normal
- Correct, happy, well functioning, father as leader, mother as helpmate
- Happy, several children, conservative/religious
- Together, cohesive, communication, loving, caring
- Intimate, help each other, support each other, democracy
- Togetherness, loving, normative, correct, compromising, good communication
- Tied by blood, normal, close, loving, whole, unblemished
- Stability, life-long relationships, strong sense of belonging, well-defined roles
- Security, consistent discipline, caring parents, working together, stability
- Happy, legitimate, a real family, normal, functional, structured, closely knit
- Dysfunctional, wicked, complex, tumultuous, rocky/shaky, childrearing problems
- Together but not unified, complex, confusion or chaotic interaction, many children
- Lots of arguing, somewhat happy, lots of children, liberal, less educated
- Confusion, dysfunction, complex
- Misunderstandings about feelings, power issues, disagreement over possessions
- Confusion, jealousy, feeling of intrusion
- Complex, negotiations, sacrifice, understanding, extra opportunity, options
- Openness to ambiguity, insecurity, more accepting of differences in others
- Conflicts, anger, confusion, children acting out, insecurities, compromising
- Chaos, confused children, conflicts in all areas, divided, stressful

The first 10 statements above were written as descriptors of nuclear families, and the second 10 described stepfamilies. Obviously, data would need to be collected from multiple and diverse samples before firm conclusions and generalizations can be drawn, but from this initial pilot study it appears that there are some clear differences in the alleged characteristics of nuclear families and stepfamilies. Of course, it not known the extent to which the participants in the pilot study subscribed to these stereotypes; all we can conclude is that the consensual, widely-held attributes of nuclear families and stepfamilies have little overlap.

Although the results of most stereotyping studies support the view that stepfamilies and stepfamily members are stigmatized, some studies have not found this to be true (Claxton-Oldfield, 1992; Dukes, 1989; Ganong & Coleman, in review). The mixed findings may be related to differences in the research methods that were used. Most of the studies finding step-family members to be stigmatized portrayed them in neutral contexts. That is, the negative evaluations of stepfamily members were based either on labels only or on neutral descriptions of an individual or family unit. The studies that have not supported the social stigma hypothesis have por-trayed stepfamily members in vignettes in which they are interacting with others or engaged in a task unrelated to family situations. For example, Claxton-Oldfield (1992) found that stepfathers were rated less positively than fathers when they were described as punishing a child, but few differences were found when stepfathers and fathers were portrayed as being affectionate with a (step)child. It may be that observers use the stepfamily status of a target person to categorize them unless more indivi-duating information is given (Leyens et al., 1994). Individuating informa-tion may serve to direct observers' attention to other, more salient, social categories to which the stepfamily member might belong, or the informa-tion may lead to a recategorization of the person if the additional informa-tion is inconsistent with cultural stereotypes. More research is needed to resolve the inconsistencies between studies.

Media Images of Stepfamilies

There is abundant anecdotal evidence, and some empirical data, that stepfamilies generally are portrayed in ways that reinforce the deficit perception of them. For example, in cinematic portrayals, for every sensi-tive, loving stepfather (*Tender Mercies*) or stepmother (*Sarah Big and Tall*), there are many more stepfathers that are murderous (*The Stepfather* and its sequels) or abusive (*Radio Flyer*), and stepmothers who are mean (*Cinderella, Snow White*) or very strange (*My Stepmother is an Alien*), and stepparents of both genders who are unwanted intruders (*My Girl, The Man of the House*). Cinematic stepfamilies are usually dysfunctional (*See You in the Morning, Table for Five*). As if there were not enough hostile terms for stepfamily positions, the movie *St. Elmo's Fire* gave us *stepmon-ster* as a way to refer to stepmothers.

Popular literature has been systematically examined by social scientists and generally shown to be consistent with professional literature in the themes covered (Coleman, Ganong, & Gingrich, 1985; Pasley & Ihinger-Tallman, 1985). One thing this means is that popular writers focus on stepfamily problems as much as clinical writers and social scientists do, to the relative neglect of stepfamily strengths (Coleman et al., 1985). Novels for children have tended to present somewhat more well-rounded images of stepfamilies and stepfamily members (Coleman & Ganong, 1988), but it has not been empirically determined how authors of adult fiction depict steprelationships.

Myths

Myths are firmly held beliefs or recurring themes that reflect cultural standards and ideals. Myths are seldom accurate, but they may contain at least some elements of truth. The main function of myths is to convey shared values. Although there have been few studies of cultural myths, clinicians and social science researchers tend to think that myths about family life are particularly prevalent.

Clinicians have long written about the impact of cultural myths about stepfamilies on stepfamily functioning (Coleman & Ganong, 1985; Dainton, 1993; Schulman, 1972; Visher & Visher, 1979). Stepfamily myths identified by practitioners include: (a) stepchildren resent and dislike their stepparents, (b) stepchildren have more problems than other children, (c) stepfamilies are just like other families, (d) stepparents and stepchildren never can learn to love each other, (e) adoption turns stepfamilies into normal families, and (f) children should be loyal to one mother and one father only (Coale Lewis, 1985; Coleman & Ganong, 1987; Leslie & Epstein, 1988; Visher & Visher, 1985).

Some myths are directionally oppositional. Two of the most often mentioned myths are the myth of *instant love* and the myth of the *evil stepmother.*

In contrast to the myth that stepparents and stepchildren can *never* learn to love each other, the myth of instant love says that stepparents should *immediately* love their stepchildren. The underlying assumption of this myth is that remarriage reconstitutes a nuclear family, and the stepparent functionally and emotionally replaces the biological parent who is no longer in the home. This myth is clearly based on a nuclear model of family life, complete with the expectation that love is both an automatic experience and a requisite emotion. Clinicians argue that the myth of instant love puts stepfamilies under great strain; stepfamily members, particularly stepparents feel pressured to feel love even when they hardly know their stepchild. On the other hand, the myth that stepparents and stepchildren can never learn to love each other is unduly pessimistic and may hamper efforts to even try to relate positively to each other.

The evil stepmother myth is widespread (Wald, 1981). In fact, folk myths about mean stepmothers are apparently common in many cultures. The Cinderella tale, or one of the 345 variations of it, has been traced to ninth century China (Smith, 1953). It has been our experience that stepmothers are disturbed by this myth and find it difficult to deal with; at the very least, they object to being saddled with a label that is associated with such unattractive characteristics.

DISCUSSION

From the early researchers who wrote about the stigma associated with stepparenthood (Smith, 1953) and the problems with stepfamily labels (Bernard, 1956), to the early clinicians who wrote about stepparents having difficulty defining their roles (Fast & Cain, 1966), societal views about stepfamilies have been seen as important elements in shaping the development of stepfamily relationships. Cultural beliefs about remarried families tend to be unhelpful, because they are almost always either negative (e.g., stepparents are mean and wicked) or unrealistic (love will occur instantaneously). Cultural beliefs, the views of "outsiders," cannot be ignored, however, because they have a number of potential implications for stepfamilies.

Children and Adults Enter Stepfamilies with Unrealistic Expectations

The most troublesome unrealistic expectation is that stepfamilies will function just like nuclear families. Such expectations may foster assumptions among remarried adults that relationships in remarried families will be good without any effort. For example, the *myth of instant love*, in which stepparents are expected to instantly feel love and affection for their stepchildren, may cause stepparents who do not experience instantaneous love feelings to feel guilty, to deny their ambivalent feelings, and to push too hard for a relationship with the stepchild rather than letting a bond with the child develop gradually, and at the child's pace. Expectations that are too high also discourage open communication and may lead to the denial of problems and the tendency to deny history, ambivalence, and conflict. Rather than confront and challenge each other when things are not going smoothly, family members avoid talking about problems, so they do not get resolved, leading to feelings of alienation and powerlessness. Rather than developing feelings of instant love, the unrealistic expectation of it may reinforce beliefs and behaviors predicted by contrasting myths (e.g., stepchildren that dislike their stepparent; stepparents and stepchildren can never learn to love each other).

Cultural beliefs based on the nuclear family model are naive to the complexity of stepfamilies. In first marriage families, the couple brings expectations to marriage that are based partly on observations and experiences in their families of origin and partly on cultural expectations regarding marriage. In stepfamilies, adults bring expectations based not only upon family experiences observed while growing up, but also upon adult experiences in prior marital/parental/family situations. Children also bring expectations, as do former spouses and extended kin. To this mix are added cultural expectations regarding remarriage and stepparenting. These competing agendas and beliefs are seldom overtly obvious to stepfamily members, making them dangerous and difficult to resolve (Leslie & Epstein, 1988; Visher & Visher, 1991).

In stepfamilies, more people and more relationships mean that there must be clear communication between members in order for the system to function smoothly. Therefore, stepfamilies, by virtue of their complexity, place greater demands on their members' problem-solving and communication skills (Nelson & Levant, 1991). The greater complexity of stepfamilies does not imply that relationships in stepfamilies are inherently problematic and distressful. Although the tendency has been for societies to assume that deviations from the nuclear family are bad, the additional complexity for stepfamilies can be an asset. Individuals and sometimes whole stepfamilies find the complexity emotionally challenging but enriching. These families would agree with a constant refrain heard from clinicians, the nuclear family model is generally inappropriate for stepfamilies (c.f., Goldner, 1982; Papernow, 1993; Visher & Visher, 1988). Attempts to recreate the nuclear family model may signify that the stepfamily and its members are devoid of imagination and creativity. Unable to take a brush to a fresh canvas, they restrict themselves to trying to color within the lines or to painting by numbers. Even if competently done, the effort will never be the same as the original.

In order to function and assume the identity of a nuclear family, stepfamilies must engage in massive denial and distortion of reality (Goldner, 1982). This takes enormous emotional energy and has considerable costs psychologically and interpersonally. It requires a forced amnesia; prior relationships must be forgotten and the family must act as if nothing that went on before the remarriage actually happened. Former spouses and their families must be cut off from children, resulting in emotional losses for adults and children alike. Feelings of abandonment, anger, guilt, resentment, and unresolved feelings of loss are likely when ties between nonresidential parents and children are severed. Sometimes, a remarried parent who severs the ties between their children and their former spouse finds that these actions have the opposite effect; children harbor resentments towards the residential parent and stepparent and fantasize about the "perfect" parent with whom they have no contact. Rather than emotionally replacing the parent with the stepparent, these children may never accept the stepparent whose presence has robbed them of knowing their biological parent. If a child refuses to accept a stepparent as a parent, then the stepparent may feel hurt and may withdraw emotionally from the child. If the nonresidential parent refuses to be replaced by the stepparent, then he or she may institute a legal custody battle over the children. As is true on most battles, wounds are common, and the resulting scars may last for years.

We need to note, however, that despite the prevailing clinical perspective on this issue, it is possible that acting like and thinking of themselves as a nuclear family unit may work for some stepfamilies. We hypothesize that the nuclear family ideology may be effective when: (a) the nonresidential parent and their kin have no contact with children in the stepfamily household, (b) the nonresidential parent was abusive or in some way an extremely negative figure to the child, (c) the children are young at the time of remarriage so that they do not remember much, if anything, about prior family life, and (d) all stepfamily members, for whatever reason, want to recreate the nuclear family and agree, implicitly or explicitly, to do so. These hypotheses have yet to be tested.

What Can Be Done?

Avoidance of terms with negative connotations may help to reduce negative attitudes and expectations. The term "stepchild" used as a metaphor for something that is unwanted or abused should be considered as inappropriate to use to illustrate a point as a racial or ethnic slur would be. Descriptors such as *real* or *natural* to refer to biological parents should also be avoided, because of the implication that stepparents are somehow unreal or unnatural.

School policies should be examined for possible biases toward nuclear families. Biased policies put a strain on stepchildren and their families and send implicit messages about how families should be. For example, official forms should include information about stepparents as well as biological parents, and school activities (e.g., father-son banquets) that assume all children come from nuclear families should be modified or discontinued.

The education of teachers and helping professionals should include training about stepfamilies. This training should be balanced, with strengths presented along with potential problems. Teachers and helping professionals should be sensitized to the needs of stepchildren and to their own biases regarding stepfamilies.

Media. A more balanced emphasis by the media on the positive and negative aspects of stepfamilies would be helpful in setting expectations and attitudes. The darker side of stepfamilies seems to be the primary focus and is not typically offset by positive examples of stepfamily life. It is not too farfetched, considering how stepfamily life is often portrayed, for stepchildren to *assume* they will be abused and unloved by their stepparent. When children do not see stepfamilies presented as normal families in their story books and on television, the subtle message is that stepfamilies are deficient in some way. Fiction for children featuring stepfamily members in positive ways should be in every school library. These stories could be helpful to stepchildren in their attempts to problem solve and they can also present information that will help children who do not live in stepfamilies develop understanding of them. The media are powerful in enhancing or downgrading a child's sense of self.

Implications for Researchers

The issue of how societies view stepfamilies is broad, and there are many related areas of study that are in need of further investigation. For example, most of the propositions that may be drawn from Cherlin's (1978) incomplete institutionalization argument have yet to be examined empirically. A number of research questions come to mind: Do stepfamilies perceive that they lack guidelines and norms for directing their behaviors? If so, what effect does this have on their interactions? What impact does the relative absence of a legal relationship have on stepparents and stepchildren? How do the policies of social institutions such as schools and health care agencies affect stepfamilies?

Similarly, the growing body of research on social stereotyping of stepfamilies and stepfamily members leads to questions regarding the pragmatic impact of stereotypes on the internal dynamics of stepfamilies and on the interactions of stepfamilies with outsiders. Under what conditions do stereotypes affect social interactions? Are impression management strategies of stepparents effective in reducing the stigmatized perceptions of others? What impact do media portrayals have on self-perceptions and stepfamily identities? A lot has been learned in the past decade about how societies view stepfamilies, but as the number of stepfamilies worldwide continues to grow, it is all the more imperative that these and other questions be addressed. The family remains society's most important avenue for socializing children. It seems only reasonable to devote intellectual and political energy into assuring that the avenue doesn't turn into a dead-end for the world's growing number of stepfamilies.

REFERENCES

Amato, P. (1994). The implications of research findings on children in stepfamilies. In A. Booth & J. Dunn (Eds.), *Stepfamilies: Who benefits? Who does not?* (pp. 81-88). Hillsdale, NJ: Erlbaum.

Bernard, J. (1956). *Remarriage: A study of marriage.* New York: Russel & Russel.

Bryan, H., Ganong, L., Coleman, M., & Bryan, L. (1985). Counselor's perceptions of stepparents and stepchildren. *Journal of Counseling Psychology,* 32(2), 279-282.

Bryan, L., Coleman, M., Ganong, L., & Bryan, H. (1986). Person perception: Family structure as a cue for stereotyping. *Journal of Marriage and the Family, 48,* 169-174.

Bryant, L., Coleman, M., & Ganong, L. (1988). Race and family structure stereotyping: Perceptions of black and white nuclear families and stepfamilies. *Journal of Black Psychology, 15,* 1-16.

Bernardes, J. (1993). Responsibilities in studying postmodern families. *Journal of Family Issues, 4,* 35-49.

Candib, L. M. (1989). Family life cycle theory: A feminist critique. *Family Systems Medicine, 7,* 473-487.

Chambers, D. L. (1990). Stepparents, biologic parents, and the law's perceptions of "family" after divorce. In S. D. Sugarman, & H. H. Kay (Eds.), *Divorce reform at the crossroads* (pp. 102-129). New Haven: Yale University Press.

Cherlin, A. (1978). Remarriage as an incomplete institution. *American Journal of Sociology, 84,* 634-650.

Claxton-Oldfield, S. (1992). Perceptions of stepfathers: Disciplinary and affectionate behavior. *Journal of Family Issues, 13*(3), 378-389.

Coale Lewis, H. C. (1985). Family therapy with stepfamilies. *Journal of Strategic and Systemic Therapies, 4,* 13-23.

Coleman, M., & Ganong, L. (1985). Remarriage myths. *Journal of Counseling and Development, 64,* 116-120.

Coleman, M., & Ganong, L. (1987). The cultural stereotyping of stepfamilies. In K. Pasley & M. Ihinger-Tallman (Eds.), *Remarriage and stepparenting: Current research and theory* (pp. 19-41). New York: Guilford.

Coleman, M., & Ganong, L. (1988). *Bibliotherapy with stepchildren.* Springfield, IL: Thomas.

Coleman, M., & Ganong, L. (1995). Insiders' and outsiders' beliefs about stepfamilies: Assessment and implications for practice. In D. Huntley (Ed.), *Understanding stepfamilies: Implications for assessment and treatment* (pp. 101-112). American Counseling Association Press.

Coleman, M., Ganong, L., & Gingrich, R. (1985). Stepfamily strengths: A review of the popular literature. *Family Relations, 34,* 583-589.

Coleman, M., Ganong, L., & Goodwin, C. (1994). The presentation of stepfamilies in marriage and family textbooks: A reexamination. *Family Relations, 43,* 289-297.

Coleman, M., Ganong, L., & Henry, J. (1984a). Children and stepfamilies. *Leadership,* October/December, 6-7.

Coleman, M., Ganong, L., & Henry, J. (1984b). What teachers should know about stepfamilies. *Childhood Education, 60,* 306-309.

Coleman, M., Marshall, S., & Ganong, L. (1986). Beyond Cinderella: Relevant reading for young adolescents about stepfamilies. *Adolescence, 21,* 553-560.

Coontz, S. (1992). *The way we never were.* New York: Basic Books.

Crosbie-Burnett, M. (1994). The interface between stepparent families and schools: Research, theory, policy, and practice. In K. Pasley & M. Ihinger-Tallman (Ed.), *Stepparenting: Issues in theory, research, and practice* (pp. 199-216). Westport, CT: Greenwood.

Dainton, M. (1993). The myths and misconceptions of the stepmother identity: Descriptions and prescriptions for identity management. *Family Relations, 42,* 93-98.

Dallos, R. (1991). *Family beliefs systems, therapy, and change.* Open University Press: Philadelphia.

Devine, P. (1989). Stereotypes and prejudice: Their automatic and controlled components. *Journal of Personality and Social Psychology, 56,* 5-18.

Dukes, R. L. (1989). The Cinderella myth: Negative evaluations of stepparents. *Sociology and Social Research, 73*(2), 67-72.

Etaugh, C., & Study, G. (1989). Perceptions of mothers: Effects of employment status, marital status, and age of child. *Sex Roles, 11,* 413-424.

Farber, B. (1973). *Family and kinship in modern society.* Glenview, IL: Scott, Foresman & Co.

Fast, I., & Cain, A. C. (1966). The stepparent role: Potential for disturbances in family functioning. *American Journal of Orthopsychiatry, 36,* 435-441.

Finch, J., & Mason, J. (1990). Divorce, remarriage and family obligations. *Sociological Review, 38,* 219-246.

Fine, M. (1986). Perceptions of stepparents: Variations in stereotypes as a function of current family structure. *Journal of Marriage and the Family, 48,* 537-543.

Fine, M. A. (1989). A social science perspective on stepfamily law: Suggestions for legal reform. *Family Relations, 38,* 53-58.

Fine, M. A., & Fine, D. R. (1992). Recent changes in laws affecting stepfamilies: Suggestions for legal reform. *Family Relations, 41,* 334-340.

Ganong, L. (1993). Family diversity in a youth organization: The involvement of single-parent families and stepfamilies in 4-H. *Family Relations, 42,* 286-292.

Ganong, L. H., & Coleman, M. (1983). Stepparent: A pejorative term? *Psychological Reports, 52,* 919-922.

Ganong, L., & Coleman, M. (1994). *Remarried family relationships.* Thousand Oaks, CA: Sage.

Ganong, L., & Coleman, M. (1996). *Effects of family structure information on nurses' impression formation.* Manuscript in review.

Ganong, L., & Coleman, M. (1995). The content of mother stereotypes. *Sex Roles, 32,* 495-512.

Ganong, L., Coleman, M., & Jones, G. (1990). Effects of behavior and family structure on perceptions. *Journal of Educational Psychology, 82,* 820-825.

Ganong, L., Coleman, M., & Kennedy, G. (1990). The effects of using alternate labels in denoting stepparent or stepfamily status. *Journal of Social Behavior and Personality, 5*, 453-463.

Ganong, L., Coleman, M., & Mapes, D. (1990). A meta-analytic review of family structure stereotypes. *Journal of Marriage and the Family, 52*, 287-297.

Ganong, L., Coleman, M., & Riley, C. (1988). Nursing student's stereotypes of married and unmarried pregnant clients. *Research in Nursing & Health, 11*, 333-342.

Glanz, D., Ganong, L., & Coleman, M. (1989). Client gender, diagnosis, and family structure. *Western Journal of Nursing Research, 11*, 726-735.

Goldner, V. (1982). Remarriage family: Structure, system, future. In J. C. Hansen & L. Messenger (Eds.), *Therapy with remarried families* (pp. 187-206). Rockville, MD: Aspen.

Guttman, J. & Broudo, M. (1988-1989). The effect of children's family type on teachers' stereotypes. *Journal of Divorce, 12* (2-3), 315-328.

Hare-Mustin, R., & Broderick, P. C. (1979). The myth of motherhood: A study of attitudes toward motherhood. *Psychology of Women Quarterly, 4*, 114-128.

Hughes, C. (1991). *Stepparents: Wicked or wonderful?* Aldershot, UK: Avebury.

Kurdek, L., & Fine, M. (1993). The relation between family structure and young adolescents' appraisals of family climate and parenting behavior. *Journal of Family Issues, 14*, 279-290.

Kurdek, L., & Fine. M. (1991). Cognitive correlates of satisfaction for mothers and stepfathers in stepfather families. *Journal of Marriage and the Family, 53*, 565-572.

Leslie, L. A. & Epstein, N. (1988). Cognitive-behavioral treatment of remarried families. In N. Epstein, S. E. Schlesinger, & W. Dryden (Eds.), *Cognitive-Behavioral Therapy with Families* (pp. 151-182). New York: Brunner/Mazel.

Levin, I. (1993). Family as mapped realities. *Journal of Family Issues, 14*, 82-91.

Leyens, J.-P., Yzerbyt, V., & Schardon, G. (1994). *Stereotypes and social cognition*. London: Sage.

Mahoney, M. (1994). *Stepfamilies and the law*. Ann Arbor, MI: University of Michigan Press.

Messinger, L. (Ed.). (1982). *Therapy with remarried families*. Rockville, MD: Aspen.

Mills, D. (1984). A model for stepfamily development. *Family Relations, 33*, 365-372.

Nelson, W. P., & Levant, R. F. (1991). An evaluation of a skills training program for parents in stepfamilies. *Family Relations, 40*, 291-296.

Nemenyi, M. (1992). The social representation of stepfamilies. In U. Bjørnberg (Ed.), *European parents in the 1990s: Contradictions and comparisons* (pp. 243-256). New Brunswick, NJ: Transaction.

Papernow, P. (1993). *Becoming a stepfamily: Patterns of development in remarried families*. Gardner Press.

Pasley, K., & Ihinger-Tallman, M. (1985). Portraits of stepfamily life in popular literature: 1940-1980. *Family Relations, 34*, 527-534.

Pill, C. J. (1981). A family life education group for working with stepparents. *Social Casework, 62*, 159-166.

Popenoe, D. (1993). American family decline, 1960-1990. *Journal of Marriage and the Family, 55*, 527-541.

Poponoe, P. (1994). The evolution of marriage and the problem of stepfamilies: A biosocial perspective. In A. Booth & J. Dunn (Eds.), *Stepfamilies: Who benefits? Who does not?* (pp. 3-28). Hillsdale, NJ: Erlbaum.

Riedle, J. E. (1991). Exploring the subcategories of stereotypes: Not all mothers are the same. *Sex Roles, 24*, 711-723.

Rossi, A., & Rossi, P. (1990). *Of human bonding: Parent-child relations across the life course.* New York: deGruyter.

Schulman, G. L. (1972). Myths that intrude on the adaptation of the stepfamily. *Social Casework, 53*, 131-139.

Schwebel, A. I., Fine, M. A., & Renner, M. A. (1991). A study of perceptions of the stepparent role. *Journal of Family Issues, 12*, 43-57.

Siebert, K., Ganong, L., Hagemann, V., & Coleman, M. (1986). Nursing students' perceptions of a child: The influence of information on family structure. *Journal of Advanced Nursing, 11*, 333-337.

Six, B., & Eckes, T. (1991). A closer look at the complex structure of gender stereotypes. *Sex Roles, 24*, 57-72.

Smith, W. C. (1953). *The stepchild.* Chicago, IL: University of Chicago Press.

Uzoka, A. F. (1979). The myth of the nuclear family. *American Psychologist,* 1095-1106.

Visher, E. B., & Visher, J. S. (1979). *Stepfamilies: A guide to working with stepparents and stepchildren.* New York: Brunner/Mazel.

Visher, E. B., & Visher, J. S. (1985). Stepfamilies are different. *Journal of Family Therapy, 7*, 9-18.

Visher, E. B., & Visher, J. S. (1988). *Old loyalties, new ties: Therapeutic strategies with stepfamilies.* New York: Brunner/Mazel.

Visher, E. B., & Visher, J. S. (1991). Therapy with stepfamily couples. *Psychiatric Annals, 21*(8), 462.

Visher, E.B., & Visher, J. S. (1996). *Therapy with stepfamilies.* New York: Brunner/Maze.

Wald, E. (1981). *The remarried family: Challenge and promise.* NY: Family Service Association of America.

Webber, R. (1991). Life in stepfamilies: Conceptions and misconceptions. In K. Funder (Ed.), *Images of Australian families* (pp. 88-101). Melbourne, Australia: Longman Cheshire.

Stepfamilies
from the Stepfamily's Perspective

Marilyn Coleman
Lawrence H. Ganong

There is considerable evidence that what individuals believe about marriage, parenting, and family life influences their expectations and behaviors
in intimate relationships (Bradbury & Fincham, 1990; Dallos, 1993; Kurdek, 1991). Individuals' beliefs about family life are influenced by experiences in their family of origin, by media, by cultural standards, by observ-
ing other families, and, in the case of remarried adults, by their
experiences in their previous families of procreation. All of these present
and reinforce, to varying degrees, a view of family life that is based on a
nuclear family idealogy. Of course, personal experiences in families and
mediated images of families are not uniform, and variations in these experiences and images help explain the wide range of family life behaviors
that may be observed. However, even personal experiences are interpreted
and evaluated within the context of a prevailing cultural ideology about
families. It is our position that a combination of idiosyncratic beliefs and
cultural perspectives/ideology influence individuals' views of their marital
and familial experiences.

In first marriages, melding marriage and family expectations with reality is a joint venture of the married couple. Together the couple negotiates
roles, rules, and power within their relationship. Although they bring their
separate prior experiences and divergent views based on such things as
gender, values, and fantasies about what *should* happen, negotiations and

Marilyn Coleman and Lawrence H. Ganong are affiliated with the University
of Missouri, Columbia, MO 65211.

[Haworth co-indexing entry note]: "Stepfamilies from the Stepfamily's Perspective." Coleman,
Marilyn, and Lawrence H. Ganong. Co-published simultaneously in *Marriage & Family Review* (The
Haworth Press, Inc.) Vol. 26, No. 1/2, 1997, pp. 107-121; and: *Stepfamilies: History, Research, and
Policy* (ed: Irene Levin and Marvin B. Sussman) The Haworth Press, Inc., 1997, pp. 107-121. Single or
multiple copies of this article are available for a fee from The Haworth Document Delivery Service
[1-800-342-9678, 9:00 a.m. - 5:00 p.m. (EST). E-mail address: getinfo@haworth.com].

constructions of marital life are usually conducted primarily by the couple. In stepfamilies the construction of family life is more complicated because there are more family members involved in the negotiations, these family members often bring widely varying prior family experiences to the deliberations, and more than one generation are involved in the negotiating. The reality of the remarried family, therefore, is a blend representing a composite of quite different realities and expectations, depending upon a number of factors, including the variety of roles that have to be created, defined, and/or negotiated in the family. The increased number of roles in stepfamilies (e.g., nonresidential stepmother, stepfather, mother, father, stepchildren, stepsiblings, half siblings) can contribute to negotiations of great complexity.

Moreover, many stepfamily roles are relatively unfamiliar to those just entering a stepfamily, and when this is so, expectations may be ambiguous. For example, the role of nonresidential stepmothers is one that probably is relatively unclear to most women, and some women may not see this as a family role at all. That is, women who marry men whose children are grown or live elsewhere may not see themselves as having any role with those children other than acquaintance.

In addition to the ambiguity of roles, stepfamily members often find themselves in relationships for which they have neither names nor any clear ideas about how to proceed. Stepparents sometimes are surprised to find themselves involved in planning children's activities with their spouse's former spouse. Adults in middle-age whose parents remarry may not know how to develop a relationship with their elderly stepparent. Stepsiblings of any age have little to guide their expectations about mutual roles and relationships.

We think it is important to try to understand the expectations that stepfamily members have for their family interactions. How the stepfamily is viewed by stepfamily members is critical to the negotiation of stepfamily life and is ultimately critical to the success or failure of the remarried family.

STEPPARENTING

Stepparents have been referred to as the "intimate outsiders" (Beer, 1992). This label evokes the image of stepparents as being members of the family as well as intruders who are not privy to the secrets and knowledge shared by family insiders. The status of being both an insider and an outsider can be unsettling and uncomfortable. Stepparenting also has been likened to setting up housekeeping on an ice flow (Peterson, 1985). The tasks of integrating into the family are indeed slippery ones, difficult to firmly grip, especially in what may be an inclement environment. Neither of these observations brings to mind the giddily happy Brady Bunch, instead, both are rather sad and poignant. Perhaps these descriptions emerge because it is difficult to parent other people's children, especially when performance expectations are often high, unrealistic, or ambiguous.

The difficulty in parenting other people's children seems to be related to a number of factors. Gender and residence are of particular importance. For example, stepmothers' views of stepfamilies differ from those of stepfathers', and residential stepparents view stepfamilies differently than stepparents whose stepchildren visit their household only occasionally. Other factors include the age of the stepparent, age and gender of the stepchildren, whether or not the stepparent has children of his or her own from a previous relationship. Because of the many structural variations in stepfamilies and step-households (Wald, 1981), attempting to draw general conclusions about stepfamilies from the stepparent's perspective is a complex and daunting task.

Considerable evidence exists that when people remarry, they expect stepparenting to work out (Ganong & Coleman, 1989). Those who have always liked children look forward to the opportunity to take a parenting role. Others give little thought to their role as stepparent, perhaps assuming things will naturally fall into place or that their spouse will guide their interactions with the stepchild. Some nonresidential stepparents may not expect to be involved with the stepchildren very much. Few stepparents are truly prepared for the challenges the stepparenting role presents because it is not a role for which people are socialized. In the absence of such socialization, most stepparents assume they will function as parents.

THE PERSPECTIVE OF THE STEPMOTHER

Stepmothers appear to have the hardest role to fill, and this is probably true whether they are residential stepmothers with major parenting responsibilities or nonresidential stepmothers who see the stepchildren only occasionally. The difficulties associated with stepmothering have been attributed to various causes. The most commonly cited cause is the widespread stereotype of stepmothers as wicked or cruel, perpetuated in fairy tales such as Snow White or Cinderella. Some of these stories go back several centuries and are firmly established in a variety of cultures (Noy, 1991; Wald, 1981). These cultural beliefs no doubt influence stepmothers' views of their roles and of their stepfamilies, and as a result some women who marry men with children actively avoid being identified as stepmothers in an effort to dodge the negatively connoted label. Although cultural stereotypes may contribute to the difficulty of being a stepmother, the challenges of this role are complex, multi-faceted, and may have as much to do with how we view the roles of mothers as they do with our view of stepfamilies or stepmothers.

It has been argued that the role of mother is central to the identity of North American women (Russo, 1979), and there is evidence that this is true for European women as well (Everingham, 1994). Feminists argue that there is a powerful "myth of motherhood" that influences the ways in which people relate to women who are mothers (Braverman, 1989; Hare-Mustin & Broderick, 1979). This myth promulgates the Madonna or whore dichotomy, the belief that mothers are either all good or all bad, perfectly loving, kind, patient, and giving, or rejecting, cold, unloving, and controlling. Although there is ample evidence in the child abuse and neglect literature that many mothers fall far short of the ideal, the role of mothers within the family is, for the most part, positively stereotyped by many cultures.

Ironically, the power of the mother stereotype is evident even among drag queens. As portrayed in the award-winning documentary, *Paris is Burning*, drag queens are shown living together in small groups that they refer to as families, and the title of mother is given to the best and most influential person in the families. In other words, the most nurturing and supportive person, the one who looks after the others, the one who most lives up to the motherhood ideal, gets the most respect from the family members, as well as the title of mother. Even among this subculture whose members have been ostracized, who may have been abandoned by their own mothers, and who are stigmatized by the broader society as dysfunctional, or bizarre at best, the role of mother reflects the cultural stereotype of the myth of motherhood. However, in the case of urban drag queens, the role of mother is *earned* or achieved through exemplary performance within the group rather than being *bestowed* or ascribed through biology or marriage.

The stepmother, on the other hand, is bestowed a role by virtue of marriage to a man who has children. This bestowed role with its negative cultural connotations has historically been seen as a replacement for a mother who died. In contrast, the modem day stepmother is most often a supplement, an extra mother, since most stepfamilies now are formed following divorce rather than parental death. Compared to married genetic/adoptive mothers, stepmothers are often thought to lack positive personal characteristics (e.g., patience, caring, dependability) and to possess many undesirable personal traits (e.g., cruelty, unreasonableness). Stepmothers also are stereotyped as less family oriented and as basically unin-terested and unskilled in raising children, at least compared to mothers. Stepmothers are even stereotyped as having fewer positive personality characteristics than women-in-general (Ganong & Coleman, 1995). It is little wonder that they often feel stressed and are reluctant to identify them-selves with the label of stepmother.

Some researchers have found that the stepfamilies suffering the most stress tend to be those in which stepchildren live with stepmothers and visits between the stepchild and the nonresidential genetic/adoptive mother are frequent (Clingempeel & Segal, 1986; Furstenberg & Nord, 1985). There are several potential explanations for this, but it may be that the mother role is so central to women's identities that the genetic mother and stepmother compete over the right to parent the children. This com-petition may lead to mutual criticism in front of the children. Because the ideal of mother is such a powerful one, it is probably difficult for children to accept criticism of their genetic mothers even though they may be abusive, irresponsible, or unfit in some other way. Even children who feel negatively towards their mother may be guilt ridden about these feelings, which in turn impedes their relationship with their stepmother. It is diffi-cult for well-meaning stepmothers to continually face rejection from their stepchildren even if they suspect the rejection may be due to loyalty conflicts within the child.

Stepmothers who bring children of their own to the stepfamily may find stepparenting even more stressful than childfree women. Single women with children sometimes develop a siege mentality, it is them and their offspring against the world. They may become fiercely protective of their children and find it very difficult to let others enter their intimate circle. This seems to be especially true of mothers and daughters. For example, we have interviewed stepmothers who became so enmeshed with their children through the divorce and single parent stage that they felt that they had to continue to protect their children's rights against the stepchildren, the stepfather, and even against their children's own half-siblings (children born to the remarried couple). Some expressed resentment because they thought that their husband preferred his own children or their mutual children to his stepchildren. Stepmothers have also expressed to us con-cerns that their husband's children (the stepchildren) were bad influences on their children, that their husband did not require his children to follow the same rules as her children, that the stepchildren sometimes had an unfair advantage in receiving more material goods than her children, and that the time she had to spend attending to the stepchildren put her own children at a disadvantage. These stepmothers expressed resentment, but at the same time they felt guilty about having such concerns.

Stepmothers' concerns and resentments about preferential treatment of stepchildren and mutual children compared to their genetic/adoptive children from a previous relationship are more likely to be expressed when other things are not going well in the remarriage. The situation can be especially perilous when stepmothers and fathers have different parenting values. For example, stepmothers are often left in charge of their stepchildren without the assurance that their husbands will back their parenting decisions. The added stress of being second guessed regarding decisions about the stepchildren only exacerbates the difficulty of being a stepmother.

In a study of 22 Canadian stepmothers, well over half expressed anger and resentment toward their husbands because they did not set limits for the children, did not support them in their parenting role, and often excluded them from the father-child relationship (Morrison & Thompson-Guppy, 1985). Eighteen of these 22 women expressed identity confusion regarding their role in the family, as well as feelings of helplessness and ineffectiveness in the home, and feelings of exhaustion or burnout. Hobart (1988) has suggested that fathers contribute to the sort of feelings expressed by the stepmothers in the Canadian study by being more lenient in discipline or more financially generous with their own children than with their stepchildren. A remarried father's wife (the stepmother) may come to resent not only him but also his children, a fact that is seldom lost on the children. Such interpersonal dynamics do not contribute to a satisfying family life.

Most stepmothers work outside the home. On the one hand, this may be a good coping strategy. If things are not going well within the family perhaps the job is enhancing their self-esteem. On the other hand, the stress of maintaining careers, attending to most of the housekeeping chores, and parenting children who are not their own and who may resent their efforts to care for them may simply be too much for some women to handle. Moreover, most stepmothers work because the family needs the income. Financial strains, particularly those that can be attributed to stepchildren, can be a source of stress and anger.

If their husbands do not back their efforts within the home and family, stepmothers are unlikely to derive support from other sources. The stepmothers we have interviewed for various studies were positive, for the most part, about their husband's involvement with his stepchildren (her children), but many were dissatisfied enough with their role as residential or nonresidential stepmother that they would advise women against marrying men who have children from previous relationships. Although they indicated that they loved their husbands, several were unsure that the remarriage was worth the stress.

Stepmothers often appear to get very little support from anyone for their stepparenting efforts, including their own children and their spouse. Viewed from the perspective of stepmothers, stepfamilies probably appear to be very difficult arrangements, providing little positive reinforcement, and presenting challenges that are often beyond their coping abilities. The stepmother role is clearly a source of considerable psychological pain to many women. It is also clear, especially in the case of nonresidential stepmothers, that the stepmothers' parenting behaviors are often the cause of their pain.

Stepmothers in our studies who expressed the most frustration were those who defined themselves as having high control needs. During interviews it was not uncommon for these women to share their attempts to "shape up" or change the behaviors of their visiting stepchildren in ways that created tremendous animosity from the stepchildren. Childfree stepmothers or those whose children were much younger than their stepchildren often expected behaviors that to us seemed unrealistic or far beyond the stepchildren's developmental capabilities. Stepmothers, especially those with no children of their own, had great difficulty accepting the messes children made, the noise and chaos children created, children's lack of gratitude for assistance, and the vying of the children for their father's attention. The husbands of these women appeared to deal with the strains between their children and their wives by taking a passive role, neither supporting the wives nor actively supporting the children in the presence of the wives. Most expressed some awareness of the inappropriateness of their wives' parenting behaviors but did not want to confront them about it. They were also unwilling to punish their children for behaviors that created problems for their wives. Although their intent appeared to be reducing rather than adding to family ferment, their passivity did little to reduce the building resentments between their partner and their children and probably contributed to diminishing couple satisfaction as well.

Over time, some of the "high control" stepmothers related that they learned to "back off" from the stepchildren and become less invested in their upbringing. It was a painful lesson, however, and many of these women still carried emotional scars from their self-perceived failure with the stepchildren. Taking a secondary or passive role in parenting children appears to be extremely difficult for many women. "Backing off" seemed to be coupled with a reduced emotional investment in the stepchildren on the part of the women we interviewed. On the other hand, many men have difficulty assuming a primary parenting role. This was especially true of nonresidential fathers. Whether driven by guilt or by the need to establish a good relationship with their children, few men in our studies have wanted to play a disciplinarian role in their limited time with their children. This role fell to the stepmother, sometimes by default and sometimes because she actively pursued it.

From the stepmother's perspective, we would have to conclude that this is not an easy family role to assume. Few expressed satisfaction with either the role or their performance of it. The most positive stepmothers were at best ambiguous about the role, and several vociferously stated that they "hated being a stepmother."

THE PERSPECTIVE OF THE STEPFATHER

Stepfathers appear to have an easier time assimilating into stepfamily life than do stepmothers. A contributing factor may be that fathers are often less involved in family activities in general, regardless of the family structure. Stepfathers may see their role with the stepchildren as quite peripheral to that of the children's mother. Although frequent interactions with children can build a sense of belonging and closeness, it also can create conflict. It is stepmothers who are likely to spend the most time interacting with stepchildren, therefore creating more opportunities for conflict. If stepfathers generally interact little and take a rather passive role in child discipline, they are less likely to come into conflict with the stepchild.

It also appears that stepfathers are less likely than stepmothers to have an agenda for the children. As noted earlier, stepmothers often see a need for shaping up their stepchildren and taking action. Although stepfathers also may comment on their stepchildren's need for more discipline, they may be less likely to impose it than stepmothers, perhaps because they are less emotionally invested in the stepchildren. Hetherington and Clingempeel (1992) described the most typical pattern for stepfathers to be one of distancing themselves from the stepchildren. They observed that when the attempts of stepfathers to bond with their stepchildren were rebuffed, the stepfathers tended to withdraw from the stepchildren. Stepmothers may find it more difficult to distance themselves from stepchildren and child-rearing activities and therefore tend to continue actively pursuing the children, often to the point of family destruction.

Of course, some men do expect to be the primary disciplinarians of stepchildren, because they see this as an important function of men's family responsibilities. Some stepfathers see their duty as rescuing their wives from being overwhelmed by their wild and disobedient children. By laying down a strict set of rules and enforcing them, these stepfathers also see themselves as rescuing their stepchildren from learning to be soft, self-indulgent slackers. The reactions of wives and children in many of these stepfamilies mirror those of parents and children in stepmother households, they range from passive resistance and resentment to outright rebellion.

In general, men probably rank their fathering role as a lower priority than women rank their roles as mothers. Society also places a higher priority on the role of mother than the fathering role. Fathering appears to be a socially-accepted secondary action within the family, and there are even fewer societal prescriptions for fathering other people's children. Thus, stepfathers, unlike stepmothers, are not as likely to feel guilty if they are not actively involved with their stepchildren.

The role that has been primary and traditional for fathers in the home is that of the breadwinner. Stepfathers also assume that role to various degrees. In a study of family obligations after divorce and remarriage, a sizable percentage of the respondents indicated that stepfathers should assume financial responsibility for those stepchildren living with them (Ganong, Coleman, & Mistina, 1995). Even though this opinion is contrary to current legislation in the United States, it is widely believed that men are financially responsible for anyone residing in their households (Ganong & Coleman, 1995). Crosbie-Burnett (1983) reported that stepfathers provided about 50% of the financial support of adolescent stepchildren in the upper-middle-class families in her study.

Giles-Sims and Crosbie-Burnett (1989) hypothesized that the greater the stepfather's financial contribution to the family in comparison to the wife's, the more power the stepfather has in the stepfamily. Although the adolescent stepchildren tended to perceive themselves as having more power than their stepfathers, Giles-Sims and Crosbie-Burnett found that stepfathers who financially supported the stepchildren did, indeed, have more influence on family decision-making. Those families in which the stepfathers agreed that their stepchildren had more power tended to be those whose adolescent children spent more time with their biological fathers. It was suggested that when adolescents have alternative sources of financial support, they are less likely to accept the power position of the mother and stepfather.

We have found that in some well-functioning stepfamilies, stepchildren appear to appreciate their stepfather's contributions, and express awareness of some obligation on their part to accord their stepfather greater respect and input into decisions about their lives. This awareness is almost never present in conflict ridden stepfamilies, and is not necessarily a widespread phenomenon in well-functioning stepfamilies.

From perusing the stepfamily literature we can conclude that the role of the stepfather in stepfamilies is perhaps even more ambiguous than that of the stepmother. There is considerable social sanction for the stepfather providing financial support to the stepfamily but little else appears to be expected of him. In other words, the stereotype of the man as breadwinner and head of the household is widely supported for stepfathers. This may be the reason that some stepfathers feel they are unappreciated and/or ignored except when a stepchild needs money for something. Some have described themselves as serving primarily as the stepchild's meal ticket although this is the perception of only a small minority of the stepfathers we have interviewed.

The adjustments of men within stepfamilies appear to differ depending somewhat on their previous parenting experiences. Men who have been fathers before becoming stepfathers seem to be able to negotiate family expectations with greater ease than those who have not. This appears to be especially true when the oldest stepchild is relatively young (Palisi, Orleans, Caddell, & Horn, 1991). Men who are fathers obviously have more experience in a parenting role. Their greater knowledge of developmental norms for children may lead to more realistic expectations regarding stepchildren's behavior which, in turn, may create a sense of trust between the children's mother and the stepfather regarding co-parenting of the children. Paradoxically, stepfathers who also have children of their own may make less effort to develop a close relationship with their stepchildren, a strategy that may ultimately lead to a mutually satisfying stepparent-stepchild relationship more than is possible when stepfathers try too hard. Men who have children of their own also are less likely to compete with the biological father for the loyalty of the children. Whether this lack of competition is due to disinterest or to shared empathy with noncustodial fathers does not seem to matter. The children are happier when their life is not impeded with loyalty conflicts; they become free to develop unique relationships with each father.

Unlike stepmothers, the stepfathers we have interviewed were much less likely to insist on taking on a parenting role (i.e., the role of father) if the genetic/adoptive father was still in the picture. Most appeared to be serving a complimentary role to that of the genetic father except when the stepchild had relatively little or no contact with the genetic father. In those cases, the stepfather usually assumed the role of the primary parent. The stepfathers showed only a little evidence of jealousy or competition with the genetic father and, in several instances, appeared to have facilitated an improved co-parenting relationship between the stepchild's genetic parents.

The men in our studies also appeared to harbor less explicit fantasies of remarried family life than the women. In Papernow's (1993) developmental model of stepfamilies, she defines the beginning period as the *fantasy stage*. It is during this stage that the biological parent hopes that the new spouse will be a better partner and parent than the previous spouse. It has been our observation that the genetic mother in stepfather families was the stronger force in maintaining the fantasy stage and that giving up the fantasy created great pain and frustration for them. It may be that women fantasize more about marriage and family than men do or that men are bereft of imagination regarding family functioning, but for whatever reason, the men seemed less likely than the women to be in the fantasy stage regardless of how long ago the remarriage occurred. Genetic mothers as well as stepmothers appeared to have been motivated to shape the children, stepchildren, and family into their image of what a family should be. Their husbands were sometimes willing to support these fantasies but more often they responded rather passively to the pressures.

Stepfathers we have studied were almost uniformly motivated to do what they perceived was best for their stepchildren although their ideas about what was best varied rather widely. Some expressed regret that their relationship with their stepchildren was not closer but few harbored the amount and types of resentment towards their stepchildren that was sometimes evident in comments shared by stepmothers. This is not to say that all stepfathers are highly motivated to be good parents. Obviously there are stepfathers who are not well intentioned and/or abusive, but they are unlikely to agree to be interviewed about their stepparenting roles.

THE PERSPECTIVE OF THE STEPCHILD

Children in stepfamilies whom we have interviewed often harbored strong emotions towards their stepparent. Sometimes these emotions were positive and sometimes negative emotions prevailed. Although often fairly inarticulate, in well-functioning stepfamilies, children were mostly appreciative of an additional parent figure. One young girl who had a close, if not enmeshed, relationship with her mother and a positive relationship with her noncustodial father, nevertheless relished having a "live-in father." As she put it, "I have a father in Missouri, and I have a father in Montana." She was clearly able to assimilate two father figures into her life. She was especially appreciative of the financial stability her stepfather provided the family, but she clearly saw him as much more than a breadwinner. When asked what role a stepfather should take in a family, she replied that "he should be just like a father." An adolescent who had a contentious relationship with his genetic father shared with us that he felt indebted to his stepfather for caring about him. "I'm not sure what would have happened to me if it had not been for _____." Another child apologized for his negative comments about his stepmother. Similar to the young girl mentioned earlier, he was able to assimilate two mothers into his family schema and felt that he had two mothers, one in Missouri and one in another state.

Some stepchildren realize how much their horizons have been broadened by their stepparents. They comment on being introduced to new hobbies, music, sports activities, and other interests that they now share with their stepparent. Some use stepparents almost as consultants. For example, one stepchild mentioned utilizing his stepfather's assistance with homework, his mother's assistance with cooking. This particular young man was estranged from his genetic father, but some stepchildren may utilize a noncustodial genetic parent as a confidant, someone to talk with when they do not want to get into trouble with the parents with whom they are living.

Clearly, not all stepchildren are so positive about their stepparents. As we mentioned previously, some stepchildren are torn with loyalty conflicts. For these children, liking the stepparent raises their anxiety and makes them feel guilty about being disloyal to their genetic parent. Paradoxically, this kind of internal conflict for children is worse when stepparents are kind, loving, and attractive to the children. Obviously, when stepparents and parents compete for children's affections, this conflict is much worse as well.

Even stepchildren who have excellent relationships with their stepparents express almost universal dislike of discipline from the stepparent. They clearly prefer that any discipline be administered by genetic parents. They also do not like to adhere to new household rules, and they resent lack of input into family changes. Most dislike rapid changes and their lack of control regarding changes. Parental remarriage, particularly of the parent with whom a child resides, usually represents a large number of big and little transitions for children. Sometimes children do not know about parents' plans to remarry in advance, and they may not have enough time to emotionally prepare for the many changes that occur when household members are added and when daily routines are altered. Stepdaughters, in particular, express disappointment at having to share their mother's time with a stepfather. Although often noting the financial concerns of their single-parent family, stepdaughters tend to refer fondly to that time in their lives.

Children in stepfamilies sometimes view the same stepparent behavior in diametrically different ways. For example, some stepchildren view stepparents who provide them with material goods as being supportive, and they are grateful. Others view material goods provided by stepparents as attempted bribes, and they are resentful of the stepparent's attempts to "win them over." These responses often make it appear that it is the stepchildren who set the agenda in the family, not the parents or stepparents. When stepchildren decide to ignore, disregard, or actively dislike the stepparent there is little that the parents or stepparents can do. Sometimes, over time, stepchildren change their minds about the stepparents. However, in some cases this is too little, too late. Stepparents, to protect their own ego and dignity, may have withdrawn from the relationship by then. Children may have truly forgotten how ugly they were to their stepparents when they were younger, they may have discounted the impact their behavior had on the stepparents, or they may not be articulate enough to fully explain their change in viewpoint. Adult stepchildren have sometimes expressed regret to us over their earlier behaviors that alienated them from their stepparents. They had come to realize that their behavior had shut them off from people who could have enriched their lives.

STEPFAMILY PERSPECTIVES AND FAMILY IDEOLOGIES

It is difficult to draw conclusions about how stepfamilies look to those who live within them. Stepfamilies are complex and extremely variable. In many ways, they differ little from other families. That is, they get up in the morning, eat breakfast, walk the dog, get ready for work and school, and do all the things that any family must do to function in society. However, unlike in first married families where these family routines develop rather naturally over time, in the stepfamily the routinizing of normal functions may take negotiation. A family of early rising, big breakfast eaters may have merged with a get-up-late-dash-out-the-door-barely-awake family. It is more challenging to live in such an atmosphere. Differences in daily routine can be negotiated through compromise. That is, everyone sleeps a little later, but all must eat breakfast or everyone gets up early one day and eats breakfast and all sleep late the next day and do not eat breakfast. Another way to develop routines is through the imposition of the standards of one of the families–all must get up early and eat breakfast. A still different solution is to keep individual traditions and let them exist side-by-side–the early risers continue to do so and the late risers continue to get up at the last minute and dash out the door. There are many solutions to the complexity created by merging two families, but the family members must be flexible and creative to be successful. The stepfamily members we interviewed expended a great deal of emotional energy trying to impose a traditional family model on a nontraditional family. It can be likened to forcing a size 8 shoe onto a size 9 foot. This can be done, but it involves much discomfort and there is little purpose to it. Rather than spending energy creating uncomfortable simulations of nuclear families, stepfamily members and professionals who regularly interact with stepfamilies need to more purposively explore the unique characteristics of well-functioning stepfamilies. This is not a new suggestion, and it is not original with us. In spite of the admonitions, however, the spotlight continues to focus on stepfamily problems. As long as the external view of stepfamilies remains negative, it is unlikely that the internal perspectives of stepfamilies will markedly improve.

REFERENCES

Beer, W.R. (1992). *American stepfamilies*. New Brunswick, NJ: Transaction.

Bradbury, T., & Fincham, F. (1990). Attributions in marriage: Review and critique. *Psychological Bulletin, 107*, 3-33.

Braverman, L. (1989). Mother guilt. *The Family Therapy Networker, 13*(5), 46-47.

Clingempeel, W. G., & Segal, S. (1986). Stepparent-stepchild relationships and the psychological adjustment of children in stepmother and stepfather families. *Child Development, 57*, 474-484.

Dallos, R. (1991). *Family beliefs systems, therapy, and change*. Philadelphia, PA: Open University Press.

Everingham, C. (1994). *Motherhood and modernity*. Philadelphia, PA: Open University Press.

Furstenberg, F.F., Jr., & Nord, C.W. (1985). Parenting apart: Patterns of childrearing after marital disruption. *Journal of Marriage and the Family, 47*, 893-904.

Ganong, L., & Coleman, M. (1989). Preparing for remarriage: Anticipating the issues, seeking solutions. *Family Relations, 38*, 28-33.

Ganong, L., Coleman, M., & Mistina, D. (1995). Normative beliefs about parents' and stepparents' financial obligations to children following divorce and remarriage. *Family Relations, 44*, 306-315.

Giles-Sims, J., & Crosbie-Burnett, M. (1989). Adolescent power in stepfather families: A test of normative-resource theory. *Journal of Marriage and the Family, 51*, 1065-1078.

Hare-Mustin, R., & Broderick, P.C. (1979). The myth of motherhood: A study of attitudes toward motherhood. *Psychology of Women Quarterly, 4*, 114-128.

Hetherington, E.M., & Clingempeel, W.G. (1992). Coping with marital transitions: A family systems perspective. *Monographs of the Society for Research in Child Development, 57*(2-3, Serial No. 227).

Hobart, C.W. (1988). Perception of parent-child relationships in first-married and remarried families. *Family Relations, 37,* 175-182.

Kurdek, L. (1991). Predictors of increases in marital distress in newly-wed couples: A 3-year prospective longitudinal study. *Developmental Psychology, 27,* 627-636.

Morrison, K., & Thompson-Guppy, A. (1985). Cinderella's stepmother syndrome. *Canadian Journal of Psychiatry, 30,* 521-529.

Noy, D. (1991). Wicked stepmothers in Roman society and imagination. *Journal of Family History, 16,* 345-361.

Palisi, B.J., Orleans, M., Caddell, D., & Korn, B. (1991). Adjustment to stepfatherhood: The effects of marital history and relations with children. *Journal of Divorce and Remarriage, 14,* 89-106.

Papernow, P. (1993). *Becoming a stepfamily: Patterns of development in remarried families.* New York: Gardner.

Peterson, M. (1985). *Mercy flights.* Columbia, MO: University of Missouri Press.

Russo, N.F. (1979). Overview: Sex roles, fertility and the motherhood mandate. *Psychology of Women Quarterly, 4,* 7-15.

Wald, E. (1981). *The remarried family: Challenge and promise.* New York: Family Service Association of America.

Stepfamily as Project

Irene Levin

A stepmother came to the airport with her eight year old stepdaughter. The stepdaughter was going to visit her mother. The stepmother had to fill out a questionnaire before departure since the little girl was travelling alone: Who followed the child to the airport? Suggestions were offered: The mother, the father, the grandparent, a sibling, a friend, the possibilities were numerous, but none for stepmother.

This little story shows part of the daily life of stepfamilies. They are hidden behind the nuclear family. The nuclear family has a kind of model monopoly when it comes to family forms. In 1973 the Norwegian sociologist, Stein Bråten, used the concept, model monopoly, in order to understand communication between two persons. One of them will have a model monopoly of what the communication is going to be about and how it should be understood (Bråten, 1973). However, model monopoly can also be useful to our understanding when applied to family forms (see also Gamache in this issue). Dorothy Smith (1993) writes about this same phenomenon. She introduces SNAF (Standard North American Family) as the ruling family form that every other family form will be compared with, either directly or indirectly. SNAF is an ideological code: "An ideological code . . . analogous to a genetic code, reproducing its characteristic forms and order in multiple and various discursive settings" (Smith 1993, p. 50). This ideological code has a normative character. We reproduce this ideological code through our language. For example, we use the term: working-mothers, but don't use the term working-fathers. Fathers who work reflect the ideological code and do not need to be expressed by a prefix.

Irene Levin is Associate Professor in the Graduate School of Social Work and Social Research at Oslo College, Oslo, Norway.

[Haworth co-indexing entry note]: "Stepfamily as Project." Levin, Irene. Co-published simultaneously in *Marriage & Family Review* (The Haworth Press, Inc.) Vol. 26, No. 1/2, 1997, pp. 123-133; and: *Stepfamilies: History, Research, and Policy* (ed: Irene Levin and Marvin B. Sussman) The Haworth Press, Inc., 1997, pp. 123-133. Single or multiple copies of this article are available for a fee from The Haworth Document Delivery Service [1-800-342-9678, 9:00 a.m. - 5:00 p.m. (EST). E-mail address: getinfo@haworth.com].

When it comes to family forms, there is a tacit understanding that indicates order or hierarchy. The nuclear family is placed highest and the rest are seen as deficient alternatives, i.e., stepfamilies, single parent families, foster families, etc. Another possible way to understand family and family forms would be to view *all* varieties of the term including the nuclear family, as non-normative. This would be compatible with Trost's dyadic perspective, family is not only formed, but constantly being reformed (Trost, 1990, 1993).

Because of the model monopoly or the ideological code of the nuclear family, our understanding of alternative family forms is seen with the eyes of the nuclear family. This prejudice affects our understanding of stepfamilies. We learn that the stepfamily is less cohesive than the nuclear family, to give one example. Father-child relationships are compared with stepfather-stepchild relationships. Anne Simon, in 1964, pointed out that comparing the household of the nuclear family with the household of the stepfamily is like comparing apples with oranges. Apples are not good because they are not orange. Apples and oranges are different entities, as are stepfamily households and a nuclear family household. In the case of the latter, the child will have both parents residing within the household. In the stepfamily household, the child will reside together with one parent, and the other parent if alive will reside in another household. The challenge is to develop a knowledge and understanding of the social reality of stepfamilies without using the nuclear family as a model.

THE STEPFAMILY AS A SECOND MARRIAGE

A popular view, even in science, has been to think of a second marriage as more or less the same as the first. A difference often mentioned is the importance of emotionally having finished the first marriage before starting a second one (Saul & Scherman, 1984, Visher & Visher, 1979). Another perspective is to highlight the importance of the structural difference between the stepfamily and the nuclear family (Coleman & Ganong, 1990). This article will focus on the *meaning* of the second marriage.

Parental behavior with a first marriage is more or less well known. Societal norms tell us what to do and what not to do. In Western societies a father may discipline a child at the dinner table. He may also decide not to do so. Both behaviors are acceptable within his role as father. But, if a stepfather disciplines his partner's children, a question arises about his role legitimacy: "You are not my father; mind your own business!"

There are no norms supporting parental roles in a stepfamily and no models (Cherlin, 1978). This makes the establishing of a stepfamily a very different process then that of a nuclear family.

In contemporary Western societies when one marries the first time, "succeeding" is very important, even though one very well knows that it is difficult to live with another person, as also the high divorce rates indicate. A lot of effort is invested into the establishment of the first marriage. When this, however, does not succeed, it can be looked upon as a "failure." This does not necessarily mean that the person defines him- or herself as a failure. But the situation itself failed to develop as originally planned. When one tries again in a new marriage, it becomes very important not to repeat the same "failure." Establishing a stepfamily can be looked upon as *a project* where an important issue is avoiding new "failure." This makes the second marriage a situation where one runs a higher risk. Accordingly the motivation to succeed is very high.[1]

The second time one is faced with a completely different situation, where "succeeding" *and* avoiding a new "failure" are both important aspects.

To further clarify, one might compare the second marriage to an exam. If one fails the first time, the reason might be seen as being bad luck. But if one fails the second time, it may be harder to maintain that kind of reasoning and one might be seen or see oneself as a seriously flawed person. On the other hand, if one succeeds the second time, the first failure will more likely be reframed as a matter of luck. What happens the second time has retrospective power and helps to permanently frame the first experience.

If one can avoid a second break up, the first one might be reframed as "she was (I was) just unlucky with that guy." The result of the second trial has retrospective power which might put the first experience in a new light.

The strong motivation both to "succeed," and to avoid a new "failure," can be likened to starting a *project*. Both are characterized by high motivation. Both lack an appropriate model. The stepfamily is not seen as being a societal institution even though several years have passed since Cherlin first wrote about stepfamilies from that perspective, in 1978. Members of stepfamilies are trapped in a very special and somewhat paradoxical situation. They have to succeed at something without knowing what succeeding in that particular situation *is*, since there is no societal model to follow.

What does one do when establishing a new household, where there are

---

1. This is the case for at least one of the couple, the one who has been previously married. In this research, when only one person had been previously married, the other partner manifested the high motivation and saw the relationship as a project.

no norms for how to be a stepparent or for how a child is to relate to and live in the same household with one parent's partner? This was one of the questions I asked in my study of stepfamilies. In my analysis of the behavior of all the members of the stepfamily household, I found three patterns of behavior. The first pattern includes various attempts to *reconstruct* a family. The second pattern reflects a *wait-and-see strategy* in order to find behavior that fits them. The third pattern is designed to *innovate* something new.

METHOD

Data comes from a qualitative study of 63 persons living in stepfamily households in Oslo, Norway. Everyone in the household aged five years and older was interviewed separately.

The sample was in part gathered by means of a snowball sampling method. Other participants were enlisted by municipal Health Centers. (In Norway every child gets several free check-ups at such centers before reaching school age.)

The method is threefold. It begins by asking informants to list who belongs to the informant's family (the family-list). Thereafter, the informant is asked to place family members on a large map using circular and triangular pieces of paper, reflecting closeness or distance to the informant (the family map). Finally, a verbal interview is conducted (Levin, 1993a and 1993b, 1994).

When children are informants the family map is substituted with a family drawing. The results and the method from the children's study are reported elsewhere (Levin 1989, 1994).

RECONSTRUCTION

For some, the behavior will be aimed at trying to reconstruct what they had in their previous marriage. Of course, they do not want to literally reconstruct these relationships since they ended in divorce. But they do not have any particular wish to create or live in a different family structure than the one they lived in before, the nuclear family. They are not concerned about the differences between the two family structures other than that they have a new partner. The mistake of the first marriage had to do with the partner, not the family structure.

Therefore they try to copy the behavior of the first marriage. As one informant stated, "I have not only built a house, but restored a family." From his point of view it seemed possible to "restore" or remake the family he had.

It is (of course) impossible to remake a nuclear family after it has broken up. This informant tries to find behavior that resembles the behavior he and his first wife had. He himself wants to be a father in the same way as he was before, and he wants his new partner to be a wife and mother the same way his ex-wife was. In order to succeed, his children must also see his new partner as a mother.

For the reconstructors, the nuclear family is not only a model it is also an ideal that they try to achieve. A stepfather is a *father substitute*. The thinking is that as an adult who lives in the same household with children, one necessarily will have parental responsibilities as a consequence. The same is true for a stepmother. It was more or less seen to be an obvious expectation for stepmothers grouped within this pattern that an adult female in a household with children does what a mother does. (For a gender perspective of the stepmother and stepfather roles, see Levin in this volume.)

Jane and John are exemplifiers of this pattern. Jane's daughter Jenniffer is living with them. When I called to make an appointment for the interview, Jane said: "We are not a stepfamily." She did not think of her household consisting of her new partner and daughter from a previous marriage, as a stepfamily. For her, the household was not different from others.

When her daughter Jenniffer, at ten years of age, asked permission to call her stepfather "daddy," the response was positive. Her request was seen as a sign that they were "on the right track." As Jane said, in their household John is the "father." He is the one who decides. Jeniffer has never lived with her biological father since her parents divorced before she was born. She sees her father regularly, but not very frequently. She has never been in his present home since his new wife does not want to be reminded of Jenniffer's father's former life.

Jane's partner John feels himself to be Jeniffer's father. He feels responsible for Jeniffer's development, and he teaches her new skills, etc. For him, taking care of another person's child makes him particularly careful. Still he knows that Jane always will be the one who gets the last word.

In that way John resembles Peter, who is the stepfather of Paula's two boys. Peter feels that he is responsible for his partner's children. He takes care of them "from a to z" when they are within his sphere. He dislikes the boys' weekly visits to their father. When not together, he is reminded of his not being in an "ordinary" family. In contrast to the previous example, Paula's two boys have a good relationship with their father.

Peter's role as a stepfather is like a father substitute; he does all that a father would do. He feels that his relationship with the boys is much better than the one he had with his own father. He also believes that he knows his stepsons better than his neighbor knows *his* sons.

Peter and John love their stepchildren. They identify themselves with them and feel pride whenever the stepchildren receive praise, and hurt when the opposite is the case.

Still, there are some dilemmas. Peter tells that he has different feelings when his own daughter sits upon his lap than when his stepsons do. Something different happens to him. Exactly what it is, he cannot tell. He really hopes it is not "biology" because then it cannot be changed. He likes to explain the felt difference as a special attribute of the young daughter. In that way he behaved according to the pattern of reconstruction.

WAIT-AND-SEE

In establishing the new household, those that wait-and-see are more pragmatic. They realize that the new relationship has to be different from the previous one, but they do not know in what way. The result will depend upon the experiences they have. In trying different ways of behaving, they will eventually find a way which feels comfortable.

The nuclear family is their model, as it is for the rest of our society, but unlike the reconstructors, it is not an ideal they try to copy. Practicing trial and error, those that wait and see are willing to invest the time it takes to get it right. For reconstructors time is something they want to shorten in order to get to the goal (being like "ordinary" families) as quickly as possible.

For those that wait-and-see the stepparent role is more like that of a friend. Since the stepparent is from a different generation, he or she also has the role of an adult in relation to the child. The stepparent's role combines being a *friend* and an *adult*.

Behavior that indicates a desire to substitute for the other parent, is not supported. "The child has two parents and does not need another," or "you never divorce your children" are terms of expression that informants from this pattern often use. Therefore the children are the responsibility of their parents.

Ruth and Roger are an example of this pattern. When they moved in together, Roger's teenage son from a previous marriage moved in together with them. Roger's daughter Rita continued living with her mother, but she saw her father's apartment as much as hers: "I live both with my mother and my father, I only live most with my mother," she said. Some years later Ruth and Roger had a child together.

In this pattern, children remain the responsibilities of their parents. Everything having to do with the children is decided by Roger and his former wife. Ruth, in a sense, remains an outsider when decisions concerning Roger's children are made.

Ruth's role as a stepmother is both a friend and an adult. She is there for them when they need her. She does housework for them, prepares food and washes clothes.

Householdmembers used time and tried out different types of behavior before fitting into their present roles. Ruth was introduced gradually. Her acceptance by Roger's son was achieved more smoothly than from Rita. Rita could not follow the process as closely, living so much of the time with her mother.

Rita said that initially she was afraid that her love for her mother would decrease if she liked Ruth too much. When I interviewed her she experienced the situation differently. Now, liking Ruth had nothing to do with her relationship to her mother. She finds that her family is now larger, to be positive. At the same time, there are more persons who have to be considered. Her brother clearly sees Ruth as a friend: "I don't need another mother," he said.

What about dilemmas in this pattern? Ruth sometimes feels uncertain about her role. When a decision is made regarding his children, Roger contacts his former wife. Ruth is not included at special arrangements where Roger's children are in focus. At the same time, Ruth is the caring person at home that prepares food for the children, washes their clothes, etc. In that respect she is no "outsider." She is sometimes inside and sometimes outside. She feels that she has duties without having any rights. When they graduate from school, she won't be invited. Sometimes she feels just like a female servant. That is her dilemma. (See also "The Stepparent Role from a Gender Perspective" in this volume.)

INNOVATION

In this pattern, the most important idea is to create something new. What the exact result will be, is not clear. They want to construct something different from what they had. They blame the previous family structure for the marital break up. That is why they want something new.

The main aim is to create a new life style. "When we moved in together the most important thing for us was not to make a family, but to change our lifestyle," as one informant said. They do not know what this new life style will be, but they are sure that they do not want to closely resemble the nuclear family. They have tried that family pattern and it did not work.

The children are clearly defined as the responsibilities of their parents. The stepparent is more like an *uncle/aunt* or a *grandfather/grandmother* that takes care of the children when they are within their sphere, otherwise they do not have any responsibilities for them.

The nuclear family is seen here as the norm for the rest of society, but it is not an ideal or a model for them. On the contrary, it's a model for how not to be.

When Eric and Esther moved in together, they bought an apartment which they divided into three parts, one part for Esther and her two daughters and one part for Eric. The kitchen and the living room were to be common areas.

Esther's two girls are her total responsibility. Sometimes Eric "baby-sits" if Esther asks him. Then he takes complete responsibility for them. The way he performs his stepfather role is similar to that of an uncle. He does not educate them, nor does he feel any responsibility for their upbringing. But when he is "baby-sitting" or whenever they come into his sphere, he will correct them if they do something he does not like.

When Eric's daughter comes visiting, she is his sole responsibility. Esther joins them only when she wants. At Yule and during other special events, Eric joins his former wife, and Esther and her children will be with their father/ her former husband.

"We started with a rather large distance, and perhaps we will move closer together after a while. In the nuclear family, you start with closeness and the distance comes later," he said.

One of the questions they faced was where the two adults should sleep. At first, Eric slept in his part of the apartment, and Esther in hers. After a while, they decided to have a common bedroom. When Eric's daughter comes to visit, she sleeps together with Esther's children.

Esther's daughters like living in this type of household. They like the idea of having more persons in their household. The oldest daughter (ten years old) tells that since their mother now is much happier than when they lived with her father, she is more satisfied with the situation. Both children want more contact with Eric than they now have. They like him very much. The oldest child was skeptical at first. However, as soon as she met Eric, her feelings changed. Her advice to others in the same situation: "Meet your mother's new partner as soon as possible! He is probably very nice."

Eric misses his daughter very much. He sees his moving out of her household as premature. Usually, the separation between parents and children occurs when the children are in their early twenties. When he is together with Esther's daughters, he feels an inner conflict, since he really wants to be with his own daughter.

The dilemma for innovators is related to the distinct division of labor, with children remaining wholly the responsibility of their parents. Esther sometimes feels like a single mother. The difference is that when evening comes, she has a partner. He can comfort her, make her tea, and they can talk and enjoy themselves. In a way, she likes this very clear division, because as it is now, she always knows who does what and what she can expect. In her former marriage, she felt a responsibility also for her husband; she constantly had to make sure that her husband did his share of the household work. This was in the middle of the seventies, when the women's liberation movement in a way made the females responsible for their husbands' liberation (Christensen, 1982). In her present relationship they have already decided who is to do what. She says that she likes this arrangement, since it saves time and avoids the wear and tear of all those tedious discussions about who should do what.

CONCLUDING REMARKS

In this paper I have argued that in establishing a stepfamily one is faced with a special situation which can be likened to that of a *project*. Highly motivated, one tries to avoid a new "failure." The problem with this particular project is that there is no institutional support (Cherlin, 1978) for what they now try to create. The nuclear family is the model, and constitutes the norm for a family in our society. The question becomes how to behave when living in a family form which differs from societal norms? What does one actually do?

The informants in this study show three differing patterns of behavior in establishing their new households. One pattern reflects the nuclear family as not only a model but also as an ideal. The adults in the household want to *reconstruct* and copy the structure of the nuclear family, and as stepparents then positions are like *father*–or *mother substitutes*.

The second pattern is more pragmatic. These couples *wait and see*, and they try various sorts of behavior in order to explore what fits them best. The nuclear family here is a model, but not an ideal. The stepparent's role is more that of a *friend* combined with the role of an adult.

The third pattern is that of *innovation*. They want to construct a new family form. For them the nuclear family is an anti-model; something they want *not* to be. The stepparent is less involved with stepchildren than in the other patterns, with a role resembling that of an *uncle* or an *aunt*. There may be other patterns in addition to those that I have found.

The patterns have been constructed by separately analyzing each member of the household. The behavior and the paradigm for different household members do not have to be identical. For example, one person might best be described as a reconstructor while others in the household might better fit into a wait-and-see paradigm. A stepfather might define his role as a friend with some adult responsibilities, i.e., a person in addition to the father. For him the social reality is clear: "The child can only have one father" while his partner, the child's mother, might see the situation differently. Through her marriage with this man she has not only gotten a husband, but a person that can fill the empty role of her former husband. In this language she is a reconstructor.

The ideas presented in this paper are not meant to indicate that one pattern is better than another. However, if there is no unity within the household about how to see role relationships–meaning which pattern they belong to–role and relational conflict will ensue. Two different ideas of the relationships might therefore lead to problems.

My data does not show any case of this sort at the time of the interview; within the households there is a unity of perspectives. The reason for this might be that the couples had been married or cohabiting for at least a year and a half. The first period of uncertainties about how to behave were over. One might expect that if the two partners have different ideas about how the new household is supposed to be, their break up will occur rather soon after moving in together; perhaps even during the period of "going steady."

The pattern preferable to members of a household in one period, might not be the one preferred in a later period. This was the case for some households in this sample. They started with the pattern of reconstruction. In one example, the wife eventually felt uncomfortable being a mother substitute. She said she was "living another woman's life." Her husband had custody over his two boys. Their mother was sick and they saw her irregularly. The stepmother changed her definition of the situation to: "a mother is someone you can tell your secrets, while a friend is a companion." This redefinition came about after she felt she had become the "wicked stepmother." She changed her role from mother substitute to that of a friend. The rest of the household followed her lead, and adopted a wait-and-see pattern.

This example shows one of the partners as not being satisfied with the situation. Another possibility is that the children are not satisfied with the decisions or role expectations of the adults. For instance, a child might rebel having an idea of the stepfather as being a friend while the stepfather sees their relationship as parent-child. This situation might lead to a break-up of the entire household. But the result can also be that the child as an adolescent moves out. White and Booth (1985) note that adolescents in stepfamilies often do just that.

I have tried to illuminate the question of models for the stepfamily. By analyzing different types of behavior into patterns, I hope to give a picture of variety and diversity. This might be a first step for the stepfamily in defining its own unique model.

REFERENCES

Bråten, S. (1973). Model monopoly and communication, *Acta Sociologica*, 16, 98-107.

Cherlin, A. (1978). Remarriage as an Incomplete Institution, *American Journal of Sociology*, 634-650.

Christensen, E. (1982). Når det første barn blir født, in E. Christensen (ed.): *Fra to til tre. En bok om det å bli foreldre*. København: Nytt nordisk forlag.

Coleman, M. & Ganong, L. (1990). Remarriage and stepfamily research in the 1980s; increased interest for an old family form, *Journal of Marriage and the Family*, 52, 925-940.

Levin, I. (1989). Barnetegninger–stefamiliens fingeravtrykk? in: I. Levin and G. Clifford (eds): *Relasjoner. Hverdagsskrift til Per Olav Tiller*. Trondheim: Tapir.

Levin, I. (1993a). Family as Mapped Realities, *Journal of Family Issues*, 14, 82-91.

Levin, I. (1993b). *Stefamilien–variasjon og mangfold*. Oslo: Aventura.

Saul, S.C & Scherman D. (1984). Divorce grief and personal adjustment in divorced persons who remarry or remain single, *Journal of Divorce*, 7, 74-85.

Simon, A. W. (1964). *Stepchild in the family*. New York: Odyssey Press.

Smith, D. (1993). The Standard North American Family: SNAF as an ideological code, *Journal of Family Issues*, 14, 50-67.

Trost, J. (1990). On becoming a family, *Family Reports*, 18, Uppsala University.

Trost, J. (1993). Family from a dyadic perspective, *Journal of Family Issues*, 14, 92-104.

Visher, E. & Visher J. (1979). *Stepfamilies: a guide to working with stepparents and stepchildren*. New York: Brunner/Mazel.

White, L. K & Booth, A. (1985). The quality and stability of remarriages: the role of stepchildren, *American Sociological Review*, 50, 689-698.

Stepfamilies from the Child's Perspective: From Stepfamily to Close Relationships

Aino Ritala-Koskinen

STEPFAMILY NEEDS CHILDREN

Looking at earlier research into the stepfamily or at the public debate that is going on about the stepfamily (see, e.g., Ritala-Koskinen, 1993), it is hard to avoid the conclusion that children are centrally important to the stepfamily; indeed the stepfamily does not really exist without children. Typically, the stepfamily is defined as a family in which at least one of the spouses has been married before, who has divorced and brought along at least one child into the new family. This means that at least one of the two parents is not the biological parent of all children in the stepfamily household. All typologies that have been presented of the stepfamily take not only the second marriage but also children as important criteria for classifying the family into this or that category: Do the spouses have children from their previous or current marriage? Do all or some of the children from the previous marriage live in this household? Do children from the previous marriage visit the household? (e.g., Essess & Campbell, 1984; Ihinger-Tallman & Pasley, 1989; Krähenbühl et al., 1986; Liljeström & Kollind, 1990; Schwartz, 1984; see also Ritala-Koskinen, 1993). Research into stepfamilies has rarely devoted specific attention to marriages in which there are no children. Clearly, researchers prefer to define stepfamilies as new families formed by adults and also including children from previous marriages.

Aino Ritala-Koskinen is Licentiate of Social Sciences and Researcher, University of Tampere, Department of Social Policy and Social Work, P.O.Box 607, FIN-33101 Tampere, Finland (E-mail: spairi@uta.fi).

[Haworth co-indexing entry note]: "Stepfamilies from the Child's Perspective: From Stepfamily to Close Relationships." Ritala-Koskinen, Aino. Co-published simultaneously in *Marriage & Family Review* (The Haworth Press, Inc.) Vol. 26, No. 1/2, 1997, pp. 135-151; and: *Stepfamilies: History, Research, and Policy* (ed: Irene Levin and Marvin B. Sussman) The Haworth Press, Inc., 1997, pp. 135-151. Single or multiple copies of this article are available for a fee from The Haworth Document Delivery Service [1-800-342-9678, 9:00 a.m. - 5:00 p.m. (EST). E-mail address: getinfo@haworth.com].

135

That children occupy such a central place in definitions of the step-family is closely related to the interpretation that children are important to the everyday life of the stepfamily. Descriptions of the distinctive charac-teristics of stepfamilies and their specific problems typically include chil-dren in a very central role. Earlier research has shown a special interest in the boundaries of the stepfamily (e.g., Pasley, 1987; Pasley & Ihinger-Tall-man, 1989; Walker & Messinger, 1979) and in step relationships: what is the stepparent's status as a parent of his or her spouse's child, what are the stepparent's rights and duties vis-à-vis that child, how can the child cope with and adapt to this kind of situation, how do new siblings in a step-family get on with each other, do adults treat them on equal terms (e.g., Santrock & Sitterle, 1987; Marsiglio, 1992). When the focus of interest is on the new couple relationship between the adults of the stepfamily and their problems in that relationship, it is clearly hard to set that relationship apart and to look at it separately as an independent object of study. Ques-tions concerning the new couple relationship are very often interwoven with the children involved in the situation (e.g., Liljeström & Kollind, 1990; Ihinger-Tallman & Pasley, 1989, pp. 63-66).

There is no doubt then that children are central to any discussion of the stepfamily; many of the questions that are typically related to the step-family will not even be asked in a study that is concerned with a family where both adults are biological parents of the children. A family is tradi-tionally thought to live together on a permanent basis in the same place, and the biological parents' rights and duties in relation to their children are hardly ever called into question. So if children are important to any discus-sion of the family, they are certainly much more so in a discussion of the characteristics of stepfamilies.

CHILDREN IN RESEARCH ON THE STEPFAMILY

Even though children are recognized as occupying a central place in definitions of the stepfamily as well as in its everyday life, mainstream research on the stepfamily has failed to give them more than perfunctory attention. Grounded in the sociology of childhood (on the general level see, e.g., Alanen, 1992; Qvortrup, 1994), this criticism insists that the life of children in mainstream research is examined mainly from an adult point of view, while the perspectives opened up by children on the stepfamily are ignored. From the very outset the research tradition has wanted to define the stepfamily from the vantage-point of the adult's new family, adhering faithfully to the nuclear family model and approaching the step-family as a unit living together and consisting of adults and children. In empirical studies the choice of interviewees, for example, will usually be based on this model. A concrete example of this orientation is provided by the research interest in stepparent relationships. Typically, this relationship will be examined as the stepparent's relationship to the child rather than as the child's relationship to his or her stepparent (e.g., Ganong & Coleman, 1994).

The orientation of mainstream stepfamily research to adults is grounded in the same notion that cuts across most sociological research: namely, that children are incapable of producing relevant information about their lives for research purposes. Sociologists have tended to think that children are not capable of a meaningful analysis of the world that surrounds them, and accordingly that the information provided by children is either pure wrong or at the very least unreliable. Psychological information about children's cognitive development and different age stages has cast further doubt on the reliability of child informants. However, there is a growing movement now within the sociology of childhood that wants to throw overboard these conventional notions and to take children seriously, as experts of their own lives (e.g., Alanen, 1992; Prout & James, 1990; Qvortrup, 1994). Applied to research on stepfamily, this so-called agent perspective holds out a promise of new angles on understanding the stepfamily. The acceptance of children as informants who understand what is going on in their own family life opens up a real chance of overturning the traditional, adult and nuclear-family based understanding. Good examples are provided by the studies of Penny Gross (1986) in the early 1980s and the more recent work of Irene Levin (1994). They have both recognized the importance of listening to children. They have found in their studies that children do not necessarily consider all people who live together in a stepfamily household as members of their own family. Also, they often define their families as including people who live outside the stepfamily household, such as biological parents living elsewhere.

Mainstream research on the stepfamily has also been characterized by a problem-oriented perspective. Starting out from psychological and pedagogic perspectives, researchers have frequently investigated the detrimental consequences caused to children by the stepfamily, often with so-called normal or nuclear families as points of reference (Ganong & Coleman, 1987). This research design has also been described as the 'deficit-comparison' model (Coleman & Ganong, 1990). A common premise of this model and a frequent result has been that, compared with children living in nuclear families, children in stepfamilies suffer from various deficits. One of the criticisms voiced by sociologists of childhood has been that research tends to look upon children as future adults rather than as children who are living their lives here and now. Indeed it has been suggested that research should learn to look upon children not as 'human becomings' but rather as 'human beings' (e.g., Qvortrup, 1994). This same criticism also applies to research on the stepfamily, where a central concern has been with the question of what kind of adverse (psychical) consequences divorces and new couple relationships can have on the child's development (towards adulthood) (Ganong & Coleman, 1987).

Further support for including the child perspective into research on the stepfamily is provided by observations in critical family studies and feminist research on how the family can mean quite different things not only to different genders but also to different generations (Alanen, 1992; Gittins, 1993). This implies not only that even the same family may appear as very different to different family members (as has been suggested in the phenomenological approach); it also implies that the family issue is anchored not to individuals but to genders and generations. Indeed the child perspective means not only that children's views on the stepfamily are taken into account but indeed that the whole perspective to exploring the stepfamily is different; we look at the stepfamily *through* children. By recognizing and adopting a child perspective we do not only want to fill in certain knowledge gaps concerning children or to generate supplementary information about stepfamilies. Rather the sociology of childhood gives to understand that the child perspective could help to create a completely new understanding of the stepfamily phenomenon (cf. Alanen, 1992; Qvortrup et al., 1994).

THE RESEARCH TASK AND THE MATERIAL

Using a qualitative interview material collected in 1994, I now move on to look at how children living in stepfamily households define their family and how they perceive their relationships with other household members. My analysis constitutes an attempt to apply a child-oriented research approach and to see whether that approach could lead to new and fruitful interpretations of the stepfamily. For reasons of space I cannot examine the interview material systematically, but I have selected extracts for closer examination that support the point I wish to make. The extracts have not been chosen by random, however, but they are representative of the whole corpus of material in terms of contents. My main concern here is to raise questions about children's stepfamilies rather than to put forward definitive conclusions concerning the whole corpus of material.

The empirical experiment presented in this article is based on interviews with 10 children living in stepfamily households. The interviewees were aged between 6 and 16 years. The interviews were carried out in the form of unstructured, focused interviews, with each interview lasting between 30 and 90 minutes. The interviewees were sampled through a family counselling centre in a middle-sized Finnish town. All the children took part voluntarily.

The context for my study is provided by the interview situation. I start out from the notion that the interview does not take place in a vacuum in which the interviewee simply produces the right responses to the interviewer's questions. Rather I understand interviews as being jointly produced by the researcher and child, as a process in which both parties are involved in producing meanings. It is important to realize that this does not by any means detract from the reliability of the material; nor does the fact that the interviewees were children mean that their responses are guided by the interviewer's questions (see, e.g., Holstein & Gubrium, 1995). My own experience is that even those children who do not talk very much will certainly turn down any "wrong" options that the interviewer tries to submit.

Before each interview I always explained to my interviewees why I was doing it. I said I was interested in the child's everyday life, in whom they lived with and what they did. I also said that I was interviewing children whose family or people with whom they live has not always been the same but where has happened changes, where someone had left, someone new had appeared. I also stressed that I knew nothing about the child's family in advance, and that whatever the children told me would remain our secret, that I would not even tell their parents.

In preparing for these interviews I devoted much attention to the way in which I was going to present my questions concerning the children's family relationships. I had been warned that by asking such a culturally loaded and sensitive question as who belongs to your family, I would not be likely to get anything other than culturally correct replies based on the nuclear family model. Consequently I would not be able to uncover the other possible ways in which close relationships were formed. However, since I was working with children, I thought the most natural approach was to operate with familiar, everyday concepts–like the family despite the problems this concept has. I also took it that people, including children, are no "cultural dopes" who are guided entirely from the outside, but they are themselves actively involved in producing cultural meanings (Prout & James, 1990, p. 24). On this basis I decided to begin the interview by asking, "Who do you count as belonging to your family?" This I followed up by asking, "Is this everyone who belongs to your family?" From these questions the conversation moved on to deal with the child's relationships with his or her family members as well as members of the stepfamily household. I was particularly interested in the relationships between children and new adults in the stepfamily household, in how the children described those relationships.

THE FAMILY OF CHILDREN IN STEPFAMILY HOUSEHOLDS

Children describe their families in different ways in interview situations. In the following we look at some of these differences by reference to three examples. All the extracts are taken from the beginning of the interviews. I am particularly interested in the question of whom the children living in stepfamily household say belong to their family and in how they produce these descriptions. The extracts have been so selected that we can examine different but at the same time a representative sample of all the family descriptions I have.

In the first description the child's family is formed of people who live together. However, it is complemented by people living elsewhere.

Extract 1[1]

A: Right. Yes erm the first thing I'd like to ask is who do you count as belonging to your family?
C: Me, then there's my brother Jaakko and Petteri and then Dad and then Liisa.
A: Let me make some notes, Matti.
C: Jaakko, Petteri and Markku, let's put it that way.
A: Markku's your Dad, right?
C: Nmn.
A: And Liisa.
C: Nmn.
A: How old are Jaakko and Petteri?
C: Well Jaakko's the same age as me and Petteri's 15.
A: So Jaakko's what about 12.
C: Yeah, 12.
A: Yes well at least you're 12.
C: Yeah.
A: Well who's Jaakko and Petteri then?
C: Well Jaakko's my brother and then Petteri he's Liisa's child.
A: I see. So what do you call Petteri?
C: Well I say Petteri.
A: Nmn. Well if someone asks you who is he what do you say?

C: This here is my stepbrother.
A: I see, but at home he's Petteri.
C: Yeah.
A: Well what about this Liisa.
C: Well I call her Liisa.
A: Aha. Do you ever call her mother?
C: No.
A: She's Liisa.
C: Yep.
A: Well what about Jaakko and Petteri, do they say Liisa too?
C: Yeah. Petteri calls her Mum.
A: Yes she's Petteri's Mum.
C: Yeah.
A: OK. Well is this everyone who belongs to your family?
C: Well there's still my mother and then two . . . my real big brother and sister.

The child replies to the interviewer's question concerning his family members by mentioning himself, his brother, his father and two other people only by their name. Further details are inquired about these people as the interview proceeds. While the interviewer is writing down the names of the people listed, Matti explains that his father is Markku. The next elaboration comes when the interviewer asks, "Well who's Jaakko and Petteri then?" The child repeats the definition that Jaakko is his brother, while Petteri is defined through Liisa as her child. Now, the interviewer uses various questions to try and get the child to define Petteri through himself, using different questions. At home, Petteri is just Petteri, but as far as outsiders are concerned he is a stepbrother. During the early part of the interview Liisa is just Liisa; she does not need to be separately defined but is understood as the spouse of Matti's father. In connection with Petteri, Liisa is described as Petteri's mother. Towards the end of the extract the discussion reverts to Liisa and mother's status. The interviewee describes Liisa precisely as Liisa. The interviewer suggests the definition that she is the interviewee's mother, but that is rejected out of hand. Motherhood is later connected with Liisa through Petteri. At the end of the extract the interviewer makes sure that everyone has been covered: "Well is this everyone who belongs to your family?" The interviewer replies by saying that his family also includes his mother, his real big brother and sister, who live elsewhere. Mother is not mentioned in this first description by her name, but simply as mother. The same applies to big brother and sister, who instead are defined as 'real,' i.e., the interviewee's biological brother and sister.

So the family of this interviewee is made up, primarily, of people who live together: the child's father, brother, the father's new partner and her son. In addition to these people who live together, the interviewee later mentions, in response to the interviewer's specific question, his biological mother and brother and sister, who live elsewhere; they appear perhaps as appendages to the family that was first described. The interesting thing about this description is the way in which the family definition is based primarily on living together, although biological ties then emerge as the criterion for 'real' membership of the family. The higher status of biological family members is also evident in the whole description, where the interviewee clearly takes distance from his non-biological family members (see also Ritala-Koskinen, 1994).

The next family description we have is a mirror image of this account, although the interviewee describes his family on the basis of the same logics of living together and biological relationships. This is particularly interesting because the description is provided by a child living in the same household.

Extract 2

A: Yes, I would first like you to tell me erm, who belong to your family, who do you count as your family members?
C: Well erm Mum erm Liisa and then I have two brothers, they like live on their own and erm.
A: Aha.
C: And then Dad he lives with his own friend.
A: And what are your brothers called?
C: They're Timo and Lauri.
A: And how old are they?
C: They're 19 and 22.
A: Hm. So they're a bit older than you are.
C: Yeah.
A: Hm, and Dad lives with a friend.
C: Yeah.
A: And what do you call Dad's friend?
C: She's Maria.
A: Yeah. And where does she live?
C: They live not far away, like, just near the bus terminal.
A: Yes so I mean pretty close to you.
C: Pretty close.
A: In the same part of town.
C: Yeah.

A: Yeah. So what I mean there's quite a few of you living together here.
C: Yeah well there's like Jaakko and Matti and then there's Jaakko's and Matti's father Markku.
A: Let me write these down so that I can keep trace here.
C: And he's like the big brother of these boys he who's in the garage, so he doesn't live here.
A: Aha, I see. Where does he live?
C: He lives with his mother and sister and she also has a boyfriend his mother.

The interview begins with the same question concerning the family members. The child says that his family consists of mother, whom he identifies as Liisa, and two brothers, who live on their own. In addition, the child's family is described as including father, who lives with his own partner, who is later identified as Maria. In this case the child's family is described primarily on the basis of biological family relationships: the child's family consists of biological parents and siblings and it has nothing whatsoever to do with living together. As the interviewer follows up by asking, "I mean there's quite a few of you living together here," the interviewee responds by listing Jaakko, Matti and their father Markku. The boy who was fixing something in the garage is described as the big brother of "these boys" who lives somewhere else. In this description Jaakko and Matti are defined as "these boys" and Markku as Jaakko's and Matti's father; in a sense he is taking distance from them. In this connection the boys and their father are not afforded the status of family members, they are just people who live in the same household.

In contrast to the previous description, the child in this interview produces a description of his family on the basis of biological family ties rather than living together. Yet both living together and biological ties are present in both descriptions. It is noteworthy that people described by reference to both criteria nevertheless belong to the child's everyday life. Also, this pair of interviewees goes to show how children living in the same household can have completely opposite views of their family.

In the following extract I want to concentrate on one particular feature that emerges from the family description, i.e., the discussion on belonging to the family. While in the extracts above the interviewee simply listed and defined the people who they thought belonged to the family, the question is here not at all as clear-cut.

Extract 3

> A: I would first of all like to ask you that what do you think, who do you count as belonging to your family?
> C: Mm Mum and Tomi. And erm, well perhaps not like Leo yet or Mika. We still haven't like known each other very long or lived together very long.
> A: Nmn.
> C: And I don't know Mika very well either.
> A: So it's like there's like this sort of vague curtain between you is that what you're saying?
> C: Ye-eah, yes. But yes.
> A: Well since when have all of you been living together?
> C: Well I was going to confirmation classes when Mum had met Leo where was it at a friend's birthday party and since then that's how it's been.
> A: They met each other there.
> C: Right, and then they decided to move in with each other.

The child replies to the interviewer's question concerning her family members by mentioning mother and Tomi (who before the interview was introduced as the interviewee's brother). She then begins to reflect upon the question more closely by considering the issue of living together. Leo, who is defined as mother's boyfriend, and Mika, whom the interviewer learned in advance was Leo's child, live in the same household. Their membership of the child's family is not taken for granted; in fact it is as yet too early to include them in this child's family. Living together is taken implicitly as the criterion for belonging to the family, but that criterion is problemized during the course of the conversation. The reasons why they are regarded as "not yet" part of the family is that they have lived in the same household for only a relatively short period of time and they do not yet know each other very well. The interviewee is clearly outlining her own set of criteria for family membership: members of the family are people with whom you live together for a long time and whom you know well. However, in this case the interviewee is also making the assumption that Leo and Mika will at some later stage be part of her family. This extract opens up a different angle on perceiving the child's family than the two previous ones. Family membership is not only a matter of belonging or not belonging, of an either-or choice; it is a matter of how far a relationship between two persons resembles a family relationship, which is something that may change with time.

The above family descriptions by children living in stepfamily households indicate that, in practice, the family is not a clear-cut, unambiguous entity as far as children are concerned. On the contrary the child's family is a group of people which may include both biological parents and siblings and people with whom you live together. Likewise, membership of a family may change over time. Biological ties and living together are important criteria in the definition of family, but different children apply these criteria differently. For instance, living together is not in itself an automatic indication that the people concerned all belong to the child's family, but in the light of our examples it does seem that biological ties can alone explain family membership (see also Levin, 1994). Some of the other children I interviewed for this study considered including grandparents and other relatives in their definitions of family, but in the end they were all excluded. On the other hand none of the children in this material defined non-relatives living elsewhere as belonging to their family. However for many children pets were important family members (see also Levin 1994); in fact in some cases they were even regarded as more important than people.

FROM STEPFAMILY TO CLOSE RELATIONSHIPS

Research on stepfamilies has often addressed the question of whether children accept the new members of the stepfamily household or how the children adapt to the new situation. The question as to whether or not children count these new people as members of their family has been seen as a clear indication of adaptation, approval and at once of this being a close relationship in a positive sense.

In her studies of how children living in stepfamily household view their family, Gross (1986) concentrated on identifying the adults (biological parents, stepparents) whom the children counted as part of their family. On the basis of her findings she proposed the following typology: (1) retention: children count both biological parents in their family but not their stepparent; (2) substitution: children exclude from their family at least one biological parent and include at least one stepparent; (3) reduction: children include in their family less people than two biological parents; (4) augmentation: children include in their family both biological parents and at least one stepparent. In this typology Gross links up family membership with the child and the new adult having a good relationship and accordingly non-membership with them having a poor relationship.

In a sense this typology is perfectly logical, and in principle the examples I have presented above could be slotted into its categories. The problem with Gross's typology is that it is a static one and is confined to certain types of family boundaries, in which people either belong to the family or do not belong to it. This means that the very approach that Gross herself is trying to avoid (i.e., the nuclear family model) becomes predominant. This typology does not take account of the reality of children, the way in which their parents' new partners can in a sense be understood as being part of the family but at the same time as outsiders.

Levin (1994) has also studied as one part of her research the ways in which children in stepfamilies look upon and define their family. The household unit is the main element of the results. Analysing the drawings made by small children of their families, Levin divides them into three categories: (1) children who do not make a distinction between mother's and father's household; (2) children who do make a distinction between mother's and father's household and who place themselves in both; and (3) children who make a distinction between the two households and place themselves in-between them. Levin's conclusion is that the family should not be defined as having a specific form. If I look only what concerns children in Levin's whole research, I would suggest that she stops short in her analysis because while it emerges clearly from what she says that membership of a family does not necessarily say anything about the quality of the child's relationship to these people, she leaves the discussion at that and fails to elaborate.

Indeed I would argue that membership of a family is a problematic indicator of the closeness of a relationship. I will try to show this by reference to the following extract. In compiling the material for my study I proceeded in the interviews (after the children had described their families) to talk with the children about the people they had identified, trying to find out what sort of relationship they felt they had with these people. The following extract has been drawn from the same interview as extract 3. The child I interviewed earlier defined her mother's boyfriend as not being part of her family; the discussion in the following focuses on the child's relationship with this man.

Extract 4

A: Nmn. What erm, otherwise what do you think about Leo, I mean it was a new man who moved in with you.
C: Well Leo to me is different from everybody else like all her previous boyfriends and I think he's really great. Like, I like him now, I you know, we get along fine and everything's fine.
A: What makes him different from the others then?
—
A: Is there any difference in what you do together with the, what you do with Leo and what you used to do with your Mum's earlier

boyfriend?

C: Well the one who lived with us longer I didn't get on with him at all. But in-between there was this one very short relationship, it was just the same really I talked about everything with him.

A: So that at least talking is something that seems natural with Leo, but not with others.

C: Nmn, nmn, yeah, that's right.

—

A: Well what about this Leo what's he like then? I mean we said earlier that you think he's different and yet you can talk with him about things.

C: Yeah, and at least he's when erm one of my friend's father he's also dead and then erm her mother's also got these boyfriends so we often talk with her and like or we both agree that it's like not nice that it's really awful you know trying really hard to be a stepfather, but like Leo he's just being himself and like or like he's really quiet, but he's OK.

A: So you feel he's not trying too hard.

C: Yeah. And because I don't want it anyway, I mean Leo is in principle my stepfather but somehow I don't like the word at all, stepfather.

A: Nmn. If you tell a friend of yours who, who he is, do you say he's your stepfather.

C: No.

A: What do you say?

C: Leo.

A: Well what if they ask who is Leo?

C: Well that he's my mother's girlfriend, no boyfriend of course.

A: Nmn, nmn. Well what do you think is he like a father to you in your everyday life?

C: No. Or I suppose sometimes he's said he would like to be my father like really, but I don't, he's no stepfather or I, I don't really know what I'd call him. We're good friends.

A: Nmn. You never call him Dad, even by accident.

C: No, no.

The conversation on mother's boyfriend starts with the interviewer's neutral talk about Leo as a new man who has moved in the household and towards the end is drawn by the interviewee towards the issues of the nature of mother's boyfriend as a father. The interviewee speaks very consciously about Leo as Leo or as mother's boyfriend and does not want to call him her stepfather or even by accident calls him father, even though the interviewer tries to suggest these categories. In her talk about Leo's nature as father, the interviewee defines Leo as her stepfather in principle, but at the same time says she positively dislikes any attempts on his part to present himself as a father. This is further confirmed by conversations with a like-minded friend. The conversation about Leo's father-nature shows how our culture tends to associate different determinants of fatherhood to mother's boyfriends and that children have also assimilated these cultural assumptions that the interviewee is here trying to refute.

So fatherhood does not provide an adequate explanation for the relationship between the child in this example and her mother's new boyfriend. The child says this boyfriend is different from mother's earlier boyfriends; he's nice and likeable. She "gets along fine" with him, he's "OK"; he also doesn't try too hard. Towards the end of the extract, to conclude the discussion on fatherhood, the relationship is crystallized in the expression, "we're good friends." So the relationship between the child and mother's boyfriend is explained on the basis of friendship rather than fatherhood or familyhood.

This example goes to show that membership of a family, for children, is not automatically the most significant criterion as far as relationships between members of stepfamily household are concerned. Their parents' new partners who live in the same household but who are not regarded as family members, may be extremely important adults in the child's everyday life. This means that significant others may remain unidentified if the definition of who are important to children is based on family memberships. On the other hand it is possible for the child to describe the new partner of his or her parent as belonging to the family even though their relationship is not a close one. In this case family membership as such comes to explain the nature of relationships. Clearly then, the family does not provide a very meaningful analytical tool where we are concerned with the relationship of children with new adults in the stepfamily household. I would argue that a deeper understanding of the life of children living in stepfamily households could be reached by taking distance from the family membership and by focusing instead on 'close relationships.'

DISCUSSION

I started this paper by pointing at the central place that children occupy in discussion of stepfamilies. I then proceeded to criticize earlier research on stepfamilies from a sociology of childhood point of view and to show how mainstream research into stepfamilies has been adult-oriented, problem-oriented and anchored to the nuclear family ideology. I set out to test whether the child perspective can open up fruitful new angles on the stepfamily.

In my empirical analysis I concentrated on the descriptions of children living in stepfamily households of their families and on how they defined their relationship to the new adults in the household. The first result of my investigation is that the definitions presented of the stepfamily in earlier research do not explain the family of children living in stepfamily households. The family of these children, in the descriptions they produce themselves, is often wider than the "nuclear stepfamily." On the other hand, living together does not qualify as an automatic criterion for family membership.

Although the adult's new family is not necessarily the child's family, the setting up of a stepfamily nonetheless means new significant relationships to children. These relationships are often explained by reference to the concepts of family and parenthood. The second result of my investigation is that as children describe their relationships to the new people in the stepfamily household, their membership of the child's family or place as a new father or stepfather does not in itself explain the nature of these relationships. The relationship between the child and his mother's new boyfriend, in the example quoted above, was not explained by family or parenthood, but by friendship. No doubt there might be other non-family determinants for the new relationships in stepfamily household. Instead of the family I am suggesting 'close relationships' as a top concept when analysing the nature of relationships children have with the members of stepfamily household.

My experiment would seem to suggest then that the sociology of childhood critique of research on the stepfamily is in the right: that a child perspective onto the stepfamily can indeed provide interesting new insights. The family may help the researcher with forming preliminary hunches, and it may be useful as an everyday concept, but for analytical purposes it is clearly inadequate. In conclusion I would like to raise the question as to what kind of consequences these new, non-family-based interpretations may have to understanding the stepfamily. Are the various definitions presented by children of their families and their close relationships an indication that the stepfamily needs to be approached from a completely different vantage-point than that suggested by the tradition of family research? Could this add new dimensions to the traditional problem-oriented interpretations of the stepfamily? There are more questions than can be answered here. However, it should at least be clear that in order to better understand the stepfamily we need to adopt new, different perspectives.

NOTE

1. All names appearing in the excerpts have been changed. Also any details that might give clues of the identity of the people concerned have been omitted, without allowing this to affect the content of the conversation. A refers to the adult interviewer and C to the child interviewee.

REFERENCES

Alanen, L. (1992). *Modern childhood? Exploring the 'child question' in sociology.* (Publication series A. Research reports 50.) Jyväskylä, Finland: Institute for Educational Research.
Coleman, M. & Ganong, L. H. (1990). Remarriage and stepfamily research in the 1980's–Increased interest in an old family form. *Journal of Marriage and the Family, 52,* 925-940.
Esses, L. & Campbell, R. (1984). Challenges in researching the remarried. *Family Relations, 33,* 415-424.
Ganong, L. H. & Coleman, M. (1994). *Remarried family relationships.* Thousand Oaks: Sage.
Ganong, L. H. & Coleman, M. (1987). Effects of parental remarriage on children: An updated comparison of theories, methods, and findings from clinical and empirical research. In K. Pasley & M. Ihinger-Tallman (Eds.), *Remarriage & stepparenting. Current research and theory* (pp. 94-140). New York: Guilford Press.
Gittins, D. (1993). *The family in question. Changing households & familiar ideologies* (2nd ed.). Basingstoke: Macmillan.
Gross, P. (1986). Defining post-divorce remarriage families: A typology based on the subjective perceptions of children. *Journal of Divorce, 10,* 205-217.
Holstein, J. A. & Gubrium, J. F. (1995). *The active interview.* (Qualitative research methods, volume 37.) Thousand Oaks: Sage.
Ihinger-Tallman, M. & Pasley, K. (1989). *Remarriage.* (Family studies text series 7.) Newbury Park: Sage.
Krähenbühl, V., Jellouschek, H., Kohaus-Jellouschek, M. & Weber, R. (1986). Uusperheet: rakenne, kehitys, terapia. In Perhe ja ammattiauttaja–perhekeskeisen työn oheisaineisto (pp. 87-101). [Stepfamilies: structure, development and professionals–supplementary reading for family-centred work.] *Sosiaalihallituksen julkaisuja 10/1986.* Helsinki, Finland: Sosiaalihallitus.
Liljeström, R. & Kollind, A-K. (1990). *Kärleksliv och föräldraskap.* [Love relations and parenthood.] Stockholm, Sweden: Carlssons.
Levin, I. (1994). *Stefamilien–variasjon og mangfold.* [Stepfamily–variation and manifold.] Oslo, Norway: Aventura.
Marsiglio, W. (1992). Stepfathers with minor children living at home. Parenting perceptions and relationship quality. *Journal of Family Issues, 13,* 195-214.
Pasley, K. (1987). Family boundary ambiguity: perceptions of adult stepfamily

members. In K. Pasley & M. Ihinger-Tallman (Eds.), *Remarriage & stepparenting. Current research and theory* (pp. 206-224). New York: Guilford Press.

Pasley, K. & Ihinger-Tallman, M. (1989). Boundary ambiguity in remarriage: Does ambiguity differentiate degree of marital adjustment and integration? *Family Relations, 38,* 46-52.

Prout, A. & James, A. (1990). A New paradigm for the sociology of childhood? Provenance, promise and problems. In A. James & A. Prout (Eds.), *Constructing and reconstructing childhood: Contemporary issues in the sociological study of childhood* (pp. 7-34). London: Falmer Press.

Qvortrup, J. (1994). Childhood matters: An introduction. In J. Qvortrup, M. Bardy, G. Sgritta & H. Wintersberger (Eds.), *Childhood matters. Social theory, practice and politics* (pp. 1-23). European Centre Vienna. Aldershot: Avebury.

Qvortrup J., Bardy M., Sgritta, G. & Wintersberger, H. (Eds.). *Childhood matters. Social theory, practice and politics.* European Centre Vienna. Aldershot: Avebury.

Ritala-Koskinen, A. (1993). *Onko uusperheestä perheeksi? Tutkimus uusperheen kulttuurisesta kuvasta suomalaisten naisten- ja perhelehtien konstruoimana.* [Could stepfamily be counted as a family? Research of the cultural representation of stepfamily constructed by the Finnish women's and family magazines.] (Reports from the Family Research Unit, No. 4.) Jyväskylä, Finland: University of Jyväskylä

Santrock, J. W. & Sitterle, K. A. (1987). Parent-child relationships in stepmother families. In K. Pasley & M. Ihinger-Tallman (Eds.), *Remarriage & stepparenting. Current research and theory* (pp. 273-299). New York: Guilford Press.

Schwartz, R. (1984). *Gift igen–Hvad med bønene.* [Married again–what about children?] Bibliotek for socialpædagoger og socialarbejdere. Køenhavn, Denmark: Gyldendal.

Walker, K. N. & Messinger, L. (1979). Remarriage after divorce: dissolutions and reconstruction of family boundaries. *Family Process, 18,* 185-192.

Stepfamilies from Siblings' Perspectives

Anne C. Bernstein

Despite an encouraging proliferation in the study of stepfamilies in the past twenty-five years, the relationship between the children of a parent's earlier partnership and the children born to a remarriage remains an under-explored area of investigation. Most of the literature investigates relationships that include at least one of the adults in the stepfamily (Pasley & Ihinger-Tallman, 1987). While a few studies assess the impact of the birth of a mutual child on the stepparent-stepchild relationship, (Ganong & Coleman, 1988; Ambert, 1986; Santrock & Sitterle, 1987); the nature of the relationship among the children is not discussed. While Duberman (1975) looked at the child subsystem, the quality of the halfsibling bond was not examined and ratings were based exclusively on adult reports of their children and stepchildren. Children's accounts of their own experience have only recently been introduced into the literature (Ganong & Coleman, 1993; Beer, 1991; Bernstein, 1989a). This relative lack of information about sibling relationships in stepfamilies is, however, congruent with the relative neglect in the study of siblings in general (Bank and Kahn, 1982).

It is difficult to accurately assess the number of children being raised in stepfamilies with halfsiblings. Based on the Current Population Report of the 1990 U.S. Census, it can be estimated that 1.6 million households consist of remarried couples and minor children from both past and pres-

---

Anne C. Bernstein is Professor, The Wright Institute, Berkeley, CA. Address correspondence to the author at 2728 Durant Avenue, Berkeley, CA 94704.

[Haworth co-indexing entry note]: "Stepfamilies from Siblings' Perspectives." Bernstein, Anne C. Co-published simultaneously in *Marriage & Family Review* (The Haworth Press, Inc.) Vol. 26, No. 1/2, 1997, pp. 153-175; and: *Stepfamilies: History, Research, and Policy* (ed: Irene Levin and Marvin B. Sussman) The Haworth Press, Inc., 1997, pp. 153-175. Single or multiple copies of this article are available for a fee from The Haworth Document Delivery Service [1-800-342-9678, 9:00 a.m. - 5:00 p.m. (EST). E-mail address: getinfo@haworth.com].

153

ent partners.[1] This figure excludes children from nonmarital relationships, minor children whose halfsiblings are currently over 18 years and halfsiblings who do not share a household, i.e., children born to the remarriage of a non-custodial father.

METHOD

The participants in this study were members of stepfamilies in which there were children from both past and present marriages, whether or not all the children were in full-time residence. Included were stepmother families, stepfather families, and complex stepfamilies (in which both adults were stepparents). An attempt was made to interview all family members over the age of three years. Interviews followed a semi-structured open-ended format designed for each the following family roles: parent, stepparent, stepchild, and mutual child. Respondents were interviewed individually, in most instances in their own homes.

Respondents included 155 people, representing 55 remarried households. In 25 of the families, between four and seven family members participated, and, in an additional six families, there were either two or three informants. Some individuals represent more than one remarried household, e.g., a mother/stepmother is interviewed both about her current family and the family of origin in which she was a mutual child, or when a child is an informant about the stepfamilies formed by both his mother's and father's remarriages. Data was collected on 26 stepmother families, 19 stepfather families, and 10 complex stepfamilies.

Participants were recruited through advertisements in general-interest publications and by using a modified "snowball" technique. and represented a wide range of SES and occupational groups. Most of the families interviewed were Caucasian and native born, but they include ethnic and racial minorities and the foreign-born. Most were Catholics, Protestants or Jews.

The group studied, however diverse, is not representative of all stepfamilies that include a mutual child. The families interviewed are clearly atypical in the high degree of post-divorce paternal involvement. Nearly 20 percent of the families had joint physical custody of the children of the

---

1. This is based on an earlier estimate by Cherlin and McCarthy (1985) of 1.3 million households, using data from the Current Population Survey of the 1980 U.S. Census. *The Statistical Abstract of the U.S.* (1994) indicates that the number of households that include either half or stepsiblings has increased 21.4% in the decade between 1980 and 1990.

first marriage. Most of the remainder were mother-custody families, but there were a few custodial fathers. While 20 percent of the remarried mothers whose children's father is alive received little or no support, and these children saw their fathers erratically if at all, all of the noncustodial fathers interviewed saw their children regularly.

Interviews were taped and transcribed in full. Transcripts were then analyzed using an amalgam model of qualitative data analysis corresponding to Weiss's (1994) description: Interviews were coded, developing concepts and categories which formed the basis for an "excerpt file," that was then sorted and resorted, creating supra- and subcategories. "Local integration," organizing and synthesizing the observations by summarizing a particular excerpt file and its coding, generated "minitheories" that were then supported or qualified by data from additional interviews, within and between comparison groups (e.g., family role or family type). "Inclusive integration," the final stage of this process, developed the framework, or "coherent story line," that combined the local integrations.

Because the nature of the sample precludes generalizations about the incidence or prevalence of particular patterns, results are described qualitatively, in accord with the aim of the study to describe the domain of relevant variables as a preliminary to later hypothesis testing.

RESULTS AND DISCUSSION

Qualitative analysis of the interview data indicates that the nature and quality of halfsibling relationships is contingent on a matrix of factors, including the stage of stepfamily development at the time of the mutual child's birth; the age and developmental issues confronting the older child(ren) at that time; the age interval between halfsiblings; the number of children in each full sibling cohort; the gender of the mutual parent/stepparent; whether it was a simple (stepmother or stepfather) or a complex stepfamily; the custody arrangement, and the amount of conflict in interhousehold relationships, both between the stepfamily household and the older children's other parent, and with caretaking grandparents.

STAGES OF STEPFAMILY DEVELOPMENT

Children's ease or difficulty in accommodating to the birth of a mutual child and the ensuing quality of the halfsibling relationship is associated with the stage of the remarriage at the time of the birth, using Papernow's

(1994) model of stepfamily development. If a new baby arrives in *Early Remarriage*, as in more than half of the families interviewed and for the majority of stepfamilies (Griffith, Koo, & Suchindran, 1984), members have not yet had time to accommodate to one change before confronting another. Children's wishful fantasies of parental reunion impede accepting a stepparent as a family member. A mutual child can now be perceived as a usurper, or replacement, especially when the older children are not full-time members of the household.

The *Middle Stages* of remarriage, when the stepparent mobilizes to bring about changes that lead to his inclusion and the recognition of his authority as an adult family member, can be a pretty tumultuous time, as the stepfamily struggles to forge a culture shared by all members, excluding none. As in *Early Remarriage*, the challenge of incorporating a mutual child can delay or even impede accomplishing this task, as stepparents, diverted by the instant gratification of taking care of their own infants, retreat from the more difficult challenge of becoming "intimate outsiders" to their stepchildren. Only in *Established Remarriage*, when intimacy and authenticity in step relationships have been achieved, is the mutual child received much as any other younger sibling would be: a mixed blessing who introduces an unknown into the family equation.

BIRTH ORDER AND AGE INTERVALS

Only and youngest children were more likely than middle and oldest children to feel more conflicted, more concerned about having to share a parent with an infant, and more invested in their role as "the baby." Middle children seemed to be more welcoming of the baby who will deprive a long-standing rival of his competitive edge, and oldest children were unchallenged in their position as firstborn.

Some age differences emerge as clearly more propitious than others for halfsibling relationships. The older children's immediate reception of the baby is only the first step in the formation of a relationship that continues to be shaped by experiences they share over the years. If we think of each child as starting out along parallel developmental tracks at different times, where they are with respect to each other at any given point also presents both possibilities and limitations.

While some intervals between children can be benign with reasonable reliability and others more predictably risky, such generalizations cannot be true for all pairs of children. Some 'developmental couplings' work particularly well at one point in time, only to become more difficult later.

The Preschool Child. Because most children in first-married families have a sibling within five years, the child who is five or under when a halfsibling is born comes closest to the situation of any child whose parents have another baby. Most parents and stepparents of children this close in age describe their later competition as "garden variety sibling rivalry," and the children voice the standard complaints of older children who resent tag-along younger siblings, who feel shunted aside, protesting that being given lesser rights and privileges is "unfair."

Primary School Age Children. Despite their greater understanding of family roles and realities, children between six and ten are more likely than their younger brothers and sisters to suffer a conflict in loyalty when a divorce remains contentious. Wallerstein and Kelly (1980) found that children in this age group are especially vulnerable to the stress of a custodial parent's remarriage. Similarly, in this study all of the children who had the most difficult time adjusting to a mutual child were between six and ten at the time of the birth.

Everything else being equal, the relationship between halfsiblings continues to be most ambivalent when they are separated by between six and ten years. Children this much older than their halfsiblings are the most vociferous in their complaints that they are discriminated against when they compare how they are treated with what happens with the mutual child. Nine years older than his first halfbrother, Jeremy, like a lot of first children, feels that his Mom has learned how to bring up children from her mistakes with him:

> Jeremy: My Mom sometimes gives in to my younger brothers and rags on me all the time. The younger kids are, I don't know, her precious pearls or something. She doesn't lock me in the cellar, but she kind of indulges them in everything. I guess 'cause they're younger.

Julia, the boys' mother, observes that Jeremy has never had an easy time with the son she and his stepfather had when he was eight, "they're still the worst two fighters in the family."

While six to nine-year-olds seem to have the hardest time accepting an infant, with girls readier for a halfsibling sooner than boys, the disruption of the mutual child's birth pales before what is to come when the mutual child becomes a preschooler just as this stepchild reaches preadolescence. Even children pleased about the birth complain about the "brat age" two to four years later. With an infant, the older child can tell that the younger has to be treated as in a different category than he himself is. When the little one begins to walk, talk, and want to play with things that still interest the older child, older children tend to treat the little ones more as peers than their development warrants. Children six to ten years older than their halfsiblings challenge them to grasp beyond their reach, tackling activities that may be too difficult or too dangerous in an attempt to keep up. Unlike still older children with more developmental savvy, they refuse to indulge the immaturity of the little ones, insisting that all players abide by the same rules.

In thinking back about the assets and debits of their parent having had more children, as they get to be teenagers, stepchildren tend to have the standard set of complaints of older siblings: parents having to divide their attention, activities constrained by the needs of the younger children, and the little ones tagging along when they are not wanted. The main difference between preteen and teen complaints about halfsiblings, as opposed to brothers and sisters who share both parents, is that halfsiblings, because their very existence can be attributed to an undesired event, a parent's divorce/remarriage, are more often objects of blame for dissatisfactions. One woman remembered her childhood family:

> Maybe the boys had nothing to do with it but I didn't get enough support and counseling and guidance from my parents when I felt I most needed it. At the time I blamed it on their being all tied up with the little guys. Maybe they just didn't think that was something that was important or necessary.

Preteen Years. Ten-to-thirteen year olds were in many ways the most receptive of all stepchildren to the prospect of a mutual child. If the developmental tasks of the previous period, a focus on acquiring new skills and moving from a family-centered life to more activities with peers, have been successfully mastered, the preteen is ready not to be "the baby." This group were the most delighted with their halfsiblings as infants, showing off pictures and regaling friends with anecdotes of baby accomplishments, enjoying the diversion of baby antics and taking pride in their ability to nurture.

Readier now to feel "grown up," only and youngest children, especially, like "the feeling of being the older person." At this age many of the older children were described by parents as "baby-happy" cuddlers and caretakers. Part of the attraction of babies for this age group may be the opportunity they provide to nurture and, in doing so, be nurtured: a source of physical closeness that gives comfort even as it saves face, because the older child is the giver of care rather than its acknowledged recipient.

The pleasures of taking care of infants and the feelings of pride in changed status can occur independent of the stage of the remarriage. When the baby quickly follows the recoupling, however, these pleasures are mitigated by having to accommodate to too much too soon. "There wouldn't have been so much jealousy with a full-blooded sister," Nathaniel said of the halfsister born when he was eleven, "because you wouldn't feel like your mother was taken." But further inquiry revealed that the person who he really felt had taken his mother was not his baby sister, but her father. Accepting a stepparent takes longer for children in this age group than for their younger brothers and sisters, and the rapid arrival of another child can feel like a further encroachment on access to the parent.

One strategy that preteens whose mothers and stepfathers have a baby in early remarriage use to counter their fear that the "family" is forming in another corner is to vie with their stepparent as to who is to be the third in the triangle whose fixed points are mother and baby. Eliot remembers how his stepson George, then ten, would fight with him about who got to hold the baby. "I would say, 'It's my first baby.' And he would say, 'It's my sister.' " Eliot recognized that by taking the baby from him and giving her to his mother, George was "forming the family with Maggie and the baby, because there was this relationship with me that was not quite the same as it was to the new baby." The mutual child, as the only consanguinal relative of all stepfamily members, belongs to everyone. But when stepparent and stepchild don't yet feel like they belong to each other, getting the baby in his corner can feel like a question of being 'in' or 'out' for both, but especially for the stepchild who already fears displacement. The older child knows that the baby legitimates the stepparent's role in the family in a new way. Wooing the baby is his insurance against extrusion. Preteens in middle stage and established remarriages also seek to fill their needs for love and closeness by becoming special caregivers to halfsiblings, but they tend to feel less "needy" than those for whom the sequence of changes has been rapid.

Their veneration by the little ones goes a long way toward enhancing the sense of competence and maturity of those a decade or so older. "I'm like a God to her," said one eleven-year-old about her toddler sister, "and she's a little munchkin." Although feeling their station in life is impressive to the much younger mutual child is an advantage for the ten to thirteen-year-old, there is also the attraction of being able to regress without shame. Susan describes how her son Carl and his friends, at twelve, thought two-year-old Eric was "a kick." "They'd get down on the floor and play with him, and played with his toys when he wasn't even there. It gave them a chance to be little kids again. He allowed everybody to have some fun."

Perhaps, too, stepchildren who are fourteen or older by the time the mutual child reaches 'the brat age' are less affected by the younger one's willfulness in that they have become more involved with what the rest of the world can provide, and are striving not for a greater share of parental attention, but for more latitude to make their own decisions. Even those who have been most involved with the mutual child as infants and tod-dlers, become not less caring, but less occupied with their halfsiblings as they enter their middle teens.

Even when they are happy to pursue their own interests in a world of their peers, teenagers who see the younger children, rather than their own evolving desires, as the reason for their getting less attention from their parents, can come to resent the early childhood focus in the remarried family with young mutual children. Yet by the time the mutual child enters school, the children ten to thirteen years older are in their middle to late teens. For most families, this is a time of decreasing rivalry and, even when they share a household, decreasing contact.

Teenagers. Older teens, more involved in separating from the family than jealously guarding their place in it, are, even in early remarriage, less apt to feel displaced by a new baby than are their younger brothers and sisters. More aware of the pragmatics of childcare and family finances, and more focussed on themselves, teenagers receive the news of another child with a view to what it's going to mean in their own day-to-day lives. Those who already have a brother or sister are less excited than those who don't, and the more children there are, the more these youngsters become concerned about lack of space, lack of money, and lack of a parent's time. Although loving both his halfsister and halfbrother, one man was clear that the strains on family life were more exacting in his father's remarried family with six children than his mother's having a third child with her new husband. For teenagers discomforted by thinking of parents as sexual just as they begin to explore their own sexuality, pregnancy and birth are obvious reminders that their parent is having a sexual life. When Sol told his teenage son Dan about his wife's pregnancy, Dan scoffed "I thought you were too old for that stuff."

While most of the teenagers disclaimed any suggestion that their rela-tionship with a halfsibling had anything to do with how they feel about the parent and stepparent who are that child's mother and father, conflict between teenager and the adults strongly influences how much contact there will be between the new child and the older ones. Adolescents who are not getting along in a custodial remarried families tend to leave, either to live with their other biological parent, or to emancipate prematurely (White and Booth, 1985). And teenagers, who have more control of their schedules, spend less time with a noncustodial parent when conflict per-sists. In either case, contact between halfsiblings is minimized.

When fourteen or more years divide a parent's first set of children from the children of remarriage, both sides of the divide feel the gulf as hard to bridge. For the mutual child, these very much older halfsiblings can begin to feel like "parent-brothers, more on the brother side," as one sixteen-year-old put it. And speaking of his mother's son, born when he was seventeen, Paul said:

I could be his father. I never fight with him. There's a big enough gap there so that most of that strife and jealousy, resentment or whatever, just isn't there. I mostly take care of the kids when I go over. It's not like being an uncle, I'm more a part of the family than that.

Yet even when there are a great many years separating the children of each of a parent's marriages, both sets of children can feel enriched by the more complex generational texture of the family.

SUMMARY OF AGE OF STEPCHILD/STAGE OR REMARRIAGE FINDINGS

Figure 1 presents a summary of how the age of the older child and the length of the remarriage combine to make the timing of the mutual child's birth either more auspicious (+) or more problematic (−).

FIGURE 1. Stage of Stepfamily Development at Mutual Child's Birth

	Early Remarriage 0-2 years	Middle Remarriage 3-5 years	Established Remarriage 4-7 years
A G E			
2-5 y.o.	Varied*	+ + + (infrequent)	+ + + + (rare)
o f			
6-10 y.o.	− − − difficult	Varied	+
C H I			
L 10-13 y.o.	−	+ +	+ + +
D			
14 + y.o.	− −	+	+ +

* The chart refers to "Varied" outcomes when it is difficult to collapse the range of either ages or marital duration to come up with a consistent prediction. For example, a three-year-old whose parent has been remarried for two years, or a six-year-old in a stepfamily that has been together for five years when a halfsibling is born, would have a relatively smooth time adjusting to this change in family membership. In contrast, the five-year-old in a brand new stepfamily, or the nine-year-old whose parent has another child only three years after remarrying can be expected to have a more difficult time of it. As a rule, the younger the child and the longer the remarriage, the better the predicted outcome.

All of the more conflictual halfsibling relationships occurred between a first mutual child and the six to nine-year-old stepchild who had been his parents' youngest child. Boys in this age group seemed to have a particularly hard time welcoming a new child, and conflict was most intense when both of the children so spaced are male. This is in keeping with earlier reports that girls show more positive behavior toward siblings than do boys (Anderson & Rice, 1992) and that sibling pairs that include a male exhibit more negative behavior (Hetherington, 1988; MacKinnon, 1989).

The age of a stepchild when a mutual child is born is inextricably linked to when in her developmental history other important family transitions occurred. For example, the child whose stepfamily has a baby by the time she is five has typically experienced her own parents' separation as an infant or toddler and has little if any memory of pre-separation family life. Acquiring a stepparent while very young facilitates her acceptance of another nurturing adult (Mills, 1988). As a result, the added stresses of stepfamily life will not be a major aggravation of the expectable difficulties that children in this age group in nuclear families have in accommodating to the birth of a sibling. At the other end of the adjustment continuum, what may make this transition more difficult for six to nine-year-olds is not their present age, but rather how old they were when they experienced parental death, divorce and remarriage. Of the boys who had the hardest time feeling secure in their own place in the stepfamily and accepting the baby, most also had experienced parental death or divorce when they were four to five-years-old, pointing to a developmental vulnerability that predisposes to difficulties with later transitions.

It is important to note that two children of the same age, same custody arrangement, same gender and even same family can have markedly different responses to a parent and stepparent having a child together. For example, the child who is closest to and most like her mother, may be less close to her stepmother than is the sister who is more attached to father and also less close to their halfbrother.

THE NUMBER OF CHILDREN FROM EACH MARRIAGE

Another important factor in how well a mutual child and a child of a parent's prior marriage get along is how many of each there are in the stepfamily. When there is only one of each, and they are each other's only brother or sister–full, step or half–attachment seems to be greater than if one or the other is a member of a group of full siblings. When two or more children share the same two parents, the center of gravity in the stepfamily will vary depending on how many offspring each marriage has produced.

Everything else being equal, the character of the stepfamily is shaped by where the heft of the children falls: a stepfamily where the majority of the children are the issue of the remarriage will feel very different to all its members than when a single mutual child is born into a family with a group of stepchildren.

The child with two remarried parents, for example, may feel closer to the halfsibling who is an only mutual child of one parent's remarriage than she does to either of the two children born to the other parent's new stepfamily. A fifteen-year-old, for example, reports of her father's daughter:

> She's really important. I don't have any full sisters, so she's the oldest any-related sister that I have, and the one I try to be the closest to. She's my sister and my friend. We share a room, so we have to be. We fight a lot like sisters of the same age, even though I'm six years older, and then we don't. We share each other's secrets.

In contrast, her mother's children form an intense unit, at least in her mind. She's glad there's a big gap between her and the two more closely spaced children.

> I think it would be really hard if I was one or two years older than Eva (her mother's next oldest child). Because I would want to be part of that crew, and in a way I wouldn't be, because they're a full sister and brother. So it's really good that I'm older than them, because instead of being the scapegoat, instead of being pushed out with 'Daddy's our father and he's not your father,' I'm pushed up and looked up to.

Her biggest, indeed her only complaint, is that her parents' divorce deprived her of the chance to have "another kid my age that has both my parents.'" The stepchild who rotates between households reports that a full sibling as travelling companion lessens the strain of navigating these transitions. According to one woman:

> It would have been much more difficult if I'd been an only child. I always felt that whatever else happens, I have my full sister, my sister who's close to me in age. If I felt threatened by my father having another child, I also knew that Bonnie and I had each other.

Divide and conquer can become the order of the day when there are two children from one marriage and only one from the other, regardless of which union had the additional child. When there is a single mutual child, the older children rival each other for the affection of the baby and enlist him in their struggles with one another. While the alliance of the two older children generally remains primary, it can be unbalanced when one is closer than the other to the mutual child, who may show amazing precocity in playing off one stepchild against the other by bestowing his affection unequally. When the older two engage in battle, the mutual child can be enlisted in the ranks, usually of the more powerful sibling. Several families reported that one of the older children would get the little one to hit his rival for him, call him names, or otherwise act as his agent in sibling rivalry. Over the years alliances can shift, so that the stepchild who was closest to the mutual child as an infant or toddler may not be the one who she spends the most time with even a few years later.

When the tables are turned, and it is the stepchild who is the only child of both his parents, the divide and conquer strategy is deployed with greater sophistication. The mother of a son from an earlier marriage and two daughters with her present husband remembers:

> For a long time, George would verbally trash Aileen and want to do things with Ellen. He was also an instigator of fights between the two of them. This was pretty equal, he didn't always side with Ellen. If one of them had something, for example, he'd say to the other one "don't you want it?"

The psychological warfare of the older child can be harder for parents to witness. It seems more deliberate and can be more finely aimed at points of greatest vulnerability. While alliances are hardly stable, the most prevalent pattern is for the stepchild to favor the younger of the two mutual children, seeing himself as her protector in her rivalry with her immediate senior. One woman remembers being very mothering towards the younger of her mother's daughters with her stepfather:

> I had to protect her from her older sister. But it wasn't really fair, it was more child abuse, because I was five years older. Whereas she was always very willing to throw the little one off the balcony, I was always very eager to catch the little one and beat up the older one, who was always ripping my dolls to shreds, and generally having a hard time of it, between the oppressive older sister and the too adorable younger sister.

When there are two or more children from both marriages, the tendency is for alliances to be made principally within full sibling groups, especially when they are not co-resident. All the children then have someone whose family circumstances mirror their own: someone who shares both their parents, is near in age, and who grows up under similar circumstances. Finding companions right at hand, children are less likely to cross the divide and become intimate with those who sometimes seem to dwell in a completely different world, especially when half a generation or more may separate them.

Regardless of the eventual numbers on each side of the marital divide, it is the two children on the frontier of the remarried family, the youngest stepchild and the oldest mutual child, whose relationship most plays out stepfamily issues. It is the youngest stepchild, who, as baby of the original family, is most vulnerable to feeling displaced by the first mutual child. And it is the first mutual child who, in finding a place for herself in the family, compares herself to her halfsibling and discovers that their differing relationships with the adults in the house color what it means to be siblings. It is the first of the mutual children who is most concerned about his halfsiblings' acceptance of him, and it is he who is most resentful at feeling abandoned by the older children. Second or later mutual children have, in their older full sibling, a layer of psychological insulation between themselves and stepfamily tensions.

GENDER OF THE STEPPARENT

All of the children who lived primarily with their mothers think that their relationship with a halfsibling depends on the gender of the shared parent. "For me, the family has always been Mom and all her kids," remarked one twenty-year-old, whose mother had two children by her first marriage, and a third with her second husband. Like the inner city kids who told their teacher that their mother's children were their "real" sisters and brothers "because you come out of the same stomach," children who share both a mother and a household feel more connected than those who have intermittent contact with their fathers. The biological connection during pregnancy can be impressive evidence of maternal primacy. While this is still more characteristic of younger children, a teenage boy speculates that he would be closer to a child born of his mother:

> When I think of Owen, I think I'm his brother, but I think of him as more Amelia's than my Dad's. My Dad didn't have him inside him for nine months. So I think he'd be more of a brother if my Mom had him, not necessarily that I'd like him any more or less.

Despite thinking they'd feel closer to their mother's child, none of the children whose fathers had had a mutual child expressed any desire for their mothers to follow suit. A seven-year-old girl was glad that her mother was not the one to give her a halfsibling, because "she would be holding it all the time." Another girl, at fourteen, concurs, saying that she "probably wouldn't like it as much, because I'd probably have to be around them all the time, you know, and take care of them when I wanted to go out or something."

In contrast, most of the children whose mothers and fathers have both had children in remarriage report that it makes little difference if it is Mommy's or Daddy's baby: what matters to them is the custody arrangement and how they feel about their stepparent. All agreed that sharing a household makes them feel closer to a new child. When the older children are in joint custody and have spent substantial periods of time in each home, most take the position, with sixteen-year-old Carl: "It's the same. They're part of the family. They're happy to see you when you come, and sad when you go. It's pretty easy to get to know them again."

In thinking about the advantages and disadvantages of a mother or a father having more children, how the older children get along with the stepparent who is the mutual child's other parent weighs heavily in the balance. One fifteen-year-old girl said:

> I think it has everything to do with whether you like who they're remarried to because if you don't like the person, then I think you'll resent your parent. Especially if they have a kid, because then this little kid is tied to you by the person that you don't even like. Other than that, I can't really see any difference, because if you think about it, Eleanor is my second mother and Arthur is my second father. So basically I don't think my Dad's kids are less my sisters and brother than my Mom's daughter.

Both of these teenagers are typical in this regard of those who have come to know and trust their stepparents over many years before the baby is born. In remarriages that have children earlier on, there is a trend, most clearly observable when both parents bring children to the stepfamily, for all the children, from all the marriages, to see stepmothers as more likely to play favorites than stepfathers. In preferring that their mothers not become repeat parents, even though they may like that their fathers already have, children may be generalizing from their experience with their stepmothers, expecting a similar loss in time, energy and emotional investment from their mothers were they, too, to have more children in a new marriage.

GENDER OF CHILDREN

Similarity of temperament and weathering crises together can forge bonds that outweigh biological ties in creating special intimacies between halfsiblings. Gender, too, can be a basis for solidarity. While parents are almost unanimous in anticipating that having a mutual child of the same sex will be more "threatening" to an older stepchild, most children downplay this consideration. Whether or not they are young enough to envision the baby as an eventual playmate, children generally prefer that the baby be as much like them as possible. Being the same sex then becomes a basis for shared activities and interests, despite the distance in years. Although now closer to her twelve-year-old brother, for instance, a ten-year-old girl thinks that as adults she and her baby halfsister will be more likely to be friends, having lunch together and sharing interests, while her brother, as a male, will be thinking and doing things that will feel foreign to her.

Almost all of the most difficult halfsibling relationships observed occurred between boys and their baby brothers. Same-sex siblings are both more likely to become close and more fiercely competitive. Aggression is not equal to lack of closeness (Dunn, 1985). Little brothers who try to be just like their big brothers, little sisters who want to play with their sister's friends, can be tag-along pests, yet the greater likelihood of shared interests is an opportunity for closeness.

CUSTODY

As noted above, sharing a household is an important determinant of the quality of halfsibling relationships. Even when opportunities for contact are rare, however, both children can find great meaning in their connection, attaching significance to their relatedness that surpasses the opportunities they are given to explore it.

"Visiting" stepchildren get a lot more excited adoration, the benefits of being an older sibling, without as much of the aggravation of accommodating to the demands of a much younger child. Because the mutual child is frequently on "good behavior" with the stepchildren who are exciting disrupters of routine, the "the brat age" is less frequently mentioned by the older children who don't have to live with a preschooler on a daily or weekly basis.

From the point of view of the mutual child, the challenge is to make sense of sibling relationships that are intermittent (Bernstein, 1988): 'Who are these big kids?' 'What are their claims to my Dad?' and, 'How important am I to them?' At four, for example, Erica was working at coming to terms with the annual visits of her halfsisters, ten and fifteen, who live in a distant state. Her mother described a conversation with Erica about the older girls' impending arrival:

> We were driving to school the day before they were coming, and she said 'I want to spend a day just with my Dad alone.' I said, 'Okay, but you're going to have to wait until Polly and Nila leave.' 'Well,' she said, 'I don't want to share him,' and she started crying, 'I don't want them to come.' I said, 'I'm not saying you shouldn't feel that way. You can. I just want you to try to understand how hard it is for Daddy not seeing Polly and Nila, and how hard it is for them not to see Daddy. It's only a week, and you get to be with him all the time.' My husband said it was going to dissipate as soon as they came, which it did. She couldn't care less about being with him right now.

Several of the mutual children whose halfsiblings never shared a household with them volunteered that had they not known of the focus of the study they would not have included them in their family drawings. When Andrea, then seventeen, was asked how she thinks it would have been different with her halfsiblings, thirteen and fifteen years her senior, had they lived together, her answer represents others in her circumstance:

> It would have been more difficult. We would have been going through the 'terrible twos' when they were going through adolescence, but I also think that we would have gotten to be closer than we are.

With joint custody, children have both enough familiarity to feel like siblings and enough distance to keep alive the issues of territoriality. For the child re-entering the home, there is the sense of having missed out on what has been happening without her, wondering if she has been missed, and thinking about what she's missing in the other home. For the child who lives there all the time, sharing space and toys and parents whom he's had all to himself takes getting used to, once again.

Parents, who generally agree that it's "rough" when the children haven't seen each other for awhile, observe that bickering seems to be concentrated around arrivals and departures. And while adults tend to think that there would be less friction between the children if the older children were in residence full time and didn't have to navigate often stormy transitions, children disagree. Not understanding that more time together would change the nature as well as the quantity of the contact, they assume that they would fight more if they were around each other more. Sixteen-year-old Larry, talking about three-year-old Owen, said:

I'd probably think of him as more of a brother than as a halfbrother if I lived here all the time. It's probably better that we're not, because when they're more your brother, you fight and get annoyed. So, I think it's good that we're just here half the time.

When remarriages end in divorce, the relationship among halfsiblings will depend on how the adults handle separation. When they share a mother and the mother retains primary custody, statistically the norm, the children will be more 'in the same boat' than ever. Because they have a relationship with their single parent that is structurally the same for all, halfsiblings who are all their mother's children, with no stepparent in the home, can be more like 'regular' brothers and sisters than they were before the divorce, since none of them has a differential tie to an adult within the household. "I never think of Andy as a half-brother," said twenty-year-old Selena, referring to the child of her mother's second marriage that ended more than ten years before, "the family has always been Mom and her kids."

When they share a father, the range of possibilities is greater. At one end of the spectrum is one man, who after his father's second divorce saw his halfbrother again only once, at the old man's funeral, and doubts whether he would recognize him if he saw him on the street. In contrast, some fathers actively strive to keep their children connected. Richard, separated from the mother of his five-year-old son, has worked out a schedule designed so that the two days his sixteen-year-old daughter is with him include at least one day when his little boy is there, too. "They're still very attached to each other," he believes, "but she, at sixteen, is less domestic."

When the remarriage, too, ends in divorce, as 50 percent are reported to do (Glick, 1984), seeing a halfsibling go through what they themselves have experienced can create a bond between children from previous and later marriages. "I feel real connected with her," said one woman of the halfsister born when she was sixteen. When the younger girl was five, their father again moved on, abandoning his younger daughter as he had left his older children seven years before.

I feel she's more than just a stranger. I'd like to get to know her better. I have this fantasy that I can understand her, and she can understand me in a way that's probably very unique. Because he did almost exactly the same thing to her that he did to me.

Telling of the time that she surprised the younger girl, then twelve, by appearing at their doorstep and announcing that she was a sister whose existence until that time had been a secret, she continued:

Within the first twenty-four hours, she danced for me, and we played sports. And my Dad's big things were music and sports. He had encouraged her along those lines as well. I have this idea that she and I share this kind of special parenting, that we had real early. In that sense, I'm glad she's there.

There are no negatives, despite her early apprehension that her stepmother's baby would be a girl who would replace her; instead, their shared experience of abandonment is a basis for solidarity.

He hasn't been there for her either, so I can't really say that she's taken him away, or in any way diminished what I've gotten from him. When I was getting ready to leave, my sister just got hysterical. I was trying to comfort her, and she just was crying and saying "Everybody leaves me, everybody always leaves me." And I knew exactly what she was talking about.

COMPLEX STEPFAMILIES

In stepfamilies to which both parents bring children from previous marriages, the mutual child can be an integrating factor for the two sets of stepsiblings who are all his halfsiblings (Duberman, 1973). And it is in these "yours, mine and ours" stepfamilies that the mutual child, while occasioning some shifts in how the family is organized, seems least disruptive. As Visher and Visher (1978) have noted, both adults have already had the experience of being a parent and a stepparent, and all the children involved have already had to deal with sharing a parent with other children. The children have already gotten used to having a stepparent who is another child's biological parent and a biological parent who is another child's stepparent. While they may still envy the child who is equally related to both adults, they are more likely to see differences as balancing out in the long run.

In the short run, however, they can vie with one another as to who is more important to the baby. Even sharing a household, stepsiblings can compete for who can lay more of a claim to insider status with the new arrival. Sometimes the competition occurs along gender lines, with girls claiming greater expertise in baby care, grabbing the baby from brothers' and stepbrothers' arms with an accusation "You'll cause mental retardation if you hold him that way."

When one set of halfsiblings are not in residence it is the absentee siblings who are more exciting to the mutual child. This can be a source of friction between the mutual child and the halfsibling who lives with him all the time. When Julia married Ben, her eight-year-old son, Josh, lived with them and his eight-year-old, Jeremy, joined them every other weekend. A year later, Ira was born. Julia tells how the triangle between the three boys created this pattern:

> Jeremy had a nice relationship with Ira. He didn't have to live with him all the time. Ira idolized Jeremy and punished Josh. If Josh refused to do something with Ira, Ira would say 'When Jeremy comes this weekend . . . ,' or when Jeremy came, he'd only want to sit next to Jeremy. Poor Josh felt awful, and then he'd beat up on Ira for the next two weeks. So, by the time Jeremy came back, he'd be ready to fawn all over Jeremy. So Jeremy got, every other weekend, this baby brother who idolized him. It was something to look forward to at our house.

The more Ira moved toward Jeremy, favoring him over Josh, the more Josh made daily life unpleasant for Ira, and, completing the cycle, the readier Ira was to wear his heart on his sleeve for the big brother who was seldom there, keeping the battle raging on the home front. Nonetheless, Jeremy and Josh did become closer to each other than they had been before Ira was born, playing with him together and then going off to pursue eight-year-old fun. Because stepsiblings are usually closer in age than any of them is to the mutual child, age may supersede blood ties in making peers more interesting to each other than a much younger child is to either of them.

BINUCLEAR FAMILY RELATIONS

Ahrons and Rodgers (1987) developed the concept of the "binuclear family" to describe the linked households created when parents divorce. Because events in one household have emotional, practical, and financial implications for the other household, a child's reception and later relationship with a halfsibling is mediated by the response of the parent they do not share to an ex-spouse having a child in remarriage.

Like the remarriage itself, the birth of a child to an ex-spouse and his new partner can be an important marker in the post-divorce relationship between the parents of the older children, introducing greater distance and further punctuating the transition from married couple to separate co-parents. As the "nail in the coffin" of hopes for marital reconciliation, the birth of a mutual child can rekindle feelings of loss in an ex-spouse. Ahrons (1987) notes, and this study confirms, that this transition is generally more unsettling to ex-wives than to ex-husbands.

In many ways, not all of them overt, children get a message from their other parent as to how they should respond to a mutual child in the stepfamily household. One five-year-old, for example, came back from her mother's house, to report: "My Mother says he's not my brother, he's my halfbrother." Another mother's response was to criticize the father who postponed a regularly scheduled visit with the older children in order to be present at the baby's birth, while a third insisted that the older children never mention the existence of the mutual child. These attempts to attenuate relationship are not lost on the child. While the mutual parent and stepparent typically encourage halfsiblings to feel as connected as possible, the child's other parent can communicate that closeness in intra-stepfamily relations is a betrayal of the parent who lives elsewhere.

Having a significant stake in the sibling bond, such as for the only child who has long yearned for a sibling, or being cognitively sophisticated enough to make distinctions between his own response and that of his parent, can help bring about a workable integration. In any case, who the children can be to one another is subject to the triangulating influence of the other parent or, in some cases, other significant parental figure such as a caretaking grandparent.

The influence of a parent outside the household on halfsibling relations can be positive as well as negative. While some ex-wives were singled out for the strongest criticism in how they responded to the birth of a child to their ex-husband's remarriage, other ex-wives received the strongest praise for generously welcoming a mutual child and encouraging their children's acceptance and affection toward a halfsibling. Ex-husbands, by contrast, were seen as more neutral in their responses to changes in the stepfamily created by an ex-wife's remarriage.

Mutual children, often intensely curious about their older siblings' hidden life in another household, are eager to know more about their halfsibling's other parent. They ask to go inside when the older children are being picked up and dropped off during custody rotations and engage in friendly conversation when given the opportunity. Personal contact between a child's nonshared parent and his halfsibling seems to help each feel more connected to the children who are so important to both.

CONCLUSION

A qualitative analysis of interview data from 155 subjects from 55 stepfamilies reveals that relationships between halfsiblings are influenced by a myriad of factors involving all members of the binuclear family system. The permutations of variables affecting the nature and quality of halfsibling relations are numerous and complex, yet some clear trends emerge.

The stage of stepfamily development at the time of the birth of a mutual child demonstrates a clear positive association with the quality of relationships between halfsiblings. The age and birth order of the stepchild interacts with the time elapsed since the remarriage to modify the strength of this association. Certain developmental "couplings" are clearly more favorable than others, both at the time of the birth and throughout the childhood of all the children.

The number of children from each marriage also informs the quality of halfsibling relationships. When there is only one child from each of two marriages, the children are likely to be closer, given similar opportunities for contact, than when either or both have other, full siblings. When there are two children from one marriage and only one from the other, "divide and conquer" strategies are used by the child who is the only child of both his parents to gain entry to the sibling system formed among the full siblings. While alliances shift, in part in response to developmental changes in all the children, the full sibling bond usually maintains primacy.

Halfsiblings who share a mother tend to feel closer and more related than those who share a father, in part because of the traditional custody arrangement that means that the former will spend significantly more time together than the latter. The traditional division of parental labor also means that children who share a mother will be more likely to see themselves as equally nurtured than will paternal halfsiblings. Halfsiblings of the same gender tend to interact more, resulting in both more conflict and more closeness. When both adults in the stepfamily are both parents and stepparents, halfsibling relationships and stepsibling relationships are mutually influential, with the amount of opportunity for contact limiting how each set of stepchildren will interact with the mutual children and with each other. The interdependence of the linked binuclear family system consisting of the households formed by divorced parents is further demonstrated by the significant impact, whether positive or negative, that the stepchild's other parent has on the halfsibling relationship between his child and the mutual child of an ex-spouse's remarriage.

REFERENCES

Ahrons, C. R. & Rodgers, R. H. (1987). *Divorced Families: A Mutildisciplinary Developmental View*. New York: W. W. Norton.

Ambert, A. (1986). Being a Stepparent: Live-in and Visiting Step children. *Journal of Marriage and the Family, 48*, 795-804.

Anderson, E. R. & Rice, A. M. (1992) Sibling relationships during remarriage. *Monographs of the Society for Research in Child Development, 57*(2-3), 149-177.

Bank, S. P. and Kahn, M. D. (1982). *The Sibling Bond*. New York: Basic Books.

Bernstein, A. C. (1994). "Women in Stepfamilies: the Fairy Godmother, the Wicked Witch, and Cinderella Reconstructed." In Mirkin, Marcia Pravder (Ed.) *Women in Context: Toward A Feminist Reconstruction of Psychotherapy* New York: Guilford Press.

Bernstein, A. C. (1990). *Yours, Mine, and Ours: How Families Change When Remarried Parents Have a Child Together*. New York: W. W. Norton.

Bernstein, A. C. (1988). Unraveling the tangles: children's understanding of stepfamily kinship. In Beer, W. R. (ed.) *Relative Strangers: Studies of Stepfamily Processes*. New York: Rowman and Littlefield.

Beer, W. R. (1988). Dynamics of Stepsibling and Half-Sibling Relations, in W. R. Beer, op. cit.

Cherlin, A. & McCarthy, J. (1985). "Remarried couple households: Data from the June 1980 Current Population Survey. *Journal of Marriage and the Family, 47*, 23-30.

Duberman, L. (1973). Step-kin relationships. *Journal of Marriage and the Family, 35*, 283-292.

Duberman, L. (1975). *The Reconstituted Family: A Study of Remarried Couples and Their Children*. Chicago: Nelson-Hall.

Dunn, J. (1985). *Sisters and Brothers: The Developing Child*. Cambridge, MA: Harvard University Press.

Furstenberg, F. F., Nord, C.W., Peterson, J. L. & Zill, N. (1981). The life course of children of divorce: marital disruption and parental contact. *American Sociological Review, 48*, 656-668.

Furstenberg, F. F. & Spanier, G.B. (1984). *Recycling the Family: Remarriage After Divorce*. Beverly Hills, CA: Sage.

Ganong, L. H. & Coleman, M. (1993). An exploratory study of stepsibling relationships. *Journal of Divorce and Remarriage, 19* 125-141.

Glick, P. C. (1984). Marriage, divorce and living arrangements: Prospective Changes. *Journal of Family Issues, 5*, 7-26.

Griffith, J. D., Koo, H. P. Suchindran, C. M. (1984). Childlessness and Marital Stability in Remarriages. *Journal of Marriage and the Family. 46*, 577-585.

Hetherington, E. M., Arnett, J.D., & Hollier, E. A. (1988). Adjustment of parents and children to remarriage. In S. A. Wolchik & P. Karoly (Eds.), *Children of Divorce* (pp. 67-107), New York: Gardner.

MacKinnon, C. (1989). An observational investigation of sibling interactions in married and divorced families. *Developmental Psychology, 25*:36-44.

Mills, D. M. (1988) Stepfamilies in context, in W. R. Beer, op. cit.

Nichols, W. C. (1986). Sibling subsystem therapy in reorganizing families. *Journal of Divorce*, 9(3), 13-31.

Papernow, P. (1993). *Becoming a Stepfamily: Patterns of Development in Remarried Families*. San Francisco: Jossey-Bass.

Pasley, K. & Ihinger-Tallman, M. (Eds.) (1987). *Remarriage and Stepparenting: Current Research and Theory*. New York: Guilford.

Santrock, J. W., & Sitterle, K. A. (1987). Parent-Child Relationships in Step-mother Families. In Pasley, K. & Ihinger-Tallman, M. (Eds.), op. cit., 273-299.

Visher, E. B. & Visher, J. S. (1978). *Stepfamilies: A Guide to Working with Stepparents and Stepchildren*. New York: Brunner/Mazel.

Wallerstein, J. S. & Kelly. J. B. (1980). *Surviving the Breakup: How Children and Parents Cope With Divorce*. New York: Basic Books.

Weiss, R.S. (1994). *Learning from Strangers: The Art and Method of Qualitative Interview Studies*. New York: The Free Press.

White, L. K. & Booth, A. (1985). "The Quality and Stability of Remarriages: The Role of Stepchildren, *American Sociological Review*, 50, 689-698.

White, L. K. & Riedmann, A. (1992). When the Brady Bunch grows up: Step-/half- and fullsibling relationships in adulthood. *Journal of Marriage and the Family*, 54(1), 197-208.

The Stepparent Role
from a Gender Perspective

Irene Levin

When a boy of seven insisted on telling me that She, the father's wife was NOT his stepmother, because she was not evil, he was relating to a myth most probably not knowing where it came from. He might not have heard the fairy tales himself, but the myth lives its own life.

Fairy tales have portrayed the role of the stepmother in an unambiguous and negative way. The Chinese were the first to introduce Cinderella around the ninth century (Yutang, 1942). Today fairy tales with an evil stepmother are known all around the world. The world has changed, but we still have fairy tales reinforcing the myth.

We relate to the myth as a truth that does not need to be investigated. It is as if we *know* what stepmothers are: evil and jealous. Stepchildren on the other hand, are helpless victims. Schulman (1972) challenges this:

> . . . both are caught in a situation that forces them to act in a certain way because of circumstances and a competitor against whom nobody can win. (Schulman, 1972, p. 135)

Interestingly, the myth is associated with the remarried female, in spite of the fact that both women and men have remarried throughout history in the Western world. Therefore both genders could have contributed to a myth. This is, however, not the case. The expression "the evil stepfather" is not used (Johnsen, 1990). The negative potential in relationships

---

Irene Levin is Associate Professor in the Graduate School of Social Work and Social Research at Oslo College, Oslo, Norway.

[Haworth co-indexing entry note]: "The Stepparent Role from a Gender Perspective." Levin, Irene. Co-published simultaneously in *Marriage & Family Review* (The Haworth Press, Inc.) Vol. 26, No. 1/2, 1997, pp. 177-190; and: *Stepfamilies: History, Research, and Policy* (ed: Irene Levin and Marvin B. Sussman) The Haworth Press, Inc., 1997, pp. 177-190. Single or multiple copies of this article are available for a fee from The Haworth Document Delivery Service [1-800-342-9678, 9:00 a.m. - 5:00 p.m. (EST). E-mail address: getinfo@haworth.com].

177

between stepfathers and children is revealed by the statistics on child abuse, but does not result in any myths.

Our knowledge about stepmothers from research is rather sparse. On the other hand stepfathers have been studied extensively (Bohannan, 1975; Wilson, Zurcher, McAdams, & Curtis, 1975; Rallings, 1976; Oshman & Manosevitz, 1976; Stern, 1978; Orleans, Palisi, & Caddell, 1989).

One reason for this may be that there are many more stepfathers. Women still most often obtain custody over children. This might also explain why there is so little research on stepmothers.

Research has mostly compared stepmothers to stepfathers, with the latter being the norm. The emphasis has been on differences between the two roles, how the stepparents or parents experience the stepparent role. The answer here is more or less unanimous: It is easier to be a stepfather than a stepmother (Bernard, 1956; Kompara, 1980; Ambert, 1986; Duberman, 1975; Fast & Cain, 1966; Visher & Visher, 1979).

Some disagree, e.g., Vemers, Coleman, Ganong, and Cooper, (1989). Their metastudy of 34 projects showed that remarried men are only a little more satisfied than remarried women. Stepfathers and stepmothers do not differ much, they are content and discontent to much the same extent.

We have a situation where stepfathers have attracted researchers' attention while stepmothers have not, even though their role has been portrayed as more difficult.

One explanation that has been put forward is the female role (Schulman, 1972). Hobart and Brown (1988) claim that since females are more sensitive, they feel conflicts more easily. That is why she has a tougher time than he. Minnich (1989) suggests that stepmothers are a symbol of the loss of the good mother. Stepmothers reactivate a vulnerability we would all rather forget, the unforeseen in our lives. Goldner (1985) is more pragmatic and mentions the one-down position when it comes to the woman's economic situation.

Looking through the literature one gets a strong feeling that gender is of importance, but in what way seems more uncertain. Often the explanations seem like critiques of women as if the difficulties were rooted in female characteristics or are their fault.

All these explanations together with the myth are rooted in our society's view of women, mirroring a contempt of women that can persist without being challenged by research.

Most research uses gender as an explanation of why relationships can be difficult, but not as a starting point for understanding. How come this situation persists and what meaning does it have? I agree with Scott (1986) who emphasizes that we have to move away from only speculating about causes and over to *meaning*. Gender often seems as an answer, an *end* and not a *beginning*. The question is rather: what are the dynamics and the processes involved?

METHOD

In a qualitative study of the social reality of the stepfamily the roles of stepparents and stepchildren have been studied. Stepfamily is here defined as a social group consisting of at least one adult-child unit and a partner-unit where one of the partners is not a parent to all of the children in the household. The adult relationship is established after at least one partner has been married or cohabiting before. The stepfamily has lived together for a period of two to eight years.

All members of the stepfamily household of five years and more are interviewed separately. In all sixty-three persons are interviewed in Oslo, Norway. The sample is recruited using a strategic sampling procedure, from a non-clinical population with the assistance of Health Centers.[1]

The method used differs with respect to adults (Levin, 1989 a and b, 1990, 1993) and children (Levin, 1989 a and b, 1993). The procedure is threefold, starting with a question of who belongs to the informant's family (the family list). Then the informant is asked to place his or her family on a large sheet of paper symbolized by circular and triangular pieces of paper according to perceived closeness and distance to the informant (the family map). Last comes a verbal interview. For the children the family map is replaced by a family drawing.

RESULTS

The results of this study show that there are many kinds of behavior in stepfamilies. Accordingly the stepparent role can differ depending on what kind of notion they have of their new family life. The whole sample has been analyzed according to patterns of behavior. Three patterns occur: to *reconstruct, to wait-and-see and to innovate*. (See Levin's article in this volume.)

The *reconstructors* have a notion of reconstructing a family similar to the one they had before, except that the partner is a different person. They

---

1. In Norway it is usual to use Health Centres in view of their regular medical check-ups of children up to school-age.

do not think of their new family as of any different type or structure than the former one. For them the nuclear family is both a model for how to relate and also an ideal. The sooner they reach the goal of reconstruction, the better. The stepparent tries to copy the role of a parent in the nuclear family, i.e., to become a *father or mother substitute*.

The second pattern emerges when stepparents try out different types of behavior in order to find the best suited for them. The *wait-and-see'ers* go slowly and learn from experience. They are pragmatic and consider their new marriage or cohabitation as something they have to use time in order to develop. Time is therefore here a positive resource, but for the reconstructors something they try to abbreviate in order to reach their goal as soon as possible. The nuclear family is not an ideal that they try to copy, but might become a model if that suits them. Here the stepparent's role resembles that of a *friend and an adult person*.

The third pattern is very clear about how they *do not* want their new marriage to be. The *innovators* want to create something new; anything but the nuclear family will be acceptable for them. The nuclear family is an anti-model. They have tried that type of relationship without success. In their first marriage they started with very close relationships and ended far apart. Now they want to start from a position of distance and see what happens. The stepparent role is more like that of an *uncle or an aunt*.

The analysis shows that there are many sorts of behavior in a stepfamily. Now I will continue to focus on the stepparent role, and show what emerges when gender is included in the analysis.

THE RECONSTRUCTORS

Berit and Bert start their relationship as reconstructors. Bert has previously been married and has custody of his two boys, Birger (12) and Bjarne (7). Berit has never been married, or cohabiting nor has she any children of her own.

Before Bert and Berit met, Bert lived alone with his two boys for a couple of years. He was accustomed to being a single parent—an experience resembling that of many women. In our culture, however, this type of experience is somewhat unusual for a man. Berit enjoyed having a partner actively involved with children, making food and participating in housework activities.

Berit's and Bert's daily life looked very much like that of an "ordinary" family except for Bert being more active than other males in their group. In that respect they had succeeded in the idea of the reconstructors in that the roles of the traditional nuclear family are models and also ideals.

However, "at the end of the day" as Bert expresses it, if an extreme situation should occur, he will support his children before his wife. Berit on her side, thinks that if necessary she can leave Bert and the children, a situation rather different than if she had been their "real" mother. These possible extreme situations are not usually in their minds at all.

When they first moved in together they were faced with a rather complex situation: First, the children had experienced a lot of turbulence in connection with custody and visiting arrangements because of their mother's chronic illness. The situation had been unstable for a while and one could perhaps describe them as "nervous." Second, they were going to move into an old house that needed quite a lot of repair and renovation.

The question was: What would be the best way for Berit and Bert to establish their household? Many solutions could be considered. Since the children had experienced a lot of turbulence, they now needed continuity that might have resulted in the father continuing as their sole caretaker. Another possibility could be that the female adult would be the one to take care of the children and do the housework.

Berit had no children and was not especially interested in children. She was not against children, by no means, but they had not been her first priority.

As a *step*-parent she need have nothing to do with her partner's children. A stepparent is "only" married to the children's parent. The prefix "step" indicates a distance compared to the parental role. To be a "step"– is in principle the same for men and women. The role of a stepparent is technically gender neutral.

"IT JUST HAPPENED"

At the time of the interview, however, Berit had been home from work for three years and had just started working. The solution she and Bert arrived at, was never discussed. "It just happened," Berit says. The result was a given. The issue of who should stay home from work in order to establish the household was never negotiated explicitly. That does not mean that there were no negotiations[2] between the two of them. These were however never explicated. They were tacit solutions as indicated in the sentence "it just happened."

---

2. Negotiations here does not, as in daily usage, indicate a situation where the parties take explicit positions. I follow Haavind (1987) and Andenæs (1989) and use it as an analytic concept which includes both stated positions, and tacit issues and behaviour that serve as premises for the explicit positions.

By acting more or less like all other households, their solution became an indication that they were on the right track. This is one reason why the question about who should stay home from work with the children was never asked. They handled the situation in the same way as nearly all other households and in that respect resembled an "ordinary" family. They also behaved according to their idea of family life, trying to reconstruct a traditional nuclear family.

That "it just happened" without any explicit negotiations is rather interesting. How come Berit was the one to be at home and not working, despite not being the mother of the children? Was her position as the partner of the father defining enough for her to be able to take that responsibility? And how come Bert was the one to work outside the house without any further negotiations?

If Berit had been the mother of the children and been the one to be home from work for three years, this arrangement would not arouse any curiosity. But Berit and Bert had different points of departure since only one of them was the parent of the children. Bert was the father and Berit was *not* the mother, but partner of the children's father. Bert was an active and responsible man. He was "a modern man" with great understanding of women's rights, also Berit's.

During the interview he said many times that he felt Berit was a "fantastic" woman. It was as if Berit showed her love through housework and he through "love talk." With this aim, behavior that served their arrangement was reinforced. By taking care of the household, Bert sees a way that Berit can show that she really accepts him and the children: "It's a way she can show her love to us," he says. Now he can travel for his business without guilt feelings. This is quite different from the situation when he was a single father. This division of responsibility fits their ideal of family: a mother, a father and children.

Berit disliked Bert's expressions of love. She insisted on looking upon herself as an evil stepmother. On some occasions when she quarrelled with the children, she underlined her position by smearing food in their faces.

Since "it just happened," their solution could be regarded as obvious and not necessary to discuss. This tacit agreement was a result of an underlying premise, and led to behavior reinforcing traditional gender roles in the nuclear family. Both enacted cultural agreements.

In nearly all relationships, "it just happens" reflects a typical cultural pattern in our society. In this way femininity and masculinity are reproduced right through new ideologies about relationships.

Berit and Bert do not themselves see that their way of reacting has anything to do with gender. On the contrary, both emphasize that Bert is an extraordinary father and different from other men. Housework adds to both identities: however, with different meaning. If she is doing housework, she is supporting her femininity, while he is becoming an extraordinary man, a modern man.

The agreement that Berit was supposed to be at home for three years, was nothing Bert had pushed Berit into. Both agreed that he had done this of free will and in the interests of both. This is part of the ideology of modern femininity and masculinity: Life consists of free choices, with the same possibilities existing for both genders.

Identity is here understood as something that is created in relation to others (Andenæs, 1989). Gender is created and maintained by the partners and helps them create their identity. Berit is confirmed and confirms herself as a woman at the same time as she is creating her identity as "a good mother." Similarly Bert is confirmed and confirms himself as a man.

If Berit and Bert had negotiated explicitly, the result would not necessarily have been any different. The premise is there as an assumption basic to their behavior and in their strong desire to create a "family."

After a while Berit experienced that the role of mother, did not suit her. She felt she was living the life of another woman. Therefore she wanted to become a different type of stepmother—more like a friend. At the same time she is also an adult. Therefore, after a while Berit and Bert changed their project and behaved more according to another pattern: wait-and-see. The stepparent role then became flexible and distant. According to the wait-and-see'ers parents are responsible for their children. In this case Bert had to contribute more.

IF THE STEPPARENT IS A MAN?

Peter and Paula are reconstructors like Berit and Bert, but in this case the male is the stepparent. Will the stepparent role here be any different?

Already when Peter and Paula first moved in together, Peter saw Paula's children as his own. He prepared food for them, played football, put them to bed and in all respects behaved as a father does towards his children.

Since he was an outsider, he could also evaluate his new wife's situation more clearly. Paula had been alone with her children for some years when Peter moved in. Peter explained to her that she had to be ready for her children when they wanted her. Since Paula often worked at home at night, she also worked with the children around her. Peter disliked what he observed. He suggested she change her relationship with the children; to be more available for them. Paula agreed, since she also had been tired and overwhelmed with guilt feelings. Moreover, by her working less, the household as a whole also "earned" less. Therefore Peter suggested that he could work more to compensate for the shortfall of income.

As with Berit and Bert, Paula and Peter did not discuss explicitly their decisions about gender roles. "It just happened." For Peter and Paula the tacit premises for negotiations led to Paula as a mother spending more time with her children, while stepfather Peter continued his career. As with Berit and Bert, Berit as the stepmother takes care of the children and the father continues his career.

Some will focus on income, who earns most? And so let the answer decide who is to work and who is to stay at home. There are many other questions to be asked. Who has the most agreeable place? For whom is it most important to work? I am not discussing these questions since Berit and Bert's solution "just happened." Bert earned more than Berit and Peter and Paula earned the same. In both cases the men were the ones to work more and the females worked less in spite of them being parent or stepparent. My point is that this is not only connected to the question of money.

WAIT-AND-SEE'ERS

Ruth and Roger are wait-and-see'ers. Roger had two children from a previous marriage, Roy (19) and Rita (14). Roy stayed with his father and Rita lived with her mother, but visited her father's household frequently.

According to the wait-and-see'ers, the children's parents are parents even though they are not married any more. The stepparent's role reminds more of that of a friend, but also an adult person. Both Roy and Rita thought of Ruth as an "extra" person. "I have one mother and do not need another one," Roy says. He was comfortable with the role Ruth had, especially since she was introduced into his life very gradually. For Rita the situation was a little different. She was very skeptical towards Ruth in the beginning. Since Ruth had taken her father from her mother, she felt he could also take him from herself. And she was also afraid that her "liking" of Ruth could diminish her love for her mother. After her half brother was born, the situation changed, and Rita also felt that Ruth was a friend: "You can't talk with your mother about boys and things like that."

Ruth experiences her role as being partially a "friend" and also an adult as a dilemma. On the one hand she has a lot to do with the children on a daily basis. She makes the food and washes their clothes. She helps them also with homework. She feels she is giving them "mom-service." On the other hand she is not invited to join when the children are performing at school at Christmas. Then she is not a mom any more.

The idea of the children being the parents' responsibility is insufficient when it comes to caring. Then Ruth's being a *woman* is more important than her not being the mother of the children. The fact that she is not the mother of the children, is only important in certain situations. Ruth herself is not the one to make that relevant.

The tacit negotiations between Ruth and Roger make Ruth a *step*mother with emphasis on first syllable. Moreover Ruth is a step*mother* with emphasis on the last part when it comes to the traditional housework.

The question arises also with the wait-and-see'ers; what about a stepfather, would he experience the same dilemmas as Ruth? Inger and Ivar are also wait-and-see'ers, but there the man is the stepparent. Inger's two boys lived with her when Ivar moved in. The boys, Ib and Ingar are also in their teens.

When Ivar moved in with Inger it was clearly as Inger's partner and not as a parent for the children. Both of the boys announced that he was not going to decide anything that had to do with them. The stepfather could give his opinion on questions about the apartment since he was a partial owner of that. When it comes to their lives, they felt he was an outsider.

Ib and Ingar were very clear about this, even though it had nothing to do with them liking Ivar or not. Both of them really liked him and respected him as well. They were rather happy with the living arrangement. Ib, the oldest, expresses that he really respects his mother for the way Ivar was introduced. She used time for the process and moved very slowly. He has never experienced that his mother has preferred her partner to him, which has been the case for several of his friends where: "the guy came first." Therefore he feels he has not lost someone, but rather gained another person. That is what counts for him.

The stepfather, Ivar, experiences his role as a stepfather as "to be himself." For him that is to not to become "a salesman that absolutely needs to get inside the door to sell his products." Very early he told the boys that he did not want to "be a stepfather, but a friend." Inger was happy that her new partner respects her boys "because they can only have one father," she says.

In one respect the three males have something in common and that is when it comes to doing housework. All three agree that they should have done more to "help" Inger, but "too bad," that is not happening. Inger on her side is very satisfied with her new partner and his contribution to the housework. She had not expected him to do anything at all with the house or the boys.

If we look at Ivar's role as a stepfather and Ruth's role as a stepmother, Ruth is getting into several dilemmas concerning caring and housework.

This is not happening for Ivar in the same way. Everything he does is better than Inger has expected from the beginning. The level of expectations is different because one relates to different standards, the cultural expression of femininity and masculinity. For Ivar the more distant role of the stepfather, which he metaphorically calls "a salesman," is not in any conflicts with the role of the father that also can be rather distant. Ruth, on the other hand, feels she is giving "mom-service." The distance in the stepparent role is relevant for Ruth occasionally. It is a discrepancy between the stepparent role and the female role. What has to do with house and home in a way "conquers" the more distant step-role and becomes decisive for the behavior.

WHAT ABOUT THE INNOVATORS?

Eric and Esther are especially interesting in this study. When they first moved in together they decided to create an alternative way of living, anything *but* the nuclear family model. With their experience the nuclear family does not work, they now wanted to make a family different from that one.

Eric sees the new marriage as a possibility to focus on his work. For many years he made the child his first priority. Now he is in a new phase of his life. His daughter lives with her mother, while Esther has her two children living with her. They are trying to create a new lifestyle. In discussions about who is going to do what, gender is not an issue.

The solution is not to create anything similar to the traditional nuclear family. For them this means that the responsibility for children lies much on each of them. Esther has two children living with her and Eric has one visiting. The apartment they divided into three: one section for Esther and one for Eric. The kitchen and the living room serve as common areas. Eric works at home so his office is in his part. Esther's children stay in her part of the house. During the day Esther and Eric live totally separate lives. In the evenings they meet in the living room and share experiences. Eric is very supportive of Esther, gives her tea and listens to her.

At first Eric and Esther also slept in each part of the apartment. After a short while they felt that was too much of a distance, and started to use Esther's bedroom as their common bedroom.

She sees her role as a single mother. In her former marriage she and her husband argued a lot about who to do what. This was their major conflict. However, contrary to her former marriage, she now knows what to expect. She feels relieved not to have all the discussions about sharing duties.

With the equality policy and ideology it was difficult for Esther to have a husband who was not willing to participate and take his share as her former husband did. The quarrels about who should do what were really tough. She also felt that the long quarrels were a major reason for the marital breakup.

In a way Esther became responsible for what her former husband had done. In periods where equity is stressed, it is the responsibility of the woman to get an egalitarian man. If she does not succeed in that, she has to take responsibility for the defeat and keep it for herself (Andenæs, 1989). If she and Eric were to manage, she had to choose between her feminist ideology and the project of succeeding the second time. Some might say that she did not have a real choice since the expenses would be too high. It looks as if the way they arranged it was partly her free choice. Modern women have to choose what other women had to accept (Borchgrevink, 1987). The modern woman knows that at the end, the responsibility still stays with her.

THE GENDERED STEPPARENT

Whether mothers or stepmothers, whether representing same or different patterns, the women's roles are very similar. Irrespectively, they take care of children and housework. The *step*mother role does not expect her to do such tasks. On the contrary; the stepparent role expects a certain distance, the female role the opposite. Between the two roles there is a dilemma. One cannot be distant and close at the same time. The result of this dilemma is that the female role "conquers" the stepparent role and becomes decisive for what to do and not. Since the female role and the mother's role overlap, her being a woman becomes the strongest in the stepparent role and not her being the partner of the parent.

Also for Bert, Peter, Ivar, Roger and Eric their roles are more or less the same when it comes to caring and housework. Peter is, however, a more active stepfather than Ivar and Eric, but the differences are not that great between them and the fathers Roger and Bert. In that respect they resemble the women. On the other hand, the stepparent role expects distance and so does the male's role. For the women there is a contradiction between the roles of stepparent and woman. For the men there are no similar contradictions. The male role and the father's role are more or less overlapping as is the female role and the mother's role. The male role is determinant of his behavior regardless of whether he is a father or a stepfather.

GENDER AS MAKING OF IDENTITY

With the project the partners give the impression that they are acting together as man and woman working towards a common goal. Another way to look at it is that they constitute each other's possibilities and limitations (Haavind, 1987). Bert does not calculate when he gives Berit compliments. He expresses how he experiences the situation. At the same time his behavior maintains ideas about how to be a man and how to be a woman, how identity is created and maintained. Gender is here a basic category in understanding women, men and power relations, as Scott (1986) expresses it.

Through their priorities, they have presupposed each other (Andenæs, 1989). Negotiations, explicit or implicit, are therefore not only about who should do what in the household, but about giving each other a mutual confirmation of identity. "Who you are as I see you and whom I am as you see me" (Andenæs, 1989, p. 688). The gender roles create and are recreated continuously in relations between women and men. When Bert is defining Berit's housework as her way of showing them love, he is defining her as a woman. He relates love to housework activities; what she does for him and the children. He adds to this by giving her expressions of love as a legitimization of the housework. She is getting a compliment that at the same time confirms her femininity. By putting her own work aside and by not questioning his, she is confirming him as a man. He is performing an honorable masculine role and can support them all.

Women are socialized to see the world from another person's perspective, while men use themselves as the basis. This gives meaning in the relationships and has consequences for the result. Women arrange themselves in the best interest of everyone. They can overlook their own personal expenses. Without such an understanding their behavior and the negotiations will be experienced as absurd by an outsider. They are, however, creating identity and strategies as the basis of a lasting couple relationship.

CONCLUDING REMARKS

This study shows that women's roles, regardless of whether they are mothers or stepmothers, are more or less the same. Women do the housework and take care of relationships anyway. This is done if she is the mother of the children, as well as if she is just the partner of the parent. The stepmother's role does not imply that she should wash clothes and dishes, but the traditional female role does. The step role suggests a certain distance–the female role the opposite. There is a dilemma in the combination of step and female roles. One cannot be distant and close at the same time. The dilemma is "solved" by the female role "conquering" the step role and becoming decisive for what to do or not to do. The stepmother lives in this dilemma. Why is *she* going to wash the clothes of *his* children or make the food? Her being the partner of the parent seems more important than him being the father of the children. Gender is here stronger than consanguinity. This dilemma does not show up for males. Their step role suggests distance and so does the male role. The men are not put in any dilemmas since both roles go in the same direction. Also for the men the gender is decisive of what to do. Only here there is no dilemma between the two roles. They are both distant.

REFERENCES

Ambert, A. M. (1986). Being a Stepparent: Live-in and Visiting Stepchildren. *Journal of Marriage and the Family, 48*, 795-804.

Andenæs, A. (1989). Identitet og sosial endring (Identity and social change). *Tidsskrift for Norsk Psykologforening, 26*, 603-615, 683-695.

Bernard, J. (1956). *Remarriage.* New York: Russell & Russell.

Bohannan, P. (1975). Stepfathers and the mental health of their children (Final report). LaJolla, CA: Western Behavioral Science Institute.

Borchgrevink, T. (1987). *Kjærlighetens diktatur* (The dictatorship of love). (magistergradsavhandling ved). Universitetet i Oslo: Institutt for Sosialantropologi.

Duberman, L. (1975). *The Reconstituted Family: A study of remarried couples and their children.* Chicago: Nelson-Hall.

Fast, I. & Cain, A. C. (1966). The Stepparent Role: Potential for Disturbances in Family Functioning. *American Journal of Orthopsychiatry, 36*, 485-491.

Goldner, V. (1985). Feminism and family therapy, *Family Process, 24*, 31-47.

Haavind, H. (1987). *Liten og stor.* Oslo: Universitetsforlaget.

Hobart, C., & Brown, D. (1988). Effects of Prior Marriage Children on adjustment in Remarriage: A Canadian study. *Journal of Comparative Family Studies, 19*, 381-396.

Johnsen, B. H. (1990). Myten om den onde stemor–fra eventyr til ukeblad (The myth about the evil stepmother–from fairy tails to popular literature). *Nytt om Kvinneforskning, 14*, 31-38.

Kompara, D. R. (1980). Difficulties in the Socialization Process of Stepparenting. *Family Relations, 29*, 69-73.

Levin, I. (1993). *Stefamilien–variasjon og mangfold.* Trondheim.

Levin, I. (1990). How to Define Family? *Family Reports, 17.* Uppsala: Uppsala University.

Levin, I. (1989a). Familie–hva er det? En presentasjon av en metode. (Family–what is that? A presentation of a method). *Fokus på familien, 17*, 25-31.

Levin, I. (1989b). Barnetegninger–stefamiliens fingeravtrykk? (Children's drawings–the stepfamily's fingerprints?). In I. Levin & G. Clifford (Eds.), *Relasjoner. Hverdagsskrift til Per Olav Tiller*, (Relationships). Trondheim: Tapir.

Minnich, E. K. (1989). Choosing Consciousness. In N. B. Maglin & N. Schniede-wind (Eds.), *Women and Stepfamilies*. Philadelphia: Temple University Press.

Orleans, M., Palisi, B. J., & Caddell, D. (1989). Marriage Adjustment and Satis-faction of Stepfathers: Their Feelings and Perceptions of Decision Making and Stepchildren Relations. *Family Relations, 38*, 371-377.

Oshman, H. P. & Manosevitz, M. (1976). Father Absence: Effects of Stepfathers upon Psychosocial Development in Males. *Developmental Psychology*, 479-480.

Rallings, E. M. (1976). The Special Role of Stepfather. *The Family Coordinator*, 445-449.

Scott, J. W. (1986). Gender: a useful category of historical analysis, *The American Historical Review*, 91, 1053-1075.

Schulman, G. L. (1972). Myths that intrude on the adaptation of the stepfamily. *Social Casework*, 131-139.

Stern, P. N. (1978). Stepfather families: Integration around child discipline. *Issues in Mental Health Nursing, 1*, 49-56.

Vemer, E., Coleman, M., Ganong, L. H., & Cooper, H. (1989). Marital Satisfac-tion in Remarriage: A Meta-analysis. *Journal of Marriage and the Family, 51*, 713-725.

Visher, E. B., & Visher, J. S. (1979). *Stepfamilies: A Guide to Working with Stepparents and Stepchildren*. New York: Brunner/Mazel.

Wilson, K. L., Zurcher, L. A., McAdams, D. C., & Curtis, R. L. (1975). Stepfa-thers and Stepchildren: An Exploratory Analysis From Two National Surveys. *Journal of Marriage and the Family, 37*, 526-536.

Yutang, L. (1942). *The Wisdom of China and India*. New York: Random House.

Stepfamily Therapy
from the Client's Perspective

Emily B. Visher
John S. Visher
Kay Pasley

INTRODUCTION

Demographers are predicting that in the United States 33% of all children will live with a stepparent before the age of 18, and stepfamilies will be the predominant type of family form by the year 2010. Since these families are considered to be at risk initially for considerable stress, it is not surprising that therapists are dealing with an increasing number of individuals living in this type of family.

Recent publications point to differences in dynamics between remarriage families and first marriage families, and raise questions about the effectiveness of traditional family therapy for these families (Browning, 1994; Pasley, Rhoden, Visher & Visher, in press; Visher & Visher, 1988; Visher & Visher, 1996). Clinicians have written extensively about the therapeutic needs of stepfamilies, and the interventions found to be particularly helpful (Visher & Visher, 1988; Visher & Visher, 1996; Bray, 1988;

Emily B. Visher is an Adjunct Faculty Member, California School of Professional Psychology, Alameda, CA. John S. Visher is Lecturer in Psychiatry, Emeritus, Stanford University, Stanford, CA. Kay Pasley is Associate Professor of Human Development and Family Studies at the University of North Carolina at Greensboro, Greensboro, NC.

Address correspondence to Emily B. Visher at 599 Sky-Hy Circle, Lafayette, CA 94549.

[Haworth co-indexing entry note]: "Stepfamily Therapy from the Client's Perspective." Visher, Emily B., John S. Visher, and Kay Pasley. Co-published simultaneously in *Marriage & Family Review* (The Haworth Press, Inc.) Vol. 26, No. 1/2, 1997, pp. 191-213; and: *Stepfamilies: History, Research, and Policy* (ed: Irene Levin and Marvin B. Sussman) The Haworth Press, Inc., 1997, pp. 191-213. Single or multiple copies of this article are available for a fee from The Haworth Document Delivery Service [1-800-342-9678, 9:00 a.m. - 5:00 p.m. (EST). E-mail address: getinfo@haworth.com].

191

Sager et al., 1983). In 1990 Elion conducted a survey of couples to determine the use of 15 interventions said by clinicians to be helpful (Elion, 1990; Visher & Visher, 1988). The present study builds on Elion's research, using a larger sample and asking additional information from the therapy clients.

Elion's sample contained 32 couples who had been in treatment with a single therapist for stepfamily issues. Her survey listed 12 areas of concern appearing in the clinical literature and then asked: What three events during therapy stand out as the most helpful in your therapy experience? Why were these helpful? What was the single most important factor, whether or not related to therapy, that brought stability to your family? Her results supported the list of interventions being evaluated. She found the most important interventions were: validation and normalization, psychoeducation, reduction of helplessness, and strengthening of the couple bond.

The present study refines and expands the concerns of participants at the beginning of therapy. We also asked respondents to identify unhelpful, as well as helpful aspects of their therapy experience. Whereas the clients in Elion's study had all seen one therapist, in our study the respondents had seen many therapists in different parts of the country. In some cases, a family saw more than one therapist in their search for help. Rather than using existing clinical categories as Elion did, the helpful therapeutic categories in our study were generated from the data. Quantitative analysis of the expanded data supports the findings of Elion's study, and increases our knowledge of stepfamily clients' experiences with therapy. A report describing these important quantitative findings that replicate and enlarge the work of Elion is in press at the present time (Pasley et al., in press).

The questions pertaining to client's therapy experiences are open-ended and as a result stepfamily adults' responses to these questions provide a wealth of information not included in the quantitative analyses. Qualitative information of this type is especially valuable at the present time because of the shift in medical practice and the concern with treatment planning and effectiveness. Two recent papers speak to the need for and the value of the type of inquiry reported in this paper (Ambert, Adler, P. A., Adler, P. & Detzne, 1995; Seligman, 1995).

METHOD

Questionnaires were sent to 1200 members of the Stepfamily Association of America, a national organization based in Lincoln, Nebraska, that provides education and support for stepfamilies.

Measures

Our interest centered on the following questions from the survey:

1. What three things during therapy standout as the most helpful to your therapy experience?
2. Was there something about the experience which you found not helpful to you?
3. What was the single most important factor, whether or not related to therapy, that brought stability to your family?

The goal was to gather information about specific therapeutic interventions that clients in stepfamilies find helpful and also to examine the unhelpful aspects of therapy reported by these same stepfamily clients. With this in mind, we used the following questions as our guide in reviewing the individual responses in the three survey areas listed above:

1. Are there differences between what men and women found helpful in stepfamily therapy?
2. Are there differences between what men and women found unhelpful in stepfamily therapy?
3. Are there differences between what remarried mothers or fathers, stepmothers, stepfathers in complex stepfamilies found helpful in therapy?
4. Are there suggestions for ways in which therapists can meet the needs for validation and normalization, psychoeducation, reduction of helplessness, and strengthening the bond between the new couple?
5. Are there specific pitfalls suggested by the respondents for therapists to avoid when working with members of remarriage families?

Sample

Thirty five percent of the questionnaires were returned, and of these 422 completed protocols 279 comprise the present sample. These include couples with a sustained, committed relationship who had sought therapy for stepfamily issues at some point during their marriage. The relevant responses for this analysis were given by women in 246 of the 279 questionnaires, and by men in 33 of the questionnaires. This group of 279 includes the 267 married couples used as the sample for Pasley's analysis plus 12 couples who had not yet married. This larger sample of 279 was selected for this inquiry because prior to their marriage many couples seek therapeutic help for stepfamily issues that can arise at any time during a committed relationship. It is important for clinicians to recognize that a marriage license is not a necessary prerequisite for interpersonal stepfamily stresses to arise.

As stated previously (Pasley et al., in press), the sample represents primarily white couples in their 40's, who are well-educated and have an average family income of $50,000 or more. These families represent an upper middle class segment of stepfamilies, with the information, motivation, and financial ability to seek therapeutic help.

RESULTS

Gender Differences in the Stepfamily Therapy Needs of Men and Women

Because of the large discrepancy in numbers of male and female respondents questionnaires were chosen at random from the 246 answered by women. The results reported here reflect questionnaires completed by 33 men and by 33 women.

Table 1 compares the two groups on four areas commonly mentioned by the respondents. Also included are the responses to the question regarding the single most important factor that brought stability to the family.

Validation of Feelings

It is clear that the greatest difference occurred in the introspective "feeling" area. Women were helped to a much greater extent than were men by the therapists' validation of their feelings, and the message that their emotions were understandable and common ones to have in stepfamily situations. Comments of these women included the following:

- "I found out I'm not weird"
- "I'm not alone in my concerns"
- "I'm not losing my mind"
- "Stepmothers feel crazy or misunderstood"
- "The therapist alleviated my guilt"
- "I learned I'm not crazy"

Fifteen percent of the 33 men made similar remarks, although none of them expressed the view that they thought they were weird or crazy:

- "I saw I was not alone in my feelings"
- "I felt supported"
- "Knowing I'm not alone helped"
- "Found out my different feelings for step and biological sons were to be expected"
- "I was supported in my feelings"

Communication

In improved communication, the direction of the trend was a reversal from the emotional area: 24.2% of the men spoke about the help that therapy provided them in communicating with the others in the family, making such statements as:

- "Helped build spousal communication"
- "Improved communication skills"
- "Our couple communication got a lot better"

Only 6% of the women made similar comments.

TABLE 1. Responses of Men and Women to Stepfamily Therapy

Helpful Interventions	Women (N)	%	Men (N)	%
Validation of feelings	(13)	39.4	(5)	15.1
Help with communication	(2)	6.0	(8)	24.2
Objectivity/authority of therapist	(2)	6.0	(7)	21.2
Psychoeducation	(9)	27.3	(9)	27.3
Most important elements for stability				
Time	(3)	9.1	(3)	9.1
Strengthening couple	(9)	27.3	(9)	27.3
Not stable yet	(4)	12.0	(1)	3.0

Authority of the Therapist

The position and authority of the therapist appeared to be more important to the men than to the women. Men commented more than three times as often on the role or personal characteristics of the therapist in this regard:

- "The opinion of an expert helped"
- "The therapist was an impartial arbitrator"
- "The therapist had a good perspective"
- "It's easier with a mediator"
- "Having a third party present is helpful"

Only two comments of a similar nature appeared in the women, and indeed there was an important element in one not found in the men's responses:

> "The therapist gave objective guidance and *my husband would listen to this third party while he wouldn't listen to me.*"

Whereas the men's comments regarding communication were varied expressions of the authority and competence of the therapist, when examining all 246 of the women's questionnaires their responses in this area were more restricted. That is, they either spoke about the objectivity of the therapist (similarly to the responses of the men) or stated, "Therapy helped because my husband doesn't believe me or listen to me and he will pay attention to what the therapist says." Men did not express this perception.

Psychoeducation

Psychoeducation clarifies issues, validates feelings and normalizes stepfamily situations, helps individuals become more realistic in their expectations for their family, and reduces helplessness by providing information and suggestions about ways to deal with the issues that are stressful for the members of the family. Clinicians have called attention to the necessity for large doses of psychoeducation when working with stepfamily members (Visher & Visher, 1988; Papernow, 1993). The fact that 27.3% of both men and women commented on its importance is noteworthy. Both men and women responded similarly in this area:

- "Normalized step situations and let us know what to expect"
- "We learned how to pro-act and follow through"

- "We learned some useful techniques"
- "She showed us the necessity for boundaries"

Women, however, also included responses reflecting the role and expectations of women in the family. They frequently spoke about learning to let go of unnecessary and unwanted responsibility, and to back off and not try so hard to make everything work out smoothly. This, of course, suggests that the men need to take added stepfamily responsibility, a task about which the men in this sample did not comment.

Most Important Elements for Family Stability

In recording the responses of the men and the women, the three most similar responses to the question were compared. These figures indicate there are two common responses for both men and women. About 9% of both men and women said that time (not related to therapy) was important to reaching family stability, and more than 27.3% of both men and women considered couple solidarity (usually a result of therapy) as the most important element bringing stability to their stepfamily. Four women stated that as yet there was no stability in the family, while one man expressed this opinion. This difference may reflect women's position of holding themselves and being expected by others to be responsible for the functioning of the family.

Dissatisfaction with Therapy

The earlier quantitative analysis of the data indicated that clients reported a number of different reasons why therapy was unhelpful or had no impact one way or the other. A larger sample is needed to compare men and women on the various reasons for their dissatisfaction. There was, however, in the original analysis one complaint made by 48.6% of those who noted something about therapy as unhelpful. This was that the therapist was not familiar with stepfamily issues and dynamics. Our examination indicates that this comment was made equally by both men and women clients. The importance of this feedback will be discussed later.

Therapeutic Effectiveness Related to Stepfamily Roles

Table 2 gives the numbers of men and women in different stepfamily roles: mother or father only, stepmother or stepfather only, dual roles of mother/stepmother, and father/stepfather. Responses from each of these

TABLE 2. Stepfamily Therapy Responses Related to Stepfamily Roles

Stepfamily Role	Validation/ Normalization		Communication		Self Understanding		Understanding Others		Couple Importance	
	(N)	%	(N)	%	(N)	%	(N)	%	(N)	%
Mother/ Stepmother N = 169	(34)	20.1	(16)	9.5	(15)	8.9	(23)	13.6	(70)	41.4
Stepmother Only N = 65	(30)	47.0	(4)	6.2	(2)	3.1	(3)	4.6	(25)	38.5
Father/ Stepfather N = 21	(4)	19.0	(3)	14.3	(0)	0.0	(1)	4.8	(8)	38.1
Mother Only N = 12	(4)	33.3	(2)	16.7	(0)	0.0	(1)	8.3	(4)	33.3
Stepfather Only N = 7	(2)	28.6	(3)	42.9	(0)	0.0	(0)	0.0	(2)	28.6
Father Only N = 5	(2)	40.0	(2)	40.0	(1)	20.0	(0)	0.0	(0)	0.0

six groups were reviewed separately. Because of the small number of mothers, fathers, and stepfathers only who were the respondents to the questionnaire, one or two responses give high percentages in these groups. Responses in five major areas are noted:

a. Validation and normalization of situations and emotional responses,
b. Help with communication,
c. Increased self-understanding,
d. Understanding of others,
e. Acknowledgment of the importance of the couple relationship.

A larger sample of stepfathers, mothers, and fathers only, is essential to give us needed information about these three groups. In our analysis, the review of these groups only gives us areas to pay attention to in future studies.

Mother/Stepmother

By far the largest group of respondents were women who were both stepparents and parents, some of them entering their stepfamily as a step-parent and then becoming a parent within this relationship. From their responses to the questionnaire it seems clear that they may have some needs relating to the role of a parent (e.g., "I learned that I didn't need to feel guilty about not feeling the same way about my stepson as I did about my own son"). However, their main concerns were related to their role as stepmothers, with their positive responses to therapy mirroring the responses given by stepmothers who were not also parents of children. Although their responses are similar, the mother/stepmother group's need for validation and normalization was somewhat less than that for the group of women who were stepmothers only:

* "Normalization of "step" situations and what to expect"
* "Knowing I'm not bad for having resentful feelings toward my step-child"
* "Husband and wife's relationship comes first and we stand as a team"

These women were invested in understanding themselves and the others in the family. They also valued their improved communication within the family more than the stepmother only group, although not to the degree stated by the father/stepfather group. In commenting on the importance of the couple 41.4% made statements such as:

"Support of us as a *couple* by the therapist above and beyond the (family) group: It was so important to have this support. The kids just wanted to split us up."

Stepmother Only

These women have no children of their own. They tend to feel isolated and alone since initially their only tie to the family unit is through their relationship with their partner. Often they have little support even from their partner who is feeling pulled by her and who also fears the loss of his children if he displeases them (Papernow, 1993). It is not surprising that it was this group of women who had strong, uncomfortable emotional reactions to their role. They also questioned themselves, their sanity, and their ability to cope. Validation and encouragement was crucial for them:

- "I felt listened to."
- "I learned that I need to get my own needs met too. It gave me courage to ask."
- "The counselor pointed out to my husband things about his relationship with my kids. I couldn't do this."
- "I felt like a failure and didn't talk about our problems much to others."
- "It gave me space to live. I could go and tell someone about what was happening."

These stepmothers had less energy directed towards understanding themselves and the others in their family, and as a group they commented less about a need for help with communication. They expressed clearly their need for a solid couple relationship. For these women it was the initial support of their therapist that felt like a "life saver." It may be that over time as stepmothers only would gain self-confidence and esteem and feel more a part of the family, their desire for family information and understanding might increase also. Initially, however, these stepmothers suggested their need was for support, normalization, and a strengthening of their relationship with their partner.

Father/Stepfather

These men are the ones with a dual role in a complex stepfamily. Their interest was in family communication, with some interest in understanding others. They did not list gaining an understanding of self as a helpful part of their therapy. This group of men were similar to the stepmother and mother/stepmother groups in their recognition of the need to work to improve their couple relationship. Indeed, 38 to 41% of these groups of mothers/stepmothers, stepmothers only, and fathers/stepfathers stressed the value of a solid couple relationship to them and to their family stability.

The Remaining Groups

Because of their small numbers, the three remaining groups can only suggest areas to be aware of in future studies. It was predominantly the men who were fathers or stepfathers only that contributed to the men's perceived need for help with communication.

Among the 33 male respondents, there was one father only who expressed the value of self-understanding. The other men did not report this. Because there are only five men in the fathers only group, the 20% given by this one response can imply more interest by this group than actually exists. It is worth noting that the women who were mothers only were similar to the men in this regard. While a few women who were mothers only expressed a desire to understand their children and partner better, they were similar to the men in not being concerned about self-understanding.

In the case of the 12 mothers only, a trend appeared. Their responses suggested that this group saw their therapy more frequently than the average of the sample as negative or non-effective. Of the 12, two (16.6%) reported that their therapy was unhelpful, while three (25%) said therapy had no impact either one way or the other. Since only 13% of the 267 respondents analyzed previously (Pasley et al., in press) rated therapy as negative, and 5% rated it as having no impact, having a total of 41.6% of women who were mothers and not also stepmothers find therapy less helpful is a finding that requires further study using a larger number of women in this position.

In addition, two other remarried mothers reported a negative aspect of their therapy experience even though they considered the experience to be positive over all. Although the sample is only 12, the fact that 7 of them (58.3%) were dissatisfied in some way points to the need to examine more carefully what the therapeutic needs are of these women and how they can better be met.

Looking at what these women found helpful, most of their comments have a different flavor from the response.

- "Therapist explained the basis of my children's conflicting behavior, so I was more able to deal with them."

- "Able to express my dissatisfaction with how things were going."
- "Recognition that stepfather needed to develop his own relationship with my daughter."
- "Resolved discipline issues between stepdad and myself. Useful because daughter played on my guilt about the divorce."
- "Safe place to talk."
- "Given permission to love biological son who went to live with his Dad, and permission to try to establish contact with him despite my husband's disapproval."

These mothers typically referred to the partner as the "stepdad" or "stepfather." In other words, they stressed his relationship to her children rather than his relationship to her. For these women, their concern centered on the stepfather/stepchild relationship and on their need to understand their children better. The final quote given reminds us of a remarried mother (not in this sample) who experienced two therapists as disapproving of her "love" for her child. She felt deeply grateful and supported when a third therapist accepted and did not question her wish to provide warmth and love for her children. These mothers did respond positively to normalization of the situations they encountered, but they did not express the same emotional turmoil and self-doubts of the women who were in a stepparent role.

For the group of fathers only, with the large number of other respondents calling attention to the need for a good couple relationship, it is noticeable that this was not included by these men. Since the couple relationship is of concern to their counterparts, this discrepancy may signal an area of tension in families of this type.

For both stepmothers and stepfathers with no children of their own, solidifying the couple relationship was important. Both groups also commented on the importance of the normalization of their situations and getting support from the therapist. They were dissimilar in general in their other types of responses. Stepfathers gave the following as being especially helpful:

- "Learning to pro-act rather than react."
- "Learning how to make decisions and follow through."
- "Found that couple communication is vital."
- "Therapy covered subjects important to us."
- "Learned coping strategies."
- "It was a safe environment in which to explore issues."

In contrast the stepmothers' responses included the following:

- "I knew we were not weird."
- "I wasn't crazy."
- "My husband showed support for me by his participation."
- "Helped me not take things so personally."
- "My husband was willing to try to work things out for everyone."
- "I can understand the other's feelings better now."
- "It was important my husband learned that our relationship came first."
- "It helped with my self-esteem."
- "He helped me not take the children's behavior so personally."

To summarize, stepparents were bewildered, discouraged, and often felt a lack of support from their partner. They found the support of a therapist as a crucial element of therapy, and normalizing their situation helped stepparents feel more adequate. Stepfathers spoke particularly about the need for information and knowledge about ways to handle stepfamily situations. Stepmothers were more inner-directed, and as well as normalizing their experience, they needed to know they "were not crazy," that their husband was supportive, and that the couple relationship was a priority.

Specific Suggestions for Therapists

Here we outline some of the specific ways noted by the respondents that therapists can provide:

1. Validation of stepfamily members' experiences
2. Normalization of stepfamily situations and challenges
3. Reduction of the adults' sense of helplessness
4. Strengthening of the couple relationship

1. Validation

- "The therapist provided support to me as a stepparent and support to my husband in his role as a parent."
- "Therapy helps to say it's your baggage that's the problem, not you as a person!"
- "It was important having a counselor understand how low I felt being considered *last* all the time. *Last*, after his kids and ex-wife. The counselor could help me *communicate* my feelings to my husband and let him know that it was important to listen to my feelings."

- "The therapist validated my feelings. I'd thought I was crazy and that I was a bad person for having negative feelings towards my stepchildren, their mother, and my role as a stepmother."

These are good examples of the type of therapeutic feedback that validates stepfamily members. It is a type of support needed particularly by stepmothers.

2. Normalization of Stepfamily Situations and Challenges

- "I was feeling inadequate and stressed although I was doing my best. It (therapy) helps you to understand even though you do your best, things don't change over night. Not for anyone! It helps you to understand the stages of stepfamily development and the myths surrounding stepfamilies."
- "As a stepmother I was assuming parental responsibility for my stepdaughter and my husband, her father, was unwittingly abdicating his parental authority to me. This was role confusion and made me anxious and angry. The therapist helped us clarify our roles and this relieved my stress."
- "The therapist helped me see that as the stepparent I didn't have to supply a year's worth of parenting (i.e., instruction, discipline, etc.) in the few weeks the kids were here. That insight helped me to relax a little concerning "his kids." The therapist also had empathy with me over my son's difficult departure to go live with his Dad and my almost immediately having to begin the stepparenting role."
- "The therapist's knowledge of "step" dynamics allowed her not to misdiagnose us as 'pathological.'"
- "The therapist gave me permission not to love my stepdaughter, so then I didn't feel guilty when love was not spontaneous."

Normalization of stepfamily situations flowed from the therapist's knowledge of stepfamily dynamics and was particularly welcomed by women clients.

3. Reduction of the Adults' Sense of Helplessness

- "Our therapist was very direct and very willing to give advice/direction . . . positive solutions to the day-to-day issues that were making us crazy. She kept us focused on those things we could control."
- "Most of our problems have been caused by my husband's ex-wife. It was real easy to just blame her and continue having problems. Our

therapist helped us focus on what *we* could do to make our situation better in spite of her, and how to avoid letting her cause these problems between us."

- "She (therapist) helped me re-define my definition of success in terms of being a good stepmother. I was trying to be Maria in the *Sound of Music*. This put so much pressure on me I was constantly stressed. I've changed my expectations of myself and them–and this has helped a lot."
- "We learned techniques for healthily handling stepfamily problems. When you're in the midst of an emotionally charged family crisis, you can't always see the issue clearly. Learning techniques of coping beforehand eased the trauma of dealing with the situations later."

Knowing what to expect and ways of dealing with stepfamily situations is of great importance to both men and women in remarriage families, though particularly to the men.

4. Strengthening of the Couple Relationship

- "She (therapist) told us to use one general rule–do what you need to do with your children to make life easier for your spouse. This puts your spouse first, and it covers *every* situation. We always go to corners over our own children and that helps us accept the fact that children will come first sometimes, and we won't always agree and, that's OK."
- "The therapist told my husband that his children, ages 5 and 7, would not need or want his time in a few years. Then my husband realized he would want to spend time with *me* when they didn't want his time, so he began treating me lots better so I would be there for him in the future–and I am!"

These comments are examples of how important it is for therapists to validate feelings, normalize stepfamily situations, help parents and stepparents understand what to expect and how to deal with the situations that arise. Another top priority is helping the adults improve their communication so they learn to understand one another and the children. As is indicated in Table 2, strengthening the couple bond was of primary importance, particularly to those who were stepparents. With the time required to form stepparent-stepchild relationships the stepparent's emotional satisfaction in the new family unit comes from the couple relationship.

Specific Suggestions of Pitfalls to Avoid

Negative comments about their therapy were made by many clients who found therapy useful, as well as by those who found it unhelpful, or that it had no impact one way or the other. Without a clear picture of stepfamily dynamics from which to work, therapists may have difficulty empathizing with stepfamily members or being able to intervene in the ways that have been illustrated. Looking at the errors stepfamily clients believe their therapists have made supports this position.

As we know from the original analysis of the 267 married couples who had therapy experience, "Most respondents (48.6%) identified the therapist's lack of training, skill, and knowledge about stepfamily issues as the most unhelpful aspect of the process" (Pasley et al., in press).

In reviewing the 279 questionnaires used for this paper, 38 respondents specifically mentioned their disappointment with the lack of knowledge about stepfamily dynamics which they perceived in their therapist. Conversely, 24 respondents spoke specifically about positive therapeutic interventions that occurred because of the fact that their therapist was knowledgeable about stepfamily dynamics. Combining these opposite, though related statements, indicates that 22% of the respondents were consciously aware of reacting in therapy either negatively or positively based on their perception of whether or not their therapist was informed in this area. Assessing the responses in 21 other questionnaires, from a therapists' point of view it appeared to us that the therapists in those cases, lacked the necessary knowledge to be as effective as they could have been. For example, in one family with many custody issues and stresses, the wife considered therapy to be helpful even though she commented, "We haven't really dealt with any 'step' issues in therapy together–(it's been) basically couples counseling and counseling to deal with handling our son's behavior." Another respondent spoke of seeing a counselor, "She seemed judgmental and she generalized too much or acted as if our problems were insignificant and we exaggerated their importance."

Therapists frequently deal with clients from diverse and unfamiliar backgrounds. While knowledge of the differences can always help, listening to the client and asking for adequate information from the client can provide a foundation on which effective therapy can proceed. Why does the therapist's lack of knowledge seem so crucial in this area? We believe it is because many times therapists are not *aware* that they are unfamiliar with "stepfamily culture." To them the picture of "family" in their head applies, and they proceed using this nuclear model rather than asking the necessary questions and accepting and not judging the answers. Numerous comments from the respondents who spoke about this particular therapeutic characteristic felt very strongly about it:

- "The therapist did not fully grasp family structure differences and their consequences for family dynamics between stepfamilies and first marriage families."
- "The therapist did not have stepfamily experience. She treated us like we were a family with children. She had no concept of the bonding problem, alienation, or loyalty problems."
- "We saw three therapists in a period of five years before we got to one who knew anything *AT ALL* about stepfamilies. Our situation continued to deteriorate, and we couldn't understand what's wrong that we couldn't be helped."
- "We were disappointed in the results because we knew more about differences of stepfamilies vs. traditional families than our therapists did. We feel the treatment would have been better had they even picked up a book and read up on stepfamilies. We saw three women, and this was the case with all of them. We feel that by lumping stepfamilies in with traditional families they do more of a disservice than a service."

Then conversely there are the positive statements:

- "We have seen several counselors. The ones who understood the differences between stepfamilies and nuclear families were the most helpful."
- "My therapist was a stepparent and he understood and could give helpful suggestions."
- "I went to a therapist who was a stepmother. I was assured that what I was feeling was normal in a stepfamily. I realized it takes time. I had had unrealistic expectations. This explained why I cried every day, yet I loved my husband so much!"

So what difficulties does a lack of stepfamily awareness produce? The following comments give us a clear idea of some of the pitfalls for therapists who the respondents felt were not familiar with stepfamily life:

- "He wouldn't allow me to talk about being a stepmother because he said I was becoming obsessed with the role."
- "The therapist treated our discipline styles like a biological family and it doesn't work."
- "The therapist believed I loved my stepchild. When I said I didn't, she couldn't quite get it. It made me feel less understood."

- "The therapist was too quick to suggest medication to me because of my anxiety and depression. He didn't recognize the real issues I was anxious about."
- "We were told to have separate rules for each set of children. We needed the same rules with each parent enforcing them."
- "We were told adding a second bathroom would solve all our problems. HAH!"
- "The therapist narrowed her work to the couple and then just to me to help me cope better. I was chosen by them to be the one with the problems, the one to change. No one else. The others talked equally about the importance of psychoeducation. It helped them get off the hook."
- "The therapist said, "Just do your own thing, just worry about your own child." 'It's not realistic."
- "We often jumped from issue to issue without making a concrete plan and agreement on how to handle them."
- "Our therapist came from a position of stepfamilies as the underdog, less than, worse off. This starts us with a negative and implies an extraordinary amount of work just to reach 'normal.'"

We believe that reading about stepfamilies and obtaining specialized training in stepfamily dynamics can allow therapists to avoid these and other remarks that produce negative therapeutic interactions. Unlike clients who can give their therapist information and understanding of the normative aspects of the culture from which they come, many stepfamily clients are not familiar with remarriage family norms. They are traditionally confused and feel helpless and hopeless. If the therapist also lacks an understanding of the stepfamily cultural norms, therapeutic confusion can reign! For clients who are aware of the dynamic differences, as their comments suggest, they feel upset if their therapist seems unaware and non-understanding. Thus, this examination of clients' responses to therapy suggests that the therapist's stepfamily knowledge is a major key to successful stepfamily therapy.

DISCUSSION

Gender Differences

There were indeed some differences and similarities in what men and women found most helpful in therapy. Women are frequently considered to be more emotional and feeling-oriented than men, while men are seen as being more "thinking" and action-oriented. Women's greater need to have their feelings validated and men's greater need for help with communication is congruent with these perceptions.

Therapists often speak of women's tendency to internalize difficulties and feel that they are responsible for their situations. Supportive of this, it was women, not men, who expressed the view that something was wrong with them and intimated this might be causing some of their stepfamily difficulties. Their relief was great when their therapist validated the legitimacy of their feelings and in essence told them, "You are not crazy."

Men, more than women, called attention to the value of having an objective third person with authority in the person of the therapist. It would be helpful to look at this perception of the therapist using a larger sample because it is an important aspect of therapy. This comparison of a small number of male and female respondents hinted at the possibility that men and women appreciate this characteristic in the therapist for different reasons. For example, even though stepfamily couples have been found to be more egalitarian than original couples (Kimball, 1988), it was women here who commented that their partner would not listen to them, but would believe the therapist when he or she supported what the woman had been feeling or saying. This points to the effectiveness of having therapy sessions with the couple alone. In these sessions the therapist can help the individuals listen to one another and become more empathetic. Several respondents commented on the importance of this listening.

Both men and women talked equally about the importance of psychoeducation. It helped them understand what was going on, it let them know what to expect, and gave them suggestions of how to deal with the intricacies of stepfamily life. This reduced their anxiety and their feelings of helplessness. They found that understanding the position of others in the family was important. A common element mentioned was the strengthening of the couple relationship. This recognition that the couple needed to work together and form a strong alliance allowed the family to gain a stability it had not had.

Regarding men and women's dissatisfaction with their therapy, they gave similar responses. In the original study of 267 respondents, 48.6% of those who found therapy non-effective or unhelpful reported that the problem was the therapist's lack of knowledge of stepfamily dynamics and issues. This lack affected both men and women similarly according to our qualitative findings reported here.

Role Differences

When comparing the effectiveness of therapy from the perspective of adults with different roles in the stepfamily, intriguing differences emerged that raise a number of considerations and indicate a need for further exploration in the area.

Since the numbers of men respondents who were stepfathers only or father only were so small few conclusions can be drawn. In the group of 12 women who were remarried mothers only more women were dissatisfied with their therapy experience than would have been expected given the number reacting this way in the total sample. This raises several therapeutic issues and points to the need for a further study with a larger group of women in this position.

Not only did these women express more dissatisfaction with therapy, they were different in several ways from stepmothers and from women who were both mothers and stepmothers. First of all, none of them referred to feeling upset with themselves. Secondly, their focus on stepfather-stepchild relationships was mentioned equally, or perhaps even more, than a focus on the couple relationship. In fact, a majority of the time these mothers referred to their partners and their child or children in terms of the stepparent-stepchild relationship rather than her relationship to them as her husband or her child.

It may be that these remarried mothers have higher self-esteem than stepmothers only or mothers who are also stepmothers. They did not think of themselves as being "crazy" or "weird" or having something wrong with them. Therefore, they do not report the relief the other women felt when they heard from the therapist that they were not crazy. Thus, these mothers may be more critical of therapy because they do not have this emotionally powerful interaction with their therapist as an important foundation of the therapeutic relationship. In addition, adults who have a single role of "parent" in a stepfamily have the security of being the only person in the household with primary emotional ties to all the others–their new partner and their children. The fact that women in the dual role of mother and stepmother express feelings and needs similar to women who are stepmothers only seems to indicate that the stepparent role becomes a greater source of stress than the role of remarried mother for women in complex stepfamilies. Because of this, the therapeutic needs of stepmothers and mothers/stepmothers appear to be more similar than the needs of remarried mothers only.

Stepmothers only express considerable concern about the new couple relationship. A further study of stepfathers only may support the suggestion that they also have the same concern. In seeing a stepfamily couple, one of whom is a mother only, and the other, initially at least, a stepparent only, the trends noted here suggest that the two adults may have different therapeutic needs: the parent wants to see an improvement in the stepparent-stepchild relationship, and the stepparent is concerned with solidifying the couple relationship. If this is so, successful therapy may depend on the therapist's understanding of these differing stepfamily concerns and his or her ability to be supportive to each of the partners and help them understand and accept the difference in their needs. Working out ways to strengthen the couple and also pay attention to developing a relationship between the stepparent and the stepchild then become important concerns of therapy.

The importance of the couple relationship is well-illustrated in this study. Omitting the three under-represented groups, 38% to 41% of the three major groups, mother/stepmother, stepmother only, and father/stepfather acknowledge the importance of the couple relationship to them and to the stability of their family. We believe that stepparents need to have a sense of security in this relationship before they can reach out and form satisfactory ties with their stepchildren.

A major question for therapists is whom to see in stepfamily therapy sessions. With this need to strengthen the couple relationship, an important way of accomplishing this may be by excluding children in sessions with the two adults prior to adequate couple bonding (Visher & Visher, 1988; Visher & Visher, 1996; Papernow, 1993; Browning, 1994). Although the majority of questionnaires indicated that couples were seen together, the responses did not in any way add to our knowledge in this area. Further study is needed to better answer this issue.

The dissatisfaction expressed by the remarried mothers raises a question of how to proceed in their therapy. Perhaps the importance to stepmothers of the couple relationship as a pre-requisite to a good stepfamily/stepchild relationship is a clue. If these remarried mothers can be shown the value of developing a close relationship with their new partner, and the stepparent can understand the importance of good stepparent-stepchild relationships to their new partner, progress towards satisfactory integration can proceed. Larger studies are needed to determine the validity of this suggestion for stepfather families, and also to explore the question for stepmother families.

CONCLUSION

Studying the responses of this sample of stepfamily clients, several strong impressions emerged:

1. This is an educated group of adults who valued their marriages and their families.

2. Many recognized the differences between their remarriage family and their previous family, but they had little understanding of what this meant as a family.
3. These families have had the strength and resolve to seek help with the pain and chaos they were experiencing.
4. For many therapy was a positive and helpful experience, but many also were disappointed.
5. In almost half of those who reported disappointment with their therapy, it was related to the level of expertise of the therapist in working with this population.
6. There is a need for special information and training about the stepfamily culture for therapists. Some responses suggested that even where clients were satisfied, therapists were not as effective as they might have been had they had more knowledge of stepfamily dynamics.
7. Without adequate stepfamily background, both the family and the therapist often operate from the nuclear family model. This can be destructive rather than constructive.
8. There are numerous questions raised by this inquiry which need further study:
   a. What are the therapy needs of remarried parents, both male and female, who have no stepchildren?
   b. What are the responses of a group of men in stepfamilies equal in number to the large number of women who responded to this study? The men's responses to this same questionnaire could be compared with the existing women's questionnaires, or a whole new study could be designed.

With the increasing number of stepfamilies, more attention needs to be given to providing adequate stepfamily therapy training and continuing education for therapists in this vital area. Paying attention to the responses of these 279 stepfamily therapy clients is a good beginning toward improving the effectiveness of this therapy with a large population of families in the United States.

REFERENCES

Ambert, A., Adler, P.A., Adler, P., & Detzne, D.F. (1995). Understanding and evaluating qualitative research. *Journal of Marriage and the Family, 57*:879-893.
Bray, J.H. (1988). Children's development in early remarriage. In E.M. Hetherington, J. Arasteh (Eds.), *The Impact of Divorce, Single-Parenting, and Step-*

parenting on Children. Hillsdale, NJ: Lawrence Erlbaum and Associates, Publishers, pp. 279-298.

Browning, S. (1994). Treating stepfamilies: Alternatives to traditional family therapy. In K. Pasley, M. Ihinger-Tallman (Eds.). *Stepparenting: Issues in Theory, Research, and Practice*. Westport, CT: Praeger, pp. 175-198.

Elion, D.A. (1990). Therapy with remarriage families with children: Positive interventions from the client perspective. Unpublished Master's Thesis, University of Wisconsin, Stout.

Kimball, G. (1988). *50-50 Parenting: Shared family rewards and responsibilities*. Lexington, MA: Lexington Books.

Papernow, P. (1993). *Becoming a Stepfamily: Patterns of Development in Remarried Families*. San Francisco: Jossey-Bass.

Pasley, K., Rhoden, L., Visher, E.B., & Visher, J.S. Successful stepfamily therapy: Client's perspectives. (in press, *Journal of Marriage and Family Therapy*).

Sager, C. J., Brown, H.S., Crohn, H., Engel, T., Rodstein, E., & Walker, L. (1983). *Treating the Remarried Family*. New York: Brunner/Mazel.

Seligman, M.P. (1995). The effectiveness of psychotherapy: The Consumer Reports Study. *American Psychologist*, (12), 965-979.

Visher, E.B. & Visher, J.S. (1988). *Old Loyalties, New Ties: Therapeutic Strategies with Stepfamilies*. New York: Brunner/Mazel.

Visher, E.B. & Visher, J.S. (1996). *Therapy with Stepfamilies*. New York: Brunner/Mazel.

Current Knowledge About Child Abuse in Stepfamilies

Jean Giles-Sims

Each year, approximately one million cases of child abuse are reported and confirmed in the United States (Finkelhor, 1994). According to most studies, child abuse occurs in stepfamilies at higher rates than in natal families, but there are many unanswered questions about the accuracy of this claim and its causes. This paper will: (a) examine major studies on rates of child abuse in stepfamilies, (b) compare theoretical perspectives applied to this issue, and (c) discuss implications for research and practice. Gaining a full understanding of this issue will contribute to the research on how remarriages influence the development of increasing numbers of children and adolescents and will provide clearer guidelines for stepfamilies and practitioners.

CHILD ABUSE RATES IN STEPFAMILIES

The first step is to determine the child abuse rates in stepfamilies and to compare these rates to the percent of children living in stepfamilies. If the child abuse percentages are significantly higher, then, stepfamilies are overrepresented and stepchildren as a group run higher risk of child abuse

Jean Giles-Sims is Professor in the Sociology Department, Box 30790, Texas Christian University, Fort Worth, TX 76129.

The author thanks members of the Family Violence Research Laboratory for helpful comments on this paper.

[Haworth co-indexing entry note]: "Current Knowledge About Child Abuse in Stepfamilies." Giles-Sims, Jean. Co-published simultaneously in *Marriage & Family Review* (The Haworth Press, Inc.) Vol. 26, No. 3/4, 1997, pp. 215-230; and: *Stepfamilies: History, Research, and Policy* (ed: Irene Levin and Marvin B. Sussman) The Haworth Press, Inc., 1997, pp. 215-230. Single or multiple copies of this article are available for a fee from The Haworth Document Delivery Service [1-800-342-9678, 9:00 a.m. - 5:00 p.m. (EST). E-mail address: getinfo@haworth.com].

than in natal families. Analyses of census data indicate that remarriages represent approximately one in five existing marriages, but approximately one-third of recent marriages (Glick, 1989). Young couples remarrying often form stepfamilies with children from at least one former relationship, and approximately 10% of children live in stepfamilies (Bumpass, Sweet, & Cherlin, 1991). Other children visit in a home with a stepparent, but do not live there all the time.

Ideally, we could compare this 10% figure to the rates of child abuse in stepfamilies from random samples in community surveys. Unfortunately, the empirical studies differ in populations, some using community surveys and others reported cases. Reporting inconsistencies and a lack of common definitions also limit the quality of information on rates of child abuse in stepfamilies. Inconsistent findings also lead to controversy about the actual rates. In addition, rates for child physical abuse and child sexual abuse in stepfamilies tend to follow different patterns, and thus need to be addressed separately.

Child Physical Abuse

Does being raised in a stepfamily increase the risk to children of being slapped, punched, beaten, seriously injured or even killed over that of those being raised in another family structure (either natal two-parent or single-parent family)? Ideally, community survey data on family violence from representative populations would answer that question.

Data from the General Social Survey Cumulative File, 1972-1984 found that both the single-parent and the stepfamily structure were significantly related to violent victimization of all kinds, and the step-father condition is more strongly linked to victimization than the mother only situation (Austen & Arthur, 1992). This included children who were victimized both in their families or outside. Thus, children are less likely to be victimized in any way when they live in two-natal-parent families. Other data on family violence across family structures do not agree. Analyses of data from the Second National Family Violence Survey found no significant differences between genetic and non-genetic caregivers in rates of severe and very severe violence towards children. In fact, the rates of violence among non-genetic offspring were slightly lower (Gelles & Harrop, 1991). Sampling problems and different assessment techniques account for some of these differences in findings. The Family Violence Surveys may also underreport the most severe forms of family violence (Johnson, 1995; Straus, 1990), but these data do raise questions about assumed higher rates of victimization in stepfamilies.

Gelles and Harrop (1991) compared their findings of relatively low rates to the higher rates reported from clinical and official reports. Both community surveys and official reports suffer some threats to external validity. Underreporting likely marks most community surveys, and this may be particularly true for stepfamily problems, but data from reported cases may overrepresent stepfamily problems due to greater visibility, scrutiny or willingness to report.

Evidence from several studies using reported cases of child abuse indicates that the risk of physical abuse, homicide, neglect, and injuries is significantly higher in stepfamilies than in two-genetic-parent homes (Burgess & Garbarino, 1983; Daly & Wilson, 1981, 1985, 1987, 1991; Gil, 1970; Giles-Sims & Finkelhor, 1984; Kimball, Stewart, Conger & Burgess, 1980; Wilson, Daly & Weghorst, 1980). Many of these studies rely on household composition to determine family structure and do not directly test the relationship between abuser and victim. For example, studying households in Canada, Daly and Wilson (1981) found that 40% of abusive households included stepparents, and in other analyses Daly and Wilson (1985, 1987) concluded that children living with stepparents were significantly more likely to become abused and/or killed than those living with two genetic parents. Data from the National Incidence Study of reported cases also indicates disproportionate rates of abuse in stepfamilies; 24% of cases involved stepparents compared to assumed rates of approximately 10% for children living in stepfamilies (Giles-Sims & Finkelhor, 1984). Additional data from 24 households with child abuse victims indicates both that stepchildren are at greater risk and that parents are more likely to abuse stepchildren in the household than their own genetic children (Burgess & Garbarino, 1983; Lightcap, Kurkland, & Burgess, 1982).

In summary, at least in the most severe cases of child abuse that have been reported and confirmed, stepchildren are overrepresented. But, these findings cannot be used to confirm greater risks for all stepchildren. While stepchildren in some stepfamilies do risk unusual rates of physical abuse, others may not because of differences in family and individual characteristics or differences in patterns of parental caregiving. Risks to some children need to be distinguished from risks to all stepchildren.

Child Sexual Abuse

Each year about 15% of the million reported and confirmed cases of child abuse and neglect are child sexual abuse cases, and a review of retrospective community surveys indicates that approximately 20% of women and 5% to 10% of United States men recall some form of child sexual abuse (Finkelhor, 1994).

Finkelhor's summary of findings also indicates that women reported that the perpetrators were family members in one-third to one-half of cases, and men reported this in 10% to 20% of cases, with most perpetrators being male, and 20% to 25% of cases actually involved oral genital contact or penetration. Finkelhor critiques existing research for the lack of clear-cut definitions, reporting inconsistencies, and samples which do not adequately reflect the general population. Most research relies on official sources of data on known or reported cases, or it relies on retrospective surveys, and thus, suffers other limitations. In addition, data on stepfamily sexual abuse may suffer from biases of reporting or greater visibility to child protection agencies.

The sexual abuse literature is more consistent than the physical abuse literature in finding that children not living with both natural parents run higher risks of child sexual abuse both from family members and others, but the exact magnitude of reported risk varies across studies (Gordon, 1989; Gordon & Creighton, 1988; Finkelhor & Baron, 1986; Finkelhor, Hotaling, Lewis, & Smith, 1989; Finkelhor, 1993; Russell, 1984). In a review of studies which employed samples of the general United States population, Finkelhor & Baron (1986) concluded that family structure, particularly living with a stepfather, increases risk of sexual abuse, but that having a stepparent is only one of a number of interrelated risk factors. In most studies, the greatest number of cases of child sexual abuse involve natal family members, but reported case analyses and retrospective surveys indicate a significant disproportionate risk for children in stepfamilies. In one retrospective study, girls abused by stepfathers who were primary parents reported 17% rates of sexual abuse compared to 2% for abuse by the biological fathers, and rates by stepfathers who were not primary parents were reported as significantly higher (Russell, 1984). In total, four of six studies based on general populations found a strong association between having a stepparent and sexual abuse (Finkelhor & Baron, 1986). Again, this increased rate of victimization extends to sexual abuse risk from other men outside the family (Finkelhor, 1980). These additional findings raise concerns about the protective capacities of at least some non-natal father families.

Research done outside of the United States finds similar patterns. In the United Kingdom, of all 198 cases of father-daughter sexual abuse in the 1983-85 registers of child abuse, approximately 46% were non-natal fathers vs. 54% natal fathers (Gordon & Creighton, 1988). Assuming again that approximately 10% of children live in stepfamilies, non-natal fathers were disproportionately represented, but stepfather rates resembled natal-fathers more than other father substitutes (Gordon & Creighton,

1988). This evidence hints that increased commitment to the stepparenting role may decrease risk of sexual abuse. This will be discussed in a later section.

Controversy also exists about comparative seriousness of types of sexual abuse which occur in stepfamilies and in natal families. In Russell's (1984) study of a probability sample of 930 women residents of San Francisco, seriousness of sexual abuse was greater in stepfamilies than in natal families, with 47% of sexual abuse cases by stepfathers in the very serious level of violation compared with 26% for biological fathers. But Gordon and Creighton (1988) report that 37% of those abused by natal fathers were subjected to intercourse compared to 16% of stepfather victims and 21% of other father substitute victims. In a study of 102 cases of incest from a mental health treatment facility, Phelan (1986) also found that biological fathers engaged in intercourse more often than non-natal fathers, that the abuse more frequently involved multiple daughters, and that biological fathers were more likely than stepfathers to abuse adolescents. Currently available data do not allow more definitive answers. These issues need further research.

Gender and age do interact with family structure to influence rates of sexual abuse in stepfamilies. Men are the most common perpetrators for both girls and boys, and the greatest risks appear to be among the younger men. Stepfathers and father substitutes are also more likely to sexually abuse early in the relationship (Gordon & Creighton, 1988). In a study of 365 adults molested as children, boys and girls were equally likely to be molested by natal fathers, but girls were more likely than boys to be molested by stepfathers, and the molestation of boys ended earlier than for girls (Kendall-Tackett & Simon, 1992).

Children also risk sexual abuse from stepgrandparents. Comparing grandparents' abuse in 95 case records Margolin (1992) concluded that: the share of sexual abuse (35%) committed by stepgrandparents is far more than expected by chance, that stepgrandparent perpetrators were likely to be sexually abusive fathers, that they abused at the milder end of the sexual severity spectrum (fondling), but were more threatening and violent than abusive grandfathers.

Changes in Rates of Child Abuse in Stepfamilies over Time

As the prevalence of stepfamilies increases, more children will be exposed to stepparents and stepgrandparents, as well as step-siblings and other non-natal family members (Glick, 1989). Demographers estimate that 50% of children will spend at least some time in a single-parent home before they are eighteen, and many will become members of at least one stepfamily and maybe a series of multiple stepfamily households (Bumpass, 1990). This suggests that the 10% figure for stepchildren will rise over the next decades, but as yet we have little evidence of changes in rates of child physical or sexual abuse in stepfamilies over time. The numbers of stepchildren abused may increase because of increased numbers of children raised by stepparents, even when the rates remain constant.

Reporting of child physical and child sexual abuse has increased dramatically in the past 20 years, but most experts attribute this increase to greater awareness of the problems and willingness to report (Finkelhor, 1987). However, some community surveys indicate higher rates of sexual abuse among the youngest respondents which may reflect actual increased rates or greater recall or revealing of memories. Evidence from the Second National Survey of Family Violence indicated lower rates of violence to children in general in 1985 than in 1975, but no comparison could be made based on stepfamily structure (Straus & Gelles, 1986; Gelles & Straus, 1987).

Most of the existing research on differences in rates of child abuse by family structure was based on cases reported during the 1970s or 1980s, and the stepfamilies of the 90s may differ from earlier samples in some respects which interact with child abuse. First, there are likely to be more middle- and upper-class stepfamilies because higher income families have increased in rates of divorce and remarriage. Most analyses indicate greater rates of child physical abuse among lower-class families (Straus, Gelles & Steinmetz, 1980), but little or no relationship exists between social class and sexual abuse (Finkelhor & Baron, 1986; Finkelhor, 1987). These issues need more investigation. We know that only a low percent of stepchildren are physically or sexually abused, but we know little about which stepfamilies are at greatest risks and why.

CAUSES OF CHILD ABUSE IN STEPFAMILIES

Child abuse in stepfamilies has attracted a good deal of theoretical attention. While many studies examine abusing populations for individual or group characteristics, others focus on trying to explain the disproportionate rates of child abuse in stepfamilies or among non-natal caregivers with social-evolutionary theory. More recently, theory and research focus on different aspects of parenting including bonding, caregiving, and the development of moral responsibility among parents for children's welfare. Each of these types of theoretical arguments is based on different assumptions and offers different implications for individual families, researchers, practitioners and social policy makers.

Individual and Group Characteristics of Abusers

Children in stepfamilies risk child physical and child sexual abuse under the same conditions that influence rates in all populations. General group risk factors for child abuse include low income, large numbers of children, unemployment, isolation, stress, and norms that support use of physical force (Straus, Gelles & Steinmetz, 1980). Individual risk factors from clinical research include higher levels of drug and/or alcohol abuse, more disturbed family backgrounds, more problems with employment, and in some cases personal pathology (Gordon, 1989; Langevin & Watson, 1991; Dadds et al., 1991; Scott & Stone, 1986). However, most studies which identify individual characteristics indicate that profiles of abusers tend not to be above the mean in pathology (Scott & Stone, 1986), and that mental illness characterizes only a small minority of cases (Finkelhor, 1978).

Can individual or group characteristics explain higher rates of child abuse in stepfamilies? Research on this question requires showing that stepfamily members have a different profile on individual or group characteristics than natal families. Unfortunately, there are few sources for this information. Stepfamilies have in the past been overrepresented in low income categories, because divorce is more common at lower incomes, but recently these patterns of divorce and remarriage have been changing so that increasing numbers of remarried families occur at higher incomes (Bumpass, 1990). Some evidence indicates that stepfamily members have more employment problems and are younger at time of first marriage and first birth (Daly & Wilson, 1985). They also experience high stress levels particularly during the early adjustment period, and they tend to be less integrated into extended families and communities (Booth & Edwards, 1992). Theoretically, these factors contribute to overall higher rates of child abuse, particularly physical abuse, among stepfamilies. However, more empirical research is needed to establish which characteristics do influence child abuse in stepfamilies and to what extent.

Useful information from a related analysis was provided by Booth and Edwards (1992). These authors tested whether five characteristics of remarriage or remarried family members' individual characteristics influence higher rates of divorce in remarriage. These same characteristics may influence child abuse rates in stepfamilies. First, remarriages are "incomplete institutions" lacking strong norms which tend to inhibit behavior such as physical and sexual abuse in natal families. Second, remarriages select for individuals with more characteristics associated with social dysfunction which may be linked to child abuse. Third, people in remarriages tend to be less integrated with parents and in-laws contributing to isolation and perhaps more "opportunity" for child abuse, and fourth, the timing and age structure of remarriages vary from norms exposing children and young adolescents to close relations with new family members who are not adequately socialized to protect their development. The final factor tested was socio-economic status. All of these factors, except socio-economic characteristics, were associated with higher marital instability in remarriages. Similar analyses need to be completed for child abuse in stepfamilies. Several of these factors, including socio-economic status, likely influence child abuse.

Other research on levels of stepfamily conflict and coercion suggest these factors also need to be studied as above. Some studies find that parents in stepfamilies tend be more authoritarian and use coercion more than parents in natal families, and also have fewer problem-solving skills (Bray, Berger, Silverblatt & Hollier, 1987; Dornbusch, Ritter, Leiderman et al., 1987). These could all influence rates of child abuse.

The stepfamily literature contributes some information on factors related to an explanation for child abuse in stepfamilies, but at this time there is no adequate model for good stepfamily functioning (Pasley, Ihinger-Tallman & Lofquist, 1994) to guide individuals, researchers, or practitioners. Most existing research lumps all stepfamilies into one category and then compares stepfamily characteristics to natal family characteristics, often with a deficit-comparison model (Coleman & Ganong, 1990). Few studies provide within group comparisons (e.g., abusive stepfamilies vs. well-functioning stepfamilies). To identify protective factors or stepfamily characteristics which reduce or inhibit child abuse, the literature needs to give more attention to well-functioning stepfamilies.

Limited research compares abusing stepparents and abusing natal parents. Scott and Stone's (1986) study of sexual abuse examined individual characteristics of natal fathers, stepfathers, mothers and adolescent sexual abuse victims. Both types of fathers showed a moderate degree of antisocial attitudes, deficits of moral conscience and rationalized behaviors. In addition, natal fathers tended to show more passive-aggression, immaturity, and unrecognized dependency needs than stepfathers, but not at pathological levels (Scott & Stone, 1986). Mothers showed a dissociative pattern consistent with other portraits of unprotecting mothers of sexual abuse victims (Scott & Stone, 1986; Finkelhor, 1978). In a more recent psychometric assessment of variables associated with father-daughter incest, all incest families indicated high conflict, low cohesion and expressiveness, and low levels of active recreation (Dadds, Smith, Webber & Robinson, 1991), but fathers and stepfathers were mixed and not compared. Other research hints that natal families with incest histories may have more problematic characteristics than stepfamilies. Gordon's (1989) comparison of natal and stepfather abuse found that personal, social, and economic stress characterized natal father families more than stepfather families with abusers. This suggests that relationships between child abuse and stress, conflict, and individual pathology in stepfamilies may differ from those in natal families. For example, thresholds or patterns of tolerance or reporting may differ.

In summary, high risk families for child physical and sexual abuse include those with low incomes (for physical abuse primarily), high stress, antisocial attitudes and lack of training for protecting children among both parents, high conflict, low cohesion, isolation from friends and community, unemployment, drugs, alcohol and some personality dysfunctions. To the degree that persons with these problems self-select into stepfamilies at higher rates than natal families through divorce and remarriage or if stepfamily adjustments involve more stress and conflict and less cohesion, stepfamilies as a group risk higher rates of abuse. These characteristics may also help identify groups of or individual stepfamilies within the total population who risk abuse.

Social-Evolutional Theory and Child Abuse in Stepfamilies

Social-evolutionary theory relies on a biosocial assumption that natal parents invest a greater amount of resources such as time, energy, care, and financial assets in their biological offspring than do non-natal parents, stepparents and other parent substitutes. Biosocial researchers hypothesize that lack of investment leads to higher rates of abuse among non-genetic caretakers. According to this perspective, natural selection processes have shaped parental behaviors so that natal parents favor their own offspring, particularly under difficult social and economic circumstances. This theory predicts that both males and females will neglect, desert, or refuse investing in non-genetic household members. Researchers also hypothesize more direct negative intervention through physical and sexual abuse of non-genetic household members, and test this hypothesis comparing natal and non-natal rates of abuse. Several sources of data indicate higher rates of child physical abuse, sexual abuse, and homicide in non-natal families as evidence of this hypothesis (Burgess & Garbarino, 1983; Daly & Wilson, 1980, 1985, 1987, 1991; Lightcap, Kurkland & Burgess, 1982; Wilson, Daly & Weghorst, 1980).

Daly and Wilson (1991) explain that the major causal determinant of disproportionate rates of abuse in stepfamilies is that stepparents lack concern for the children's well-being and thus, children are subject to all kinds of increased risk of harm. This theory offers no explanation for abuse from natal caregivers. The basic tenet of the biosocial perspective, lack of investment, is only tested indirectly through abuse statistics. Gordon and Creighton's (1988) analyses of natal and non-natal fathers as sexual abusers in Great Britain do find higher rates of sexual abuse among non-natal fathers. But their analyses also indicate that stepfathers resemble natal fathers more than other father substitutes. This suggests that investment is malleable and can be learned or developed over time. These authors go on to emphasize that commitment to the father role (as distinctly learned) may be the neglected variable in studies of paternal caregivers. Commitment to the father role likely varies on some continuum across both natal and non-natal fathers. This concept of commitment to the father (or parent) role offers an opportunity to test the theory of investment more directly. Gordon and Creighton's (1988) findings also suggest more attention to parenting in general.

Caregiving, Parental Bonding and Child Abuse in Stepfamilies

Recent research on remarriage and stepparenting and/or child abuse emphasizes directing attention to the related concepts of parental bonding (Parker & Parker, 1986; Williams & Finkelhor, 1995), commitment to the parenting role (Gordon & Creighton, 1988; Herman, 1981), and to the learning and expression of care, the self-other orientation, and moral responsibility to other family members (Byrd & Smith, 1988; Giles-Sims, 1994; Gilgun, 1995; Smith, Goslen, Byrd & Reece, 1991).

In early research on sexual abuse, Herman (1980) found that the incestuous families she studied adhered to a very strong traditional division of labor, with men as providers having very little commitment to the caregiving dimension of the father's role. Since this time many other studies have furthered work on her insight. In Gordon and Creighton's study (1988), 49% of natal fathers reported sharing care-giving, 70% of stepfathers did, but only 39% of father substitutes did. The authors mention that natal incestuous fathers may have problems in bonding with their child victims. Stepfathers reported the highest rates of caregiving, differing significantly from father substitutes. This suggests that time in the relationship and commitment to caregiving likely influence rates of abuse. In a study comparing incestuous and non-incestuous fathers, Parker and Parker (1986) found that incestuous fathers spent less time in the home during the child's first three years than non-incestuous fathers, and they participated in less caregiving. This intriguing finding was explored in another comparison between incestuous fathers and non-incestuous fathers (Williams & Finkelhor, 1995). Again, low involvement with caregiving increased the risk of incest. In Williams & Finkelhor's (1995) analyses of two different samples, incestuous fathers fell into the low-care group more often than non-incestuous fathers (44% vs. 25% in one comparison and 46% vs. 17% in another). The relationship with caregiving became even stronger when other factors were controlled.

All of this research emphasizes the importance of parenting feelings and caregiving experiences. Does care-giving develop a self-other orientation between parent and child that reduces chances of abuse? If so, this would help explain the dramatically lower rates of child sexual abuse among women, but leave physical abuse by women to other explanations.

Three recent articles show the usefulness of the self-other orientation, and particularly the development of care to general theories of remarriage and stepparenting (Byrd & Smith, 1988; Giles-Sims, 1994; Smith et al., 1991). This perspective emphasizes the importance of whether partners (or parents and children) do or do not meet each other's needs fairly in interactions. Recent research on how incest perpetrators account for their behaviors used the justice and care perspective (Gilgun, 1995). In this study, most perpetrators claimed through their own descriptions of motivations that love and care characterized their relationships with daughters. But their refusal to stop when children wanted to stop belies this self-other orientation (Gilgun, 1995). This research concludes that the incest literature lacks a critical understanding of how incest perpetrators apply or avoid applying principles of justice and care.

Why has care and caregiving been a relatively neglected concept in this literature? Researchers and practitioners find that mothers provide most of the caregiving, and tend to neglect men's roles as caregivers. Our society also tends to take women's caregiving for granted, and thus deemphasize it's importance. In fact, only women's lack of care and protection has received much attention over time in the child abuse literature (Finkelhor, 1978). Care and relational morality can and must be learned. This suggests attention to norms about caregiving for males, and for stepfathers in particular. It also suggests training, monitoring and rewarding of caregiving, because good caregiving may reduce or inhibit child abuse in all types of family structures.

RESEARCH AND PRACTICE IMPLICATIONS

Research on Family Structure and Child Abuse

The remarriage and stepfamily literature has examined outcomes of family structure for children extensively. In a review of this literature Coleman and Ganong (1992) concluded that self-esteem (a frequent and important indicator of outcomes for children) and other important markers for child development do not differ significantly by family structure. Other research finds that parenting style and other variables such as family conflict have more impact on children than family structure (Dornbusch et al., 1987; Fine, Donnelly & Voydanoff, 1991; Fine, Kurdek & Hennigan, 1992; Kurdek & Sinclair, 1988). Coleman and Ganong (1992) recommend the alternative path of examining within-group comparisons. This suggests comparing abuse rates with an emphasis on parenting and household characteristics rather than simply on the basis of family structure. In addition, research can assess outcome variables for children in different family structures under different conditions (e.g., abuse experience, gender, stepparent-stepchild relationship, marital quality and parenting style). This will help eliminate the tendency to assume that all children in stepfamilies risk high rates of child abuse. We must identify which children are at higher risk rather than stereotype a whole family structure. Currently, accounts of child abuse risks in stepfamilies unnecessarily increase the existing negative attitudes and stereotypes associated with stepparenting (Ganong, Coleman & Jones, 1990).

Research on child abuse in stepfamilies needs to increasingly use standard definitions and measures, larger representative samples, and within-group comparisons. The theoretical arguments discussed in this paper also suggest including multidimensional theories to the analysis of the problem. For example, when commitment to the parenting role is taken into consideration, differences by family structure can be largely explained without relying solely on biosocial assumptions. Other suggestions include: (1) focus on the developmental stage of the individual and the stepfamily, and (2) increased attention to the dynamics of self-other orientation such as the development of moral responsibility in relationships. Additional suggestions can be found in Fine and Kurdek's (1994) outline of a four-dimensional model of stepfamily adjustment.

Practice Implications

Several of the factors identified by Fine and Kurdek (1994) provide specific cognitive foci for family practitioners. These include raising awareness both among stepfamily members and practitioners of the importance of clarity of role perception, having realistic perceptions, balanced causal attributions, reasonable beliefs about stepfamily identity and uniqueness, and parenting skills. Dealing with these basic issues both in educational and intervention programs could reduce the conditions that make some stepchildren risk abuse.

The care and justice perspective also offers a significant dimension to enhance practice and educational programs. Stepfamily members do or do not meet each other's needs and treat each other with relational morality. Gilgun (1994) found that sexual abusers indicate a rationality which distorts or denies the well-being of children. Direct implications of this include teaching morality and family justice using principles of care, self-other orientation, and a focus on how the other's needs are being met, rather than principles which can easily be distorted.

The care and justice perspective involves gender analysis and critique. Since most sexual abuse perpetrators are male and most victims female, the gender analysis is crucial to research, theory and practice when sexual abuse is the topic. This suggests continuing to focus on male dominance as it relates to feelings of ownership and rights to daughters, and imposing appropriate censure or penalty for sexual victimization of a dependent, either male or female. We must hold all caregivers responsible for their behavior in regards to the needs of children.

Most research finds that stepfamilies with girls have more adjustment problems than those with boys (Vuchinich, Hetherington, Vuchinich & Clingempeel, 1991). This observation of adjustment problems for girls could partly explain the greater risks to girls in stepfamilies and it also indicates that stepfamilies with girls may need more intervention than those with boys. Length of remarriage, boundary ambiguity within the family system, quality of the stepparent-stepchild relationship, and relationships with non-custodial parents and other family members also likely influence risks of adjustment problems and possible abuse for girls in stepfamilies. However, this does not suggest that boys' needs and experiences be overlooked. Each gender runs specific risks and may need unique interventions.

In summary, most studies of child abuse in stepfamilies indicate higher risks to children, particularly for sexual abuse of girls. For practice, this suggests more remarried family education, and opportunities for intervention. It does not mean that all children in stepfamilies are at risk. The factors that increase risk in stepfamilies likely include the same factors that put other children at risk, plus some individual and group characteristics that are more common in stepfamilies, and also a general lack of understanding and training for parental care and a morality which stresses the needs of children in the United States. All families would benefit from raising awareness and commitment to children.

REFERENCES

Austen, R.L. & Arthus, J. (1992). Family disruption, violent victimization and protest masculinity. *International Review of Victimology, 2,*(2), 103-125.
Booth, A., & Edwards, J.N. (1992). Starting over: Why remarriages are more unstable. *Journal of Family Issues, 13,* 179-194.

Bray, J.H., Berger, S.H., Silverblatt, A.H., & Hollier, A. (1987). Family process and organization during early remarriage: A preliminary analysis. In J.P. Vincent (Ed.), *Advances in family intervention, assessment, and theory* (pp. 253-279). Greenwich, CT: JAI Press.

Bumpass, L.L. (1990). What is happening to the family? Interactions between demographic and institutional change. *Demography, 27*, 483-498.

Bumpass, L., Sweet, J.A., & Cherlin, A. (1991). The role of cohabitation in declining rates of marriage. *Journal of Marriage and the Family, 53*, 913-927.

Burgess, R.L., & Garbarino, J. (1983). Doing what comes naturally? An evolutionary perspective on child abuse. In D. Finkelhor, R. Gelles, M. Straus, & G. Hotaling (Eds.), *The Dark Side of Families: Current Family Violence Research* (pp. 88-101). Newbury Park, CA: Sage Publications.

Byrd, A.J., & Smith, R.M. (1988). A qualitative analysis of the decision to remarry using Gilligan's ethics of care. *Journal of Divorce, 11*(3-4), 87-102.

Coleman, M. & Ganong, L.H. (1990). Remarriage & stepfamily research in the 1980s: Increased interest in an old family form. *Journal of Marriage, 52*(4), 925-940.

Coleman M., & Ganong, L.H. (1992, April). *Effects of remarriage on children: Clinical implications.* Presentation at the 6th International Congress on Family Therapy, "Divorce and Remarriage Interdisciplinary Issues and Approaches," Jerusalem, Israel.

Dadds, M., Smith, M., Webber, Y. & Robinson, A. (1991). An exploration of family and individual profiles following father-daughter incest. *Child Abuse & Neglect, 15*(4), 575-586.

Daly M. & Wilson, M. (1981). Child maltreatment from a sociobiological perspective. *New Directions for Child Development, 11*, 93-112.

Daly, M. & Wilson, M. (1985). Child abuse and other risks of not living with both parents. *Ethnology and Sociobiology, 6*, 197-210.

Daly, M. & Wilson, M. (1987). Evolutionary psychology and family violence. In C. Crawford, M. Smith and D. Krebs (Eds.), *Sociobiology and Psychology* (pp. 293-309). Hillsdale, New Jersey: Lawrence Erlbaum Associates.

Daly, M. & Wilson, M. (1991). A reply to Gelles: Stepchildren are disproportionately abused, and diverse forms of violence can share causal factors. *Human Nature, 2*(4), 93-98.

Dornbusch, S.M., Ritter, P.L., Leiderman, P.H., Roberts, D.F., & Fraleigh, M.J. (1987). The relation of parenting style to adolescent school performance. *Child Development, 58*, 1244-1257.

Fine, M.A., Kurdek, L.A., & Hennigen, L. (1992). Family structure, gender, perceived ambiguity of (step)parent roles, and perceived self-competence in young adolescent. *Family Perspective, 25*, 261-282.

Finkelhor, D. (1987). The sexual abuse of children: Current research reviewed. *Psychiatric Annals, 17*(4), 233-241.

Finkelhor, D. (1993). Epidemiological factors in the clinical identification of child sexual abuse. *Child Abuse and Neglect: The International Journal, 17*(1), 67-70.

Finkelhor, D. (1994). Current information on the scope and nature of child sexual abuse. *The Future of Children, 4*(2), 31-53.

Finkelhor, D. & Baron, L. (1986). Risk factors for child sexual abuse. *Journal of Interpersonal Violence, 1*(1), 43-71.

Ganong, L.H., Coleman, M., & Jones, G. (1990). Effects of behavior and family structure on perceptions. *Journal of Educational Psychology, 82*, 820-825.

Gelles, R.J., & Straus, M.A. (1987). Is violence toward children increasing? A comparison of 1975 and 1985 national survey rates. *Journal of Interpersonal Violence, 2*, 212-222.

Gelles, R.J., & Harrop, J.W. (1991). The risk of abusive violence among children with nongenetic caregivers. *Family Relations, 40*(1), 78-83.

Gil, D. (1970). *Violence against children: Physical Child Abuse in the United States.* Cambridge, MA: Harvard University Press.

Giles-Sims, J., & Finkelhor, D. (1984). Child abuse in stepfamilies. *Family Relations, 33*, 407-414.

Gilgun, J.F. (1995). We shared something special: The moral discourse of incest perpetrators. *Journal of Marriage and the Family, 57*(2), 265-281.

Glick, P. (1989). Remarried families, stepfamilies, and stepchildren: A brief demographic profile. *Family Relations, 38*, 24-27.

Gordon, M. (1989). The family environment of sexual abuse: A comparison of natal and stepfather abuse. *Child Abuse & Neglect, 13*(1), 121-130.

Gordon, M. & Creighton, S.J. (1988). Natal and nonnatal fathers as sexual abusers in the United Kingdom: A comparative analysis. *Journal of Marriage and the Family, 50*(1), 99-105.

Johnson, M.P. (1995). Patriarchal terrorism and common couple violence: Two forms of violence against women. *Journal of Marriage and the Family, 57*(2), 283-294.

Kendall-Tackett, K.A. & Simon, A.F. (1992). A comparison of the abuse experiences of male and female adults molested as children. *Journal of Family Violence, 7*(1), 57-62.

Kimball, W.H., Stewart, R.B., Conger, R.D., & Burgess, R.L. (1980). A comparison of family interaction in single versus two parent abusive, neglectful and normal families. In T. Field, S. Goldberg, D. Stern, & A. Sostek (Eds.), *Interactions of high risk infants and children*, 43-59. New York: Academic Press.

Kurdek, L.A., & Sinclair, R.J. (1988). Relation of eighth graders' family structure, gender, and family environment with academic performance and school behavior. *Journal of Educational Psychology, 80*, 90-94.

Langevin, R. & Watson, R. (1991). A comparison of incestuous biological and stepfathers. *Annals of Sex Research, 4*(2), 141-150.

Lightcap, J.L., Kurland, J.A., & Burgess, R.L. (1982). Child abuse: A test of some predictions from evolutionary theory. *Ethology and Sociobiology, 3*, 61-67.

Margolin, L. (1992). Sexual abuse by grandparents. *Child Abuse and Neglect: The International Journal, 16*(5), 735-741.

Parker, H., & Parker, S. (1986). Father-daughter sexual abuse: An emerging perspective. *American Journal of Orthopsychiatry, 56*, 531-549.

Pasley, K., Ihinger-Tallman, M. & Lofquist, A. (1994). Remarriage and stepfamilies: Making progress in understanding. In K. Pasley & M. Ihinger-Tallman (Eds.), *Stepparenting: Issues in Theory, Research, and Practice* (pp. 1-14). Westport, CT: Greenwood.

Russel, D.E. (1984). The prevalence and seriousness of incestuous abuse: Stepfathers vs. biological fathers. *Child Abuse and Neglect, 8,* 15-22.

Scott, R.L. & Stone, D.A. (1986). MMPI profile constellation in incest families. *Journal of Consulting and Clinical Psychology, 54*(3), 364-348.

Smith, R. M., Gosley, M.A., Byrd, A.J. & Reece, L. (1991). Self-other orientation and sex-role orientation of men and women who remarry. *Journal of Divorce and Remarriage, 14*(3/4), 3-32.

Straus, M.A. (1990). Injury and frequency of assaults and the "representative sample fallacy" in measuring wife beating and child abuse. In M.A. Straus & R.J. Gelles (Eds.), *Physical Violence in American Families: Risk Factors and Adaptations in 8,145 Families* (pp. 49-73). New Brunswick, N.J.: Transaction Books.

Straus, M.A., & Gelles, R.J. (1986). Societal change and change in family violence from 1975 to 1985 as revealed in two national surveys. *Journal of Marriage and the Family, 48,* 465-479.

Straus, M.A., Gelles, R.J. & Steinmetz, S.K. (1980). *Behind Closed Doors: Violence in the American Family.* New York: Doubleday/Anchor.

Vuchinich, S., Hetherington, E.M., Vuchinich, R., & Clingempeel, W.G. (1991). Parent-child interaction and gender differences in early adolescents' adaptation to stepfamilies. *Developmental Psychology, 27,* 618-626.

Wilson, M., Daly, M., & Weghorst, S.J. (1980). Household composition and the risk of child abuse and neglect. *Journal of Biosociological Science, 12,* 333-340.

Stepfamilies from a Legal Perspective

Margaret M. Mahoney

I. INTRODUCTION

Within many stepfamilies little attention is paid to the legal aspects of the stepparent-child relationship until a particular problem arises. This article focuses on the ways in which stepfamily members in the United States can take greater control of this dimension of their family life. In many cases, advance planning can prevent legal problems from arising at a later time.

The starting point in any discussion about planning for stepfamilies is an understanding about their status under the laws that regulate family relationships. The question then becomes whether effective steps can be taken by the family to modify the relationship imposed by law. In fact, the U.S. legal system limits the scope of private planning available for many important family issues.

This article focuses on several legal aspects of the stepparent-child relationship where the question of advance planning may arise: the financial support of minor children, the disposition of the stepparent's estate in the event of his or her death, and the custody of minor stepchildren in the event of the custodial parent's death. As to each of these economic and custodial issues, some individuals may prefer sets of rights and duties different than those currently imposed by state law. This article describes the underlying rules of law regulating the stepparent-child relationship in these areas, and the manner and extent to which they can be modified in the individual stepfamily by private action.

Margaret M. Mahoney is Professor of Law, School of Law, University of Pittsburgh.

[Haworth co-indexing entry note]: "Stepfamilies from a Legal Perspective." Mahoney, Margaret M. Co-published simultaneously in *Marriage & Family Review* (The Haworth Press, Inc.) Vol. 26, No. 3/4, 1997, pp. 231-247; and: *Stepfamilies: History, Research, and Policy* (ed: Irene Levin and Marvin B. Sussman) The Haworth Press, Inc., 1997, pp. 231-247. Single or multiple copies of this article are available for a fee from The Haworth Document Delivery Service [1-800-342-9678, 9:00 a.m. - 5:00 p.m. (EST). E-mail address: getinfo@haworth.com].

Many of the underlying rules of law discount the role of the stepparent in the family. Thus, as a general rule, stepparents have no legal child support responsibilities. Under the laws of inheritance, stepchildren are not regarded as heirs entitled to inherit their stepparent's property. Further, in the event of the death of a custodial parent, legal custody generally passes to the surviving parent, without regard for the stepparent-child relationship. Within this framework, some families may desire to create a more significant legal role for the stepparent.

As to some of these issues, the presence of the noncustodial parent directly impacts the ability of stepfamily members to enhance the stepparent's legal status. For example, the power of the custodial parent and stepparent to make arrangements for the child's custody in the event of the custodial parent's death is severely limited by the legal rights of the remaining biologic parent. Absent the noncustodial parent's cooperation, it is difficult to prevent the automatic award of custody to the surviving biologic parent upon the death of the custodial parent. On the other hand, as to other issues, the presence of the noncustodial parent is irrelevant. For example, the presence or absence of the second biologic parent has no effect upon the stepparent's freedom to execute a will that benefits the stepchildren.

The presence of the noncustodial parent directly impacts another important matter, namely, the decision whether the stepparent will adopt the stepchild. In the eyes of the law, the adoptive stepparent must take over the legal role of the noncustodial parent. While the adoption decision has many complex aspects, from a legal perspective it is the ultimate planning device for establishing legally binding relationships within the stepfamily. Notably, adoption transforms the role of the stepparent from that of quasi-stranger to that of legal parent, with all of the rights and obligations of biologic parents. The adoptive stepparent has full custodial authority and full economic responsibility for the child, thus obviating any need for the issue-by-issue planning described in this article. Therefore, the stepparent adoption decision is discussed below before the specific issues of planning for child support, inheritance, and custody within the stepfamily.

II. THE ADOPTION DECISION

A significant portion of all adoptions in the United States occur within stepfamilies (Hollinger, § 1.05(2)). Still, most stepparents do not adopt their minor stepchildren. The considerations that enter into the decision by a stepparent and custodial parent to formalize the family in this fashion are multiple and complex. From a legal perspective, the stepparent must be willing to make a commitment to the child comparable to the assumption of rights and obligations by parents in the traditional family. In addition, the custodial parent (the stepparent's spouse) must agree to this change in family status, since state adoption laws require such concurrence. In the case of older stepchildren, their consent may be required as well (UAA, § 4-103). Finally, the child's legal relationship with the other biologic parent must be terminated before stepparent adoption can take place. Such termination can be based on either voluntary consent to the adoption or the decision by a court to involuntarily terminate the noncustodial parent's rights. Where the noncustodial parent has played an active role in the child's life, by spending time together and/or providing economic support, a judge will be very reluctant to sever the biologic parent-child relationship. Indeed, in these circumstances, well-established statutory and constitutional standards generally protect the noncustodial parent who objects to a proposed stepparent adoption (Clark, 888-894).

A recent proposed change to state adoption laws may affect the way that family members think about the appropriateness of stepparent adoption in particular cases. The National Conference of Commissioners on Uniform States Laws, which worked for many years on a comprehensive code to govern all aspects of the adoption process, finally made their Uniform Adoption Act available in 1994 for enactment by the state legislatures. One of the controversial issues discussed during the drafting process was open adoption, a proposed model whereby the biologic parents would be permitted to play an ongoing role following adoption of their child. This model involves a significant deviation from the current adoption model, which requires the complete legal termination of parental interests prior to adoption. In the end, the only version of open adoption incorporated into the Uniform Act appears in the section describing stepparent adoption. Section 4-113 provides that the adoption court may include in its order an enforceable provision permitting the noncustodial parent (or grandparents or siblings) to communicate or visit with the child following a stepparent adoption.

Within the first year of its completion, bills proposing to enact the Uniform Adoption Act were introduced in six state legislatures (Family Law Reporter, 1328). Widespread adoption of the Act would constitute a radical change in the laws that regulate post-adoption visitation. To date, only a handful of state lawmakers have exhibited any willingness to move beyond the traditional notion that the stepparent who adopts must totally displace the natural parent in the eyes of the law (Mahoney, 181-189 (collecting statutes and cases)). Even these exceptional provisions generally require the agreement of all parties at the time of the adoption before visitation rights can be recognized. The Uniform Act, by way of contrast, provides that "[i]n addition to any agreement approved [by the adoption court], the court may approve the continuation of an existing order or issue a new order permitting the minor adoptee's former parent . . . to visit or communicate with the minor . . ." (§ 4-113(c)). Not surprisingly, the Act authorizes the court to enter a post-adoption visitation order, with or without the agreement of the parties, only if it would serve the best interests of the child.

The topic of open adoption is complex and controversial, both as a general model and specifically as applied in the stepfamily context. On the one hand, opponents argue that the adoptive family needs a "fresh start," free of uninvited interference from biologic family members. Furthermore, the child needs a single line of parental authority, which must be provided by the adoptive parents. And finally, the availability of future lawsuits by the noncustodial parent opens the door to the undesirable continuing involvement of the legal system in the newly formalized adoptive family. On the other hand, the recognition of a limited future relationship between the child and the natural parent, whose rights are otherwise terminated prior to the adoption, may have positive effects for the child. Especially where the child is older and has an established bond with the parent, post-adoption visitation enables important family relationships to continue. In all cases, continuing contact between the parties enables the child to know about his or her biologic roots. The drafters of the UAA apparently found the latter set of arguments to be compelling enough in the stepfamily setting to permit the adoption courts to fashion and enforce orders regarding parental visitation based on the child's best interests.

If the UAA visitation provision is enacted at the state level, to what extent will such a change affect the decisions of stepparents to seek adoption, the decisions of noncustodial parents regarding consent, and the decisions of the courts who must decide whether adoption petitions should be granted? The drafters of the UAA stated that the post-adoption visitation provision may increase the number of stepparent adoptions (Introductory Comment to Article 4). While the matter is somewhat speculative, there is reason to believe that the decisions of all of the relevant players may be affected in a manner that will encourage adoption.

First, the drafters of the UAA stated that the noncustodial parent may be more likely in some cases to consent to a proposed stepparent adoption and the termination of his or her parental rights, if the adoption order contains an enforceable provision regarding future visitation. It remains to be seen, however, exactly what weight will be assigned to such visitation rights if problems arise down the road, such as interference by the adoptive family with visitation arrangements. The Act provides for judicial enforcement "only if the court finds that enforcement is in the best interest of a minor adoptee." (§ 4-112 (e)). In other words, enforcement is not guaranteed. Still, the availability of a formal visitation order, coupled with the termination of child support responsibility and all other economic and custodial rights and obligations, may prove to be an attractive new option for many noncustodial parents. If so, then the prediction of the Uniform Act's drafters regarding an increase in the number of noncustodial parents consenting to stepparent adoptions will be realized.

The impact of the post-adoption visitation provision in *contested* stepparent adoption cases is also speculative. Here the question is whether courts might be more willing to terminate the rights of the noncustodial parent and order a stepparent adoption, in spite of the noncustodial parent's objections, if continuing visitation becomes a legal option. In the past, most decisions to deny adoption petitions in contested cases have focused on preservation of the biologic parent-child relationship (Hollinger, § 2.10(3)(c)). It is possible that judges will be more willing to order stepparent adoptions if state law recognizes a post-adoption visitation right for the noncustodial parent.

Finally, the views of stepfamily members themselves about the desirability of adoption may be influenced by the enactment of the open adoption provision of the UAA. To the extent that the custodial parent, stepparent, and child welcome and value the child's association with the other biologic parent, the current adoption model may seem inappropriate to them. A new model like the UAA, which sanctions an ongoing legal tie with the noncustodial parent following stepparent adoption, may encourage such families to think more seriously about adoption. On the other hand, if the noncustodial parent is regarded as an unwelcome intruder in the stepfamily, the model that contemplates his or her continuing participation in the child's life may be less attractive to the custodial parent and stepparent than the current law of adoption. Where the stepparent seeks adoption but objects to parental visitation, the Uniform Act provides that the judge must consider any objections by the stepfamily in deciding whether visitation would be in the child's best interests (§ 4-112(d)). Another important factor that enters into the adoption decision for many stepfamilies, relating to child support responsibility, is left unaffected by the Uniform Adoption Act. No doubt, the release of the noncustodial parent from all economic responsibility under state laws will remain a significant consideration that cautions against adoption in many stepfamilies. Thus, it remains to be seen whether the enactment of a post-adoption visitation provision by the state legislatures will increase the number of stepparents seeking to adopt their stepchildren.

When a stepparent adoption occurs, the stepparent becomes the second legal parent for all purposes, including economic and custodial responsibility. This major transition negates the need for the type of stepfamily planning in the areas of support, inheritance and custody that are described in the remainder of this paper. These issues remain relevant in the large majority of stepfamilies, however, because most stepparents never adopt their stepchildren.

III. CREATING AN ENFORCEABLE CHILD SUPPORT DUTY

The issue of financial support for minor stepchildren is a vital one in many stepfamilies. This section first describes the manner in which the child support laws allocate responsibility between the two biologic parents and the stepparent. Notably, these laws create enforceable legal duties which may not necessarily coincide with the actual responsibilities voluntarily assumed by the adults in many families. Next, the discussion outlines the extent to which adult stepfamily members are able to take steps to create enforceable stepparent support obligations in addition to those imposed by the child support laws, and the situations where this type of economic planning may be desirable.

The child support laws in every state in the United States impose strict duties on both of the biologic parents, including the parent who does not reside with the child in the stepfamily. By way of contrast, stepparents are rarely required to make any financial contribution. Currently, only ten states impose a support duty on all stepparents who share a home with their spouses' minor children. Another eight states create the stepparent support duty only in families where the child would otherwise be destitute. In the remaining states, stepparents are not required to support their stepchildren (Mahoney, 38-40 (collecting statutes)). A key aspect of the law in every state, including those that impose stepparent obligations, is the stepparent's clear right to end all contributions as soon as the stepparent and stepchild cease to reside in the same household.

Against the backdrop of laws requiring no financial contribution, many stepparents do in fact help to support the stepchildren with whom they reside, either through direct contributions to the child's personal expenses or through contributions to general household expenses such as food and shelter. The stepparent here is regarded as a person voluntarily standing "in loco parentis" or "in the place of a parent." As defined by the courts, the in loco parentis doctrine permits the stepparent to withdraw support at any time. Furthermore, such voluntary contributions by the stepparent do not, at least as a theoretical matter, reduce the amount of the parents' obligation. As a result, the noncustodial parent is not permitted to reduce the amount of a court-ordered support obligation on the ground that the custodial stepparent contributes to the child's support (Mahoney, 41-45 (collecting cases)). Thus, the imposition of formal support responsibility exclusively on the natural parents has numerous legal ramifications, even in families where the stepparent actually contributes to the support of stepchildren.

Although state child support laws largely leave the question of child support to the stepparent's discretion, two important federal programs, which assist families on the basis of financial need, make a blanket assumption that all stepparents support their stepchildren. First, the Aid to Families with Dependent Children [AFDC] Program provides income assistance to needy families with minor children. Second, several federal programs make financial aid for higher education available to students based on the amount of income in the household of the custodial parent (Higher Education Resources and Student Assistance). The blanket assumption about stepparent contributions to stepchild support effectively reduces the amount of public assistance and financial aid available to stepchildren whose custodial stepparent has income and/or resources. Such a reduction of benefits may operate as an indirect incentive to the stepparent to actually provide support to minor stepchildren who are ineligible for AFDC or older stepchildren who fail to qualify for educational loans and grants. Where the incentive does not work in this way, however, stepchildren are left with neither the protection of a state law requiring stepparent support nor the right to federal need-based benefits.

In planning for the financial well-being of minor stepchildren, the primary resources available are likely to be the income and assets of the responsible adults. Steps should be taken to assure, to the extent possible, that anticipated contributions from both natural parents will indeed be available in the future. For example, the purchase of life insurance protects against the risk of parental death while the child is still dependent. Furthermore, the custodial parent, on behalf of the child, is able to obtain and enforce a child support order in the event that the noncustodial parent does not voluntarily provide support. The discussion here, however, focuses not on the income and resources of the two natural parents, but on the status of the stepparent as a source of child support. Specifically, in light of the discretion conferred upon stepparents by state law to determine whether or not they will undertake any financial responsibility, is it desirable and/or feasible to create binding stepparent obligations?

A private contract is the most effective means available for creating a legal obligation that binds the stepparent to provide future child support. Typically, the parties to the contract would be the stepparent and the custodial parent, who may reach such an agreement prior to marriage (an antenuptial or prenuptial contract), during the marriage, or in preparation for divorce (a separation agreement). Under contract law, the stepparent's voluntary promise regarding child support becomes legally enforceable when it is made in exchange for promises by the custodial parent regarding other matters. The stepparent's motivation to voluntarily assume a financial obligation may be complex and varied. First, the stepparent may be moved by concern for the well-being of the child and the custodial parent. Additionally, the promise to support a stepchild may be made in exchange for the waiver of other financial rights by the spouse, such as the right to certain property at the time of divorce. In many cases, the emphasis is likely to shift away from the altruistic, and more toward the bargained financial exchange, when the contract is made at the time of divorce.

To assure enforceability, the stepparent's promise to undertake stepchild support duties during the marriage or following a divorce should be in writing. Although unwritten contracts about voluntary family support are recognized in many states, it is frequently difficult to obtain enforcement absent a writing. Thus, in a number of reported cases, stepparents have made oral statements before or during marriage that they will "take care of" stepchildren and "treat them as my own children." Courts have generally refused to find a binding promise in here, even if the custodial parent made concessions to the stepparent in exchange for these financial commitments. The courts have ruled that the stepparent's oral statements merely demonstrate an intention to assume "in loco parentis" responsibility, which can be set aside by the stepparent at any time, and nothing more (Mahoney, pp. 27-31 (collecting cases)). These results highlight the importance of a clear, written agreement to provide child support under designated circumstances.

Of course, to many individuals, the execution of a written contract is the antithesis of the love and trust that they experience as the basis of their family life. Nevertheless, the practice of making contracts prior to marriage, or sometime into the marriage when divorce is not an issue, is becoming more common. First, the process of reaching an express understanding about important financial issues can be beneficial, especially in nontraditional families where the "family tree" tends to be complicated. Second, a growing number of people entering marriage prefer to anticipate and prepare for the future at a time when the parties are still "on the same wavelength" regarding responsibilities in their family. If their planning for the future includes the assumption of child support responsibility by the stepparent, then the discussion should focus, among other things, on the amount and duration of the stepparent's responsibility. For example, do the parties anticipate that the stepparent will contribute to the child's higher education? Do they anticipate that the responsibility will continue in the event that the marriage terminates either by divorce or by the death of the custodial parent? While detailed rules of law define the scope of the support duty of biologic parents under all of these circumstances, there is no corresponding legal reference point for stepparents. To the extent that the parties seek to create a stepparent support duty, they must carefully spell out their understanding in the contract. Of course, private contracts can be updated or terminated at any time in the future with the consent of both parties.

In the absence of a contract, state laws generally do not require the stepparent to provide support following divorce from the custodial parent. The exceptions to this rule are extremely limited (N.D. Cent. Code § 14-09-09; Mahoney, 31-38 (describing the doctrine of equitable estoppel)). The stepparent may, however, voluntarily agree to assume such responsibility in a contract executed at any time prior to or during marriage, or following divorce. The contractual obligation differs from the post-divorce duties of natural parents in several respects. For example, the amount of support owed by natural parents is generally determined by reference to the law of child support, including state child support guidelines; the stepparent's obligation will be determined solely by reference to the contract terms. Similarly, the body of law creating avenues of enforcement for parental child support obligations, including imprisonment for contempt, does not apply to the contract obligations of stepparents; rather, separate remedies are available to enforce promises to pay money as a matter of contract law. In other words, the parties can create an enforceable contract, but they cannot do what the state has failed to do: impose a true post-divorce child support duty on the stepparent. Still, the assumption of contractual responsibility is a serious matter, to be undertaken by the stepparent only if he or she determines that such a step makes sense either from the point of view of family commitments or as part of a deal in which adequate financial consideration is exchanged.

IV. ESTATE PLANNING

Estate planning is an important financial and legal concern in many families, and this is especially true in stepfamilies. The purchase of life insurance and the writing of wills by adult family members are the most common elements of a family estate plan, designed to provide economic protection for the survivors in the event that one family member dies. This section focuses specifically on the laws in the United States regulating the disposition of the stepparent's estate. First, in the absence of a will, the state inheritance laws dictate those persons who will receive the decedent's property, and stepchildren are uniformly excluded from this benefit. Furthermore, the owner who makes a will is limited by other laws that guarantee a share of the estate for the surviving spouse and biologic or adopted children. Careful planning and drafting of the stepparent's will can assure that his or her goals regarding economic protection for surviving family members are achieved in light of these regulations.

State inheritance laws identify the closest surviving relatives as the heirs of every person who dies without a will. When both a spouse and children (or grandchildren who are the children of a deceased child) survive, they share the estate after the payment of taxes and creditors. When there is no spouse, the children inherit everything. Conversely, when there are no children, the spouse is usually the sole heir. Finally, when there are no children and no spouse, the property passes to more distant relatives, such as parents and siblings. As noted in Section III, the adoption of stepchildren during the stepparent's lifetime lifts their status to that of "children" for this purpose. Absent adoption, however, the stepchildren are not regarded as relatives and do not inherit from their deceased stepparent (Mahoney, 53-60 (collecting statutes and cases)).

Of course, the stepparent is able to set aside this statutory plan of distribution by executing a will. In the stepfamily, the desire to directly benefit minor or adult stepchildren at death can be accomplished only in this manner. The stepparent's will must be carefully drafted in order to overcome the assumption in the law that stepchildren are not "natural objects of bounty" like those relatives named in the inheritance statute. In a number of reported cases, stepparents who apparently intended to benefit their stepchildren failed to do so because the language of the will was not clear enough to overcome the preference in the law for members of the traditional family. For example, a bequest "to my children" is generally presumed to include biologic and adoptive children but not stepchildren (Restatement (Second) of Property § 25.6). To avoid confusion, the will should name each stepchild who is an intended beneficiary. Thus, stepparents are able to make bequests to stepchildren as long as the will carefully spells out this intention.

In planning for the distribution of property at death, the owner's freedom to make a will is limited by two family-related rules. First, state laws provide that a minimum share (frequently one-third or one-half) of the estate must pass to the surviving spouse, even if the testator prefers some other distribution (Gregory et al., 59-60). In the stepfamily where the stepparent is married at the time of death to the custodial parent of step-children, it seems unlikely that this restriction will seriously interfere with the desire to provide for surviving family members. The second type of limitation, which exists in less than half the states, prevents the disinheritance of minor children who are the beneficiaries of an outstanding child support order at the time of their parent's death (Gregory et al., 269; Uniform Marriage and Divorce Act § 316(c)). The amount of the children's claim is determined by reference to the amount of child support the parent owed to them. This type of provision could affect estate planning within the stepfamily if the stepparent has children from another relationship, living in another household, who are entitled to assert such a claim.

Within this legal framework, a number of factual scenarios can be envisioned where a will is necessary to accomplish the economic goals of the stepparent for surviving family members. First, where the custodial parent, stepparent and stepchildren reside together as a stepfamily, it may appear that the inheritance laws would protect the stepchildren by passing a significant portion of the stepparent's estate to the custodial parent (the stepparent's spouse) who would be naturally inclined to share it with the children. Even in this situation, however, the stepparent may desire a different distribution of the estate in order to guarantee the welfare of the children. For example, the stepparent may choose to make a gift to the stepchildren specifically earmarked for their education. The law of wills permits this type of arrangement; a simple distribution of the estate to the surviving spouse does not similarly guarantee that the assets will be used for this purpose.

Furthermore, if the stepparent dies without a will, the surviving spouse must share the estate with any surviving biologic or adoptive children. These may be the children that the spouse and the decedent had together, or they may be the decedent's children from a prior relationship. If the stepparent is survived by children from a prior relationship who reside in another household, the law of inheritance would distribute a significant share of the estate to those children, and out of the stepfamily, upon the stepparent's death. In some cases, the stepparent may prefer a different distribution, and the law of wills would permit this type of control. Even in the minority of states that recognize compulsory claims against the estate by children with outstanding child support orders, the amount of such claims may be less than the children's share as heirs.

Perhaps the most compelling situation arises when the custodial parent (the stepparent's spouse) predeceases the stepparent who thereafter assumes continuing responsibility for the stepchildren. In the absence of a will, on the stepparent's death, the inheritance laws in every state would distribute the estate to the stepparent's other relatives. The stepchildren would not benefit at all from the estate. A will enables the stepparent to leave property to the stepchildren subject only to the possible claims of biologic children if they have outstanding support orders, and the surviving spouse if the stepparent has remarried.

Another scenario in which, in the absence of a will, the stepchildren receive no direct benefit from the stepparent's estate and no indirect benefit through a surviving custodial parent involves the family where the parent and stepparent have divorced before the stepparent's death. Here, neither the parent's former spouse nor the stepchildren are heirs under state inheritance laws. The stepparent who has maintained a caring relationship with his or her stepchildren following divorce may desire to provide for them in the event of death. The only way to accomplish this financial goal is through a will.

Of course, the subject of estate planning in the stepfamily is much more complex than this discussion suggests. As a general rule, the spouses (custodial parent and stepparent) make these types of plans together, executing wills that provide for various contingencies, including the death of each before the other. Ideally, where there is a noncustodial parent of the stepchildren, some coordination with that person takes place as well. And where the stepparent is responsible for additional children who reside in a different household, financial planning for the extended family also involves the custodial parent of those children. Within this complex picture, however, the stepparent must understand that unless a specific bequest to stepchildren is made by will, they will not be included among the direct beneficiaries of the stepparent's estate.

Finally, this discussion has addressed for the most part the scenario where the stepparent dies while the stepchildren are still dependent minors residing in the stepfamily. Most people, however, die only after their children and stepchildren have reached adulthood and established independent lives. Within the stepfamily, as well as other families, individual and family economic goals may change over time, and estate plans may be updated following major changes in family status, such as the death of a spouse, marriage of a child, or birth of grandchildren. A will can be easily revoked at any time and replaced by a new will reflecting current testamentary goals. Notably, the rules of inheritance in the absence of a will are the same whatever the ages of the parties. The surviving spouse and children (or grandchildren who are the children of a deceased child) inherit everything. The stepchildren, whether they are minors or adults with children of their own, become beneficiaries of their stepparent's estate only if they are named in the stepparent's last will.

V. STEPPARENT CUSTODY

The process of making a will, discussed in the last section, causes many parents to focus on an important nonfinancial issue, namely, the custody of minor children in the event of parental death while the children are still young. In families where the children reside with just one of the biologic parents, such as the stepfamily, the parent's death frequently creates a legal crisis. The underlying legal rules provide that a court must decide who will care for minor children when the parent/custodian dies, and there is a very strong presumption that the next custodian will be the other biological parent if he or she is still alive. As described in this section, the ability of stepfamily members to override this legal scheme and designate the surviving stepparent as the future custodian is extremely limited.

The two biologic (or adoptive) parents are the "natural guardians" of their children, which entails the numerous privileges and responsibilities of legal parenthood. In the intact family, when one parent dies, the survivor simply continues in the role of natural guardian. Here, there is no reason for the children to come to the attention of the state. On the other hand, where both parents in an intact family die, there is no surviving guardian and the courts are empowered to name a new guardian. Judges must exercise this authority according to the best interests of the child in each case. Although state laws enable the parents to name a guardian in their wills, the courts do not automatically defer to parental wishes in this situation. Nevertheless, the independent judicial assessment of a child's interests typically places great weight on the wishes of the parents, because they are presumed to know what is best for their children (Weinstein, § 13.48). As a result, judges usually appoint the guardian named in the parents' wills, although in exceptional cases another person may be appointed (*In re* Russell, 1988).

These rules describing the guardianship appointment process when neither biologic parent is alive apply in the stepfamily if, for whatever reason, the noncustodial parent is not in the legal picture. The noncustodial parent may be dead; his or her legal rights vis-à-vis the child may have been terminated in a legal proceeding; or an unmarried father may never have been identified. In these situations, the custodial parent (spouse of the stepparent) has a great deal of control over the future custody of the children in the event of the parent's death. The parent's testamentary nomination of the stepparent, or any other fit person, will receive deference from the court that must appoint a guardian after the custodial parent's death. The exceptional cases in which courts have not deferred to the surviving parent's wishes involve competing requests by a third party, usually a relative, for appointment as the guardian. If the stepfamily members anticipate that a stepparent guardianship may be opposed by other relatives, they may take steps to deter such opposition. Thus, if the concern of relatives is that they will lose contact with the child in the event of a stepparent guardianship, prior assurances of future access may deter a guardianship contest. Even where the stepparent's nomination is contested, the court will likely follow the parent's wishes if the stepparent is fit for custody and has, in fact, shared custodial responsibility prior to the parent's death. Of course, the custodial parent should nominate the stepparent only if the stepparent desires to continue in a custodial role and the parties believe that the child's interests would be served by such an arrangement.

The custodial parent's testamentary wishes regarding the appointment of a guardian for minor children are much less likely to receive judicial deference if the other biologic parent is still a legal player in the child's life. As a general rule, all parents have protected rights as the "natural guardians" of their children. Furthermore, the courts presume that the interests of children are best served by custody with a biologic parent rather than a third party. These general principles regarding the interests of parents and the well-being of children apply even in situations where the child has been out of the parent's custody for an extended period of time. Thus, if the parent who has custody of a child–either by court order or by de facto arrangement between the parties–dies or otherwise becomes incapable of continuing custody, the other parent is usually entitled to take over the custodial role (Mahoney, 137-147 (describing the various legal standards that favor the natural parent in custody contests with stepparents)).

Can effective legal steps be taken in advance to assure that the stepchild will continue to reside with the stepparent following the death of the custodial parent in spite of the underlying rules that prefer the surviving parent? This is an area where the power of stepfamily members is severely circumscribed, for the two policy reasons embodied in the underlying rules. First, there is nothing the custodial parent and stepparent can do to destroy the rights of the other parent. And second, the courts will not allow anyone to take from them the function of protecting children. Nevertheless, stepfamily members are not totally powerless. First, a guardianship nomination of the stepparent in the custodial parent's will may have some impact on the decision of the guardianship court. And second, the execution of a contract with the noncustodial parent, wherein he or she promises not to fight for custody, may also add weight to the stepparent's later custody claim.

The precise weight assigned to the custodial parent's nomination of a person other than the noncustodial parent seems to vary from one case to the next. At the one extreme, the guardianship courts never defer totally to the parent's testamentary wishes in this matter. At the opposite extreme, courts have on occasion stated that the provision in the custodial parent's will is totally void when the other parent survives and requests custody (Guardianship of Stremel, 1983). Most of the time, however, judges take the position that the custodial parent's wishes are a factor in determining what future custody arrangement will best serve the child's interests (Marriage of Russell, 1988). Especially where there are indications that the surviving parent is not a very suitable parent, the nomination of another person by the deceased custodian may influence the court's decision. Thus, in the stepfamily, the nomination of a surviving stepparent as guardian enhances the likelihood that the desires of stepfamily members will be accommodated.

The stepparent is least likely to prevail if the surviving parent actively seeks custody. As a planning strategy, the custodial parent and stepparent may try to eliminate the prospect of any objection by the surviving parent to the stepparent's appointment as guardian. On occasion, noncustodial parents have signed contracts wherein they agree to permit a third party, such as the stepparent, to assume custody of their children. Such a contract may take the form of an agreement not to contest the testamentary nomination of a third party guardian upon the death of the custodial parent. The contract, like the guardianship nomination itself, is not a totally reliable planning device within the stepfamily. The contract is not binding because the welfare of children is involved. If the parent subsequently changes his or her mind, the court will listen to any objections raised by the parent against the nomination of the stepparent as guardian. Although the parent's past agreement may be a factor suggesting that he or she is not the best custodian, the contract does not eliminate the need for a judicial determination of the child's best interests (Potter v. Potter, 1950). In summary, the contract option is worth pursuing in combination with a testamentary guardianship nomination of the stepparent. The noncustodial parent may, in fact, adhere to the contract terms, which will greatly enhance the chances that the court will appoint the stepparent as guardian. Even if this is not the case, the existence of the contract will detract from the parent's claim for custody. However, like the guardianship appointment itself, the contract is not a certain way to plan for the future custody of stepchildren.

Indeed, the only certain method is the termination of legal rights of the noncustodial parent, with or without that person's consent, followed by a stepparent adoption. Following adoption, the stepparent assumes the rights of a natural parent regarding custody and all other matters. In the event of the custodial parent's death, the adoptive stepparent would become the sole legal custodian of minor stepchildren. As discussed in Section II, the adoption decision involves the consideration of many issues besides the particular question of custody. Short of a stepparent adoption, the stepfamily must rely upon the uncertain methods of guardianship nomination and contract law to plan for the child's future custody.

VI. CONCLUSION

As to many legal matters, including child support, inheritance, and child custody, state laws largely discount the stepparent-child relationship. Scholars in law and the social sciences have begun to ask how this nonrecognition in the eyes of the law actually influences feelings and behavior in the stepfamily (Chambers, 103-109; Fine, 55; Mahoney, 5-7). At this point in time, the answers to the question are speculative. Furthermore, it is unlikely that state laws will undergo any radical change in the near future that would raise the stepparent-child relationship to the level of a significant legal status.

Within this legal framework, stepfamily members may desire to attach more certainty and more significance to the stepparent-child relationship. Family members may vary the terms of their legal relationships through the use of such devices as contracts, wills, guardianship appointments, legal proceedings to terminate parental rights, and adoption. The extent of private autonomy within the stepfamily as to issues of child support, inheritance and child custody is limited, however, by the state policies that justify the legal rules in the first place. Within these parameters, and with careful planning, stepfamilies in the United States can "take control" of their legal situation in a manner that empowers the family.

REFERENCES

Aid to Families with Dependent Children Act, 42 U.S.C. §§ 601-615 (1988 & Supp. V 1993).

Chambers, D.L. (1990). Stepparents, Biologic Parents, and the Law's Perception of "Family" After Divorce, in *Divorce Reform at the Crossroads* (S. D. Sugarman & H. H. Kay, eds.), 102-129. New Haven, CN: Yale University Press.

Clark, H.H., Jr. (1988). *The Law of Domestic Relations in the United States.* Minneapolis, MN: West Publishing Co.

Family Law Reporter (May 16, 1995). Washington, D.C.: Bureau of National Affairs.

Fine, M.A. (1989). A Social Science Perspective on Stepfamily Law: Suggestions for Legal Reform. *Family Relations* 38, 53-60.

Gregory, J.D., Swisher, P.N. and Scheibel, S.L. (1993). *Understanding Family Law.* New York City: Matthew Bender.

Higher Education Resources and Student Assistance Act, 20 U.S.C. §§ 1070a, 1070a-1 to 1070a-3 (1988 & Supp. V 1993).

Hollinger, J.H. (1994). *Adoption Law and Practice.* New York City: Matthew Bender.

Mahoney, M.M. (1994). *Stepfamilies and the Law.* Ann Arbor, MI: University of Michigan Press.

N.D. Cent. Code § 14-09-09 (Supp. 1995).

Potter v. Potter, 219 P.2d 1011 (Okla. 1950).

Restatement (Second) of Property § 25.6 (1988).

In re Russell, 523 N.E.2d 193 (Ill. Ct. App. 1988).

Guardianship of Stremel, 660 P.2d 952 (Kan. 1983).

Uniform Adoption Act (1994). 9 *Uniform Laws Annotated* 1 (Supp. 1995).

Uniform Marriage and Divorce Act (1970). 9A *Uniform Laws Annotated* 18 (Supp. 1995).

Weinstein, M. (1988). *Summary of American Law.* Rochester, NY: Lawyers Cooperative Publishing Company.

Stepfamilies from a Policy Perspective: Guidance from the Empirical Literature

Mark A. Fine

A number of legal scholars in the United States (US) have expressed concerns about the uncertain status of stepfamilies in the law (Mahoney, 1994; Ramsey, 1994). Stepfamily members are typically not granted a number of rights and the accompanying responsibilities that are afforded members of biological families. In addition, their treatment under the law varies depending on the issue and, because laws affecting families in the United States are decided at the state level, geographic location. For example, Mahoney (1994) shows that the stepparent-stepchild relationship has received its greatest legal recognition in the area of Worker's Compensation law, which addresses who receives benefits in the event of injury or death in an industrial accident. By contrast, this relationship has received relatively little legal recognition in the area of inheritance, where, in the absence of a will, stepchildren are seldom allowed to inherit from their stepparents.

Thus, the status of stepfamilies in US law is somewhat ambiguous and inconsistent across issues and states. The most common generalization is that stepfamily relationships are not legally recognized. As Mahoney (1994) stated, the "stepparent-child relationship is not regarded as a legal status" (p. 232). Given the inconsistencies in legal status and the general lack of recognition, one might think that there would be strong pressures to invoke policy reforms. However, this does not seem to be the case, as

Mark A. Fine is affiliated with the Department of Human Development and Family Studies at the University of Missouri, 31 Stanley Hall, Columbia, MO 65211 (Internet: hdfsfine@mizzou1.missouri.edu).

[Haworth co-indexing entry note]: "Stepfamilies from a Policy Perspective: Guidance from the Empirical Literature." Fine, Mark A. Co-published simultaneously in *Marriage & Family Review* (The Haworth Press, Inc.) Vol. 26, No. 3/4, 1997, pp. 249-264; and: *Stepfamilies: History, Research, and Policy* (ed: Irene Levin and Marvin B. Sussman) The Haworth Press, Inc., 1997, pp. 249-264. Single or multiple copies of this article are available for a fee from The Haworth Document Delivery Service [1-800-342-9678, 9:00 a.m. - 5:00 p.m. (EST). E-mail address: getinfo@haworth.com].

there have not been major changes in recent years in how family law in the US treats stepfamilies (M. A. Fine & D. R Fine, 1992). When changes have been made, they seem to have been relatively minor and have occurred as a part of changes affecting other third parties. For example, when stepparents are granted more rights vis-à-vis stepchildren, it is often as a result of rights granted third parties, including grandparents, and not those specifically afforded to stepparents.

How might policies affecting stepfamilies be changed? One possible mechanism is that empirical findings pertaining to stepfamily functioning could be used to formulate more effective and sensitive legislation (see Monroe, 1995, for an overview of how empirical findings may play a role in the policy process). Despite the claims of a number of scholars that empirical findings pertaining to stepfamilies could inform legislative change (M. A. Fine & D. R Fine, 1992; Ramsey, 1986; Mahoney, 1994), social science research has not commonly been used for this purpose.

To my knowledge, there have been no previous attempts in the literature to draw policy implications from empirical findings generated from a number of lines of stepfamily research. Accordingly, the primary purpose of this paper is to explore how the empirical literature may provide guidance in the process of policy reform in the US. Before addressing this purpose, however, I provide the necessary context by briefly reviewing the state of policies pertaining to stepfamilies.

REVIEW OF POLICIES PERTAINING TO STEPFAMILIES

Most of the attention that has been devoted to laws and policies affecting stepfamilies has been directed to stepfamilies that have been disrupted by divorce. Relatively less attention has been directed to stepfamilies that are still intact. One of the reasons why intact stepfamilies have received less policy attention is that, partly because family interactions are considered private matters that should not be intruded upon by the state (Mahoney, 1994), family law in general is primarily concerned with circumstances that occur following major (and public) family changes, such as divorce or death. However, this has had the unfortunate consequence of reducing the amount of effort that has gone into attempting to devise policies that help existing stepfamilies function more effectively.

Policies Pertaining to Intact Stepfamilies

With respect to intact stepfamilies, most attention has been directed to the rights and responsibilities of stepparents vis-à-vis their stepchildren.

As examples (see Mahoney, 1994, for a detailed analysis of laws affecting stepfamilies in these and other areas), in most states, stepparents are not legally obligated to financially support their stepchildren, although most choose to do so; a child's name can be changed to that of the stepparent only if the nonresidential parent consents; stepparents have received mixed treatment in terms of whether they are responsible for damage caused by their stepchild; stepparents can adopt their stepchild only if the nonresidential parent is declared "unfit," because adoption effectively ends the parenting rights and obligations of the nonresidential parent; and stepparents acting *in loco parentis* (see below) have the same rights to physically discipline their stepchild as do biological parents, although they are also subject to the same laws prohibiting physical and sexual abuse.

Policies Pertaining to Stepfamilies Disrupted by Divorce

In reviews of laws affecting stepfamilies, M. A. Fine and D. R Fine (1992) and Mahoney (1994) concluded that courts and legislatures have not generally recognized the stepparent-stepchild relationship as one that can endure after the divorce of the biological parent and stepparent. Although there is variation across states, stepparents are unlikely to be legally obligated to support stepchildren following divorce and, if they wish to maintain contact with their stepchildren following divorce, they may have difficulty doing so. M. A. Fine and D. R Fine (1992) noted, however, that there had been some progress toward recognizing the potential importance of the stepparent-stepchild relationship, particularly in the area of granting stepparents visitation rights following divorce.

POLICY GUIDANCE FROM THE EMPIRICAL LITERATURE

The relatively recent increase in the amount of research on stepfamilies (Coleman & Ganong, 1990) has provided important new information on stepfamilies that may have policy implications. In this section, six key lines of research on stepfamilies are reviewed that have policy implications for stepfamilies in the US. My intent is not to be exhaustive, but rather to highlight several key research areas. For each of the six areas, the relevant findings are presented, followed by the policy implications.

Quality of the Stepparent-Stepchild Relationship

Perhaps the most central issue in formulating policies affecting stepfamilies is the extent to which the stepparent-stepchild relationship is important and meaningful to the parties involved. Research findings generally suggest that the perceived quality of stepparent-stepchild relationships is lower than that between parents and children. For example, Fine, Voydanoff, and Donnelly (1994) found that biological fathers reported that they had higher quality father-child relationships than did stepfathers and that biological mothers reported that they had higher quality mother-child relationships than did stepmothers. However, the differences between groups were quite small in magnitude.

Not only do differences in the perceived quality of stepparent-stepchild and parent-child relationships tend to be small, there is also evidence that many stepparents and stepchildren have very positive relationships (Coleman & Ganong, 1990). In the Fine et al. (1994) study described above, the mean scores on the perceptions of quality measure for the stepfather-stepchild and stepmother-stepchild relationships were above 5.9 on a 1 (*very poor*) to 7 (*excellent*) scale. It should be noted that, while the stepparent-stepchild relationship can be enduring and meaningful, White (1993) found that this is not typically the case into adulthood; based on analyses of the National Survey of Families and Households, she concluded that stepparents and stepchildren are not generally supportive of each other when the stepchildren are adults.

Policy implications. The finding that the stepparent-stepchild relationship can be mutually beneficial and important has several policy implications. In terms of intact stepfamilies, policies should be implemented that give stepparents the *option* (but not the *requirement*) of becoming more involved in the lives of their children by assuming parental rights and responsibilities. For example, as noted by Crosbie-Burnett (1994), school systems can be more supportive of stepchildren by being more sensitive to the potentially important role that stepparents may play in the children's lives.

In terms of stepfamilies that have been disrupted by divorce or death, these findings pertaining to the quality of the stepparent-stepchild relationship suggest that there should be a mechanism established to ensure that this relationship can continue if desired by both the stepparent and the stepchild and if the relationship has been meaningful to both parties. Elsewhere, a colleague and I (M. A. Fine & D. R Fine, 1992) argued that stepparents who have had such meaningful relationships with their stepchildren should have visitation rights following divorce and should have the option of contesting custody in certain selected circumstances.

Similarly, careful consideration should be given to allowing stepchildren who had meaningful relationships with their stepparents to inherit from their deceased stepparent. I am not arguing that the stepparent-stepchild relationship should be given the same degree of legal recognition and status as the biological parent-child relationship; rather, in certain cases, the step-relationship should be given greater consideration and recognition than it currently is.

Typically, the standard used for determining when the stepparent-stepchild relationship should be legally recognized is the *in loco parentis* doctrine. Under this doctrine, a person who intentionally acts as if he or she were the child's parent may be considered to have some of the rights and responsibilities that parents do. However, this standard has several significant limitations, including that it is not based on the actual quality of the stepparent-stepchild relationship, it can be terminated at will by the stepparent, and it does not protect the stepparent-stepchild relationship in many situations (e.g., stepchildren whose stepparents stood in loco parentis to them are not able to inherit, unless specifically written into a will) (Mahoney, 1994).

As a result of the limitations of the in loco parentis standard, some have called for a standard that is more sensitive to the actual nature of the stepparent-stepchild relationship (see M. A. Fine & D. R Fine, 1992). Bartlett (1984) has proposed that an adult-child, including a stepparent-stepchild, relationship should be legally recognized when the following criteria are met: (a) the adult has had physical custody of the child for at least six months; (b) mutuality is present, meaning that the adult genuinely intends to provide care for the child and the child perceives the adult's role to be that of a parent; and (c) the adult must prove that his or her relationship with the child began with the consent of the child's legal biological parent or with a court order. It may be useful to consider whether Bartlett's proposal could be the foundation for a new standard to replace or complement the in loco parentis doctrine. However, before it could be used with stepfamilies, this proposal would require modification. For example, because few stepparents would meet the first criterion, this criterion might be changed to indicate that the stepparent and stepchild must have lived in the same residence (or had a meaningful relationship if they have not lived together) for at least six months.

Norms Pertaining to Financial Obligations in Stepfamilies

A second key issue in policy discussions pertaining to stepfamilies is the extent to which stepparents should be financially obligated to support stepchildren, both during their marriage to the child's biological parent and, should the marriage end, after it terminates. To address this issue, it is important to know individuals' perceptions about stepparent financial obligations. These perceptions are important because they represent normative beliefs that policy makers need to consider (Fine, 1989).

While it has been argued that normative obligations to support biological children are stronger than those to support stepchildren (Rossi & Rossi, 1990), it is not clear how strong the obligation is for stepparents to support their stepchildren. To address this issue, Ganong, Coleman, and Mistina (1995) assessed perceptions of obligations that biological parents or stepparents have to financially support a hypothetical child's need for special tutoring. In a sample of adults from a Midwestern state, Ganong et al. (1995) found that, when they were living with their stepchildren in an intact remarriage, stepparents were considered to be as obligated to support stepchildren as were biological parents. After the termination of the remarriage (and the stepfamily), stepparents were considered to be much less obligated to financially support the child's tutoring needs than were biological parents. Thus, after termination of the remarriage, the financial obligation is perceived to lessen substantially and becomes more voluntary.

Policy implications. Ganong et al.'s (1995) findings suggest that requiring stepparents to support stepchildren during the existence of the stepfamily is unlikely to meet with much resistance. In fact, given that remarriage greatly improves divorced single mothers' economic status (Folk, Graham, & Beller, 1992), it is apparent that most stepparents choose to support their residential stepchildren. However, Ganong et al.'s findings also suggest that there could be considerable resistance if legislation were passed requiring stepparents to support stepchildren following termination of the remarriage. Whereas resistance to legislation by those affected is not the only factor that needs to be considered in forming policy, it does need to be taken into consideration.

If it is determined that a stepparent does have an obligation to support a stepchild following divorce, a thorough and carefully constructed explanation of why this determination has been made needs to be provided to the stepparent (and, ideally, to stepparents-to-be before they marry the child's biological parent). Elsewhere, a colleague and I (D. R Fine & M. A. Fine, 1992) argued that the standard that should be used to determine support obligations following divorce for stepparents is *equitable estoppel*. According to this theory, stepparents would have a support obligation if they consciously established an expectation on the part of the biological parent and/or the stepchild that the stepchild would financially rely on the stepparent. We also argued that the standard of proof to establish a support obligation should be that the expectation of reliance was "clear and convincing," which is more difficult to meet than other possible standards (e.g., "preponderance of the evidence").

Clarity of the Stepparent Role

A third research area pertains to how clear or ambiguous the role of the stepparent is to stepfamily members. Schwebel, Fine, and Renner (1991) asked college students to respond to a series of 16 hypothetical case scenarios that involved a situation calling for some type of parental behavior. In each scenario, respondents were asked to rate how likely it was that a parental figure *would* engage in a designated parental behavior relevant to the scenario and to what extent the parental figure *should* engage in the parental behavior.

In terms of policy, two findings from this study have particular relevance. First, Schwebel et al. (1991) found that respondents believed that stepparents were less obligated and less likely than were biological parents to engage in the parenting behaviors called for in the scenarios, which supports the notion that stepparents are perceived as being less active in parenting than are biological parents and that they should be less active.

Second, to determine the extent to which people agree about the role of the stepparent, the variabilities in the *should* and *would* ratings of biological parents and stepparents were compared. The greater the variability, the less consistency there was in participants' ratings; we believe that a lack of consistency in ratings reflects a lack of clarity in the role of the parental figure. Results indicated that there was generally greater variability in ratings of what stepparents would do and should do than there was in ratings of what biological parents would and should do, although this varied somewhat by the gender of the rater. These findings suggest that there is less consensus in how stepparents do and should act than there is in reference to biological parents.

There is also some empirical evidence that stepchildren regard the stepparent's role as more ambiguous than biological children regard the biological parent's role. In a study of 7th and 8th grade children, Fine, Kurdek, and Hennigen (1992) found that children rating stepfathers reported more role ambiguity than did those rating biological fathers. Furthermore, children rating stepmothers reported more role ambiguity than did those rating biological mothers.

Not only does there appear to be greater role ambiguity for stepparents than for biological parents, but there is limited empirical evidence to suggest that the extent of role ambiguity is negatively related to the adjustment of stepfamily members. Kurdek and Fine (1991), in a study of mothers and stepfathers from 27 stepfather families, found that perceptions that the role of the stepparent was ambiguous were related to mothers' reports of low family/marital/personal life satisfaction and stepfathers' reports of low parenting satisfaction. With respect to adolescent stepchildren, Fine, Kurdek, and Hennigen (1992) found that adolescents living with stepmothers reported high self-competence to the extent that they perceived the stepmother's role as clear.

Policy implications. The presence of ambiguity regarding the stepparent role and the possibility that this ambiguity negatively impacts stepfamily members suggest that policies should be pursued that help clarify the stepparent role to whatever extent possible. Elsewhere, I (Fine, 1989) have argued that it is conceivable that reducing the legal ambiguity surrounding the stepparent-stepchild relationship may help clarify perceptions of the stepparent role. As noted earlier, developing a standard that is more sensitive than the *in loco parentis* doctrine to determine when the stepparent-stepchild relationship is mutually beneficial may help reduce the legal ambiguity surrounding this relationship. It also may be useful to consider whether the English system (described below) may be helpful.

Family Processes and Adolescents' Adjustment in Stepfamilies

A fourth research area relates to how processes in stepfamilies, such as parenting behaviors and family climate, are related to children's and adolescents' adjustment in stepfamilies. In a sample of early adolescents living with either stepfathers or stepmothers, Fine and Kurdek (1992) found that perceptions (by the adolescent) of authoritative parenting (by the biological parent) were positively related to several adjustment dimensions (i.e., lack of health problems, lack of drug usage, self-esteem) and perceptions of authoritarian parenting (by both the biological parent and the stepparent) were negatively related to adjustment. These findings are consistent with those from studies that have assessed similar relations in first-marriage (Maccoby & Martin, 1983; Steinberg, Elmen, & Mounts, 1989) and stepfather families (Hetherington & Clingempeel, 1992).

With respect to family processes (the climate within the family system as a whole), all of the family process variables were related to adjustment in at least some subgroups of adolescents. As has been found in previous studies based mostly on first-marriage families (see Fine & Kurdek, 1992), adjustment was positively related to supervision, warmth and interest, and order, and negatively related to conflict. These findings support the argument that the relations between adolescent adjustment and family processes are similar in first-marriage and stepparent families (Hetherington & Clingempeel, 1992).

An especially interesting pattern was that the relations between the family process variables and adjustment were strongest among girls living with stepmothers. Clingempeel, Brand, and Segal (1987) have suggested that girls in stepmother families acquire a privileged status because fathers are granted custody of girls only in cases of very close father-daughter and/or conflictual mother-daughter relationships. Because of this status, girls may find the addition of a stepmother into their family as particularly disturbing and invasive. Thus, because of the tensions endemic to the stepmother-stepdaughter relationship and/or the father-daughter relationship, family climate may have more potent effects on this group of adolescents than on others.

Policy implications. These findings suggest that stepparents can play an important parenting role in stepfamilies and that they, like parents in first-marriage families, are important contributors to family processes that affect children and adolescents. As discussed earlier, legally clarifying stepparents' rights and responsibilities may provide needed support for stepfamilies. The findings pertaining to girls in stepmother families, if replicated in other studies, suggest that policymakers need to consider that interactions within stepfamilies may have more potent effects on some groups of stepchildren than others.

Longitudinal Changes over the Lifecourse of Stepfamilies

A fifth research area pertains to changes that occur over time in stepfamilies. All too often, researchers have studied stepfamilies at one point in time and have drawn general conclusions about stepfamilies without taking into consideration that stepfamilies change over time. Papernow (1993), in a qualitative study, showed that stepfamilies pass through a series of stages over their lifecourse and that, even for those stepfamilies that successfully negotiate these tasks, adjustment takes seven years or more.

Recently, there have been several well-designed and well-controlled empirical studies that have shown that adjustment and relationships in stepfamilies change over time. Hetherington (1993), based on analyses from the Virginia Longitudinal Study of Divorce and Remarriage, found that stepparents' behavior had different effects on stepchildren at different points in time following formation of the stepfamily. For example, when remarriages occurred before the children reached adolescence, stepchildren responded most positively to stepfathers who attempted to develop an affectionate relationship with the child, who supported the mothers' discipline, and who did not independently establish and enforce rules. However, for stepfamilies with adolescent stepchildren, stepparents who immediately acted in an authoritative (e.g., they disciplined their stepchildren, as well as showed support and affection towards them) way had better relations with their stepchildren than those stepfathers who were initially more distant. Similar findings were reported by Bray and Burger (1993), who also found that child behavior problems in stepfamilies were magnified when stepchildren reached adolescence, regardless of their ages when their stepfamilies were formed. Children's adjustment appears to be promoted when stepparents, at least initially, do not take an active role in discipline

Policy implications. Legislation needs to be sensitive to important changes that occur in stepfamily relationships over time, as well as in individual stepfamily members over time. Policies will not be effective if they are insensitive to developmental changes in stepfamily members and relationships.

Variability in Stepfamilies

A sixth and final research area pertains to the heterogeneity of stepfamilies. Variability is endemic to stepfamilies in numerous ways. At the most basic level, there are a multitude of types of families that can be categorized as stepfamilies. For example, Clingempeel, Brand, and Segal (1987) identified nine types of stepfamilies and Burgoyne and Clark (1984) identified 26 types. By contrast, two-parent first marriage families do not share this level of structural heterogeneity. It should be noted that these estimates of the number of stepfamily types include only partners who are married; if one counts cohabiting and/or gay and lesbian relationships that are not sanctioned by marriage, the number of stepfamily types is even larger.

The variability in stepfamilies is not limited to structural characteristics. There is also variability in family processes that occur in stepfamilies and in how stepfamily members adjust to their changing family circumstances. In fact, some of the inconsistency in the results of previous studies may be due to the fact that different investigators study different types of stepfamilies. For example, although most investigators have found that children in stepfamilies are more poorly adjusted on some dimensions (e.g., behavioral problems, social competence, substance abuse) than those in first-marriage families (Dawson, 1991; Dornbusch et al., 1985; Zill, 1993), others have not found differences for either boys or girls (Kurdek & Sinclair, 1988) or have found them for girls only (e.g., Needle, Su, & Doherty, 1990; Santrock, Warshak, Lindberg, & Meadows, 1982). Perhaps differing samples are one explanation for these divergent findings. Another possible explanation for these inconsistent findings pertains to the fifth research area discussed above–stepfamily dynamics change over the lifecourse of the stepfamily.

Within stepfamilies, there are also variations in adjustment and the quality of stepparent-stepchild relations based on the gender of the stepparent, the gender of the stepchild, the age of the stepchild at the time of remarriage, the stepchild's current age, and the extent of involvement of the nonresidential parent (Bray & Burger, 1993; Hetherington, 1993). Findings such as these demonstrate that there is no uniform experience for members of stepfamilies.

Policy implications. Given the tremendous variability in stepfamilies, we need to balance having policies that affect all stepfamilies with a consideration of the unique aspects of each particular stepfamily. Certainly, it is unreasonable to expect that each and every stepfamily should be treated differently in legal and policy contexts. However, perhaps more than other family forms, there is a need for social policies to be sensitive to heterogeneity within stepfamilies.

LESSONS FROM GREAT BRITAIN

With respect to intact stepfamilies, it is instructive to consider a system recently implemented in Great Britain. England's Children Act 1989 (1989), which took effect in 1991, established a new concept in English law: *parental responsibility*, maintaining as its theme the notion that parenthood involves continuing and enduring responsibility. The Act regards children no longer as their parents' property (thus eliminating the notion of *custody* in the law), but rather as their parents' responsibility. Because most parental responsibility can be exercised only while a parent is caring for a child, the Act dictates that the court's powers should be directed to allocating the time the child spends with his or her parents and not with dividing responsibilities and obligations between the parents (Cretney & Masson, 1990). Thus, the expectation is that both parents will retain parental authority following divorce and, consequently, that the courts will be concerned primarily with determining the residence of the children (Duquette, 1992).

The Children Act 1989, as it does for any adult who cares for a child, provides an opportunity for stepparents (who have been married to the child's parent for at least two years) to have a legal relationship with their stepchildren by petitioning the court for a "residence order." If such an order is granted, and the petition can be granted even over the objections by the nonresidential parent (Masson, 1992), that adult has many of the same rights and responsibilities as do the child's biological parents. In such a circumstance, the child may actually have legal relationships with three adults, both parents and the stepparent, all of whom have both parental responsibilities and obligations. In the United States, if the stepparent adopts the stepchild, the child still has legal ties to only two adults, as adoption generally terminates the parenting rights and responsibilities of the nonresidential biological parent.

Reactions to the Children Act 1989 in Great Britain

Although I am unaware of any empirical studies that have assessed the effects of the Children Act 1989 on stepfamilies in Great Britain, there has been some speculation about how it might affect stepfamilies (see Dimmock, 1992). Although several commentators had high hopes for the legislation as it was being formulated, some have expressed disappointment that the legislation did not do more to improve the plight of those living in stepfamilies. Among the concerns raised by Masson (1992) were that: (a) the Act does not specifically use the term *stepparent* or *stepfamilies*; (b) the Act does not give stepparents any special rights or impose new obligations on them, except for those who seek a residence order; (c) except for those with a residence order, a stepparent is in the same legal position as is any other person who may be caring for a child; (d) the Act does not impose a financial responsibility on stepparents to support their stepchild, nor does it confer inheritance rights; (e) the Act does not give stepparents the right to make major decisions about adoption or guardianship; (f) the new phrase *parental responsibility* is not clearly defined; and (g) it is unclear how many stepparents (and their spouses) will seek a residence order, particularly given that such an order may be unnecessary if the two biological parents and the stepparent are able to cooperate in matters related to the children.

Applicability of the British System in the United States

Ramsey (1994) has pointed out that the process of legal reform requires that there be some agreement on the desired goals of the reform. She lists a number of possible goals, including promoting the child's welfare, supporting the residential parent-child relationship, supporting the new remarriage, protecting the rights of the nonresidential parent, and promoting the welfare of the stepparent. The direction one wishes to take in legal reform will depend on which of these goals one adopts. In the discussion below, I take the position that addressing two pressing issues will address at least several of the goals listed above.

These two issues requiring policy reform in the United States are:

(a) clarifying the legal rights and responsibilities of stepparents and (b) developing a more sensitive standard to determine when the stepparent-stepchild relationship is mutually beneficial to the stepparent and the stepchild. At least for those stepfamilies in which the stepparent obtains a residence order (or some variant), the British system may at least partially address each of these issues.

With respect to clarifying stepparents' rights and responsibilities, stepparents who seek and obtain a residence order would have a relatively clear set of rights and obligations. If the British system were implemented in the United States, the exact nature of these rights and responsibilities would need to be determined (see Ramsey, 1994, for a discussion of how a residence order could be used as a mechanism to support stepfamilies and particularly stepchildren). However, the clear potential benefit of the British law is that a mechanism would be in place to clarify the legal status of the stepparent vis-à-vis the stepchild *for those stepparents who obtain a residence order.* A residence order provides additional flexibility in that it provides an option that lies somewhere between no legal relationship and adoption. Unlike adoption, it also increases the number of adults who have parenting responsibilities, which is likely to provide additional support for stepchildren.

With respect to the development of a new standard for determining when the stepparent-stepchild relationship is mutually beneficial, the British system may also be of some benefit in the United States. Stepparents who have a residence order (or some equivalent) would seem to be more likely to have an enduring and meaningful relationship with their stepchild than those who did not obtain such an order, although it is possible that stepparents may seek such orders for reasons other than to solidify their relationships with their stepchild (e.g., logistical and practical factors, such as allowing the stepparent to make some parenting decisions in the absence of the biological parent). Despite the variety of reasons why a stepparent may seek such an order, it may be beneficial to use the presence or absence of a residence order as one standard, perhaps among several, to use in making the determination if the stepparent-stepchild relationship is mutually beneficial. Thus, when determining such issues as whether the stepparent should have visitation rights following the termination of the remarriage and whether the stepchild should be allowed to inherit from a deceased stepparent, the presence or absence of a residence order would be one important consideration.

CONCLUSIONS

The recommendations for policy reform in this article are relatively modest. Unfortunately, we lack the empirical foundation to propose more sweeping legislative reforms. For example, as detailed elsewhere (Fine, 1989; M. A. Fine & D. R Fine, 1992), even within the current legislative and policy climate, there is a pressing need for studies to help us learn more about such areas as: (a) stepparent-stepchild relationships, how they develop, and the conditions under which they become mutually beneficial even after the termination of the remarriage; (b) how finances are typically managed in stepfamilies, both during and after termination of the remarriage; (c) the beliefs of stepparents and biological parents regarding the nature of stepparents' responsibilities, obligations, and rights; and (d) how changes in stepparents' rights and responsibilities may impact upon other important areas of family life, such as the remarriage rate and the role of the nonresidential parent.

In addition, there is a need for research into what the potential impact would be of a system like the British one, where more than two adults may have parenting responsibilities for the child. What proportion of stepparents would seek residence orders? Of those who do, what are their reasons for doing so? Of those who do not, why do they chose not to? What are the long term implications for stepparent-stepchild relationships when the stepparent has a residence order? Because the British system has been in place for a number of years now, it is ripe for thorough study. Systematic studies into the British experience may provide very useful information to help those desiring to reform policies affecting stepfamilies in the United States.

REFERENCES

Bartlett, K. T. (1984). Rethinking parenthood as an exclusive status: The need for legal alternatives when the premise of the nuclear family has failed. *Virginia Law Review, 70,* 879.

Bray, J. H., & Berger, S. H. (1993). Developmental Issues in StepFamilies Research Project: Family relationships and parent-child interactions. *Journal of Family Psychology, 7,* 76-90.

Burgoyne, J., & Clark, D. (1984). *Making a go of it.* London: Routledge and Kegan Paul.

Children Act 1989, England and Wales.

Clingempeel, W.G., Brand, E., & Segal, S. (1987). A multilevel-multivariable-developmental perspective for future research on stepfamilies. In K. Pasley & M. Ihinger-Tallman (Eds.) *Remarriage and stepparenting: Current research and theory* (pp. 65-93). New York: Guilford.

Coleman, M., & Ganong, L. H. (1990). Remarriage and stepfamily research in the 1980s: Increased interest in an old family form. *Journal of Marriage and the Family, 52,* 925-940.

Crosbie-Burnett, M. (1994). The interface between stepparent families and schools: Research, theory, policy, and practice. In K. Pasley and M. Ihinger-Tallman (Eds.), *Stepparenting: Issues in theory, research, and practice* (pp. 199-216). Westport, CT: Greenwood Press.

Dawson, D. A. (1991). Family structure and children's health and well-being: Data from the 1988 National Health Interview Survey on Child Health. *Journal of Marriage and the Family, 53*, 573-584.

Dornbusch, S. M., Carlsmith, J. M., Bushwall, S. J., Ritter, P. L., Leiderman, H., Hastorf, A. H., & Gross, R. T. (1985). Single parents, extended households, and the control of adolescents. *Child Development, 56*, 326-341.

Dimmock, B. (1992). *A step in both directions? The impact of the Children Act 1989 on stepfamilies*. London: National Stepfamily Association.

Duquette, D. N. (1992). Symposium, child protection legal process: Comparing the United States and Great Britain. *University of Pittsburgh Law Review, 54*, 239-294.

Fine, M. A. (1989). A social science perspective on stepfamily law: Suggestions for legal reform. *Family Relations, 38*, 53-58.

Fine, D. R, & Fine, M. A. (1992). Learning from social sciences: A model for reformation of the laws affecting stepfamilies. *Dickinson Law Review, 97* 49-81.

Fine, M. A., & Fine, D. R (1992). Recent changes in laws affecting stepfamilies: Suggestions for legal reform. *Family Relations, 41*, 334-340.

Fine, M. A., & Kurdek, L. A. (1992). The adjustment of adolescents in stepfather and stepmother families. *Journal of Marriage and the Family, 54*, 725-736.

Fine, M. A., Kurdek, L. A., & Hennigen, L. (1992). Perceived self-competence and its relations to stepfamily myths and (step)parent role ambiguity in adolescents from stepfather and stepmother families. *Journal of Family Psychology, 6*, 69-76.

Fine, M. A., Voydanoff, P., & Donnelly, B. W. (1994). Parental perceptions of child well-being: Relations to family structure, parental depression, and marital satisfaction. *Journal of Applied Developmental Psychology, 15*, 165-186.

Folk, K. F., Graham, J. W., & Beller, A. H. (1992). Child support and remarriage: Implications for the economic well-being of children. *Journal of Family Issues, 13*, 142-157.

Ganong, L. G., Coleman, M., & Mistina, D. (1995). *Family Relations, 44*, 306-315.

Hetherington, E. M. (1993). An overview of the Virginia Longitudinal Study of Divorce and Remarriage with a focus on early adolescence. *Journal of Family Psychology, 7*, 39-56.

Hetherington, E. M., & Clingempeel, W. G. (1992). Coping with marital transitions: A family systems perspective. *Monographs of the Society for Research in Child Development, 57* (2-3, Serial No. 227).

Kurdek, L. A., & Fine, M. A. (1991). Cognitive correlates of adjustment for mothers and stepfathers in stepfather families. *Journal of Marriage and the Family, 53*, 565-572.

Kurdek, L. A., & Sinclair, R. J. (1988). Adjustment of young adolescents in two-parent nuclear, stepfather, and mother-custody families. *Journal of Consulting and Clinical Psychology, 56*, 91-96.

Maccoby, E.M., & Martin, J. (1983). Socialization in the context of the family: Parent-child interaction. In E.M. Hetherington (Ed.), P.H. Mussen (series Ed.), *Handbook of child psychology: Vol. 4. Socialization, personality and social development* (pp. 1-101). New York: Wiley.

Mahoney, M. M. (1994). *Stepfamilies and the law.* Ann Arbor: University of Michigan Press.

Masson, J. (1992). Stepping into the Nineties: A summary of the legal implications of the Children Act 1989 for stepfamilies. In B. Dimmock (Ed.). *A step in both directions? The impact of the Children Act 1989 on stepfamilies* (pp. 4-16). London: National Stepfamily Association.

Monroe, P. A. (1995). Family Policy Advocacy: Putting Knowledge to Work, *Family Relations, 44*, 425-438.

Needle, R. H., Su, S., & Doherty, W. J. (1990). Divorce, remarriage, and adolescent substance use: A prospective longitudinal study. *Journal of Marriage and the Family, 52*, 157-169.

Papernow, P. L. (1993). *Becoming a stepfamily: Patterns of development in remarried families.* San Francisco: Jossey-Bass.

Ramsey, S. H. (1994). Stepparents and the law: A nebulous status and a need for reform. In K. Pasley and M. Ihinger-Tallman (Eds.), *Stepparenting: Issues in theory, research, and practice* (pp. 217-237). Westport, CT: Greenwood Press.

Rossi, A., & Rossi, P. (1990). *Of human bonding: Parent-child relations across the life course.* New York: Aldine de Gruyter.

Santrock, J., Warshak, R., Lindbergh, C., & Meadows, L. (1982). Children's and parents' observed social behavior in stepfather families. *Child Development, 53*, 472-480.

Schwebel, A. I., Fine, M. A., & Renner, M. A. (1991). An empirical investigation of perceptions of the stepparent role. *Journal of Family Issues, 12*, 43-57.

Steinberg, L., Elmen, J.D., & Mounts, N.S. (1989). Authoritative parenting, psychosocial maturity, and academic success among adolescents. *Child Development, 60*, 1424-1436.

White, L. (1993). Stepfamilies over the life course: Social support. In A. Booth & J. Dunn (Eds.), *Step-families: Who benefits? Who does not?* (pp. 109-137). Hillsdale, NJ: Erlbaum.

Zill, N. (1993). Understanding why children in stepfamilies have more learning and behavior problems than children in nuclear families. In A. Booth & J. Dunn (Eds.), *Step-families: Who benefits? Who does not?* (pp. 97-106). Hillsdale, NJ: Erlbaum.

Stepfamily Policy from the Perspective of a Stepfamily Organisation

Erica De'Ath

THE HISTORICAL CONTEXT

Stepfamilies are not a new phenomenon. For centuries the lives of many children have been interrupted by the death, separation or divorce of their parents. Where children were separated from both parents by death or destitution they were cared for up by friends or family, apprenticed or adopted into other families or brought up in orphanages, foster families or residential care.

Since the creation of the institution of marriage there has always been the potential for remarriage for a variety of reasons and, if one partner already has children, the formation of a stepfamily. Where a parent was alone it was likely that they would remarry bringing a stepmother to look after the household and provide child care, or a stepfather to provide the finances and discipline the children. In the past stepfamilies were more likely to arise after the death of a spouse, often to create a substitute parental figure for the children as well as companionship between the couple.

Historical records give us a tantalising glimpse of remarriage and family life over the centuries. Laslett (1977) describes the household survey of Clayworth in 1688 which recorded 39% of couples with at least one partner who had been widowed and 57% of orphaned children living with a step-parent (p. 166-170); and, a sample of seventeenth and eighteenth

Erica De'Ath is Chief Executive, National Stepfamily Association, London.

[Haworth co-indexing entry note]: "Stepfamily Policy from the Perspective of a Stepfamily Organisation." De'Ath, Erica. Co-published simultaneously in *Marriage & Family Review* (The Haworth Press, Inc.) Vol. 26, No. 3/4, 1997, pp. 265-279; and: *Stepfamilies: History, Research, and Policy* (ed: Irene Levin and Marvin B. Sussman) The Haworth Press, Inc., 1997, pp. 265-279. Single or multiple copies of this article are available for a fee from The Haworth Document Delivery Service [1-800-342-9678, 9:00 a.m. - 5:00 p.m. (EST). E-mail address: getinfo@haworth.com].

century parish registers showed half the widowers and a third of the widows who remarried did so within a year. Such remarriages could result in large families and increasingly complex stepfamily relationships. Buried in Bath Abbey is Sir Philip Frowde, who died in 1674 having been married three times. His first wife bore no children, his second gave him 4 daughters and a son, and his third 4 more sons. Burchardt (1989) recounts that Lord John Russell (1792-1878) married a widow with four children, had two children with her and after her death remarried and had four more children. Bringing up one's own children and other people's (even if those of your spouse) can have its own difficulties and Hardyment (1983) in her history of parent and child care manuals describes how Mrs. Sarah Ellis, author of *Mothers of England* in 1843 considered writing a sequel *Hints to Stepmothers* (p. 44). In the first decade of this century it is estimated that there were 70 people remarrying after being widowed for every person remarried after divorce (OPCS, 1990).

Marital disharmony and breakdown are also not new as evidenced in the case studies of separation and divorce in England in the period 1530-1987 (Stone, 1990) and 1660-1753 (Stone, 1993). However, during the early middle-England period, 1603-04, remarriage after divorce was still contentious with second marriages subject to a financial penalty (Stone, 1990, p. 305).

The increase in divorce in England and Wales, particularly since 1970, has led to much public discussion about the breakdown of a lifelong commitment to marriage, the undermining of the stability of family life and the effects upon children. However, remarriage is probably no more or less common than in the previous century. Marriage cohorts indicate little change in the percentage of marriages which ended within twenty years either by death or divorce, calculated since 1826 at 36%, 1896 at 30% and 1980 at 32%. There was a significant dip during the inter-war and immediate post-war period with the 1921 marriage cohort as low as 17%. The major difference with the 1980 cohort is that it was projected that all but 3% of the marriages would end because of divorce rather than death (Anderson, 1983).

THE CURRENT CONTEXT

There have been other changes in society which affect families and stepfamilies. Families have fewer children; over one third of children in Britain are born to unmarried parents, but often there are four or even five generations alive simultaneously, sometimes in the same household. The role of women has changed. Patterns of employment and unemployment, of mobility and housing, of expectations of marriage and relationships have altered the roles and responsibilities of men and women both as a cohabiting or marital couple and as parents. Such major changes in the very structure and formation of families requires greater understanding by policy makers, legislators and practitioners.

This paper seeks to highlight some of the ways in which legislation and policy shapes and fails to acknowledge key issues relating to remarriage and stepfamilies both as private and public concerns. There is a practical urgency to address such matters. Current figures suggest that second and subsequent marriages are more at risk of breakdown than first marriages, so children will experience another major disruption during their childhood.

The most recent figures for Great Britain (Haskey, 1994) show that 8% of all families with dependent children under 16 years contained one or more stepchildren, and that 52% of these stepfamilies have at least one child born into the stepfamily, giving a figure of over one million children. In addition, a similar number will have a part-time stepfamily where they visit their other remarried parent. Many stepfamilies will, therefore, have three sets of children: his, hers and theirs. Many men have a triple parenting role: separated parent, step-parent, parent in the new marriage. Many women also have a triple but slightly different role: resident parent of children from previous relationship, part-time step-parent, parent in the new marriage.

A POLICY FOR STEPFAMILIES

There is no concept of a stepfamilies policy in Britain anymore than there is a clear policy on families or the family (Pugh, De'Ath & Smith, 1994; APPG, 1994). Indeed, the word stepfamily only entered the *Concise Oxford Dictionary* in July 1995 after representation by the National Stepfamily Association.

> *We define a stepfamily as a family created by two adult partners one or each of whom already has a child from a previous relationship; the offspring from a former marriage ended by separation, death or divorce, a former cohabitation or an extra-martial affair. A stepfamily may include resident stepchildren or partially resident stepchildren who live primarily with their other birth parent, and children of the two adults, who are half-siblings to the stepchildren. The stepfamily relationship exists even when the adults and children have*

not met each other or lived together and extends to grandparents, aunts, uncles and cousins.

Although the majority of children still grow up with both their birth parents (70%) significant numbers do not. Our social and family welfare polices and legislation are, however, still heavily influenced by the model of the nuclear family where a man and woman marry, have children and live together in the same household.

Whilst many recent changes in policy have moved away from the notion marital status and towards parental status there is still very little recognition of the movement of children between family households or of any other people acting in a parental role and as extended kin. Policies need to be considered in terms of the various roles, functions, obligations and relationships within stepfamilies:

• blood ties, birth parents and extended family rights and responsibilities;
• household realities, children may be members of more than one household;
• reciprocity, notions of obligation may go beyond blood ties or household membership (Finch, 1994);
• parenting, as a discrete function whether regularly or irregularly.

At present, there are numerous examples of inconsistency, inappropriateness and contradiction arising from post-separation parenting and step-parenting. Where there is actual physical (50:50) shared care of a child one parent must still be named as the primary carer in order to be the holder of the universal child benefit; it cannot be shared. A cohabiting father who is named and has signed a birth certificate still needs to acquire parental responsibility; it is not automatic. A full-time stepmother with actual day-to-day care of a stepchild may find that her signature on a routine medical form or school trip agreement is not adequate. An ex-daughter-in-law may feel an obligation to a frail elderly ex-mother-in-law who helped her with child care, which does not legally exist, but not to a frail elderly step-mother recently acquired through her father's remarriage where a financial responsibility may be sought.

There is a particular ambiguity about stepfamilies and the role of step-parent. A step-parent may be seen as a saviour or an intruder. A stepfamily is rarely portrayed as a positive re-investment in family life but rather as a threat to marriage and an encouragement to divorce. In the past, it has been portrayed by some politicians as a solution to the financial and housing needs of single parent families. The presence of a strong male figure can provide discipline, especially for boys. At the same time, there is still the image of the wicked stepmother from fairy stories and the abusive stepfather.

HOW CURRENT POLICIES AFFECT STEPFAMILIES

It needs to be stated from the start, that any policies which affect two-parent households with dependent children will also affect stepfamilies. Some specific areas where policy makers need to re-examine current policies, legislation and regulations to determine the impact and implications for stepfamilies are listed below.

Collection and Collation of Formal Statistics and Information

Any changes in legislation and policy should be based on up-to-date information, informed research and the views of those most likely to be affected. The term remarried, for example, is rarely, if ever, used in any breakdown of categories for marital status.

Stepfamilies have to exercise the rights and responsibilities that any family has for dependent children. Information should be requested on the existence and age of any children at the registration of a marriage. This would identify some, but not all, stepfamilies who could receive appropriate information on where to seek advice and help if needed, set out any responsibilities for dependent children, as well as provide us with valuable statistics. It would also be an opportunity to explain some of the unique and complex characteristics of stepfamily life so that individuals do not feel they are personal failures when they encounter difficulties which may arise from the realities of stepfamily life, as well as highlight key tasks they should undertake such as making a will, appointing guardians for their respective children and restrictions on other activities such as changing family names.

The proliferation of Charters has encouraged the public to believe that services are designed to meet their needs and there is, therefore, more attempt to consult consumers. When new legislation is proposed, unless there is an active pressure group or a professional lobby, it is often difficult for members of the public to ensure their views are conveyed to policy makers. Stepparents and stepchildren are not mentioned at all nor do they appear to have been overtly considered within the Children Act; although representation was made by the National Stepfamily Association to Ministers, necessary statistical information on separated and remarried parents was not available, sought or considered in drafting the Child Support Act;

and, despite a formal response to the consultation paper on the review of adoption, no attempt was made to commission research or information from stepfamilies when considering a major review of step-parent adoption despite the overwhelming proportion of annual applications; and, the consultation on Divorce Reform makes virtually no mention of the existence of or possible additional needs arising from second and subsequent divorces and arrangements for different sets of children.

Integrated Income Policy

As the responsibilities of the welfare state are reduced, a review of the inter-dependency between generations and family households is urgently needed in considering distribution of income and assets, whether child support, child care, elder care, benefit entitlement, pensions, or tax allowances. The introduction of a formula for assessing child support payments which encompasses so many of these elements means that a change in the income level or responsibilities of an individual within one family household can have an immediate impact on the income of another. Which should take precedence, child support or elder care?

Anomalies within the formula have created bitterness and a polarised attitude between first and second families. For example, it is presumed that a residential parent, even if remarried, is entitled to a carer's allowance for looking after the children whereas the non-residential parent's new partner, the stepmother, even if also a mother at home looking after the children, not only was not allocated a carer's allowance within the formula but was also assumed to pay her own housing costs and those of her children. This was based on the assumption that every child would have two parents and no thought was given nor acknowledgement made of those stepchildren whose father had died, was abroad or in prison, and no child support or carer's allowance would be forthcoming.

The retrospective nature of this legislation has led to actual bankruptcy, debt, stress, redundancy and marital breakdown for many stepfamilies, some suicides, and increased levels of conflict and animosity between many separated parents not helped by the chaotic administration and 50% error rate of the early assessments. There are still major problems in integrating the implementation of, or any changes in, child support payments and benefit entitlements. The anticipated accuracy of assessments and procedures is still only 75%.

The three year phasing in of this legislation, now extended beyond the projected April 1996, means that children within the same stepfamily are subject to different regulatory procedures. Some will have child support assessed and allocated under the previous Court administration, and others within the new formula-based agency scheme. The consequence is again to create confusion, anger and a sense of unfairness.

The reality for many stepfamilies is that the child support going out of the stepfamily under the new scheme is significantly higher than the amount coming into the stepfamily, if any child support is received at all. No systemic attempt has been made to try and resolve this, nor to link the assessment procedure of families where there is such a discrepancy. It has been stated that any linkage, even where a change in one stepfamily will inevitably create a change for another, is not administratively possible despite the high financial investment in computers.

Family Welfare

Families with dependent children are at an economic disadvantage, and over one third of children in Britain are growing up in poverty. Whilst stepfamilies are, on balance, better off than most lone-parent families, they are more likely to live in local authority housing, to have a lower income, and heads of households are less likely to have a degree (GHS, 1993). Many of the differences found between a group of stepfamilies and other families could be accounted for by socio-economic variations (Ferri, 1984). Financial investment in children needs to be made for all families as a national policy and priority. The impact of the Child Support Act, as outlined above, has led to a re-distribution of finance from one family to another, often reducing the income of both due to a lack of any financial disregard for some families.

Community and Family Care

The presumption of community and family care in Britain is still based primarily on the notion of the nuclear family with women being at home and available to look after children, or anyone within the family who is disabled, terminally ill, elderly or frail. With the majority of mothers now in paid employment and with less time and availability to meet these responsibilities, it is hard to see how this will be possible and where such obligations begin and end. Not only may there be obligations based on reciprocity, as mentioned above, but an increasing number of people for whom one is expected to take responsibility. For example, if both your parents remarry there are four not two to consider, and if your partner has remarried parents you may find yourselves responsible for eight elderly adults. It is highly unlikely that the average wage will be able to sustain three sets of children–his, hers, theirs–and four sets of parental figures.

Housing

Stepfamilies are often "flexi-families" (Walker, 1992a) with five or six children coming or going, compared to the average static 1.5. Whether we look at allocation or allowances, the housing needs of stepfamilies are not routinely considered. The Child Support Act was recently amended to take into account the housing costs of a new partner and any stepchildren, which had previously been ignored. Public housing, which is where the majority of stepfamilies live (GHS, 1993), is planned on the norm of two adults and two children and is rarely sufficient for stepfamilies. Personnel in the Armed Forces are allocated accommodation based on household size not parental responsibility, which may ignore the need of a separated or remarried parent for room for visiting children and thereby reduce opportunities of maintaining contact with them.

Parental Roles and Responsibilities

Changes in child care legislation (Children Act, 1989, implemented in 1991) were designed to help families rear their children and manage their affairs with minimal intervention from the State and to ensure that any arrangements for children are related to the child's needs, wishes and feelings. Married parents, normally, will each have for their child parental responsibility which is automatic and continuous.

Little thought or debate seems to have been given as to how possible it is for two people, who have chosen not to live together, to share the care of their children from a distance and where they each have the right of independent action without any requirement to consult (Masson, 1992). Some have even questioned if it is possible (Walker, 1992a, 1992b). In particular, it gives greater rights than before to non-resident parents, with the stepfamily and step-parent by definition relegated to a less central role in relation to post-divorce parenting. This may be disruptive to stepfamilies by enabling non-resident parents to participate to a much greater extent in decisions relating to their birth child, such as determining the mobility of a stepfamily (James, 1992).

The focus on independent shared parental responsibilities may cut across new family boundaries and the privacy of family life although step-parents can often be key mediators in stepfamilies (Walker, 1992b). The potential for a disruptive and abusive separated parent can also undermine the potential for a stepfamily to offer stability and continuity (Adcock, 1992), and there are already concerns that in some cases 'contact at all cost' is proving not to be in the interest of some children or their stepfamily.

Marriage to a child's parent does not confer any automatic step-parental role or status. However, there are three possible ways to formalise a step-parent's legal relationship with a stepchild. If the parent holds a residence order they may appoint the step-parent as guardian giving parental responsibility in the event of the resident parent's death but not during their lifetime. The step-parent can acquire parental responsibility through seeking a residence order and this does not end the separated parent's parental responsibility. Or, the couple (parent and step-parent) can apply to adopt the stepchild and become an adoptive- rather than a step-family.

The Children Act 1989 and the Child Support Act implemented in April 1993 impose no financial obligations on step-parents. However, in the event of the stepfamily breaking down the step-parent can be held liable for child support through the courts if they have treated the stepchild as a child of the family (Masson, 1992). Another ambiguity which undermines rather than supports and underpins the stepfamily as a reinvestment in family life and responsible step-parenting.

Education

The growing use of the term parental responsibility, in place of parent or guardian, is already creating misunderstanding and difficulties. Many schools still use the term parent or guardian when seeking authority for school activities, medical examinations or immunisations. The Education Reform Act requires schools to hold a register of those with parental responsibility for use in parent ballots. In the summer of 1992 one local education authority anxious to implement all elements of the Children Act and the Education Act sent out a questionnaire to many thousands of parents with a child attending any of their schools asking who had parental responsibility for the child in question, particularly where parents were separated or remarried. Many parents did not know what was meant, many step-parents immediately wanted to have it whatever it was, and as a result of being overwhelmed with calls they set up a Helpline, and numerous local radio shows ran items and phone-ins to address the topic.

In seeking information from the Department of Education and Science (now the Department of Education and Employment) a number of other issues of policy and procedure were identified where guidance was lacking: Does the education legislation entitle everyone with parental responsibility for a child to vote on school policies? If each person with parental responsibility can act autonomously, who does the school consider to have the ultimate parental authority if they disagree, for example, on health issues such as a measles immunisation programme, on removing a child from sex education, or giving permission for a school trip?

Criminal Justice

Similarly, the Criminal Justice Act 1991 makes parents directly accountable for a child's criminal behaviour, through being fined or bound over to ensure that the child does not re-offend. There is no clear statement of whether that liability extends to a step-parent (without parental responsibility but with whom the stepchild lives), particularly if the resident parent has no income and is unable to pay a fine. Is the other birth parent liable for the fine even if the child was not in their care at the time of the offence?

Social Security

Legislation is sometimes contradictory as well as seeming unfair and illogical to many stepfamilies. Under social security legislation a couple are seen, for the purposes of housing costs, as a unit. Initially, under the Child Support Act, now amended, a couple were seen for the purposes of assessment as separate. The new partner and step-parent, whether cohabiting or married, were presumed to provide for themselves whether or not they had any income. And yet, if the new partner did have an income this was then included in the total available household income to determine final calculations of child support payments.

Some understanding of obligations and costs and the pattern of economics and financial responsibilities where there have been second and subsequent marriages needs to be charted to ensure we are not drawing even more families and children into poverty by withdrawal of state benefits (De'Ath, 1992).

Support of Young People

Research on stepfamilies has frequently focused on the early home leaving of stepchildren. Many young people are already disadvantaged due to poor education, lack of employment and lack of access to any form of financial allowances. Where child support is minimal or non-existent, and may well cease at age 16 years, this can add further stress to the relationship between stepparent and stepchild, especially if the stepchild is felt to be a drain on the family finances.

Children's dependency on their parents has been extended with parents expected to support their non-employed young people aged 16-18 years.

Like other low income families with younger dependent children, step-families are not alone in addressing this problem. A programme to work on youth unemployment would benefit all families.

WHAT WE HAVE LEARNED
FROM CALLS TO OUR HELPLINE

An analysis of over 300 calls to our Helpline, in addition to the many letters we receive, gives our organisation a unique view of some of the issues affecting stepfamily life. They are neither a clinical sample, nor are they a random representation of stepfamilies. They do provide an insight into the day-to-day realities that many stepfamilies grapple with, some of which could be alleviated by better understanding and knowledge that might influence and improve legislation and policies affecting all families (Batchelor, Dimmock and Smith, 1994). Key findings relevant for this paper challenge many of the assumptions and myths about stepfamily life and include:

- the family is not under threat and the majority of problems between stepparent and stepchildren are exacerbated by the lack of an agreed understanding of the role and responsibilities of step-parenting;
- variable contact and residence over time are not necessarily dysfunctional or disruptive arrangements for children in stepfamilies. Children are more flexible than figures and research on custody would suggest. More children change residence, move between households, and siblings choose to share themselves between parents;
- stepfamilies are different from nuclear families; there are certain key transitions which have an impact on stepfamily structure and process which could provide useful entry points for informal help or intervention;
- the impact of a new baby can disrupt even long standing and smooth arrangements between separated parents and their children, as well as be a unifying event;
- legislation designed to limit state intrusion into family life has left many step-parents even more confused about their role now that non-resident parents supposedly retain parental and financial responsibility for their children;
- a high level of distress was noted in stepfamilies resulting from death, which challenges the perception of stepfamilies only arising from divorce, and that parental death must be easier for children to cope with;

- intergenerational issues are not widely discussed or acknowledged leading to distress for many grandparents.

ADVICE TO POLICY MAKERS

Stepfamilies have been around for a long, long time and they are unlikely to go away. Indeed, estimates based on current trends predict that by the year 2010 in Britain it will be the norm for couples to cohabit, marry, divorce and remarry with an emerging pattern of a dispersed extended family (Northcutt, 1991). And, despite continual rhetoric by both major political parties emphasising the importance of the family, there has been a clear policy drift away from recognising the actual costs and demands of parenthood (Utting, 1995). Any family household, whether with one or two adults, with dependent children has increasingly found themselves on the wrong side of the growing divide between rich and poor with adverse consequences for children. Stepfamilies are as disadvantaged as any other two-adult household with dependent children with the added factor that their family finances are likely to have to stretch to additional children outside the household. It seems essential, therefore, that serious attention is given to planning for stepfamilies and the increasing numbers of children moving into stepfamilies, being born into stepfamilies, and struggling to grow up within stepfamilies.

Stepfamilies are complex and diverse, and the collection of statistics is of limited but important value. The National Stepfamily Association has attempted to describe stepfamily household formation and responsibilities based on two generations (adults and dependent children), previous marital and parental status, residence of any children, and current parental status. This gives 72 permutations (De'Ath, 1995) and, if we focus on residency, 16 stepfamily household types (Batchelor et al., 1994). Clearly, this ignores many other factors that would be important in addressing demographic, practical or research issues, such as the number and gender of children, extended family, contact with other parent, age at which they entered or left stepfamily, religious, geographical and cultural factors, legal position and many more. It highlights the enormous difficulty of calculating numbers of stepfamilies–who and what would we be counting? But it clearly is important if policies are made in ignorance or on assumptions that are no longer accurate or appropriate.

Topics for an agenda for such activities would include:

- developing agreed and common definitions of the role and responsibilities of step-parenting

- collecting and collating formal statistics to identify the characteristics and flow of children into and out of stepfamilies
- identifying the nature and duration of second and subsequent marriages
- using normative-adaptive perspective (Ganong & Coleman, 1994) rather than a deficit model for stepfamily functioning
- consulting the client group–the stepfamily members
- conducting a rigorous analysis and critique of past research on stepfamilies identifying clearly the limitations, the contradictory findings and any underlying presumptions and assumptions
- subjecting legislation which affects all families to stepfamily impact statements in order to ensure that stepfamilies are supported as a reinvestment in family life and not undermined to the extent that further family breakdown is likely.

The information and views arising from our Helpline calls and contacts are that:

- The family is not under threat, parents and grandparents, stepparents and stepgrandparents are concerned to uphold and ensure stability and continuity for children but need help and support to do this.
- The lack of formal statistics, information and awareness of stepfamily formation and functioning reaffirms their invisibility in policy formulation.
- Opportunities for public education and family support intervention are not identified; for example, recording at registration children brought into a marriage, or providing informal information and signposts to helping agencies.
- Distributing finances between families redistributes poverty and can create further conflict rather than encouraging a renewed investment and stability in family life.

IN CONCLUSION

It is clear that there is little awareness of stepfamily issues at a policy level. Laws and policy can define and shape normalcy and deviancy. Excluding collection of information on stepfamilies re-affirms their invisibility and reinforces the notion that their situation is a private matter and not a public concern. In 1991, over one million dependent children under 16 years old were growing up in a stepfamily, 8% of families with dependent children were stepfamilies and 52% of them had at least one child born into the stepfamily (OPCS, 1993). If these trends continue it is expected that 1 in 8 children will spend part of their childhood in a stepfamily. Stepfamilies could be seen as pioneers in the projected dispersed extended family of the future if only policy makers, practitioners and politicians were prepared to harness the belief in marriage and family life in the complex and diverse world of stepfamilies.

REFERENCES

Adcock M (1992) *The Children Act, Public Law and the Stepfamily: the child care system and steprelationships* in Dimmock B (Ed) (1992)

All Party Parliamentary Group on Parenting & International Year of the Family UK (1994) *Parliamentary Hearings.* Exploring Parenthood, London

Anderson M (1983) *What is new about the modern family: an historical perspective,* OPCS Occasional Paper 31, The Family, 5. HMSO

Batchelor J, Dimmock B & Smith D (1994) *Understanding Stepfamilies, What can be learned from callers to the STEPFAMILY Telephone Counseling Service.* STEPFAMILY Publications.

Burchardt N (1989) Structure and relationships in stepfamilies in early twentieth century Britain, *Continuity and Change* 4 (2), p293-322

De'Ath E (1992) (Editor) *Stepfamilies: what do we know? what do we need to know?* STEPFAMILY Publications, London

De'Ath E (1995) Keeping in Touch: 'Looked after' children and their stepfamilies, in *Families in Transition: Keeping in touch when families part,* De'Ath (Ed), STEPFAMILY Publications, London

Dimmock B (1992) (Editor) *A Step in Both Direction: The Impact of the Children Act 1989 on Stepfamilies.* STEPFAMILY Publications, London

Ferri E (1984) *Stepchildren: a national study.* NFER-Nelson

Finch J (1994) Responsibilities, Obligations and Commitments, Chapter 3 in *The Future of Family Care*

Ganong LH & Coleman M (1994) *Remarried Family Relationships.* Sage Publications

General Household Survey 1991 (1993) HMSO

Hardyment C (1983) *Dream Babies, Child Care from Locke to Spock.* Oxford University Press

Haskey J (1994) Stepfamilies and stepchildren in Great Britain, *Population Trends,* 76. p17-28. HMSO

James A (1992) Continuity, Change and Contradiction: the Children Act 1989 and the stepfamily, in Dimmock (1992) ibid.

Laslett, L (1977) *Family Life and illicit love in earlier generations.* Cambridge

Masson J (1992) Stepping into the Nineties: a summary of the legal implications of the Children Act 1989 for stepfamilies, in Dimmock (1992) ibid.

Northcutt J (1991) *Britain in 2010, The PSI Report.* Policy Studies Institute, London

OPCS (1990) *Marriage and divorce statistics. Historical Series, England and Wales, 1837-1983.* OPCS Series FM2, no 16. HMSO, London

Pugh G, De'Ath E & Smith C (1994) *Confident Parents, Confident Children: policy and practice in parent education and support.* National Children's Bureau.

Stone L (1990) *Road to Divorce, A history of the making and breaking of marriage in England.* Oxford University Press

Stone L (1993) *Broken Lives, Separation and Divorce in England 1660-1857.* Oxford University Press

Utting D (1995) *Family and parenthood: supporting families, preventing breakdown.* Josephine Rowntree Foundation, York, England

Walker J (1992a) Divorce, remarriage and parental responsibility, in De'Ath (Ed) (1992)

Walker J (1992b) Stepfamilies and Parental responsibility: who makes the decisions? in Dimmock B (Ed) (1992)

Family Life Education Programs for Stepfamilies

Robert Hughes, Jr.
Jennifer D. Schroeder

Stepfamilies are an increasingly common family form in American society. The latest census data provide a portrait of the growing number of stepfamilies. In 1980 there were 3.9 million married couple households containing at least one stepchild under 18 in the United States. By 1990, that figure had risen to 5.3 million and this population comprises 20.8 percent of all married couple family households with children in the United States (U.S. Bureau of the Census, Current Population Reports, 1992). Population experts project that the number of stepfamilies will increase through the remainder of this decade (Glick, 1989).

In the growing body of research on stepfamilies there are common themes regarding the stressful nature of the formation of a new stepfamily. In part, members of stepfamilies must face the many negative stereotypes that are commonly held regarding stepparents (Ganong, Coleman, & Kennedy, 1990). Although there is a growing body of research that indicates that not all stepfamilies have problems (e.g., Kelly, 1994) and that there can be many positive outcomes for adults and children as the result of remarriage, there is also accumulating evidence about the challenges faced by stepfamilies. By following a group of families over time Hetherington

Robert Hughes, Jr. is Associate Professor and Extension Speialist in the Department of Family Relations and Human Development, The Ohio State University, 1787 Neil Avenue, Columbus, OH 43210. Jennifer D. Schroeder is a Marriage and Family Therapist at Catholic Social Services, UFMC 600 Sager Avenue, Danville, IL 61832.

[Haworth co-indexing entry note]: "Family Life Education Programs for Stepfamilies." Hughes, Jr., Robert. Co-published simultaneously in *Marriage & Family Review* (The Haworth Press, Inc.) Vol. 26, No. 3/4, 1997, pp. 281-300; and: *Stepfamilies: History, Research, and Policy* (ed: Irene Levin and Marvin B. Sussman) The Haworth Press, Inc., 1997, pp. 281-300. Single or multiple copies of this article are available for a fee from The Haworth Document Delivery Service [1-800-342-9678, 9:00 a.m. - 5:00 p.m. (EST). E-mail address: getinfo@haworth.com].

(1993) and Bray (Bray & Berger, 1993) and their colleagues have documented the stressful nature of the remarriage transition and the complexity of stepfamily formation. These researchers have demonstrated that the early years of stepfamily life are especially difficult and that those families with young adolescent children face significant challenges. There is growing consensus that children in stepfamilies have more behavior adjustment problems than children who have not experienced family changes (Zill, Morrison, & Coiro, 1993).

In response to this growing population and the difficulties presented by these families, family life educators have given increased attention to developing appropriate strategies and programs for assisting these families. Recently, there have been important efforts to review empirical findings and offer suggestions to practitioners regarding this body of knowledge. There have been reviews of the empirical literature to identify the key issues facing stepfamilies that should be central to clinical applications (Pasley, Dollahite, & Ihinger-Tallman, 1993; Walsh, 1992), an analysis of specific family therapy strategies for working with stepfamilies (Browning, 1994) and considerations of ways in which schools can contribute to supporting stepfamilies (Bray & Berger, 1992; Crosbie-Burnett, 1994). Despite these important contributions to the development of effective intervention with stepfamilies, it is important to look carefully at the structure and content of specific family life education programs that have been designed for stepfamilies and to consider the effectiveness of these efforts.

In this paper we will review and analyze family life education programs that have been developed to assist stepfamilies and examine the evaluation studies that have considered their effectiveness. The analysis of the programs will involve a comparison of the content of the programs with the clinical and research literature and examine the extent to which programs address these issues. The analysis of the evaluation studies will consider the substantive aspects of the programs as well as the methodology. The final section will include recommendations for both programs and evaluation. The paper is organized into three sections based on the target client in the stepfamily system: child-focused, adult-focused, and family-focused interventions.

ISSUES FACING CHILDREN AND ADULTS IN STEPFAMILIES

There have been several important reviews of the research and clinical literature in regards to the issues and problems confronting these families. In this paper we have not attempted to review this literature ourselves, but are relying on these reviews as a basis for a synthesis of this literature. Ganong and Coleman (1987) sought to compare the research and clinical literatures with regards to common themes and questions. In their review of the clinical literature Ganong and Coleman found over 70 issues that therapists identified as confronting stepfamilies. They organized these issues into five major categories: family dynamics, transitional adjustments, incomplete institution, emotional responses and stepfamily expectations. More recently Walsh (1992), Pasley et al. (1993) and Ganong and Coleman (1994) have provided additional summaries of the issues confronting stepfamilies based on both the research and clinical literature. The issues raised in these more recent reviews can be roughly categorized into the same categories that were identified earlier by Ganong and Coleman (1987). Table 1 provides a summary of the issues confronting stepfamilies.

Family Dynamics

There are numerous issues regarding family dynamics including the issue of closeness, competition for time, and the variety and complexity of the various relationships within the family. There are also specific issues within the various dyadic relationships within families. A central task for biological and stepparents is establishing an effective co-parental partnership within the stepfamily. The new marital relationship requires attention especially in understanding how this relationship is affected by the parenting demands in the stepfamily. Issues surrounding the continuing relationship with non-residential parents also affect these families. Conflict and competition may pose special difficulties for stepfamilies. Children may have to work through new ties with stepsiblings or deal with other sibling issues.

Transitional Adjustment

Another important area of concern to stepfamilies is transitional adjustments. Some of these adjustments are due to the formation of the new family such as a lack of shared history and rituals, but some issues such as the entry and exit of children due to visitation in several households are ongoing. Also, stepfamilies are likely to have special adjustments due to life cycle incongruencies such as having a new baby at a time when a person is expected to be past the age of childrearing.

Incomplete Institution

Stepfamilies also face some unique issues due to what Cherlin (1978) described as their status as an "incomplete institution" which refers to the

TABLE 1. A Summary of Issues Facing Children and Adults in Stepfamilies

Issues	Children	Adults
Family Dynamics	Stepfamily systems are less close (Ganong & Coleman) Biological parent-child bond predates spousal bond (Ganong & Coleman) Many types of relationships (Ganong & Coleman) Competition for time (Ganong & Coleman; Walsh) Extended Kinship Network (Walsh) Sexual conflicts (Walsh)	Stepfamily systems are less close (Ganong & Coleman) Biological parent-child bond predates spousal bond (Ganong & Coleman) Many types of relationships (Ganong & Coleman) Competition for time (Ganong & Coleman; Walsh) Extended Kinship Network (Walsh) Sexual conflicts (Walsh)
Parent-Child Relationships	Name for the new parent (Walsh) Discipline by the stepparent (Walsh)	Discipline of children (Walsh) Teach stepparents how to support and assist the parent in the parental role (Pasley et al.)
Marital Relationship		Effects of parenting on the new marital relationship (Pasley et al.; Walsh) Build parental coalition; strengthen marital relationship (Ganong & Coleman; Pasley et al.)
Non-residential Parent Relationship	Idealized absent parent (Ganong & Coleman)	Sharing responsibility across households (Ganong & Coleman) Continuing adult conflict (Walsh) Competition of the nonresidential parent (Walsh) Reduce loyalty conflicts and triangulation of children (Pasley et al.)
Sibling Relationships	Sibling conflict (Walsh)	

TABLE 1 (continued)

Issues	Children	Adults
Transitional Adjustments	No shared rules or rituals (Ganong & Coleman) Instant love of new family members (Walsh) Fantasy about old family structure (Walsh) Changes over time (Walsh) Exit and entry of children (Ganong & Coleman; Walsh) Increase family flexibility early in the remarriage/stepfamily (Ganong & Coleman; Pasley et al.) Life cycle incongruencies (Ganong & Coleman)	No shared rules or rituals (Ganong & Coleman) Instant love of new family members (Walsh) Fantasy about old family structure (Walsh) Changes over time (Walsh) Exit and entry of children (Ganong & Coleman; Walsh) Increase family flexibility early in the remarriage/stepfamily (Ganong & Coleman; Pasley et al.) Life cycle incongruencies (Ganong & Coleman)
Incomplete Institution	Confusion over family roles & boundaries (Ganong & Coleman; Walsh) Society's concept of the remarried family (Ganong & Coleman; Walsh) Organizational practices that interfere with stepfamily functioning (Ganong & Coleman) Less support by friends and family (Ganong & Coleman) Lack of legal ties (Ganong & Coleman)	Confusion over family roles & boundaries (Ganong & Coleman; Walsh) Society's concept of the remarried family (Ganong & Coleman; Walsh) Financial concerns (Walsh) Explore adaptable roles (Pasley et al.) Organizational practices that interfere with stepfamily functioning (Ganong & Coleman) Less support by friends and family (Ganong & Coleman) Lack of legal ties (Ganong & Coleman)
Emotional Responses	Affection for the new parent and the absent parent (Walsh) Loss of the natural parent, nuclear family (Ganong & Coleman; Pasley et al.; Walsh) Instant love of new family members (Walsh) Share family histories to reduce jealousy, misunderstanding and favoritism (Pasley et al.)	Instant love of new family members (Walsh) Resolve grief over losses and changes in family relationships (Ganong & Coleman; Pasley et al.)

TABLE 1 (continued)

Issues	Children	Adults
Stepfamily Expectations	Unrealistic expectations about family/parents/stepparents (Ganong & Coleman) Use of nuclear family as model (Ganong & Coleman) Familial self-concept (Walsh) Individual self-concept (Walsh) Normalize the emotional, social and economic realities of remarriage and stepfamily (Pasley et al.)	Unrealistic expectations about remarriage/family/children (Ganong & Coleman) Use of nuclear family as model (Ganong & Coleman) Familial self-concept (Walsh) Individual self-concept (Walsh) Normalize the emotional, social and economic realities of remarriage and stepfamily (Pasley et al.)

lack of societal support and norms of behavior for these families. Ganong and Coleman (1994) and Walsh (1992) note that members of stepfamilies are expected to develop family roles and negotiate boundaries between roles for which they have little experience and can find few examples in society. Likewise, many organizations have procedures that either do not recognize the requirements of a stepfamily or actually interfere with its functioning (e.g., schools in many cases do not provide an easy way for more than two adults to be involved in school decisions or activities). The lack of legal ties between the stepparents and stepchildren can also lead to a weakened sense of responsibility for children or to frustration over not being included in decision making of the children within one's own household.

Emotional Responses

Although all of the concerns and issues already described can lead to emotional responses that must be handled within the stepfamily, there are some major emotional adjustments that clinicians and researchers have identified that are especially important in the adjustment of stepfamilies. This includes resolving grief over various kinds of losses experienced by all members of the stepfamilies. Also, there are issues of affection between stepparents and stepchildren and for children dealing with feelings of love for an additional adult while maintaining loyalty to one's biological parents. Dealing with feelings of jealousy may be especially important for stepfamilies.

Expectations

Lastly, stepfamilies must deal with a variety of expectations regarding family both from their own perspective as well as from others. Ganong and Coleman indicate that having unrealistic expectations about how the family will function, in particular, dealing with the "the nuclear family ideal" is important to developing healthy relationships over time. Both children and parents must also confront their own expectations regarding what parents are and what they are supposed to do without embracing models of behavior that will not work in a stepfamily situation. Pasley and her colleagues indicate that a crucial first step in helping stepfamilies is to assist them in understanding that many of their experiences are common to stepfamilies and part of a developmental process rather than some aberrant behavior or reaction.

This brief summary of the issues facing children and adults in stepfamilies provides a basis for examining the educational interventions that have been developed for stepfamilies. In the following sections, we will compare the existing programs to these concerns to consider the extent to which the programs match the needs of stepfamilies.

FAMILY LIFE EDUCATION PROGRAMS: CONTENT, METHODS AND EFFECTIVENESS

Child-Focused Intervention

A common way to provide prevention services is by creating programs that will reach children through the schools or in community settings such as religious institutions or youth groups. Our search of the literature only yielded two programs that were identified for children in stepfamilies.

Content. Before looking directly at the specific content of these programs, it is worth noting that these programs were designed for general classroom use, not just for children in stepfamilies. Thus, the purpose of these programs is to provide insight for all children about stepfamilies. Crosbie-Burnett and Pulvino (1990) have designed a program that deals with family dynamics in stepfamilies including issues surrounding parent-child relationships with both the residential parent and non-residential parent, parents' dating, stepparent relationships, and stepsibling relationships. There is also some discussion of the various transitional adjustments and emotional adjustments that are likely following divorce or remarriage. This program generally does not deal with issues surrounding the incomplete institution or expectations regarding stepfamily life.

Another program designed for children at school is *Shapes: Families of Today* (Geis-Rockwood, 1990) which is a four-part series for both school-age children and adolescents. The overall purpose of this program is to teach children that there are many different types of families. The major topics are emotions that accompany changes in families and a discussion of communication and problem-solving techniques.

Methods and delivery. Both programs that have been identified are designed to be used in classrooms during four 45-60 minute class periods with all students rather than just students who are in stepfamilies. This is different from programs that have been designed for children of divorce which have usually involved meeting only with the children who have experienced divorce (e.g., Pedro-Carroll, Alpert-Gillis, & Cowen, 1992). That is, these are not programs in which children are pulled out of class to deal with unique issues. The teaching methods in both programs rely on the presentation of brief lectures and discussion with students. There are some group activities and role plays to illustrate some of the concepts.

Evaluation. Neither of these programs report any evaluation results, although Geis-Rockwood reports that the program has been taught to over 2,000 children which suggests that the program has been well received. As an initial first step it would be useful to know more about the children who have participated in these programs and their satisfaction with the program. Both authors provide some ideas about ways to measure satisfaction among participants.

Summary of children's programs. While these programs seem useful, they are clearly not designed to address children in stepfamilies directly. The program designed by Crosbie-Burnett and Pulvino addresses more of the issues affecting stepchildren, but still does not cover many of the issues identified by research and clinical literature. Overall, the teaching methods seem appropriate for children, but the programs seem better designed for children in the upper elementary grades rather than primary grade children or teens. The lack of evaluation of either program leaves open the questions as to the effectiveness of the programs. There is clearly a need for both program development and evaluation of children's programs.

Adult-Focused Intervention

When attempting to strengthen or intervene with the stepfamily, the most common unit of intervention is the adults in the family. Adults are a likely focus of intervention both because they have much influence on family adjustment and because parenting is often listed as a significant source of stress among remarried couples (White & Booth, 1985) which may motivate them to participate in programs. A total of eleven programs were identified that focus on adults.

Content. In contrast to the children's programs, programs for adults are specifically designed for stepfamilies and most of the programs deal with many of the issues that are important for stepfamilies. All eleven of the programs identified address issues related to family dynamics. Several programs discuss the general pattern of family dynamics such as developing a sense of closeness and building a sense of a common experience (e.g., Burt, 1989; Currier, 1982; Einstein & Alpert, 1986; Larson et al., 1984; Nadler, 1983; Pill, 1981). Also, the programs often discussed difficulties around the variety and complexity of family ties.

Several of the programs place special emphasis on parent-child relationships (Brady & Amber, 1982; Dinkmeyer et al., 1987; Larson et al., 1984; Nelson & Levant, 1991). Each of these programs devotes much of the time to helping adults in stepfamilies develop an understanding of the motivations and problems of children and the skills of communication, discipline and problem-solving that will be useful to parents.

In terms of the other significant family relationships there are variations in the degree to which marital, non-residential parent and sibling relationships are addressed. Increasingly, program developers are recognizing the importance of the marital relationship on stepfamily relationships. Einstein and Alpert (1986) and Currier (1982) devote at least one session to the couple relationship. Another interesting program by Kaplan and Hennon (1992) focuses on couples' role expectations and issues between the partners regarding ideas about family and parenting with considerable attention to developing a common language and understanding of their expectations for each other. The least likely relationship to be addressed is the relationship between the stepfamily household and non-residential parents, although Burt, Currier and Dinkmeyer et al. address these issues briefly.

Transitional adjustment issues and emotional responses to the stepfamily are covered by many of the programs. Feelings of loss, affection, and guilt are covered by most of the programs. Einstein and Alpert provide the most in-depth coverage of transitional adjustment issues and emotional responses to stepfamily adjustments. In regards to issues surrounding stepfamilies as "incomplete institutions" there is discussion of roles and boundaries in many of the programs, but few programs address the legal, financial and societal practices that can make stepfamily living problematic. One exception to this general pattern is the program by Lown, McFadden, and Crossman (1989) that incorporates a substantial section on financial management along with the program developed by Einstein and Alpert. Given the many complications in stepfamilies around financial issues this is an important addition. Most of the programs also deal with myths about stepfamilies and expectations about what "normal" stepfamily life should be like. Interestingly, the content of the programs has changed little over the past decade. The topics included in Pill (1981) and

Nadler (1983) are remarkably similar to the topics considered in more recent programs (e.g., Burt, 1989).

Methods and delivery. The primary mode of delivery of these programs is a workshop format. The target audience is the adults in stepfamilies. Interestingly there are variations in terms of whether both adults or only one adult is included in the programs. Although most seem to encourage both to participate, Nelson and Levant only had one member from each family in their program. The length of the programs ranges from 3 to 8 sessions and 8 to 24 hours. All of the programs include some lecture and discussion with several of the programs providing very structured activities including homework assignments (e.g., Dinkmeyer et al., 1987; Einstein & Alpert, 1986; Nelson & Levant, 1991). The program by Burt is designed more or less in a self-study format for families, although there is a support group manual (Winter & Tompkin, 1987) that offers guidelines for creating stepfamily support groups that could use the Burt book as a basis for discussion.

Effectiveness. There has been very little information provided about the effectiveness of these programs. Five of the programs (Burt, Currier, Dinkmeyer et al., Kaplan & Hennon, and Lown et al.) provide no evaluation data about even the client characteristics, utilization of the program or participant satisfaction. Pill (1981), Anderson, Larson and Morgan (1981) and Nadler (1983) provide brief information about the characteristics of the participants and their reactions. These reports indicate that their samples included mostly middle-class parents and that their overall reactions to the programs were positive.

There have only been three outcome evaluation studies that were designed to measure client change as a result of participation in the program. Brady and Ambler (1982) examined the effects of a four-session program dealing primarily with parenting issues. Thirty-three participants were randomly assigned to either a treatment condition or a wait-list control group. Each completed the Family Environment Scale and an experimenter-designed measure of stepparenting beliefs. Program participants completed the measures before and after the intervention and the control group completed the instruments at the same time intervals. The results indicated that there was one slight change on one dimension (out of 10) on the Family Environment Scale and no change on the stepparenting scale. These results suggest that generally there was little measurable change on these family life dimensions.

In another effort Turner-Bielenberg (1991) examined the effectiveness of the Einstein and Albert (1986) curriculum with stepfamilies. A group of 15 couples were recruited that were committed to remarriage within one year (n = 7) or married for less than one year (n = 8) with no major adjustment problems. There was no control group. Participants were primarily White, middle-class, suburban, and college-educated couples. Participants met for 6 sessions of 1.5 hours each week and were composed of 5 couples each. Data from the Family Environment Scale's Cohesion subscale, the General Health Questionnaire, the Parenting Social Support Index, and the Ways of Coping Scale were collected before the program, immediately after the program and again at a two-month follow-up. The results indicated that following the program and at two-months post-program participants had less anxiety, greater satisfaction with their social ties and more extensive social networks. There were no changes in family cohesion and the small changes in styles of coping present immediately after the program were not evident at the two-month follow-up. While these results suggest some modest success of the program, the results are limited by the lack of a control group which would more soundly demonstrate that the changes were the result of the program and not just the result of typical adjustment gains that would occur without the program over time.

Nelson and Levant (1991) also conducted an evaluation of their program that focuses on parent-child relationships. This program is based on both behavioral and communications approaches to family relations. Using an experimental design, the authors compared participants in four-session programs that were each six hours in length with a wait-list control group. Participants were primarily White parents who had been remarried a mean of seven years and who had children who were in their early teens. Only one parent from each stepfamily attended training. The experimental group included 14 families, while the control group had 20 families. Participants completed the measures before and after the program and the control group was assessed at the same time interval. Communication skills (Sensitivity to Children Scale), children's perception of parent's behavior (Children's Report of Parental Behavior Inventory and Kinetic-Family Drawing), and family adaptability, cohesion, and satisfaction (Family Adaptability and Cohesion Evaluation Scales, II) were measured. Results indicated that trained stepparents improved their communication skills and that children reported somewhat more close feelings with their parents. There were no significant differences between experimental and control groups on family adaptability, cohesion, or satisfaction. These results suggest that the program was moderately successful in teaching parents to change their styles of communication. Other family relationship patterns may be influenced over time but not immediately after the program.

Summary of parents' programs. Overall these programs are well-designed and address many of the issues that are relevant to stepfamilies. There are some significant gaps in the content regarding the effects of the non-residential parents on stepfamilies and there is little attention in most programs on how legal and financial issues affect families. The major difference in content is whether the focus was on general family dynamics or specifically on parent-child relationships. Since much of the recent research documents the influence of one relationship in the stepfamily on other relationships (e.g., Bray & Berger, 1993), it will be important to know if programs that only deal with parenting issues are more or less effective than those that deal more generally with the dynamics within the total stepfamily. In terms of the methods of program delivery there was little variation or innovation in these programs or their instructional methods. At present there is insufficient evaluation data to come to any conclusion about the overall effectiveness of these programs.

Family-Focused Programs

A third approach to addressing stepfamily issues is to work with the entire family. In view of the importance of building ties among family members (Visher & Visher, 1988), this seems like an especially appropriate method of working with stepfamilies. Four programs were found that work with all members of stepfamilies.

Content. Two of the four programs identified take an approach that is quite similar to the programs for parents (Borup, Campbell, & Wise, 1989; Bosch, Gebeke, & Meske, 1992). These programs address family dynamics, especially those concerning the couple and the parent-child relationship. Each devotes at least one session to each of these types of relationships. There is almost no discussion of issues regarding non-residential parents. Interestingly, despite the presence of parents and children, there is no emphasis on sibling relationships or on how parents' behavior can affect sibling relationships.

There is also much discussion in these programs of transitional issues (e.g., roles, rules) and expectations (e.g., myths, societal views). There is little discussion of legal or financial issues or the effects of social ties or institutions (e.g., schools, youth groups) on the stepfamily. There is also little attention to matters of helping families deal with emotional issues such as losses and/or feelings of guilt, jealousy or affection.

Two other programs take unique approaches to working with stepfamilies. Duncan and Brown (1992) take a "strengths" perspective on stepfamilies. They address family caring, communication, family pride, family unity and social ties. From this perspective they deal with some of the general family dynamics, expectations, and transitional issues. There is less attention to any of the dyadic relationship issues (e.g., marital, parent-child, sibling) because the focus is clearly on the family as a whole. Due to the emphasis of this program on family unity and togetherness, this program runs the risk of failing to help stepfamilies understand the unique challenges and the normal developmental process of stepfamilies (Papernow, 1993).

Another unique program is described by Mandell and Birenzweig (1990). They describe a program for parents and children of stepfamilies in which there are six general themes for the groups, but the specific content is dependent on the families in the program. Several of the themes would foster discussion of family dynamics, transitional issues, and expectations (e.g, the child's perspective, roles and expectations, parenting, marriage), but clearly the direction of each group would depend on the membership of the group. Developing communication and problem-solving skills were the overall program objectives.

Methods and delivery. Three of the four programs (Borup et al., Bosch et al., Mandell & Birenzweig) use a workshop model involving the entire family, but each uses a different approach. Bosch and her colleagues conduct the program with parents and children together throughout the program. Borup and his colleagues begin and end each session with parents and children together, but have a middle period in which children are together by age group (elementary, school-age and teens) and couples are together. Mandell and Birenzweig have adults and children in separate groups for the first five sessions and then bring them together for the last session. These three programs also vary in length. The Bosch et al. program is 12 hours (6 sessions of 2 hours each), the Borup et al. program is 12 hours (4 sessions of 3 hours each), and Mandell and Birenzweig's program is 9 hours (6 sessions of 1.5 hours each).

In contrast to these workshop models, Duncan and Brown's program is a home-study format. Families are given a series of activities that they can conduct on their own. Each of the five major topics includes 8 to 12 activities that can be conducted in an evening or over several days. The authors suggest giving families about three months to conduct the program.

Three of the programs (Borup et al., Bosch et al., Duncan & Brown) provide fairly structured programs with activities, brief lectures and handouts. The program by Bosch and her colleagues, however, is less structured and seems to present some difficulties. It is unclear how the program works with children and parents together. The lectures and activities seem designed for adults and little guidance is given for how adults and children should handle these activities together. The thematic program described by Mandell and Birenzweig makes the most demands on the facilitator because there is limited guidance about how to address the specific issues that arise during the group. This program would require a very knowledgeable and skilled facilitator.

Effectiveness. None of the four programs provide evaluation results. Duncan and Brown offer a family strengths instrument that can be used as a pre- and post-test measure, but indicate that extensive program data have not been collected. Borup and his colleagues include a sample consumer satisfaction form, but provide no data on past experience with the program. This lack of information leaves open the question of the effectiveness of these programs.

Summary of family-focused programs. In terms of content and delivery, these programs offer some promising directions for working with adults and children of stepfamilies together. Having adults and children together in a program provides a special opportunity to deal with issues between children in families and between the biological parent and stepparent in regards to children, yet none of these programs take advantage of this situation. The format employed by Borup and his colleagues of having adults and children together at the beginning and end of each program seems especially useful. Neither the Bosch et al. or Mandell and Birenzweig programs seems to consider the difficulties that might be encountered by having children within a wide age range involved either as a group or with adults. Finally, without some minimal utilization and consumer satisfaction data it is impossible to begin to evaluate stepfamilies' responses to these programs.

ANALYSIS OF THE INTERVENTIONS

Despite the substantial growth in the numbers of stepfamilies, there are only a handful of intervention programs that are designed to help families with this important transition. There is much work ahead for family life educators interested in stepfamilies. Strengthening family life education for stepfamilies will require improving the content, delivery and teaching methods as well as conducting more rigorous evaluations.

Content

As a first step towards improving the content of the programs there should be attention to rationales that structure the programs. Most of the existing programs are built on atheoretical or eclectic approaches to stepfamilies. There are now several authors who have presented stepfamily development models (Goetting, 1982; Papernow, 1993) or task descriptions (Visher & Visher, 1988) that could serve as important conceptual frameworks for designing family life education programs.

Whether considering child-, adult-, or family-based intervention, there were several programs that addressed many of the broad issues that researchers and clinicians have identified as important to healthy stepfamilies. Nevertheless, most of the programs were designed in the 1980s prior to some of the most important theory development and research findings regarding stepfamilies.

Recent research provides several important insights about parent-child relationships in stepfamilies. Hetherington (1993), for example, has documented the special difficulties that stepfamilies with adolescents face. Also, Kurdek and Fine (1992) isolate some of the significant family process variables that influence how children adjust. Researchers have also begun to understand changes in the relationship between marital and parenting relationships within stepfamilies (Bray, Berger, & Boethel, 1994).

Beyond the immediate family, researchers have begun to understand the importance of extended family relationships and the effects of schools on stepfamilies (Hetherington, 1993). Perhaps the most important area of research is the effects of non-residential parents on stepfamilies. Although almost all the programs mention the importance of families developing appropriate ties to the non-residential parents, recent research provides special insights into what makes these relationships work and fail (Depner & Bray, 1993).

Few programs consider the special financial and legal issues that face stepfamilies. An important component of future family life education programs would be the addition of material on these topics.

Methods

Participants. Programs for children are the most underdeveloped. Although there are many programs for children of divorce, we found few efforts aimed at children in stepfamilies. The growing body of knowledge regarding the issues faced by these children provides an ample foundation for creating programs to assist these children. Also, the growing body of evidence regarding the special difficulties encountered by adolescents in stepfamilies suggests that this would be an especially important target group.

Beyond the children, there are important segments of adults in stepfamilies that would benefit from some special attention. There is accumulating evidence that stepmothers (both residential and non-residential) face some unique challenges and often report being under great stress. This should signal family life educators to design programs that focus on this group's special needs.

The current descriptions of programs provide little insight about the social class and ethnicity of participants. From the intervention samples most participants appear to be middle-class, well-educated and White. As this work evolves it will be important to consider content and delivery issues that influence the participation of more diverse stepfamilies.

Delivery methods. Most of the programs are delivered through workshops. The one exception was the Renew program (Duncan & Brown, 1992) which was designed in a self-study format. Although workshops are a common format for family life education, there is a need to consider alternative types of delivery. Home study programs, newsletters, and other methods can provide people with alternative ways of getting information.

Program support materials. There was a wide variety of program support materials with each program. Some program manuals provided a considerable amount of information on implementation and guidance for conducting the programs (e.g., Borup et al., 1989; Geis-Rockwood, 1989) and other programs provided very little information about how to operate programs for stepfamilies. All of the programs would benefit from more attention to the instructional and implementation process as well as background materials for program presenters (Hughes, 1994).

Evaluation

The most disappointing finding is the meager attention to the evaluation of stepfamily programs. Applying Jacob's (1988) model for evaluating family life education, program developers should begin by developing needs assessment information, followed by measuring client satisfaction and ultimately to examining short- and long-term outcomes. Overall, there were no reports regarding needs assessment and few reports of satisfaction and outcomes. To advance our ability to effectively serve stepfamilies more attention needs to be paid to examining the effectiveness of these efforts. A clear agenda of evaluation is sorely needed.

First, a comprehensive needs assessment should be conducted that identifies the emotional, parenting, family, financial and legal issues that face children and adults living in stepfamilies. This assessment should take into consideration the views of all family members both residential and non-residential as well as biological and step-status in these families. This data will provide critical information about the content for future programs as well as information about strategies for reaching families.

Next, new and existing programs would benefit from the careful collection of utilization and client satisfaction information. Program developers need to understand what is currently working. This too will provide a basis for designing more effective interventions.

The third phase in establishing effective intervention is for program developers to document the implementation process and to provide detailed information about the instructional process. For example, several program developers acknowledge difficulties in recruiting participants. By documenting the recruitment process it would be possible to build a database about what works and what doesn't. Likewise, it would be helpful to have more information about the success of the various teaching activities within programs so that these could be refined. This process of program analysis needs to be conducted with each of the three types of programs for children, adults and the entire family because there are likely many variations depending on which of these groups is the focus of intervention. A comparison of these different formats would also be important.

Lastly, as program process data becomes available there need to be careful outcome studies. Only three outcome studies were found. All of these studies have substantial conceptual and methodological limitations. The most troublesome issue is the lack of appropriate outcome measures. In part this is due to limited knowledge about stepfamilies generally, but at present much better outcome data could be collected. Any rigorous outcome study should include the following general types of measures: (1) program specific measures of knowledge and skills that fit the program content, (2) measures of child and adult mental and physical health, (3) measures of family process including both cohesion and adaptability, and (4) measures related to stepfamily issues and developmental tasks such as those suggested by Papernow (1993) and Visher and Visher (1988) among others. Finally, to clearly establish the effectiveness of family life educational interventions with stepfamilies, there needs to be more rigorous testing with experimental designs that include appropriate control groups that assess change just after the program as well as at a follow-up time. Ultimately, to advance our knowledge of interventions we will need to develop and test theoretical models that indicate which programs are effective for which clients under what conditions.

CONCLUSIONS

Despite the clear need to provide information and education to stepfamilies as they negotiate challenges and adjustments, there is a lack of solid intervention programs. The accumulation of research data over the past decade and the initial educational programs described in this review provide a preliminary basis upon which to build more effective interventions. In the short term, there is a critical need to develop new programs, especially programs for children that incorporate the latest research evidence. These new programs need to consider both traditional workshop methods as well as the use of innovative methods including video and computer technologies. Additionally, family life educators who are currently teaching stepfamilies need to begin documenting implementation and instructional processes that are effective. Each of these efforts needs to include evaluation strategies to strengthen our understanding of what is effective. Finally, these interventions focus on stepfamilies themselves as the issue; however, there is also a need to consider the ways in which schools (Crosbie-Burnett & Skyles, 1989), youth organizations (Ganong, 1993) and other aspects of communities are supportive or not supportive of stepfamilies. In the long-term, the health of stepfamilies will depend not only on how they adapt to their circumstances, but also how society evolves to provide a supportive context.

REFERENCES

Bray, J. H., & Berger, S. H. (1993). Developmental issues in the Stepfamily Research Project: Family relationships and parent-child interactions. *Journal of Family Psychology, 7*, 76-90.

Bray, J. H., Berger, S. H., & Boethel, C. (1994). Role integration and marital adjustment in stepfather families. In K. Pasley & M. Ihinger-Tallman (Eds.). *Stepparenting: Issues in theory, research and practice* (pp. 69-86). Westport, CT: Greenwood Press.

Borup, J. H., Campbell, S. C., & Wise, G. M. (1989). *Blended family workshop guide*. Ogden, UT: Jerry H. Borup.

Bosch, G., Gebeke, D. R., & Meske, C. M. (1992). *Stepping together*. Fargo, ND: North Dakota State University and the Center for Parents and Children.

Brady, C. A. & Ambler, J. (1982). Therapy with remarriage families: Use of group educational techniques with remarried couples. In J. C. Hansen & L. Messinger (Eds.), *Therapy with remarriage families* (pp. 145-157). Rockville, MD: Aspen Publications.

Browning, S. (1994). Treating stepfamilies: Alternatives to traditional family therapy. In K. Pasley & M. Ihinger-Tallman (Eds.). *Stepparenting: Issues in theory, research and practice* (pp. 175-198). Westport, CT: Greenwood Press.

Burt, M. (Ed.). (1989). *Stepfamilies stepping ahead*. Lincoln, NE: Stepfamily Association of America.

Cherlin, A. (1978). Remarriage as an incomplete institution. *American Journal of Sociology, 84*, 634-650.

Crosbie-Burnett, M. (1994). The interface between stepparent families and schools: Research, theory, policy, and practice. In K. Pasley & M. Ihinger-Tallman

(Eds.). *Stepparenting: Issues in theory, research and practice* (pp. 199-216). Westport, CT: Greenwood Press.

Crosbie-Burnett, M., & Pulvino, C. J. (1990). Children in nontraditional families: A classroom guidance program. *The School Counselor, 37,* 286-293.

Crosbie-Burnett, M. & Skyles, A. (1989). Stepchildren in schools and colleges: Recommendations for educational policy changes. *Family Relations, 38,* 59-64.

Currier, C. (1982). *Learning to step together: A course for stepfamily adults.* Baltimore: Stepfamily Association of America, Inc.

Depner, C., & Bray, J. (Eds.). (1993). *Nonresidential parenting: New vistas in family living.* Newbury, CA: Sage.

Dinkmeyer, D. , McKay, G. D., & McKay, J. L. (1987). *New beginnings: Skills for single parents and stepfamily parents.* Champaign, IL: Research Press.

Duncan, S. F. & Brown, G. (1992). Renew: A program for building remarried family strengths. *Families in Society, 1992,* 149-158.

Einstein, E., & Albert, L. (1986). *Strengthening your stepfamily.* Circle Pines, MN: American Guidance Service.

Ganong, L. H. (1993). Family diversity in a youth organization: Involvement of single-parent and stepfamilies in 4-H. *Family Relations, 42,* 286-292.

Ganong, L. H., & Coleman, M. (1987). Effects of parental remarriage on children: An update and comparison of theories, methods, and findings from clinical and empirical research. In K. Pasley & M. Ihinger-Tallman (Eds.), *Remarriage and stepparenting today: Current research and theory* (pp. 94-140). New York: Guilford.

Ganong, L. H., & Coleman, M. (1994). *Remarried family relationships.* Thousand Oaks, CA: Sage.

Ganong, L. H., & Coleman, M., Kennedy, G. (1990). The effects of using alternate labels in denoting stepparents or stepfamily status. *Journal of Social Behavior and Personality, 5,* 453-463.

Geis-Rockwood, W. (1989). *Shapes: Families of today.* Santa Barbara: Stepfamily Association of America, Inc.

Goetting, A. (1982). The six stations of remarriage: Developmental tasks of remarriage after divorce. *Family Relations, 31,* 213-222.

Hetherington, E. M. (1993). An overview of the Virginia Longitudinal study of divorce and remarriage with a focus on early adolescence. *Journal of Family Psychology, 7,* 39-56.

Hughes, R., Jr. (1994). A framework for developing family life education programs. *Family Relations, 43,* 74-80.

Jacobs, F. H. (1988). A five-tiered approach to evaluation: Context and implementation. In H. B. Weiss & F. H. Jacobs (Eds.), *Evaluating family programs* (pp. 37-68). New York: Aldine de Gruyter.

Kaplan, L. & Hennon, C. B. (1992). Remarriage education: The Personal Reflections program. *Family Relations, 41,* 127-134.

Kelly, P. (1994). Healthy stepfamily functioning. *Families in Society, 1994,* 579-587.

Kurdek, L. A., & Fine, M.A. (1992). The adjustment of adolescents in stepfather and stepmother families. *Journal of Marriage and Family, 34*, 725-736.

Larson, J. H., Anderson, J. O., & Morgan, A. (1984). *Effective stepparenting.* New York: Family Service America.

Lown, J. M., McFadden, J. R., & Crossman, S. M. (1989). Family life education for remarriage focus on financial management. *Family Relations, 38*, 40-45.

Mandell, D. & Birenzweig, E. (1990). Stepfamilies: A model for group work with remarried couples and their children. *Journal of Divorce and Remarriage, 14*, 29-41.

Nadler, J. H. (1983). Effecting change in stepfamilies: A psychodynamic/behavioral group approach. *American Journal of Psychotherapy, 37*, 100-112.

Nelson, W. P., & Levant, R. F. (1991). An evaluation of a skills training program for parents in stepfamilies. *Family Relations, 40*, 291-296.

Papernow, P. (1993). *Becoming a stepfamily: Patterns of development in remarried families.* New York: Gardner.

Pasley, K., Dollahite, D. C., & Ihinger-Tallman, M. (1993). Bridging the gap: Clinical applications of research findings on the spouse and stepparent roles in remarriage. *Family Relations, 42*, 315-322.

Pedro-Carroll, J. L., Alpert-Gillis, L. J., & Cowen, E. L. (1992). An evaluation of the efficacy of a preventive intervention for 4th-6th grade urban children of divorce. *Journal of Primary Prevention, 13*, 115-130.

Pill, C. J. (1981). A family life education group for working with stepparents. *Social Casework, 62*, 159-166.

Turner-Bielenberg, L. (1991). A task-centered preventive group approach to create cohesion in the new stepfamily: A preliminary evaluation. *Research on Social Work Practice, 1*, 416-433.

U. S. Bureau of the Census. (1992). *Marriage, Divorce, and Remarriage in the 1990's.* Washington, DC: U.S. Government Printing Office.

Visher, E. B., & Visher, J. S. (1988). *Old loyalties, new ties: Therapeutic strategies with stepfamilies.* New York: Brunner/Mazel.

Walsh, W. M. (1992). Twenty major issues in remarriage families. *Journal of Counseling and Development, 70*, 709-715.

White, L. K., & Booth, A. (1985). The quality and stability of remarriage: The role of stepchildren. *American Sociological Review, 50*, 689-698.

Winter-Tamkin, M., & Winter-Tamkin, E. (1987). *Manual for leaders of mutual help and stepping ahead groups.* Lincoln, NE: Stepfamily Association of America.

Zill, N., Morrison, R., & Coiro, M. J. (1993). Long-term effects of parental divorce on parent-child relationships, adjustment, and achievement in young adulthood. *Journal of Family Psychology, 7*, 91-103.

Step- and Foster Families:
A Comparison

Pauline-Irit Erera

A comparison between step-families and foster families seems both logical and long overdue. Foster families are at the same place that step-families were before studies in the late 1970s and the early 1980s revealed that, contrary to what practitioners and researchers had assumed, step-families are a distinct family structure, not just a variation on nuclear families. The literature on foster families reflects a similar bias, reminiscent of early descriptions of step-families as representing the restoration of a two-parent family (Wald, 1981). This article, comparing foster and step-families, shows the structure of the foster family as having, in some respects, much more in common with the step-family than with the nuclear family.

Family scholars have studied a number of alternative family styles. These include step-families, cohabiting, single-parent families, joint-custody families, gay and lesbian families, childless families, and adoptive families, to mention a few. Foster families, however, have not received the same attention. Rather than being examined as a family structure in its own right, foster families have been considered primarily in the context of child welfare. From that perspective, foster families are seen as nuclear families temporarily hosting an additional child. The fact that this "temporal hosting" significantly alters the foster family's structure has been overlooked by child welfare and family studies scholars alike.

There are several reasons for this lack of attention to the structure of

Pauline-Irit Erera is on the Faculty at the University of Haifa and Visiting Professor at the University of Washington. Address correspondence to the author at University of Washington School of Social Work, 4101 15th Avenue NE, Seattle, WA 98105-6299 (e-mail address: ererap@u.washington.edu).

[Haworth co-indexing entry note]: "Step- and Foster Families: A Comparison." Pauline-Irit Erera. Co-published simultaneously in *Marriage & Family Review* (The Haworth Press, Inc.) Vol. 26, No. 3/4, 1997, pp. 301-315; and: *Stepfamilies: History, Research, and Policy* (ed: Irene Levin and Marvin B. Sussman) The Haworth Press, Inc., 1997, pp. 301-315. Single or multiple copies of this article are available for a fee from The Haworth Document Delivery Service [1-800-342-9678, 9:00 a.m. - 5:00 p.m. (EST). E-mail address: getinfo@haworth.com].

foster families. The central concern of child welfare professionals is the foster child, not the host family. The foster family is regarded as a temporary means for promoting the child's well-being, not as a family in its own right. This view of the foster family as a temporary residence reflects the strong belief–supported by studies on human development and attachment–that the birth family is the child's true family. It is consistent with the current thrust of child welfare policy toward family preservation, reunification and permanency planning. This emphasis is reflected in Public Law 96-272, the Adoption Assistance and Child Welfare Act of 1980, as well as in numerous studies (Courtney, 1994; Folaron, 1993; Maluccio, Fein & Olmstead, 1986; Pecora, Whittaker & Maluccio, 1992). Focusing on the structure of the foster family conveys a recognition that such families are not always "temporary," and runs counter to the advocacy of the birth family as the appropriate family for the child. In reality, foster placements may continue for years, and some foster families adopt the foster children. In those instances where placements are short term, the foster family may have a succession of foster children, rendering their status as foster families a permanent one.

Child welfare and family studies, despite their common concerns, are distinctly specialized and separate disciplines, with little inter-disciplinary sharing. There is a strict compartmentalization between the study of foster families and step-families, with foster families being addressed in the child welfare literature, and step-families in the family studies literature. While there are good reasons for this division, it is worth noting that child welfare issues arise in all kinds of families, step-families included, and as this article suggests, foster families deserve study as families in their own right. The respective literatures on foster- and step-families focus on different aspects of family life. The step-family literature shows an impressive body of knowledge based on empirical studies as well as clinical reports, about the step-role (Ahrons & Wallisch, 1987; Erera, forthcoming; Ganong & Coleman, 1986; 1994; Henry, Ceglian & Ostrander, 1993); the step-relations (Brand & Clingempeel, 1987; Crosbie-Burnett, 1991; Fine & Kurdek, 1992; Orleans, Palisi & Caddell, 1989; White, 1992), and about the remarried couple (Brand & Clingempeel, 1987; Crosbie-Burnet, 1984; 1991; Ganong & Coleman, 1994; Gold, Bubenzer & West, 1993; Ihinger-Tallman & Pasley, 1987).

In contrast, the literature on foster families, although mostly descriptive, has much to say about the child and his/her dual relationships with both birth and foster parents (Hess, 1988; Hess & Proch, 1993; Kadushin & Martin, 1988; Maluccio, Warsh & Pine, 1993; Petr, 1994); on the non-residential birth parents (Hämmig, 1991; Hess, 1988; Hess & Proch, 1993;

Kadushin & Martin, 1988; Mech, 1985; Pecora et al., 1992), and on interventions with the child and the birth parents (Grigsby, 1994; Pine, Warsh & Maluccio, 1993; Simms & Bolden, 1991). Comparing the accumulated knowledge from one discipline to another can shed new light on the way we look at both these family styles. My focus here, however, is on applying insights from the step-family literature to reveal the foster family in all its complexity. The foster family is arguably a style or structure in search of a theory. Applying Messinger's (1984) pioneering conception of the step-family to the foster family, "a new definition of family has to be created . . . [with] its own range of normality" (pp. 160; 163). This comparative analysis suggests some of the directions such theory might take.

Family studies scholars have usefully compared different forms of families, including single-parent families to nuclear families, and step-families to both single-parent and nuclear families (Kushnir, 1993; Schwebel, Fine & Renner, 1991; Zeppa & Norem, 1993). Such comparative studies have provided new understanding and recognition of a host of alternative family styles. For example, Furstenberg (1979) and Messinger (1984) have suggested that problems posed by remarriage provide insight into the general family system expanding our understanding of what a family is. A comparison of the structure of foster families, with the more familiar family structure of step-families, can enhance our understanding of foster families, while enriching our understanding of issues confronted by various diverse family types.

Step-families and foster families differ from each other in significant respects. So much so that a comparison may seem out of place. However, there are also major similarities, as discussed below. Before examining the similarities, let us first consider the differences.

DIFFERENCES BETWEEN STEP- AND FOSTER FAMILIES

A comparison between foster and step-families reveals the greater marginality of the foster child than either the stepparent or the step-child. First, whereas foster families are created by the placement of a child, following the decision of an external agent—usually the social caseworker—step-families are created by the love and mutual decision of the spouses. While love is regarded as a normative reason for establishing a family, at least in the Western world, placing a child who cannot continue living with his or her own birth family is regarded, instead, as a disruption of the family rather than a normative basis for creating a new family. Second, the relationship between the foster family and the foster child is defined as temporary, and the love and caring for the child are expected to be conditional. In contrast, the normative expectation is that step-families establish permanent kin-relationships, and provide their children with unconditional love. One can argue, however, that with foster children who may remain very many years, and with 60 percent of the remarriages ending in divorce (Glick, 1989), both foster and step-families are not that far apart on a continuum of stability and permanence. Third, in the foster family the new member is a child, whereas in the step-family, the joining family member is an adult (the stepparent), who, being an adult, has more authority. Finally, in the foster family neither residential parent is a birth parent, while in the step-family, there is one residential birth parent. The absence of any residential birth parent suggests that the foster child has less support and backing than his or her counterpart in the step-family.

The relative marginality of the foster child and his birth parents is reflected in the different expectations placed upon the stepparent and the foster child. Whereas the stepparent is expected to generate changes in the family (Bernstein, 1989; Larson & Allgood, 1987), the foster child is expected to adjust to the current family style (Kadushin & Martin, 1988). Similarly, the non-residential birth parents of the foster child are recognized and labeled as malfunctioning in some way, while this is not necessarily the case with the non-residential birth parent in the step-family. The child welfare literature suggests that foster parents tend to look down at the foster child's birth parents. They believe that birth parents are unfit (Kadushin & Martin, 1988); they perceive them as neglectful or abusive (Seaberg, 1981), and as morally and behaviorally repulsive (Kadushin & Martin, 1988). Foster parents often regard birth parents' visitation as a threat to the foster child (Kadushin & Martin, 1988; Mech, 1985; Ryan, McFadden, Rice & Warren, 1988), and attempt to discourage it (Simms & Bolden, 1991). There are no similar descriptions of the noncustodial divorced parent in the literature on step-families.

Bearing in mind these differences, let us examine the structural characteristics that step-families and foster families share in common.

SIMILARITIES BETWEEN STEP- AND FOSTER FAMILIES

Families Created by the Joining of an Additional Family Member

Both step- and foster families are systems created by the joining of at least one additional family member: an adult and sometimes children in step-families (the stepparent and his or her birth children), and a child (or more) in foster families. Both this joining member and the "absorbing" family have their own family connections, rituals and habits. Due to this joining to a well-established family, step-families and, most probably, foster families constitute, at least in their early stages, distinct sub-systems: the "veteran" or "absorbing" family members constitute one sub-system, and the "newcomer"–a separate sub-system. In step-families, the residential birth parent, usually the mother may, in some cases, form a coalition with "her" children, "protecting" them from the step-fathers (Anderson & White, 1986; Hobart, 1987; Visher & Visher, 1988). The joining foster child, like the stepparent, might similarly be excluded from the foster family sub-system while feeling deeply connected to his or her non-residential birth family.

Families Created by the Disruption of Previous Families

Both step- and foster families are created on the basis of the disruption of previous families. The loss of family members, shared by both step- and foster families, sets them both apart from nuclear families. Step-families are founded on the basis of divorce or widowhood in the nuclear family. Foster families are founded on the basis of the disruption of the birth family, and the placement of the child in a foster family. The literature on both step-families and on foster care address this history of loss and separation from both the parent's and the child's perspectives. Nevertheless, there are some distinct differences in the way the two disciplines treat this issue. First, while studies on step-families come at it from the residential parent's perspective (Ahrons & Wallish, 1987; Clingempeel & Segal, 1986; Crosbie-Burnett, 1991; Visher & Visher, 1990), the literature on foster care addresses this issue from the non-residential parent's perspectives (Hess & Proch, 1993; Kadushin & Martin, 1988; Pecora et al., 1992). Second, although both disciplines examine the child's perspective, the literature on foster care does so much more elaborately, linking the child's sense of loss to theories of attachment and bonding (Grigsby, 1994; Kadushin & Martin, 1988; Maluccio et al., 1986).

The different emphasis on loss may stem from the fact that while the step-child resides with one birth parent, and possibly with biological siblings as well, the foster child is usually cut off from his or her entire birth family. In addition, step-families regard the child's home base with his or her residential birth parent, while child welfare theorists regard the child's home base with his or her non-residential birth parents.

Residential and Non-Residential Family Members

Both step- and foster families are comprised of residential and non-residential family members. In the step-family, the residential members are two parents (a birth parent and a stepparent), birth- and step-children ("his" and/or "her" children). The non-residential members in the step-family are often a birth parent (the noncustodial parent), and at times also an additional stepparent (the current spouse of the noncustodial parent), as well as birth- and step-siblings (of the current spouse and the noncustodial parent). In foster families, the residential members usually include one or two foster parents, their birth children and one or more foster children. The non-residential family members in foster families are usually one or two birth parents (the foster child's parents), and the foster child's biological siblings.

Furthermore, in both instances, the residential family consists of a unique combination, in which at least one residential parent is not a birth parent. In the foster family, neither foster parent is a birth parent of the foster child, while in the step-family, the stepparent is not the birth parent of the step-child. This constellation is represented by the fact that often different family members who are sharing the same household maintain different surnames. According to Messinger (1984), these different sur-names within the same family contribute to maintaining separate identities and loyalties.

The presence of residential and non-residential family members sug-gests that family membership in both step- and foster families extends beyond the family's household (Furstenberg & Spanier, 1984). This means that the physical boundaries of these families are incongruent with their psychological boundaries (Pasley, 1987; Pasley & Ihinger-Tallman, 1989). Family theorists have defined this situation as family boundary ambiguity (Boss & Greenberg, 1984; Pasley, 1987; Pasley & Ihinger-Tallman, 1989; Rodgers & Conrad, 1986), a concept that would equally apply to foster families.

Multiple Parental Figures

Step- and foster-families usually include more than two parental fig-ures: two residential parents (birth, step, or foster) that perform their parental role on an everyday basis, and at least one non-residential parent, who performs as a parent on a partial basis. The presence of non-residen-tial parents, especially if they are involved in their children's lives, sug-gests that residential parents need to share parental responsibilities and authority with the non-residential birth parents. This task interdependence may lead to conflict, especially if the interdependent parties have different goals or priorities (Ahrons & Wallisch, 1987; Ambert, 1986; Visher & Visher, 1983). Indeed, studies on step-families have indicated that the relations between residential and non-residential family members are often charged with tension and feeling of threat (Hobart, 1988; Messinger, 1984), as well as with conflicting and ambiguous expectations (Ahrons & Wallisch, 1987; Ambert, 1986). Similarly, studies on foster care suggest that the relationship between foster- and birth parents is inherently conflicted (Kadushin & Martin, 1988; Seaberg, 1981); and that visitation is the most prevalent arena for this mutual antagonism, tension and competitiveness, and is regarded by foster parents as undesirable (Kadushin & Martin, 1988; Simms & Bolden, 1991).

Studies of foster care suggest that the problematic relationship between foster parents and non-residential birth parents is also fueled by the non-residential birth parents. They tend to compete with foster parents for the affection and loyalty of the child, they tend to dislike foster parents and be jealous of them (Kadushin & Martin, 1988; Simms & Bolden, 1991). When collaboration between foster and birth parents is discussed, it is presented as an ideal role prescription in which the foster parents serve as helpers to the birth parents, providing them with information, emotional support, and teaching them parenting skills (Maluccio et al., 1993; Pecora et al., 1992; Ryan et al., 1988; Seaberg, 1981). Similarly, although the parental authority in foster care is shared with the caseworker, collaboration between foster parents and caseworkers is usually not considered as shared responsibility (Hess & Proch, 1993; Maluccio et al., 1993; Pecora et al., 1992; Pine, Warsh & Maluccio, 1993). In that sense, the literature on foster families implies that although expected to coordinate with caseworkers and birth parents, foster families are basically independent of the birth parents. Rather than a "complementary family," foster families are essentially portrayed as a "substitute family" that, in the process of rearing the foster child, "forgets" that it is not the birth family (Hämmig, 1991; Hess, 1988).

This need to share parental responsibilities with non-residential parental figures characterizes both step- and foster families, and distinguishes them from nuclear families.

Ambiguous Role Expectations

The literature on step-families stresses that stepparents have no clear behavioral guides, norms or models to turn to for assistance in their performance of the step-parental role (Ahrons & Wallisch, 1987; Clingempeel, Brand & Levoli, 1984; Ihinger-Tallman & Pasley, 1987). Like stepparents, foster parents, too, lack clearly defined behavioral guides about their relationship with the foster children. They too need to define their role from a wide range of possibilities (Ahrons & Wallisch, 1987; Erera, forthcoming; Miles, 1984; Visher & Visher, 1990). The literature on foster care, while addressing the legal aspects of the foster parents' performance, mentions little about parenting ambiguity, by implication suggesting that foster parents follow the parenting models of nuclear families. To do so, however, may place them in a bind. If foster parents do act as if they were the birth parents, they are likely to experience conflicts with the child (Ganong & Coleman, 1994; Mills, 1984; Visher & Visher, 1990). If they don't, they are likely to experience role ambiguity.

Divided Loyalties

From the step- or foster children's perspective, being raised by non-birth parents (step- or foster), while at least one of their birth parents lives elsewhere, may cause both an idealization of the non-residential parent (Kompara, 1980), and a sense of divided loyalty. Children tend to view loyalty to the step- or the foster-parents as disloyalty to the non-residential birth parent (Ahrons & Wallisch, 1987; Ambert, 1986; Ganong & Coleman, 1994; Erera, forthcoming; Hobart, 1987; Kadushin & Martin, 1988; Maluccio et al., 1986). In contrast to these family structures, neither divided loyalties nor idealization of parents is characteristic of nuclear families.

Furthermore, the relationship between children and their non-residential parents may affect the bond between children and their step- or foster parents. The direction of this influence seems to be dependent on such factors as whether the contact is measured by frequency or by quality, and by the gender of the parent. Some studies found that good relations with the non-residential parent hinder the stepparent-step-child bond (Ahrons & Wallisch, 1987); others found the opposite (Pink & Wampler, 1985; Santrock & Sitterle, 1987), while still others found that contacts with the non-residential parent had no effect on the stepparent-step-child bond (Clingempeel & Segal, 1986; Furstenberg, 1987). Clingempeel et al. (1987) hypothesized that close contact with the non-residential parent reduces the child's fears that the stepparent is a parental replacement, and therefore generates positive step-relations. Alternatively, such frequent contact can confuse the stepparent, and consequently prevent intimacy with the step-children.

The literature on both step-families and foster families examines the relationship that children have with their non-residential parents. However, the literature on step-families focuses on the influence that this relationship has on the bond with their stepparent, while the literature on foster care has focused on the impact of visitation on the bond with the non-residential birth parents (Folaron, 1993; Hess & Proch, 1993; Maluccio et al., 1986; Pecora et al., 1992; Seaberg & Tolley, 1986). In addition, studies on foster care found that the cooperation of foster parents influenced the frequency of birth parents' visits (Gean, Gillmore & Dowler, 1985; Hess, 1988; Simms & Bolden, 1991).

Payment for Raising Children

Both step- and foster families may receive payment for raising children. Whereas the foster family receives it from the welfare agency, step-families are expected to receive payments from the non-residential birth parent in the form of child support. The literature on foster care addresses the issue of payments quite extensively. In contrast, rather than addressing this issue in the context of the step-family, family scholars usually address it while discussing the noncustodial divorced parent (King, 1994; Paasch & Teachman, 1991; Seltzer, 1991).

In both instances, payment may engender a sharing of the parental role with the non-residential parental figure–the non-custodial parent, or the caseworker and the social welfare agency. It becomes a medium for discussions about the child's well-being as well as a source of conflict for both step-families and for foster families.

Although the receipt of child support distinguishes step- and foster families from nuclear families where no payments are received for child-rearing, there are significant differences between foster and step-families in this regard. In foster families, child-rearing is conditional upon receiving payment, while in step-families it is expected that the parenting will continue regardless of whether child support is received or not. Indeed, studies based on national samples indicate that between 40 to 60 percent of the divorced noncustodial fathers in the US do not pay child support, and do not visit their non-residential children (McLanahan & Casper, 1994; National Commission on Children, 1991; Seltzer, 1991). Receiving money from public funds, foster families represent a general societal responsibility, whereas step-families' payment reflects the privatization of parental responsibilities. It is worthy of mentioning that the US differs from many industrialized nations in this regard. Other countries commonly provide child support payments irrespective of whether the non-residential parent pays or not, thus assuring continuity of support. Government agencies then collect or seek to collect the payments from the non-residential parent.

CONCLUSION

This comparative analysis of the foster family extends our notion of what constitutes a family, and how it is defined. It also demonstrates the overpowering strength of the paradigm of the traditional nuclear family. This construction lingers despite evidence that the nuclear family has lost its place as the most prevalent type (Glick, 1989). In reality, the nuclear family is but one of numerous alternative family structures. Since all families tend to be viewed against a "template" of the nuclear family, other family structures fall into two broad stereotypical categories: the deviant, and the variant nuclear family.

The deviant stereotype is assigned to families that seem much too different to be regarded as a variation of the nuclear family. These have included in the past the single parent family, and at present, teen mothers, gay and lesbian families, and childless families. Deviant implies not only that these families are different, but that they are bad or wrong in some way. The deviant family needs somehow to "prove" its legitimacy.

The second stereotype views alternative families more positively, considering them as essentially nuclear families, but with a difference. Families that tend to be labeled as nuclear–but variant–usually have two parents of the opposite gender who reside with children in the same household. These include adoptive families, step-families, and foster families. While lacking the negative connotation attached to deviance, this "positive" stereotypical labeling is also disadvantageous to these families. It establishes unrealistic normative expectations based upon the model of the nuclear family. Since such families are not quite nuclear when measured against the template, they are left feeling that they are falling short in some respects. Such families need to redefine themselves, once they realize that their pseudo pathology stems from inappropriate standards. In doing so, however, they may lack clear guidelines and models. If they consider themselves as nuclear families, they may never measure up. If, alternately, they claim legitimacy as a distinctive family type, they may a lack a clear model of family life.

The limitation of "one size fits all" stereotypes is illustrated in the case of family boundaries. Family boundaries distinguish the family system from other social groups while defining who belongs in the family and what functions they will perform in that system (Boss & Greenberg, 1984; Pasley, 1987; Pasley & Ihinger-Tallman, 1989). Lack of boundary clarity is recognized as a source of stress and dysfunction (Boss & Greenberg, 1984; Rodgers & Conrad, 1986). Nuclear families that are uncertain whether a member does or does not belong, "who is in and who is out," are indeed experiencing family boundary ambiguity. But what may be problematic for nuclear families does not apply to step-families. Comprised of family members who are living in different households, with residential parents sharing parenting with non-residential birth parents, with half siblings and step-children, these families need to maintain "ambiguous" family boundaries that will allow these different family members to function in an adaptive, satisfactory manner.

In a similar vein, the foster family, too, needs to claim its legitimacy as a family with its own standards and role-expectations. Like step-families before them, foster families are wrongly regarded as nuclear families. This stereotypical assumption is incorrect on two grounds. First, with the addition of the foster child, it becomes a unique form of a bi-nuclear extended family. Second, the foster family was not necessarily a nuclear family even before the joining of the foster child. Foster families come in all varieties, including kin-families (relative foster families), single-parent families, step-families, and gay and lesbian families.

Foster families have not achieved recognition as a distinct family structure because they are assumed to be temporary, and relatively rare. Furthermore, such families are likely to be drawn from the least powerful segments of society. However, with 60 percent of nuclear families divorcing, one may argue that they, too, are "temporary." With about 500,000 children in foster care in the US (Pecora et al., 1992), foster families are, in fact, a widespread social phenomenon.

The example of the "discovery" of the step-family by family studies scholars is a reminder of how a once-familiar phenomenon may suddenly appear quite different when viewed through a new lens. The foster family, like the step-family twenty years ago, has not received the attention it deserves as a family in its own right. This comparative analysis of foster families and step-families is a first step toward including foster families among other family styles. Bringing foster families within the purview of family studies opens the way for the examination of this unique family structure. Family studies, the forefront in examining diverse family styles, seems particularly suited for the study of the foster family.

REFERENCES

Ahrons, C. A. & Wallish, L. (1987). Parenting in the binuclear family: Relationships between biological and stepparents. In K. Pasley & M. Ihinger-Tallman (Eds.), *Remarriage and stepparenting: Current research and theory* (pp. 225-256). New York: Gilford Press.

Ambert, A. M. (1986). Being a stepparent: Live-in and visiting stepchildren. *Journal of Marriage and the Family, 48,* 795-804.

Anderson, J. Z. & White, G. D. (1986). An empirical investigation of interaction and relationship patterns in functional and dysfunctional nuclear families and stepfamilies. *Family Process, 25,* 407-422.

Bernstein, A. C. (1989). *Yours, mine, and ours: How families change when remarried parents have a child together.* New York: Scribner.

Boss, P. & Greenberg, J. (1984). Family boundary ambiguity: A new variable in family stress theory. *Family Process, 23*, 535-546.

Brand, E. & Clingempeel, W. G. (1987). Interdependencies of marital and step-parent-stepchild relationships and children's psychological adjustment: Research findings and clinical implications. *Family Relations, 36*, 145-155.

Clingempeel, W. G., Brand, E. & Levoli, R. (1984). Stepparent-stepchild relationships in stepmother and stepfather families: A multimethod study. *Family Relations, 33*, 465-474.

Clingempeel, W. G., Brand, E. & Segal, S. (1987). A multivariable-developmental perspective for future research on stepfamilies. In K. Pasley & M. Ihinger-Tallman (Eds.), *Remarriage and stepfamilies: Current research and theory* (pp. 65-93). New York: Guilford Press.

Clingempeel, W. G., & Segal, S. (1986). Stepparent-stepchild relationships and the psychological adjustment of children in stepmother and stepfather families. *Child Development, 57*, 474-484.

Courtney, M. E. (1994). Factors associated with the reunification of foster children with their families. *Social Service Review. 68*(1), 81-109.

Crosbie-Burnett, M. (1984). The centrality of the step relationship: A challenge to family theory and practice. *Family Relations, 33*, 459-463.

Crosbie-Burnett, M. (1991). Impact of joint versus sole custody and quality of co-parental relationship on adjustment of adolescents in remarried families. *Behavioral Sciences and the Law, 9*, 439-449.

Erera, P. I (Forthcoming). On becoming a stepparent: factors associated with the adoption of alternative stepparenting styles. *Journal of Divorce & Remarriage.*

Folaron, G. (1993). Preparing children for reunification. In B. A. Pine, R. Warsh & A. N. Maluccio (Eds.), *Together again: Family reunification in foster care* (pp. 141-154). Washington D. C: Child Welfare League of America.

Fine, M. A. & Kurdek, L. A. (1992). The adjustment of adolescents in stepfather and stepmother families. *Journal of Marriage and the Family, 54*, 725-736.

Furstenberg, F. F. (1979). Recycling the family: Perspectives for researching a neglected family form. *Marriage and Family Review, 2*, 12-22.

Furstenberg, F. F. (1987). The new extended family: The experience of parents and children after remarriage. In K. Pasley & M. Ihinger-Tallman (Eds.), *Remarriage and stepfamilies: Current research and theory* (pp. 42-61). New York: Guilford Press.

Furstenberg, F. F. & Spanier, G. B. (1984). *Recycling the family: Remarriage after Divorce.* Beverly Hills, CA: Sage.

Ganong, L. H. & Coleman, M. (1986). A comparison of clinical and empirical literature on children in stepfamilies. *Journal of Marriage and the Family, 48*, 309-318.

Ganong, L. H. & Coleman, M. (1994). *Remarried family relationships.* Thousand Oaks, CA: Sage.

Gean, M. P., Gillmore, J. L. & Dowler, J. K. (1985). Infants and toddlers in supervised custody: A pilot study of visitation. *Journal of the American Academy of Child Psychiatry, 24*(5), 608-612.

Glick, P. C. (1989). Remarried families, stepfamilies, and stepchildren: A brief demographic analysis. *Family Relation, 38*, 24-27.

Gold, J. M., Bubenzer, D. L. & West, J. D. (1993). Differentiation from ex-spouses and stepfamily marital intimacy. *Journal of Divorce & Remarriage, 19*(3-4), 83-96.

Grigsby, R. K. (1994). Maintaining attachment relationships among children in foster care. *Families in Society: The Journal of Contemporary Human Services, 75*(5), 269-277.

Hämmig, Y. (1991). *Participation of the birth family in foster care from the Swiss point of view.* International Foster Care Organization Conference, Jönköping, Sweden, 1991.

Henry, C. S., Ceglian, C. P. & Ostrander, D. L. (1993). The transition to step-grandparenthood. *Journal of Divorce and Remarriage, 19*(3-4), 25-45.

Hess, P. (1988). Case and context: Determinants of planned visit frequency in foster family care. *Child Welfare, 67*(4), 311-325.

Hess, P. & Proch, K. (1993). Visiting: The heart of reunification. In B. A. Pine, R. Warsh & A. N. Maluccio (Eds.), *Together again: Family reunification in foster care* (pp. 119-139). Washington D. C: Child Welfare League of America.

Hobart, C. (1987). Parent-child relations in remarried families. *Journal of Family Issues, 8*, 259-277.

Hobart, C. (1988). The family system in remarriage: An exploratory study. *Journal of Marriage and the Family, 50*(3), 649-661.

Hunter, J. E. & Schuman, N. (1980). Chronic reconstitution as a family style. *Social Work, 25*, 446-451.

Ihinger-Tallman, M. & Pasley, K. (1987). *Remarriage.* CA: Sage Pub.

Kadushin, A. & Martin, J. A. (1988). *Child welfare services.* New York: MacMillan, 4th. ed.

Kushnir, T. (1993). Emotional reactions and coping activities of divorced and married mothers in Israel during the Gulf War. *Journal of Divorce & Remarriage, 21*(1-2), 1-21.

King, V. (1994). Nonresident father involvement and child well-being: Can dads make a difference? *Journal of Family Issues, 15*(1), 78-96.

Kompara, D. R. (1980). Difficulties in the socialization process of step parenting. *Family Relations, 29*, 69-73.

Larson, J. H. & Allgood, S. M. (1987). A comparison of intimacy in first married and remarried couples. *Journal of Family Issues, 8*(3), 319-331.

Maluccio, A. N., Fein, E. & Olmstead, K. A. (1986). *Permanency planning for children.* New York and London: Tavistock.

Maluccio, A. N., Warsh, R. & Pine, B. A. (1993). Family reunification: An overview. In B. A. Pine, R. Warsh & A. N. Maluccio (Eds.), *Together again: Family reunification in foster care* (pp. 3-19). Washington D. C: Child Welfare League of America.

McLanahan, S. & Casper, L. (1994). *The American family in the 1990s: Growing diversity and inequality.* Walferdange, Luxembourg: Luxembourg Income Study, Working paper No. 115.

Mech, E. V. (1985). Parental visiting and foster placement. *Child Welfare, 64*, 67-72.

Messinger, L. (1984). *Remarriage: A family affair.* New York & London: Plenum Press.

Miles, D. M. (1984). A model for stepfamily development. *Family Relations, 33*, 365-372.

National Commission on children (1991). *Speaking of kids: A national survey of children and parents.* Washington, D. C

Orleans, M., Palisi, B. J., & Caddell, D. (1989). Marriage adjustment and satisfaction: Their feeling and perception of decision making and stepchildren relations. *Family Relations, 39*, 371-377.

Paasch, K. & Teachman, J. D. (1991). Gender of children and receipt of assistance from absent fathers. *Journal of Family Issues, 12*(4), 450-466.

Pasley, K. (1987). Family boundary ambiguity: Perceptions of adult stepfamily members. In K. Pasley & M. Ihinger-Tallman (Eds.), *Remarriage and stepparenting: Current research and theory* (pp. 206-224). New York: Guilford Press.

Pasley, K. & Ihinger-Tallman, M. (1989). Boundary ambiguity in remarriage: Does ambiguity differentiate degree of marital adjustment and integration? *Family Relations, 38*, 46-52.

Pecora, P. J., Whittaker, J. K. & Maluccio, A. N. (1992). *The child welfare challenge: Policy, practice and research.* New York: Aldine De Gruyter.

Petr, C. G. (1994). Crises that threaten out-of-home placement of children with emotional and behavioral disorders. *Families in Society: The Journal of Contemporary Human Services, 75*(4), 195-204.

Pine, B. A., Warsh, R. & Maluccio, A. N. (1993). Training for competence in family reunification practice. In B. A. Pine, R. Warsh & A. N. Maluccio (Eds.), *Together again: Family reunification in foster care* (pp. 35-50). Washington D.C: Child Welfare League of America.

Pink, J. E. T., & Wampler, K. S. (1985). Problem areas in step-families: Cohesion, adaptability, and the stepfather-adolescent relationship. *Family Relations, 34*, 327-335.

Rodgers, R. H. & Conrad, L. M. (1986). Courtship for remarriage: Influences on family reorganization after divorce. *Journal of Marriage and the Family, 48*, 767-775.

Ryan, P., McFadden, E., Rice, D. & Warren, B. (1988). The Role of Foster Parents in Helping Young People Develop Emancipation Skills. *Child Welfare, 67*(6), 563-572.

Santrock, J. W., & Sitterle, K. A. (1987). Parent-child relationships in stepmother families. In K. Pasley & M. Ihinger-Tallman (Eds.), *Remarriage and stepfamilies: Current research and theory* (pp. 273-299). New York: Guilford Press.

Schwebel, A. I., Fine, M. A. & Renner, M. A. (1991). A study of perceptions of the stepparent role. *Journal of Family Issues, 12*(1), 43-58.

Seaberg, J. R. (1981). Foster parents as aides to parents. In A. N. Maluccio & P. A. Sinanoglu (Eds.), *The challenge of partnership: Working with parents in foster care* (pp. 209-220). Washington D. C: Child Welfare League of America.

Seaberg, J. R. & Tolley, E. S. (1986). Predictors of the length of stay in foster care. *Social Work Research and Abstracts*, 22(3), 11-19.

Seltzer, J. A. (1991). Relationships between fathers and children who live apart: The father's role after separation. *Journal of Marriage and the Family*, 53(1), 79-101.

Simms, M. D. & Bolden, B. J. (1991). The family reunification project: Facilitating regular contact among foster children, biological families, and foster families. *Child Welfare*, 70(6), 679-690.

Visher, E. B., & Visher, J. S. (1983). Stepparenting: Blending families. In H. I. McCubbin & C. R. Figley (Eds.), *Stress and the family* (pp. 133-146). Vol I: Coping with normative transitions. New York: Brunner/Mazel.

Visher, E. B. & Visher, J. S. (1988). *Old loyalties, new loyalties: Therapeutic strategies with stepfamilies*. New York: Brunner/Mazal.

Visher, E. B. & Visher, J. S. (1990). Dynamics of successful stepfamilies. *Journal of Divorce & Remarriage*, 14(1), 3-12.

Wald, E. (1981). The remarried family: Challenge and promise. New York: Family Service Association of America.

White, L. K. (1992). The effects of parental divorce and remarriage on parental support for adult children. *Journal of Family Issues*, 13, 234-250.

Zeppa, A. & Norem, R. H. (1993). Stressors, manifestations of stress, and first-family/stepfamily group membership. *Journal of Divorce & Remarriage*, 19(3-4), 3-24.

Index